A **NAOMI SCHNEIDER** BOOK

Highlighting the lives and experiences of marginalized
communities, the select titles of this imprint draw
from sociology, anthropology, law, and history, as well
as from the traditions of journalism and advocacy, to reassess mainstream
history and promote unconventional thinking about contemporary
social and political issues. Their authors share the passion, commitment,
and creativity of Executive Editor Naomi Schneider.

Riding Like the Wind

Riding Like the Wind

THE LIFE OF SANORA BABB

Iris Jamahl Dunkle

UNIVERSITY OF CALIFORNIA PRESS

University of California Press
Oakland, California

© 2024 by Iris Jamahl Dunkle

Cataloging-in-Publication data is on file at the Library of Congress.

ISBN 978-0-520-39544-2 (cloth : alk. paper)
ISBN 978-0-520-39547-3 (ebook)

Manufactured in the United States of America

33 32 31 30 29 28 27 26 25 24
10 9 8 7 6 5 4 3 2 1

Unless otherwise noted, all photographs are from the Sanora
Babb Papers, Harry Ransom Center, the University of Texas at
Austin, and are used by permission of Joanne Dearcopp.

publication supported by a grant from
The Community Foundation for Greater New Haven
as part of the **Urban Haven Project**

For Joanne Dearcopp, who kept her promise to her friend
Sanora, and for my grandmother, Marilouise Kirby, who knew
the true story of the Dust Bowl because she lived it

The real revolution must occur in the human heart, not on the streets.

—SANORA BABB

This is a collective history told by people who lived it. Memory in America suffers amnesia. Here the memory is blown from the ashes and glows in the city.

—MERIDEL LE SUEUR

Contents

Acknowledgments

Thank you, first, to Sanora, who lived a life that has taught me so much about what the word *fortitude* means and what it means to be a writer.

Thank you to my grandmother Marilouise Kirby, who shared many of her experiences surviving the Dust Bowl and starting a new life in Atwater, California. She is the one who first alerted me to the fact that *The Grapes of Wrath* is not a Dust Bowl novel. I only wish I could have shared Babb's novel *Whose Names Are Unknown* with her while she was still alive.

The journey of this book could not have happened without the support of Joanne Dearcopp, Sanora Babb's friend and literary executor. It was Joanne who helped connect me with the people who knew and loved Sanora Babb during and after her lifetime, and who was always available for a call or even a visit to clarify facts about Babb. I'm also grateful to Roxana Ma Newman, who provided detailed information about her own relationship with Babb and the friendship between her mother, Lotus Ma Lee, and Babb, and who carefully cataloged their decades of correspondence. I'll never forget the day I first met Pauline Hodges. When I picked her up from her care facility, I had no idea what a treasure I'd come across. Pauline brought the historical town of Forgan, Oklahoma, to life. It's been an honor to get to know her over the years I've been writing this book.

Thank you to Doug Wixson, whom I never had the opportunity to meet in real life, but whose careful notes from his interviews with Babb helped lay the groundwork for this book.

Thank you to Kathleen A. Kelly, who first cheered on this project and helped me develop my first concept of the book.

Thank you to the staff at the Harry Ransom Center Special Collections, who were incredibly helpful as I worked with Babb's collection, including Kathryn Millan, who always welcomed me to Austin, and Adrienne Sockwell and the rest of the Reference Team, who helped me find what I was looking for in the Sanora Babb Papers: Elizabeth Garver, Hartlyn Haynes, Hamza Iqbal, Cristina Meisner, Maggie Mitts, Adrienne Sockwell, Kayleigh Voss, and Courtney Welu.

Special thanks to Amy D. Wagner, who helped me navigate the Sanora Babb Papers each time I visited Austin, and to the other members of the Reading Room team: Andi Gustavson, Michael Gilmore, Jeremy Aguilar, Lincoln Howard, Lucy Mears, Gabby Sanchez, Sean Dudo, Alejandra Gracias, Juhyun (Josh) Lee, Raikolf Lopez, Fatima Raja, Favour Udegbunam, Joana Villarreal, Sara Armendariz, Brooke McKinney.

Thank you to CrossFit Central in Austin, Texas, for giving me a home away from home, a place to work out and clear my head after long hours in the archives.

Thank you to my agent, Laura Mazer, who believed in this book when many did not and who helped me find Naomi Schneider at the University of California Press, where this book has bloomed under her care. Naomi's dedication and editorial leadership helped me shape Sanora's story and led me toward creating the book I've always wanted to write. Thank you also to all of the amazing people I've gotten to work with at the University of California Press, including Aline Dolinh. Thanks to Emily Park for careful project editing and to Emily Grandstaff and Teresa Iafolla for support with the publicity and marketing of this book. Thank you to Kevin Barrett Kane for creating such a striking cover. Thank you to Victoria Baker for the time and attention she spent developing an index for this book.

Thanks to Todd Fuller, curator of the Western History Collections at the University of Oklahoma, for hosting me at the University of Oklahoma and for helping me map out my tour of Red Rock and the surrounding areas. Thank you also to the Cherokee Strip Museum in Perry, Oklahoma, and to the First Americans Museum in Oklahoma City.

Thank you to Jan Beatty and Jennifer Steinorth, whose workshops at Lit Youngstown helped me navigate my way through my family's connection to the Dust Bowl and my trepidation about challenging John Steinbeck's novel *The Grapes of Wrath*.

Thanks to Timothy and Leslie Hume for their hospitality, for helping me find the spot where Babb's family dugout was located, and for helping me learn to appreciate the beauty of the land on which Babb and her family lived in Baca County, Colorado. Thank you to Kent Brooks for historical knowledge about Baca County. Thanks to Lidia Gray for helping me find Konkie's buffalo grass–covered grave, and for her support of this project. Thank you to the Morton County Museum, which helped me imagine life in Elkhart, Kansas, in the early 1900s (with a special thanks to M. K. Barnes for helping me find early photographs of Elkhart). Thanks also to the J. Plummer Museum in Beaver, Oklahoma. Thanks to Mike Conklin, who helped me understand the early newspapers of the Oklahoma Panhandle. Thanks to Carol S. Loranger for insight into Babb's poetry. And thanks to all of the contributors to *Unknown No More: Recovering Sanora Babb* for incredible scholarship.

Thanks to the Margaret Herrick Library in Los Angeles, and to my friend Nan Cohen, who let me stay with her while I researched Babb's time in the area. Thank you to Evie King, daughter of Dolph Sharp, who helped me learn more about the writing group Babb formed with Sharp and Ray Bradbury.

Thank you to Don Lee, who helped me better understand Babb during the last years of her life. And thanks to Alan Wald for an insightful interview with Babb and for answering all of my follow-up questions. Thanks to Steinbeck scholar Kevin Hearle for the contextualization surrounding Steinbeck's life and work. And thanks to Larry Ceplair for helping me understand more about Paul Jarrico.

Thank you to Dayton Duncan for an incredible interview that helped shed light on how word about Babb and her book *Whose Names Were Unknown* was spread through Ken Burns's documentary. And thanks to Ken Burns for the work he did to bring back Sanora's story. Thank you to *Catamaran* for publishing the first piece that would become this book: "Sanora Babb: Challenging a Single Story of the Dust Bowl."

Thank you to Biographers International for the generous Caro Grant that helped me fund research travel, and to all of my Patreon donors, Substack subscribers, and the private donors who helped support this important project. Thank you to Vermont Studio Center, where many of the early chapters of this book were born. Thank you also to Millay Arts, where I had the space and time to work on several chapters and then again to revise and finish copy edits. Both of these places filled me with inspiration (the Gihon River's icing over, then the ice suddenly breaking and flowing past, the ghost of Edna St. Vincent Millay, the moss-covered walk to her grave), but it was the artists I met in these creative places who helped me see my project differently.

My writing groups were the safe spaces where I was able to either sit with others to write or where I could bring drafts of chapters to workshop and improve. Thanks to the Matrix Prose Group—Nicole Callihan, Ruth Ellen Kocher, and KP Kaszubowski—and my biography group: Humera Afridi, Kari Miller, Mary Chitty, Mike Ashcroft, Rachel Greenfield, Sarah Dorsey, Terese Svoboda, and Wanda Little Fenimore.

Thank you to my CrossFit Northgate family, where I cleared my head and felt the strength of community as I wrote this book, and to my new fitness family at the Barn.

Finally, thank you to my sons, Max and Jack, to my husband, Matt, and to our dogs, Shirley Jackson, Griffen, and Yeti, for supporting me at home.

Introduction

I knew from a very young age that I wanted to be a writer. But when I was growing up in the 1970s and '80s in rural Northern California, I was rarely assigned women writers to read in class. Having grown up in the West, I've always been drawn to writers who wrote about the West. When I was assigned books by Jack London, John Steinbeck, and Wallace Stegner, I was mesmerized by how they wrote about the land on which I lived. Judging by their depictions of the West, as well as those presented in film and on television, however, someone like me, a woman, had little to do with the West, and we certainly had never received much acclaim for writing about it.

My grandmother grew up in the panhandle of Oklahoma, and she and her family were forced to leave their farm when dust storms destroyed their crops. It was a tough journey, one that would scar my grandmother with its trauma for the rest of her life. My grandmother was proud of her survival, but she didn't want to talk about it, and she most certainly didn't want others to tell her story for her incorrectly.

When I was in high school, we were assigned John Steinbeck's *The Grapes of Wrath*. After I read it, I rushed home to call my grandmother to tell her about it. "Grandma, did you know they wrote a book about us?" She told me Steinbeck got it all wrong. She said he made her and her family look like helpless victims. She said not to mention the book ever again.

For a long time, I was confused by my grandmother's reaction. Why was she so upset about this great author's work? How had Steinbeck gotten it wrong? In my schooling up to that point, I had been trained to prioritize the published fictional account written by Steinbeck (a man) over my grandmother's firsthand (and of course more accurate) real-life experience. I had no idea how right my grandmother's reaction was.

When I first stumbled upon and read Sanora Babb's novel *Whose Names Are Unknown,* written in the late 1930s while she was volunteering with the Farm Security Administration, which built resettlement camps for Dust Bowl refugees, I was overwhelmed with emotion. I found mention of her book while I was watching Ken Burns's award-winning documentary *The Dust Bowl,* which features extensive excerpts from Babb's notes and reports and showcases Babb's unique knowledge of the Dust Bowl and its victims. Burns introduces Babb as someone who, like the refugees, had grown up in the affected area around the Oklahoma Panhandle (sometimes called No Man's Land) and was deeply committed to "establish[ing] a trust and respect" with the refugees "that extended both ways."[1]

Babb's was a story that humanized the experiences of those who had suffered through the worst natural disaster the United States had ever faced: a version where we got to know the characters before the worst days of their lives, when they had to flee to California to find work; where we saw the lives of women and children through their own eyes; and where we saw Black, Mexican, and Filipino workers in the fields and organizing strikes side by side with whites. Here was a book that told a version of the Dust Bowl story that aligned with the one my grandmother had told me.

Babb was a writer who reported the human truth. As her friend the poet Ann Stanford wrote about her work, she "represents the truth about life, even in its rough beauty."[2] By the time I finished reading *Whose Names Are Unknown,* I had become fascinated with Babb and knew that she had to be my next biographical subject. I had decided to write my first biography, *Charmian Kittredge London: Trailblazer, Author, Adventurer,* about Jack London's wife, an amazing woman who disregarded gender norms, when I found out that she had helped write many of her husband's novels and had never been given credit for her work. That biography was used as a source for a remodel of the museum at Jack London State Historic Park, housed in Charmian's previous home, The House of Happy Walls. Now, when young girls visit the park they will be introduced to two writers: Jack London and Charmian Kittredge London. This physical representation of my work has motivated me to commit my career to unearthing the stories of women who have been forgotten or misremembered. The more I learn, the more I research, the more I realize how many women have been erased not only from the history of the West, but from human history.

It is an arduous task to tell the story of a life. Babb hated writing biographical statements and was cautious of any biographer who wanted to take on the task of writing a biography of her husband, the Academy Award–winning cinematographer James Wong Howe, after he'd died. Thankfully Babb left a wide trail of materials, mainly at the Harry Ransom Center at the University of Texas at Austin: everything from the pair of beaded moccasins Chief Black Hawk gave her when she was a five-year-old living in Red Rock, Oklahoma, to drafts of her novels, memoirs, poems, and short stories, to long letters to and from friends, to boxes and boxes of photographs.

But while Babb could control what she left as her personal archive, she couldn't control how others would remember her. The word *archive* comes from the ancient Greek *arkheion,* "the house of the ruler." That means that what is placed in or what is left out of the archive is a political act. When you read the biographies of Babb's contemporaries—the novelists Ralph Ellison, William Saroyan, John Fante, and Carlos Bulosan, whom she supported and who were her literary equals—you rarely see Babb's name mentioned. The omission of her name and of many of her contemporaries' names has had a lasting effect.

Women's stories, especially those of women who were inspired by the likes of protofeminists like Edna St. Vincent Millay to cast off the monogamous, heterosexual gender norms that had been placed on them, were written out of the record after World War II, during the "Silent Decade," when women's lives were subjected to "the isolation of suburban domesticity beneath a decorative façade of respectability and resentment."[3] This, combined with the blacklisting that occurred during the Red Scare, left many once-popular female leftist writers of the 1930s and '40s unpopular and at odds with gender norms.

My research made me wonder what would have happened if I had been assigned Babb's *Whose Names Are Unknown* in school in addition to or even instead of *The Grapes of Wrath.* Not only would I have seen my own family's experience within the history I was being taught, but I also would have been given an example of a foremother: a woman writer who was writing about the West.

This biography aims to correct the record by returning to the archives with the intent of writing Sanora Babb's name back into the canon that has forgotten her. The life of Sanora Babb teaches us something about how to better understand the story of the American West. Hers is the story of a strong woman who was not deterred by those who wished to tell her story for her, or by those who would not let her tell her own story. This biography challenges the set canon of the American West by adding Babb's name to that elite and ever-growing list.

1 *Cheyenne Riding Like the Wind*

The writer Sanora Babb was only seven years old when, on an early fall morning in 1914, she boarded a westbound train with her younger sister Dorothy and her mother, Jennie, bound for a place she'd never been in Eastern Colorado. She had no idea what future she was heading toward. She'd left her home in the small town of Red Rock, Oklahoma, a place where she knew almost everyone and felt at ease, for a place she couldn't even imagine.

As the train picked up speed, young Babb rested her small forehead against the chilled glass.[1] The vast plains that whisked past the window were cold and stark. It was autumn, and each night winter threatened with lower temperatures and frost powdering the prairie. Bored from hours on the train, I imagine Babb nudged the seat in front of her, her small feet clad in soft worn moccasins. The shoes had been a present from the Otoe-Missouria Chief Black Hawk, and she treasured them.[2] In fact, she'd keep these moccasins her entire life. Even though she wore her shoes every day, the tiny white and turquoise beadwork still decorated each foot. She was sad to leave her pinto pony and the Otoe community that had welcomed her when she needed to escape her troubled home.[3] She must have wondered what life would be like in Colorado. She, her mother, and her sister had been separated from her father, Walter, for five months as he gambled the small wealth they had amassed running a popular bakery on purchasing a 160-acre plot of bare, unclaimed grazing land in Eastern Colorado. A week before they'd boarded the train, a simple letter arrived in the mail that brought Babb's mother to her knees: "Dear Jennie, bought a place. Sell all the stuff. Close down the bakery. Be ready to leave when you hear from me."[4] Then, a few days later, the telegram arrived that sent for them. Babb's father's closest friend, Asa, who was also an employee at the Babbs' bakery, had helped Jennie sell most of their belongings, let the staff of the bakery go, and helped shut it down. Asa hated to see them go, but he knew once Walt had an idea in his head, there was no stopping him. "Don't worry," he reassured Jennie and the girls, "you'll be back. That homesteading fever will soon pass. Don't give up."[5]

· · ·

Babb's parents had first arrived in Red Rock in 1905. When Walt and Jennie Babb pulled into the depot at Red Rock in the Oklahoma Territory, the train was surrounded by a dozen Otoe-Missouria men galloping alongside on horseback. Jennie, who had grown up in Lansing, Kansas, and who had little interaction with Native Americans prior to this event, screamed when she looked out the glass window of the train and saw the horses galloping and the long-haired men pumping their arms in the air and yelling. She was sure it was a train heist.[6] Babb would reimagine this journey as retold by her mother in a later short story, "Run, Sheepy, Run." When the protagonist looked out of the window of the train, she

> saw twenty or thirty [Native Americans] . . . [who] wore their long hair in braids, and it was black as a horse's tail. Bright blankets were drawn around their shoulders and moccasins were on their feet. Their faces were dark and impassive.

Laurie felt stiff with terror. She flung herself against Clete and whispered, "What will they do to us?"

"Nothing. They rode by to see the train come in." Clete raised the window and called out names, and two young men rode over, their horses moving along with the train. "Outfielder and second basemen," Clete said to Laurie, and then to the [Native Americans], "This is my wife, Laurie. Ben Good Bear and Lester Crazy Snake."[7]

At the station, Walt and Jennie boarded a rickety wagon and drove down Red Rock's dusty main street to Doc Sweeney's café, where they would live in Doc's wife's old rooms, as she'd recently left him.

A few months before, Doc, who was the first baseman on the town's semiprofessional baseball team, had offered Walt (the pitcher) the job of running the bakery. Walt had learned the baking trade from his father, who had run bakeries off and on in the Oklahoma Territory and in Kansas. At the center of Doc's café was a huge oven in which Walt would bake bread, cakes, and pastries. The town was next to Otoe-Missouria land. Most of the white residents of Red Rock baked their own bread, but many from the Otoe-Missouria tribe loved to buy Walt's doughy creations. His shop buzzed with the Jiwere language, and he swiftly learned to speak with his customers in their own language.[8] Walt's travels around the Oklahoma Territory playing baseball brought him in contact with Native Americans from many tribes, including the Osage, Caddo, Kiowa, Comanche, and Wichita, and Walt had become fluent in several of their languages. Soon after his arrival in Red Rock, the lot behind the bakery was transformed into a makeshift baseball diamond where Walt practiced his fast pitch and taught bakery visitors how to play baseball. Many of the Otoe-Missouria loved the sport, and it was in the lot behind the bakery that the Native American Red Rock baseball team was born.

On that first night, Doc welcomed the newlyweds with open arms and invited them to a meal. Exhausted, Jennie was relieved to sit down, even at the dirty table. Light filtered in through the dusty glass windows as Doc handed Jennie a hot cup of coffee in a greasy mug. She breathed on the scalding liquid, and right before she took a sip, looked down to see a fly floating in her drink. Then Doc placed a plate in front of her: a steak with French fried potatoes with a fly cooked into the steak. Jennie felt sickened by the food and worried about the place she would be living, but she ate anyway because she didn't want to appear ungrateful to her new host, who seemed little bothered by the black flies that buzzed in clouds around them and lay dead on all surfaces. She was only a child herself, just fifteen years old, and that night she cried herself to sleep.[9]

Walt's love letters to Jennie had made the small frontier town seem like a major metropolis, and she had been excited to leave her boring family-oriented life in Lansing, Kansas, where their existence was ruled by her father, who was a judge. Red Rock was located in the northern part of the territory, near the Otoe-Missouria reservation and the Miller Brothers' 101 Ranch, a vast 110,000-acre ranch famous for its Wild West shows.

The Otoe and Missouria tribes were originally from the Great Lakes region, but the tribes had both migrated to the lower Missouri River Valley in the 1600s. As more settlers began to trespass on their land, conflicts arose. In 1855 the Otoe-Missouria people were confined by the United States government to a reservation on the Big Blue River in southeast Nebraska. For three decades, the Otoe tribe suffered on the Big Blue Reservation before being forcibly relocated to another reservation in the area that would become Red Rock. But no sooner had they begun to settle in this new location than the land was taken away piece by piece, much of it leased to the Miller brothers when they established the 101 Ranch on the Salt Fork River. Then in 1887 the U.S. government passed the Dawes Act, which provided for the subdivision of tribally held lands into individually owned parcels. This broke up the Otoe-Missouria reservation and opened land deemed as "surplus" to settlement by non–Native Americans and development by railroads. When the Atchison, Topeka and Santa Fe Railway built a railroad line through this part of the state, a trading post began to operate near Red Rock Creek. The railroad ran through the trading post; however, the land remained a part of the reservation until July 20, 1903, when "surplus" lots were offered for sale. It was not long before Native Americans had lost half of their allotted land due to the arbitrary and exploitative practices of their so-called guardians, white citizens who managed Native Americans' financial holdings, supposedly with their best interests in mind. Soon, banks and stores opened, and the town of Red Rock began to grow. By 1905, when twenty-five-year-old Walt and his fifteen-year-old wife moved to Red Rock, there were three hundred white residents.

Just a week before he and Jennie arrived in Red Rock, Walt had traveled aboard a Southern Kansas Railway train back to Jennie, and the two were married by a judge at the courthouse in Leavenworth, Kansas, on November 1, 1905, at 3:00 p.m. Jennie's parents were present, and her siblings, but Walt's father, Alonzo Babb, refused to attend. He was often at odds with his son, and he didn't approve of Walt's marrying such a young girl. He knew his son wasn't cut out to be a good husband.

At the wedding, Jennie—who weighed a mere ninety-eight pounds, and whose tiny waist measured just twenty-one inches— wore a navy blue silk dress with a light blue velvet hat that Walt had bought for her. He loved to spend money on new clothes. He had also splurged on his own clothes: he wore a new black broadcloth suit with a white vest, a black hat, and black shoes.[10] After the brief meeting with the judge, they were officially married, and the couple and Jennie's family returned to Lansing, where Jennie's closest confidant and sister, Mae, had cooked the newlyweds a chicken dinner. It was the last time Jennie would see her family for months; however, instead of being sad, Jennie was pulsing with excitement.

Now that she'd seen and experienced Red Rock, however, Jennie was utterly disgusted. She wasn't one to give up easily though, and she tried hard to adapt to her new life. She put up curtains and swept out the ever-present dust that the train sent into their meagerly furnished room. But she often found herself alone for days at a time. Although Walt had become a baker in Red Rock to please his new wife, he hadn't given up his true love—gambling—and he often found his way to the back room of the Yellow Dog Saloon on Main Street, playing card games that lasted hours and even days.[11]

Walt had learned to gamble at an early age by watching older players play poker in the smoky saloons in the town of Mulhaul in the Oklahoma Territory, where high-stakes games were played day and night in back rooms. Walt's mother, Laura Davis, had only been married to his father Alonzo for five years when she suddenly died. One snowy night, the two had eloped and gotten married at the St. George Hotel in Weston, Missouri. They'd been happily married and when Laura died giving birth to their third child, Alonzo lost himself in grief and took to drink, leaving his surviving young children to be raised by their grandparents. Walt hadn't ever felt at home with either set of his grandparents, so he found another family in the back rooms of saloons, where, if he played his cards right, he felt powerful and in charge. For the majority of his life Walt would use the skills he had gained watching these games, and gambling became his passion. His other passion was baseball, a game he'd play semiprofessionally for most of his twenties and thirties in the Western League. Walt had learned how to play baseball when he was in his early teens from a classmate who'd "played in the Big League" and who would teach him whenever he returned home at the close of baseball season.[12] After three years of training Walt, his mentor sent him to play in the Western League, where Walt was drafted and soon known for his "great spit-ball delivery."[13]

About a month after their arrival in Red Rock, Walt and Jennie had their first serious fight. Doc Sweeney had hired a young girl to wait tables and to help in the kitchen. In the afternoons, when the café was quiet, Walt would ask the girl to play cards with him. He never played cards with Jennie because he knew she didn't know how to play. But the girl insisted on dealing Jennie in. Jennie stumbled though her first hand and Walt cruelly mocked her. During the game he made fun of every card she chose to put down. Jennie was so upset that she stood up from the table and ran to their room. She crawled into the closet, sat on her trunk, and cried. Even tucked into the closet, she could hear Walt and the girl laughing through the thin walls of the café. That night, Jennie wanted desperately to go home. She was sick about the decision she'd made to leave her family and live in this rough town that was filthy with black flies and dust, with a man who treated her like she was a fool. She locked the door. A few hours later, Doc Sweeney came by and knocked gently, asking her, "You're not mad at me, runt, are you?" Jennie did not open the door but assured him she wasn't. She told him she hated Walt. A few minutes later, she could hear the repercussions of her words as Doc scolded Walt, warning him that if he didn't start treating his new wife better, she'd end up leaving him like his own wife had done. Walt just barked back "Let her leave" as he walked out the door of the café to head to the saloon. That was the first night Walt didn't come back. Jennie had never slept anywhere by herself before that night; she was so scared in the middle of the night that she unlocked the door and stepped out of their room into the moonlit café. Everything was shadowed and dark. Jennie vowed she would go home but she didn't know how she'd pull it off. She had to get out of the situation she'd gotten herself into.[14]

A month later Jennie had gathered enough money to purchase a train ticket and took the train home to visit her family. While she was there, she begged her mother to take her back. But her mother was traditional; her daughter had married and she believed she needed to stay with her husband no matter the circumstances. Instead of welcoming her troubled daughter, she responded to Jennie with words that were seared into her mind for the rest of her life: "You made your bed hard. Now lie in it." So after just a few days of reprieve, Jennie returned to Red Rock and faced her life with Walt. For fun, when he was at the saloon, Jennie would play Run Sheepy Run (a game of hide-and-seek) with the kids in town. Later, as the relationship between Walt and Jennie continued to deteriorate and became more violent, Jennie's mother regretted that she'd been so hard on her daughter.[15]

A few months after Jennie's return, Walt's father, Alonzo, came to stay with Jennie and Walt. Jennie knew he didn't really like her, but she was desperate for company. When he got off the train, he was lugging nothing but a bedroll and an empty five-gallon can that had held currant jelly. On the train ride, the jelly had spilled, leaving the bedroll stained red and sticky. When Alonzo laughingly shoved it at his son, joking that now he'd have to sleep with the newlyweds, Walt didn't laugh in return. Instead, he was furious. He'd never forgiven his father for abandoning him when he was a child. He grabbed the ruined bedroll, marched to the bakery, and threw it into the blazing oven.

Walt, who hated working for others, wanted to start his own bakery. He found an empty store he could rent from Barney Woolverton, who was a fellow Red Rock baseball player and the owner of the Yellow Dog Saloon. With Alonzo around, Walt was almost entirely freed from his duties at the bakery. Alonzo baked the breads and his specialty, cakes, and Jennie ran the cash register. Most of the patrons who frequented the bakery came from the Otoe-Missouria reservation, and Jennie, now over the initial shock of her first day in Red Rock, began to form close friendships with many of the Native American women who frequented the bakery. Alonzo's cakes, which he decorated with exquisite detail, were a huge hit and were ordered for every encampment or powwow. Local celebrities, including a young Will Rogers, also frequented the shop when they visited the Wild West show at nearby 101 Ranch.[16]

Since they'd begun dating, Walt had made it clear to Jennie that he didn't want to have children. But with no birth control available to them, Jennie soon found herself pregnant. It wasn't an easy pregnancy; the first few months, she suffered constant nausea, and she once became so violently ill that she vomited blood. When she asked Walt to come with her to find the town doctor, he instead left to play in a baseball game. Given Walt's lack of enthusiasm and his unpredictable nature, Jennie was afraid that she would be alone when she went into labor, so when she was seven months pregnant, she decided to face her mother and return home to have her baby. Thankfully, this time her mother didn't refuse her. In fact, when she found out Jennie was pregnant, she insisted that Jennie return to Kansas immediately so that baby would be born in an actual state, rather than in the Territory of Oklahoma.

When she arrived, Jennie unpacked the layette she'd been putting together for her baby. She had only just learned to sew and was teaching herself. Her mother was a tailor, and when she caught sight of the work her daughter had done, she shook her head and ripped out the seams. Together, she and Jennie's sister Mae remade all of the clothes for Jennie's baby. Jennie's father, the judge Green Berry Parks, had a close friend who was a doctor at St. John's Hospital in Leavenworth, and he arranged to have his daughter admitted to the prestigious institution to give birth. On April 21, 1907, Sanora Louise Babb was born at 9:30 a.m. A few days later, Jennie dressed her newborn in a silk dress the doctor's wife had sewn for her and wrapped her in a baby blanket crowned in ribbons and left the hospital to return to her elm-tree-shaded family home, where she spent six blissful weeks with her mother and sister helping her care for her new baby. Jennie didn't want to return to Red Rock, but each day another letter arrived from Walt in which he claimed to be sorry for all he had done. He revealed to her he'd been terrified that she was going to die during childbirth, just like his mother, and he was so relieved she had survived that he promised he would change. He professed his love and claimed that he couldn't live without Jennie and begged her to return. Jennie was only seventeen years old. She began to remember the handsome man she'd first seen working at the bakery and fallen in love with, the man who had walked her home from church and told her stories of his travels around the Midwest playing baseball. Walt was persistent when he wanted something and stubbornly did everything in his power to make it happen. And after six weeks, Walt's relentless letters worked, and Jennie returned to Red Rock.

Babb and her mother boarded the train with Babb's grandfather, Green Berry Parks. On the way to Red Red Rock, the three stopped to buy Jennie and her new child some furniture for their rooms. Then Judge Parks left his daughter and new grandchild at the station to catch a train headed back home, and Jennie was completely alone with her daughter for the first time. Looking out the train window on her way back to her life in Red Rock, Jennie couldn't shake the weight of the sadness that had sunk into her. She wanted to believe that Walt would grow into being a father and a better husband and that having a baby together would bring them closer, but she couldn't completely convince herself of the possibility. She held Babb's small form close to her chest, trying to ward off the sadness that sank deeper each mile the train got closer to Red Rock.

As expected, fatherhood didn't change Walt. The train whistle that rang through town on the hour still made him long to wander. He managed the town baseball team and all summer he'd travel around the state, leaving Jennie alone to tend for their child and manage the bakery. In her first few months, Babb cried incessantly. When Walt was home, Jennie paced up and down in their small rooms, trying to get the baby to sleep before Walt's anger erupted. Alonzo told his son to "settle down," and when he was tired of picking up the slack at the bakery for what his son wouldn't do, Alonzo would shout "God dang my wild cat!"[17] In the evenings, Alonzo would sit on the back steps of the bakery and quietly smoke his pipe by himself. Jennie was always comforted by the red glow she saw out the window because it meant she wasn't alone.

But the truth was, once she had her daughter, Jennie's life was too busy to complain about. She woke at 4:00 a.m. to begin her work in the bakery. She mopped the floors and washed the showcases where they displayed their breads and cakes, then filled them with fresh delicacies. She kept Babb in a baby carriage behind the register, where she could watch her while she ran the shop. She also had to run their home. She washed and ironed clothes and diapers and prepared each meal they ate. Her hands were always raw and chapped. She was exhausted every second of the day. She became friends with another young woman in town, Grace Carpenter, and every once in a while Grace would take Jennie on an outing, giving her a vacation from her hard life. One Christmas they took the train to Ponca City to go Christmas shopping, and a few Sundays Jennie accompanied Grace to church, where a handsome preacher gave sermons. But whenever Jennie returned from such an outing, Walt would berate her with insults and accuse her of infidelity, so she rarely went.[18]

From the start, Babb was an outgoing child. By ten months she was walking and greeting every customer that came into the bakery with a wave. By the time she was two, she was the team mascot for her father's baseball team. Walt had a small jersey sewn for her to wear at games. He began to call his daughter by his pet name, Cheyenne, a name that he'd call her for the rest of his life. Once Babb was on the go, Jennie couldn't run the bakery and watch her, and Babb began to wander around the block where the bakery was located. Soon she knew all of the shopkeepers in town.

During one of Walt's many trips around the state with his baseball team, he caught smallpox. Jennie, who grew up in a state where children were vaccinated, was immune to the disease, but Babb hadn't yet been vaccinated, and when Walt returned home, she caught the disease. The Babbs were ordered by the sheriff to close the bakery for six weeks. By this time, Oklahoma had become a state and regulations against smallpox were strongly enforced. A big yellow sign was posted on the bakery door.[19] The Otoe-Missouria residents were terrified of smallpox and wouldn't even walk on the same side of the street as the bakery while the yellow sign loomed. Young Babb was covered in sores, and Jennie had to bind her arms in order to stop her from scratching and scarring her skin. For weeks, she carried her daughter around on a little pillow in order to try to make her feel comfortable.

A few weeks later, Jennie received the terrible news that her father was dying. She bundled up her daughter and caught a train to the hospital in Fort Scott, where she, her mother, and her siblings took turns sitting by her father's bedside. He lasted only a few days, but Jennie was relieved she arrived in time to see him one last time. While she was away, Walt found an opportunity to run a bakery in the nearby town of Waynoka, and he was eager for Jennie to return so they could move. Once again, Walt had his mind set on something and wouldn't relent until he got what he wanted. Jennie was unable to stay for her father's funeral and instead was forced to leave her family on the day that her father died.

Compared to Red Rock, Waynoka was a bustling town, as it housed Oklahoma's largest rail yard. Trains were constantly coming and going, twenty-four hours a day. The Babbs moved into a small house with a wraparound porch. Soon, Jennie was thrilled to find out that her brother was also moving to Waynoka, to start a butcher shop. When he disembarked from the train in Waynoka, he asked where the Babbs lived and was told to look for the house with clotheslines filled with diapers. Jennie's life continued to be hard. She managed the new bakery, which was bustling with customers. She took care of her husband, her child, Alonzo, and whomever else Walt brought home (one summer the entire baseball team lived with them). But she did have one joy: she'd been able to acquire a piano, which she loved to play. In the evenings, she played the songs her father had loved, which helped soothe her grief about his loss.

In late 1908, Jennie started to feel sick and realized she was pregnant with a second child. As her pregnancy progressed, she kept telling herself that with two babies, Walt would finally settle into being a better father. She was only eighteen years old, and naïve. But Walt had no interest in changing his ways. On March 28, 1909, Dorothy Marcella Babb was born at the hospital in Waynoka. From the start, Dorothy was the opposite of her sister. When Babb saw adventure, she ran to it; when Dorothy saw adventure, she hid from it. Though different, the two sisters were inseparable as children.

Soon after Dorothy was born, Walt again became restless and uprooted the family to return to Red Rock, where he would once more run the bakery they'd left behind and a baseball team. Within a few months of moving back to Red Rock, Alonzo moved on to another "opportunity" in Eastern Colorado, where he planned to live on a homestead and sober up. Now Jennie found herself running the bakery alone and taking care of two children. She wrote her sister Mae often, and even visited her a few times. Mae adored her nieces and sewed them gorgeous clothes: she made Dorothy, whose hair had grown in white blonde, an Easter bonnet. Mae told her sister that if anything ever happened to Jennie, she would gladly raise the girls. But on August 12, 1911, Jennie received the worst news of her life: she found out via telegram that Mae had died suddenly of typhoid fever.[20] Jennie was devastated. Her sister had been her closest confidant in the world, and she had been the buoy keeping Jennie afloat through the early tumultuous years of her marriage. It was a loss she'd never get over.

With her mother consumed with running the bakery and taking care of her little sister, Babb, now five years old, found herself free again to wander around the town of Red Rock. She knew all the shop-keepers from her family's previous stint in Red Rock, but the people she connected with the most were those of the Otoe-Missouria tribe. Many of the Otoe-Missouria children were being forcibly removed to a boarding school, where they were taught "white ways" and were threatened and coerced into abandoning their heritage, including the Jiwere language. It's likely the community embraced Babb be-cause many within it missed their own children. Chief Black Hawk was especially fond of young Babb. All her life, Babb liked to recall the story her father had told her about the chief's wish to buy her and the gifts he gave her. One day when the chief came in to the bakery to buy his favorite rolls, he asked Walt in all seriousness if he could buy his daughter. Walt laughed and told Chief Black Hawk that his daugh-ter was not for sale. But Chief Black Hawk was persistent, and each day he visited the bakery he'd bring Babb a small present. First he brought her feathers and handmade rattles. As she grew older, he be-gan to bring her larger gifts: handsewn moccasins with exquisite beadwork, and other clothing. Finally he arrived with a pinto pony. Five-year-old Babb's face lit up when he led her outside by the hand and she saw the pony tied to a post outside the bakery.[21]

"She's your pony now," Chief Black Hawk told her as he lifted Babb onto the pony's bare back and untied the reins from the post so he could walk her around the town.

Just then, a gunshot went off nearby and the pony lurched into a full gallop. Chief Black Hawk lost the reins and Babb clung desper-ately to the pony's mane as he shot like a comet out of town toward the Otoe-Missouria encampment. Chief Black Hawk had his own horse nearby, and he quickly mounted and galloped after Babb and her runaway pony. When he caught up to them, Babb was shaking, but the chief couldn't help but laugh. He lifted Babb down from the pony and said, "You did very good staying on your new pony even though he was running like the wind! Your name is now Cheyenne, Riding like the Wind."

The name stuck. For the rest of the time she and her family spent in Red Rock, Babb went by the name.[22] As soon as she could ride on her own, Babb began spending increasing amounts of time with the Otoe-Missouria people because they treated her with more love and compassion than she found in her own home. Her mother was young, stuck, and depressed, and her father was out all night most nights, gambling. When her parents were together, they would fight, often violently, leaving her mother with black eyes and bloody lips. In contrast, Babb saw that the Otoe-Missouria people were "wonderful with their children; gentle, kind, dignified. Scolding is rare and punishment non-existent. . . . I was incredibly happy. There was much violence at home." Even as a five-year-old, Babb would ride out to the Otoe-Missouria land on her new pony and sometimes stay for days at a time. As Babb remembered, Chief Black Hawk "used to hold me on his lap. He smoked so much; his clothes smelled of tobacco. Whenever I've smelled such an odor since I remember him."[23]

In 1914, Walt became restless for a new adventure. Ever since Alonzo had left to stake a claim in Eastern Colorado, he had been sending Walt letters romanticizing his new pioneer life. In each, he proselytized about how invigorating his new life was, proving-up his claim, learning dry-land farming, and living in a one-room dugout near Two Buttes. One day, on a whim, and without consulting his wife, Walt set out on his own to join his father, telling Jennie that he'd send for her and their daughters as soon as he'd settled and set up a place for them to stay.

·   ·   ·

The whistle rang out, the massive weight of the train came to a full stop, and steam veiled the windows. They had finally reached the town of Lamar, the first stop on their journey to their new home in Eastern Colorado. Seven-year-old Babb took her sister Dorothy's small hand in hers and followed her mother down the train car to the open door. Framed in the doorway was her father. Dorothy, whose world revolved around her father, dropped her sister's hand and ran to jump into her father's arms, but Babb hung cautiously back, close to her mother. She didn't yet trust the new life her father had chosen for them. When they stepped onto the platform the first thing she noticed was that all of the people there were white, so different from the majority Native American population she'd lived with in Red Rock and Waynoka. Her father's eyes shone. He'd clearly missed his family. Her mother stood tall and rigid in her large-brimmed straw hat, until a wind scooped it up and set it soaring toward the tracks. A nice gentleman ran for it and brought it back to her.[24] The Babbs gathered their things, and Jennie revealed to Walt that she hadn't had the heart to sell her most precious belonging, her piano, and had instead brought it with them on the train. Walt was irate. "We're fifty miles from here. I'll have to hire a wagon to come after it! Goddamn."[25]

Walt tried to swallow his anger, as they didn't have time for a fight. He led them to a black Ford touring town car that was parked next to the platform. It was stuffed with so many passengers that there was no place for the girls to sit. Dorothy was placed on her mother's lap, while Babb was left to sit on the floor with everyone's high-buttoned shoes and the cold draft drifting in from the floorboards. Her seat cut her off from seeing the new world that she'd now inhabit. For two hours she sat and imagined the world that was unfurling past outside the car. Suddenly the car stopped, and they unfolded themselves from the packed seats. In front of them was the small town of Two Buttes, named after the two mounds that rose sharply from the flat land in the distance. They hired a wagon to the isolated place where their homestead was located.

For as far as Babb could see in the dimming light there were no trees, just a cold, flat starkness that threatened to swallow her up. The wagon carried them farther and farther away from the town. The cool air smelled like sage. In the distance she finally saw a dim light coming from the ground; she couldn't figure out what it might be. When the wagon stopped, a dog began barking incessantly. A door in the ground opened up and out walked her grandfather, Alonzo. How had he crawled out of the ground? she wondered. Then she saw a staircase leading down behind him, and she realized this was their new home: a hole in the ground.[26]

Babb's shift from the bustling frontier town of Red Rock to the desolate plains of Eastern Colorado was shocking to her: "This was an empty land. A primordial loneliness was on it; the train carried us backward in time."[27] Indeed, the years Babb spent on the "empty land" of the high plains of Colorado would haunt her for the rest of her life. But this empty land would prove fruitful as it awakened in her a sense of curiosity and wonder. This place would be the source for her first novel, written in the 1930s, *Whose Names Are Unknown,*[28] and her memoir, *An Owl on Every Post.* As she would later recall, "Living in a true wilderness as a child had a profound influence on me."[29] But most of what Babb wrote about this time was romanticized and purged of many of the most troubling details. These omissions exist because her time in Eastern Colorado was a time when she, in many ways, began to come into her own. She became her own person, and as conditions began to worsen due to her father's rash choices and ill temper, she began to fight back. "It was I who challenged him, even as a child, causing his furies to soar. Behind my back he boasted of my spirit, but in the fray he was my enemy and I was his."[30] Later, in a letter to her cousin Lillie Pollard, Babb elaborated on the terrible conditions they endured and her relationship with her father: "My sister and I began as very healthy youngsters and were quite sturdy looking until my father took a notion to do a little pioneering in an unsettled part of Colorado, and the several hopelessly failing years there, when we were all starved into shadows and broken by his furious vents of temper at misfortune, took such a toll on our young bodies that we have never really known health since."[31] From 1914 until 1917, Babb's family would not only be extremely isolated, they would suffer her father's abuse and would nearly starve to death on a number of occasions.

To say that the Babb family's accommodations in the dugout were rustic would be an understatement. A dugout, or pit-house, was a common structure used by earlier pioneers. In Laura Ingalls Wilder's fictional account about homesteading in Minnesota, *On the Banks of Plum Creek,* she describes her protagonist's first impression of the dugout that was soon to become her home: "Over the edge of the bank, the path turned and went slanting down close against the grassy bank that rose up like a wall. Laura went down it cautiously. The bank rose up beside her till she could not see the wagon. Laura went a step farther, then one more step. The path stopped at a wider, flat place, where it turned and dropped down to the creek in stair steps. Then Laura saw the door. It was like a house door, but whatever was behind it was under the ground." In the midwestern U.S., the dugout home was used as a temporary shelter to weather the first few winters, or as a subsistence dwelling for pioneer farmers in the mid-1800s. "'It's only till I harvest the first wheat crop,' said [Laura's] Pa. 'Then you'll have a fine house.'"[32] Like the fictional Laura and her family, many settlers in the expanding region of Baca County in Colorado found temporary or semipermanent shelter in dugout houses.[33]

However, Alonzo's dugout that Babb, her sister, and her mother were moving into would turn out to be anything but temporary (although Walt would claim he had a plan to soon build them a house on his newly purchased land). Babb described their dugout as "a square hole in the ground, dirt floor, with a 2 or 3 ft. wooden wall and roof. No amenities of any kind, save two windows which look onto the ground."[34] The first time she and her mother and sister entered the dugout, Babb recounted, "The air above the ground was sharp and dry, [but] in the dugout a dank earth dampness pressed into our breath, chilled our bones. The slant door had been let down. We were trapped. 'This place is like a grave,' Papa said."[35]

2 A Dugout on the High Plains

In May 1914, when Babb, her sister, and her mother moved into the dugout on her grandfather's land south of Two Buttes, there were only two beds, so Babb slept in one of them with her grandfather. This troubled seven-year-old Babb, for the grandfather she'd grown up with had been a drunk. But the night they arrived, weary from the long journey, she didn't have a choice, so she lay down next to her grandfather's tall, thin body. As the hours passed, she heard her grandfather's regular breathing next to her, and far outside in the distance, muffled by the dugout's earthen walls, she could hear the sound of coyotes howling. Then another sound from inside the dugout came to her attention: "I heard the fast ticks of little feet running up and down the walls. Once a thump on my blanket and the feet continuing on the floor. . . . Then something bit me. Without thinking, I scratched the bite, felt a small fat bug, and smelled a revolting odor. I cried out. I could not help it." Startled by her scream, her grandfather woke up and quickly ordered that someone light the kerosene lamp, and in the light, Babb saw what had bitten her. There were "oval brown bugs running over our pillows and up the walls, hurrying away from the light." Her mother, who had also been awakened by her daughter's scream, asked Walt what the bugs were, and he explained, "Bedbugs. They came with the new lumber. Dad's lived alone so long he doesn't care, didn't even try to get rid of them."[1]

Jennie was horrified. She stood abruptly, scooped up some blankets, grabbed her daughters by the arms and pulled them up the stairs, where she swung open the heavy door and exited, exclaiming to the men, "We'll sleep in the wagon." Babb's father tried to protest, claiming it was "too cold" and safer underground, while Babb's grandfather warned of coyotes and wolves. But Babb didn't even hear her parents fighting. When the hatch opened and she stepped outside into the cold spring air and looked up at the night sky, "it seemed the stars were falling down upon us."[2] The stars seemed infinite above them. On that first night, Babb felt the solace of nature, a balm that would soothe her countless times during the trials she and her family would face over the next three years. Safely outside, Jennie set up a pallet in the flat bed of the wagon Alonzo and Walt had borrowed, and the three of them tried to sleep, listening to the sound of coyotes far off in the distance.

The next morning, Babb awoke to a frosty dawn. The dark place they had seen at night under thousands of stars had been transformed. Endless miles of tall grass were painted pink under a grenadine-colored sunrise. The sharp scent of sagebrush, intensified by the dry ground, filled their nostrils. "The air was of such purity that we stood breathing deeply for the simple pleasure of breathing."[3] The land around the dugout contained, Babb explained, "only range cattle, long empty plains, a few farms miles and miles from one another. Desolation."[4] The only thing that rose up from the wide flat horizon that surrounded them were the pointed summits of Two Buttes Mountain, which towered three hundred feet above the prairie. Babb mistakenly thought the formation was left over from a silver mine, but the strange double-peaked mountain was naturally formed. That morning, as she was standing in the yard outside the dugout, she looked to the horizon "wondering, dreaming. I recall thinking: one day I will lift up the sky and go into the world and wander all over that world."[5]

Walt had purchased the 160 acres of desolate land sight unseen based on the recommendation of his father, paying the enormous sum of $750.[6] He hadn't wanted to be tied down to the five years of farming that was required to obtain the land for free through the Homestead Act of 1862.[7] Buying the land outright was a huge gamble, one that would nearly cost his family their lives. Babb's grandfather Alonzo—who now went by Konkie, a nickname Babb had given him when she was too young to be able to pronounce his name—hadn't purchased his land outright. Instead, he was "proving up" his acreage. According to the Homestead Act, "Every citizen, and every foreigner who asked for citizenship, [had] the right to claim government land. The law said each man could have sixty-five hectares. If he built a home on the land, and farmed it for five years, it would be his."[8] And so Konkie had moved onto two plots equalling 320 acres of government land a few miles from the town of Two Buttes, built a small dugout, and planted a crop of broomcorn. Konkie was following in the footsteps of his own father, John Babb, who had claimed government land in the Kiowa-, Comanche-, and Apache-ceded lands in Yukon, Oklahoma Territory, in 1901.[9] Little did Konkie and Walt know that that they were trying to settle arid land, land that according to geologist and explorer John Wesley Powell was under the constant threat of recurrent drought. When Powell had surveyed the land east of the Rockies in the 1800s, he "was convinced that settlement had already reached as far west as it could go without grave risks to both settler and the land."[10] In his monumental book *The Great Plains,* historian Walter Prescott Webb describes how "the Great Plains offered such a contrast to the region east of the ninety-eighth meridian, the region with which American civilization had been familiar until about 1840, as to bring about a marked change in the ways of pioneering and living."[11]

Instead of building a structure on his own land, as his father had done, Walt just moved his family into his father's dugout. He was deeply disappointed by what he claimed his father had lured him into, but not disappointed enough to save his family from the disaster of joining him there. Walt fought constantly with his father but never wanted to leave him. In fact, Konkie would live near Babb and her family until close to the end of their stay in Colorado three years later.

As Babb would recount:

> The time here is the end of . . . pioneering, long after pioneering had passed. Before WWI, the government opened up large areas of range land on the high plains, east of the Rockies, the fenceless grasslands valued by cattle ranchers. . . . These were the margin lands, treeless, and all but rainless. One was lucky to get one crop out of five, a starvation existence. . . . People came, not many, and on that vast plain, a few fenced farms appeared, the families far and distant from one another, unwelcome by the even more far distant ranchers, whose herds overran the fences or were withdrawn to other free ranges to the west; and so, it seemed to the new settlers, unwelcome to the whole of nature. The summers were dry and hot, almost rainless; the winters were fierce with blizzards; the year round was wild with the winds. There was no water for crops or gardens; few could afford the deep and expensive wells. Most were "starved out"; a few struggled for years. There were no schools. A store and a post office were miles away.[12]

Cooking in the dugout, like everything else, was rustic. That first morning, Jennie left the girls to explore the land around the dugout while she went back into the dark hole in the ground, where the men still snored, to boil water for coffee and learn how to cook on the small monkey stove. Monkey stoves are general-purpose stoves with two small burners. The Babbs kept theirs stoked with firewood and, when that ran out, dried cow patties they found littering the plains, which were used to free-range cattle. That first day was anything but easy, with Walt and his father, the master bakers, bickering about teaching Jennie how to cook using the rustic device. Soon, though, she had learned how to use the stove proficiently enough to bake cinnamon rolls and bread for her family.

After breakfast, Jennie ordered everyone in the family to haul the contents of the dugout out into the cold morning sun. Soon the yard was strewn with mattresses and the iron bedsteads. To get rid of the bugs that had visited them the night before, Jennie wiped down the bed frames and soaked the feet with coal oil. Then she aired out the mattresses. She opened the two dirty windows at the top of the dugout and refused to close them even when the family had hauled everything back in at the end of the day and gone to sleep that night, so as to air out the stench of the two men combined with the smell of the burning cow patties in the small stove. She made a paste from flour and water and used it to glue the pages of the *Denver Post* she'd brought with her to the walls of dugout, text that would later prove useful to Babb when she learned how to read. Jennie did this in order to keep at bay the feeling of living underground in what was like a grave. She also swept the hard-packed earthen floor until it was as clean as it would get. Somehow swept dirt felt cleaner than loose dirt.

The dugout was so small for the five of them that they were forced to be outside whenever the weather permitted. Babb's grandfather Konkie would escape to the small makeshift barn he had built in back of the dugout, a barn made out of cedar logs he'd hauled back from the far-off mountains, while Babb and her sister would explore the plains around them. When the family had to go to the bathroom, they visited a rustic outhouse around the back of the dugout. And if someone wanted to take a bath, they used "a wash tub out in the yard with as little water as possible."[13]

This homestead on the desolate Colorado plains, though bleak, was a place Babb would come back to repeatedly in her thoughts and in her writing. Babb's early experiences in Colorado would later form what scholar Jessica Hellmann, drawing from a term developed by Aldo Leopold, has called Babb's "land ethic."[14] Babb lived on a homestead, yet she wrote against the grain of the myths of the American West. When you and your family begin to starve, the ideal of rugged individualism goes out the window. What Babb learned while living in Colorado was that she and her family were not conquerors of the land; rather, they had to live under the land's terms, or they would never survive. As Babb later wrote in the epilogue of *An Owl on Every Post,*

> I always felt grounded in the plains. The impact of those years is still potent.
>
> I treasure the deep influence of those years: a sense of living on a grand earth under a big sky, not within walls. The darkness on the plains was as black as space and the stars so thick and brilliant they seemed touchable while they seemed eons away, all of this mysterious and awesome. Long before I read that everything in the universe is connected, that all life is One, I knew it intuitively when I was seven years old. This was an awareness, not a discovery. It gave me a mystical sense of being in the universe, related, belonging, as transient as a flower but just as welcome. It gave me freedom from the need for specific beliefs and dogmas. It gave me tolerance. Perhaps it was the bigness of the plains and the sky that stretched my thoughts.[15]

Often Babb's descriptions of her life during this time period, though, would be seen through the sepia of nostalgia. She'd change facts to make the poverty and trauma her family experienced less prominent. For instance, the reason they had trouble farming was the sheer fact that their homestead had no water source and the family had no money to dig a well. When Babb writes about their first day in *An Owl on Every Post*, she claims they already had two horses and that they hitched them to the wagon to ride the two and a half miles to Horse Creek to gather water in barrels. The truth was that on that first day, there were no horses. Instead, the whole family, including seven-year-old Babb and four-year-old Dorothy, trekked to their neighbor Old Man Hoopies's well three miles away, carrying a gallon syrup bucket in each hand. Empty on the way there and full on the way back. It wasn't until after the first broomcorn harvest that they were finally able to purchase two horses and a wagon complete with water barrels. From that point on, they no longer had to hike the three miles to their neighbor's well. Instead, they hitched the horses to the wagon and drove to the Knox Ranch, where they filled their large barrels with water and then drove them home.

One of the two horses they purchased was named Fred; strangely, he had two quarters embedded under the skin on his hips. Years later, when the horse died, Konkie cut out the quarters and gave them to Babb and her sister as keepsakes. Sadly, the girls had to give them back in order to buy food for the family when times got really tough. The horses were dear to them, and when Fred died, they mourned him as if he were a member of their family: "When Fred's carcass was stripped by wolves and coyotes and his bones whitened, we put them back in order and on Sundays often walked the long way to visit his bones and to eat our lunch nearby. On those Sunday walks, often ten miles, we found arrowheads and passed buffalo wallows, and Konkie and Papa told us of the Indians who were so lately driven from their land."[16]

Konkie and Walt's land was located near the small community of Blaine and the town of Two Buttes. Their first trip to town, which took place before they owned horses, was made in a borrowed wagon. Babb remembered that although the trip happened just two weeks after their arrival, it felt like they had been living in isolation for years. Two Buttes had less than a hundred residents, but it housed J. V. Sayler's general store and pharmacy, a post office, and a café, and most importantly, it offered other people to look at and talk to. In Red Rock and Waynoka, Babb had spent her days playing with other children, visiting shops, or completely away from her family, out on Otoe-Missouria land. In those first two weeks stuck with only her immediate family in a one-room dugout, she felt claustrophobic.

During the three years Babb would spend living in Eastern Colorado, she would develop a close relationship with her grandfather, one that would save her by counteracting the tense and argumentative relationship she had with her father. In *An Owl on Every Post,* Babb claims that it was here in Colorado that she first met her grandfather, but this isn't true. Her grandfather had been a part of her life since Red Rock. The grandfather she met in Colorado, though, was quite different than the one she had known in Red Rock: he was sober. It is this fact that makes her introduce him as a new character in her life in her writing about that time. As she describes him, "He was most uncommunicative, and the only gesture of affection he made toward me was a rare small thump of knuckle on my shoulder. This I treasured greatly."[17]

Babb's grandfather had dark skin and dark eyes. When she asked, hopefully, if he had indigenous blood, he answered that he did not, claiming instead he was "Irish and Welsh, Spanish-dark from the Armada days, perhaps."[18] His explanation for his otherness was a common one in the early 1900s; claiming to be "black Irish" was a way to pass as white in a racist society.

Neither Babb nor her sister would be able to regularly attend school while they lived on the homestead. Instead, they used whatever they found around them to learn. Konkie read to them from the only book they had, *The Adventures of Kit Carson.* Narrated by the illiterate frontier "hero" Carson, the book offers the classic version of the West put forward by Frederick Jackson Turner: a man conquers the indigenous people and the land. By the time this dime novel was published, Kit Carson had made a name for himself as an American frontiersman while working in the fur trade. He was hired by army officer John Charles Frémont as a guide during several expeditions west of the Rockies. Frémont would later record Carson's life story as Carson told it to him, and that text would eventually become the best-selling book Babb and her sister would use as their reading textbook.[19]

Strangely enough, though Babb read this book hundreds of times, its themes did not inform her psyche. The West that Babb would later describe in her writing was the West she had grown up in, a place where women and men both had agency, and where everyone had to work together to survive. Nonetheless, the book proved to be extremely useful, as Babb recalled: "[It] gave me also my first formal source of education. I studied it to learn words; I copied from it to learn to spell; I read it to myself and aloud; I copied numbers from its pages; I wrote lessons on what I had read. We wore that book out."[20]

Another source of reading material were those pages of the *Denver Post* her mother had pasted to the dugout's bare soil walls. The pages would not only provide her with reading material, but they would also act as a gateway to the world that existed beyond their small dugout. "Grandfather selected short pieces for me to read from the *Denver Post* pasted on the walls. Others he ignored, which meant he forbade, but I read them when he wasn't around. I was fascinated by all the pieces in the newspaper; each showed me a facet of the world beyond that far circle of horizon. Everything existed out there and I would someday find it."[21]

In addition to the *Denver Post* and Kit Carson's book, each week Jennie's mother sent the girls columns of Thornton Burgess's famous animal stories clipped from the *Kansas Star and Times* and enclosed in her letters. Babb and her sister loved animals and these columns only intensified their commitment; they'd cry every time their father killed a chicken, and they improvised funerals for the chicken heads. Decades later, after she'd published a number of stories herself, Babb wrote Thornton Burgess a fan letter thanking him for his stories and explaining the value his weekly columns had for her and her sister when they had little else to read and lived so isolated on the plains.[22]

To help Babb learn arithmetic, her grandfather would draw figures in the hard ground with a stick. He'd hand the stick to Babb and ask her to solve it. Or he'd ask elaborate word problems like the one Babb remembers in *An Owl on Every Post:* "If a rancher had 9,000 acres of grazing land, and an electric storm came up and lightning struck the ground and started a prairie fire, burning 587 acres, how many acres of good grass were left for the stock?"[23] They'd also have spelling bees and competitions reciting multiplication tables. But none of this makeshift instruction could compare to the greater education Babb received walking around the plains and learning from the land. Babb memorized the flora and fauna that she observed as a young child, and those plants and animals would stay with her for the rest of her life, resurfacing in many of the stories and poems she'd later write.

Soon after their arrival in Colorado, life got busy with the arduous work of planting and farming broomcorn. Broomcorn is a type of sorghum that is used for making brooms. The crop was first introduced in Baca County in 1887 and thrived as the area's leading crop well into the 1970s, due to the fact that the plants need little water to survive. Wealthier farmers would hire crews to do the work of planting and harvesting, but the Babbs and most other new settlers in the area didn't have that luxury. Instead, farmers would pool their resources, traveling to each other's farms to assist with these activities.

To start the crop, rows were cleared and seeds were planted. Before tractors, this work was done with a horse harnessed to a plough. During their first planting, the Babbs would have had to have borrowed a neighbor's horse and hand-steered plough. Once the fields were plowed, the tiny broomcorn seeds were planted by hand, two inches apart, in long furrows that were four feet apart. At first, broomcorn grows slowly, then once the stalks are about a foot tall, they begin to shoot up in height. By harvesttime in late August, the stalks tower ten to eighteen feet. The Babbs' first crop of broomcorn "matured without mishap of prairie fire or drouth." Those first few months, the weather had been extreme, but "the fertile soil had stored its winter moisture well." When it came time to harvest, even the children participated, as "every hand was needed."[24]

On the first day of the harvest, Babb's grandfather showed her how to take "hold of the stalk with my left hand, grip the broom with my right, and quickly break it free."[25] Each family member took a row and began pulling the stalks, leaving them to cure in small piles along the rows. Neighbors came by to help.

During the next phase, even more neighbors came to help: "Men and women enjoyed a release from isolation and loneliness in the hard shared work and the big meals usually served in yards on new pine planks resting on sawhorses. Seats were long planks supported by nail kegs and lard cans." They built a fire outside to do the large-scale cooking this required (as the monkey stove in the dugout was too small). Luckily, Jennie had the help of Bettie Gatlin, a nearby farmer's wife (who would soon become her dear friend), to do the cooking for the harvest crew.[26]

The pulled broomcorn was stacked in small piles on a flatbed wagon. Everyone wore long-sleeved shirts and pants to protect their skin from the itchy fibers. Babb walked alongside the wagon, carrying water for the men who were laboring in the field. Rattlesnakes were their greatest danger, as the snakes hid napping under the shady piles and were startled when the men grabbed the stalks.

The piles of broomcorn were hauled to the west end of the field, near the road, and stacked in ricks, like firewood, to cure for six to eight weeks. This is when it came in handy that they lived in a land of little rain. As Babb's grandfather explained, "The greener we can cure this straw, the higher price we'll get."[27] One of the famers who lived nearby, Van Houten, who went by the name Dutch, owned a seeder and baler. Once the eight weeks of curing had passed, he came by with his equipment. Again, all of the farmers returned to help with the final stage of the harvest, carrying the broomcorn stalks from the ricks to the seeder, "a large turning cylinder with spikes." Under the hot sun, the men "held onto the stalks" and turned them "until all of the seeds had fallen away."[28] Then the stalks were placed in the baler and bound in bales that weighed half a ton. That first year, the Babbs were able to produce sixteen bales, equaling four tons, which they sold in the town of Holly, Colorado, near the Kansas border, for fifty dollars a ton.[29]

After their first good harvest of broomcorn, everyone's spirits were lifted. Debts at Sayler's General Store and Mrs. Denny's Royal Café in Two Buttes were paid off, Doctor Verity's bills were paid, and fresh groceries were purchased. It's at this time that the Babbs were able to afford to buy a wagon and two horses, which would ease the burden of hauling water. Walt being who he was, though, didn't stop with just a standard wagon: he also acquired a surrey. The surrey, a light four-wheeled carriage with two seats facing forward, was luxurious and highly impractical for a life of farming, but it was far more comfortable to ride in than a standard wagon. It had black leather seats and small kerosene lamps that you could light at night. During a visit with Walt's sister, Stella, in Liberal, Kansas, Walt had seen the old surrey in the barn and had been thinking about it ever since. That fall, when the Babbs visited Stella again, Walt offered to trade his gold pocket watch for the vehicle.

There were a few brief weeks of pleasure that fall, including a multiple-week trip back to Red Rock, Oklahoma, so the girls could attend a few weeks of school before they returned to freezing weather and were sealed into the dugout. There were record snowfalls in early December. One night, so much snow fell as they slept that the dugout door wouldn't open in the morning. The family remained trapped in the dugout for three days. As Babb recalled, "We were used to the silence of the plains, but the snowed-in silence had a different quality."[30] With the windows blocked by snow, the dugout remained black as night all day. They burned their small lamp to combat the darkness. To go to the bathroom, they dug a hole in the dirt in the corner of the dugout. By the second and third days, they could hear the cattle above them bawling out of hunger. All of the grasses they grazed on were covered with snow. Finally, on the third day, Babb's father, mad with claustrophobia, threw his entire weight against the hatch and managed to push it open. He crawled through it into a bank of snow.

As the long winter continued, Walt's cruelty increased. Winter brought isolation, and Babb and her sister were very lonely. One evening, her father sweetly asked his daughters if they would like to have two little white calves. The girls eagerly nodded their heads yes. He instructed them to run around the dugout seven times, claiming that when they finished, they'd magically see two white calves appear behind them. The girls were thrilled and happily followed their father's instructions, running in circles around the dugout. When they stopped and breathlessly turned around to see their new calves, they saw nothing except their father, his face red with laughter. As Babb later recalled, "Of course this wonderful magic did not materialize the calves that we dreamed of. When he laughed at our shocked faces and pointed to the calves of our legs we burst into tears and ran to the barn to cry about our loss."[31]

Somehow that winter, Walt and Jennie found enough time alone to have sex, and Jennie became pregnant with her third child. Walt, who had never been supportive of her pregnancies, acted differently this time because he was convinced from the start that this baby was going to be the boy he had always wanted. "Papa wanted a son,"

Babb remembered, "a baseball player, and when Mama became pregnant, he was incredibly happy, making plans for his son, Rex. Rex was a full member of the family from conception. Papa told us how Rex would do this and that, be this and be that; Papa would train him for the big-league baseball and there was never any doubt about his future."[32]

By late spring they had burned through all of their harvest money and were again living on simple, inexpensive foods like hardtack, a type of biscuit made from flour, water, and a bit of salt and popular with sailors and pioneers due to its long shelf life. Hardtack never went bad. Konkie preferred it to most food as he could take it with him whenever he'd set off on one of his multiday jaunts, during which he walked the plains by himself, but Babb and her sister hated it. Thanks to this limited diet, no one in the family was getting the nutrients they needed, especially not pregnant Jennie.

On one of their rare trips to town, Jennie went to see the town doctor, Dr. Verity, who suggested that she at least add some milk to her diet so as to protect her good teeth. When a pregnant mother is malnourished, it isn't the baby who suffers. The baby will gather whatever nutrients it can from the mother. If Jennie wasn't eating anything with calcium in it, the baby would leech whatever calcium she had in her body. Jennie was struck by what the doctor said, so the next day she and her daughters put on freshly ironed dresses and sun bonnets and went to make arrangements to begin purchasing milk from their neighbors, the Haupmans, at a far better-off farm nearby. Babb carried a "a shiny gallon pail for milk" and her mother "pulled a long-handled child's cart" in which Dorothy sat. It was a clear summer day without any wind. Walking away from the dugout, they passed by their field where "the good stand of broomcorn" was beginning to grow.[33]

They walked four miles through the long open range before they saw the dark green, fragrant alfalfa fields that surrounded the

Haupmans' farmhouse.[34] The Haupmans had a water source and therefore could easily irrigate their crops. When Jennie and the girls got to the front of the house, one of the daughters, Maxine, ran out to meet them, waving her arms in a warm welcome.[35] She escorted them through "a back screened porch into a large room adjoining the kitchen." Inside, the girls took in the yeasty aroma of baking bread, a scent that had once filled their childhoods at each of the bakeries their father and mother had run. Now the smell made their mouths water and their stomachs growl. Everything in the house was neat and clean; there wasn't a spot of dust to be found.[36]

Jennie wrapped her arms around her huge belly and told Maxine that they had come to get some milk. Maxine smiled, accepted the bucket, and took Babb and her sister with her to the milk house. It was a large, cool room next to the family windmill. As they walked in, Babb could hear the creak of the windmill's wheel slowly turning. The milk was kept cold in a trough of running water. The amount of water the Haupmans had was shocking to the two young girls, who were often admonished for wasting a drop at their own home. They followed Maxine back into the house, where she poured them each a tall glass of buttermilk and handed them a slice of the freshly baked bread, slathered thick with butter. Both girls grinned at each other over the luxurious food before they began furiously eating.

From the kitchen Mrs. Haupman scolded, "Maxine!" before she walked in, dried her hands on her apron, and shook Jennie's hand. "I'm pleased to meet you Mrs. Babb. You'll have to excuse me that I don't have time to visit. But I'm sure the girls will keep you company."

Mrs. Haupman returned to the kitchen and her daughter took the guests over to a round table covered in oilcloth. The other Haupman daughter, Pearl, appeared and they all sat together, drinking mug after mug of buttermilk and eating the thick, buttered slices of bread.

After they'd had their fill, the Haupman girls gave Jennie and her two daughters a tour of their home: the dark formal living room where a piano sat, the long hallways with multiple bedrooms. Babb couldn't believe how much space this family occupied. Compared to the dugout, the Haupmans' home seemed like a mansion. The only home Babb had visited that compared to this was her Grandma Park's house in Lansing, Kansas. However, it had been a long time since they'd visited their grandmother.

The few hours they spent at the Haupmans' felt like a vacation from their everyday lives. They chatted and giggled. Babb couldn't believe how relaxed and at ease her mother seemed in the other girls' presence. Maxine was in love with a cowboy, and Jennie was in her element giving her advice about love and life. Then the booming voice of Mrs. Haupman broke in from the kitchen and interrupted their fun: "Girls! Girls! . . . Time is going by."

Mrs. Haupman walked out, looked at Babb and her sister and asked, "Did you girls have a good visit?"

Babb and her sister nodded yes.

Mrs. Haupman continued, "Well, that's nice, but you forgot the time. It is nearly suppertime, and Mrs. Babb will have to be getting home."

Jennie blushed and said, "Is it that late? I'm sorry."

Maxine and Pearl tried to cover up for their mother's rudeness, blurting out, "It doesn't matter."

"It is clouding up," Mrs. Haupman continued, her eyes looking out the window, "and they'll want to be going home before supper."

Jennie was embarrassed at the insinuation that she'd stayed late to get a free meal. "We didn't come for supper. . . . I do want to buy a gallon of milk if you can spare it."

Thunder cracked outside. A loud roll of thunder followed. The bright sunlight they'd seen on their way over had been washed away by a steel curtain of clouds.

"You mustn't go!" Maxine insisted, seeing the weather outside and knowing how quickly a dangerous storm could blow in on the flat plains.

But Mrs. Haupman shook her head and repeated, "It is nearly suppertime." She looked out the window at the sky and insisted, "It is far-off yet."

Jennie was humiliated. She took a dime out of her pocket and gave it to Mrs. Haupman for the bucket of milk. Mrs. Haupman accepted the dime and placed it in her apron pocket.

Jennie swallowed her pride, smiled, and said, "Thank you all for a lovely visit."

They all stepped outside. Jennie placed Dorothy in the cart and gave Babb the bucket of milk to carry. After a few waves and goodbyes, the three set off toward home, which lay four unsheltered miles away.

As they walked, they began to notice how the horses in the fields were "running around crazily." Then, suddenly, the sky opened up and large drops of rain began to fall fast. There was another loud clap of thunder. Clouds covered the sun, inking the day so it looked like night. The storm had arrived. With no protection, Jennie and her daughters began to run. The wind picked up. The clouds boiled above them. Lighting struck a nearby fence. Jennie scooped up Dorothy and told Babb to drop the metal bucket of milk and run. Jennie, now carrying Dorothy on her hip, kept slipping on the wet mud and falling to the ground. She'd fall, then get up, then fall again. The rain beat down so hard they could barely see what was in front of them.

Suddenly, they heard a new thunder: the sound of hoofbeats in the distance. Soon their wagon came into view with Walt at its helm, pushing the horses to a breakneck speed. When he pulled up next to them as they huddled against the storm, he shouted, his face contorted with anger, "Didn't you have sense enough not to start out in this storm?"

Jennie just looked up at him, defeated.

Walt dropped the reins and leaped out of the wagon. He scooped up Babb and her sister and nearly threw them into the cab of the wagon. Then he carefully sat Jennie down next to him on the wooden seat. "I wouldn't have seen you at all if it hadn't of been for the lightning just before the rain. I saw you running. Damn fools. You should have stayed," he scolded as he urged the horses on, back to the dugout.

Babb couldn't take it anymore. She knew her mother would never rat out Mrs. Haupman, but she would. "Mrs. Haupman told us we had to go," she shouted over the rain and galloping horses.

Walt wouldn't believe her. "No one would ever do that!" he said.

"She did," Babb stated.

"Well, I heard she was stingy, but damn it to hell, that's the goddamn limit," Walt scowled.

He turned to Jennie, his voice softening. "Are you all right, [Jennie]?"

Jennie said she was and that he needed to calm down. "That's just the woman's way whether we like it or not."

By the time they arrived at the dugout, Konkie was pacing back and forth anxiously, waiting for them. As soon as the wagon stopped, he asked each of them if they were all right. Everyone said they were, and they quickly descended into the shelter of the dugout, the girls to change into dry clothes and Jennie to lie down and rest. By the time they got settled inside, the storm had miraculously passed and the sky looked down on them with a big blue grin, as if nothing had happened and they'd imagined the whole thing.

But that night, the effects of the storm and their flight began to take root. Babb woke to a horrible low moaning sound. Her grandfather told her to get up. Walt brought Dorothy over to her bed and covered her with a blanket. "Tell your sister to stay there and be quiet," Walt ordered. Babb covered her sister and got up.

On the monkey stove, a pot of water boiled. Babb walked over to her mother, who lay in her bed, her face covered in sweat. Her mother told her not to be scared, that she'd be all right. Then her body began to contort into contractions. Babb's father screamed at Jennie, "Hold him back, hold him back!" He knew that if Jennie pushed into her contractions, his long-dreamed-about son would be born premature and would die. Babb knew what was happening right away. She had snuck into the room when her mother had given birth to her younger sister because she'd been curious.

That night Babb's mother gave birth to her baby boy, Rex, and he did not survive. Her father was so devasted that he wept openly in front of all of them. As Babb would later recall, "Papa wrapped him well and tenderly and buried him on the plain. We heard his great sobs until dawn when he rose from sitting by the grave and came back to the dugout. He shook his fist in the direction of the other farm and shouted in a terrible voice, 'I curse you, Mrs. Haupman, I curse you!'"

It's likely that Jennie miscarried her baby due to a placental abruption. The trauma of fleeing from the storm may have sheered the placenta from the uterine wall, leading to her baby's demise. For the next few months, Dr. Verity would come by once a week to care for Jennie. Neighbors such as Bettie Gatlin also came by in the first few weeks, to take care of housework so that Jennie could rest and recover from her loss. But the story of her lost brother would haunt Babb. She would write about it in both her novel, *Whose Names Are Unknown*, and her memoir, *An Owl on Every Post*. The most devastating version is found in *Owl*, where Babb goes with her father to bury her brother: "This boy, who would have carried his name, aroused thoughts of his own existence that I found in Papa's notebook later. He had waited for Rex, and Rex's life and death had been all in an instant. It made him aware of every suffering life on earth." Her father changed after the stillbirth of his son: "He was neither violent nor gay, but darkly moody, when he was in the dugout, he shut us all out by a low whistling of sad songs."

3   *The House on Horse Creek*

The Babbs' second year of broomcorn farming in Eastern Colorado did not go as well as the first, despite the heavy snow that had alleviated the risk of drought. And without the cash from a successful crop, Walt couldn't afford to pay the taxes on his newly purchased land, let alone buy food for his family. That fall, there was no trip back to Oklahoma so the girls could attend school. There were just the lonely plains that surrounded them and the sound of the wild geese circling. After several foreclosure notices were published in the *Springfield Herald* throughout November 1913, on November 28 of that year, Walt lost the property into which he had sunk all of their family savings because he didn't pay his taxes. Jennie was suffering from the depression caused by losing her baby, and she felt trapped in her life with Walt on the prairie. If they lived in town, she could take a job or do something else to support their family. But here on the plains, all she could do was wait and watch her family starve. When they'd first moved to the dugout, Jennie had insisted on bringing her piano at an outrageous expense (that Walt never forgave). Now, the keys of her piano, her only solace, were beginning to stick from the damp air of the dugout. As Jennie would later recall, "I can't understand a man who would rather starve than work. I couldn't work, there wasn't any there. . . . It's the worst life I've ever lived."[1]

That winter, food and clothes became increasingly scarce. Babb remembered that their "clothes wore out and could not be replaced" and she and her sister "grew afraid of strangers." When a rare visitor stopped by, she and Dorothy "hid behind the barn to watch and listen. Papa was disgusted by our behavior, but our mother was sensibly worried."[2] When the grocery bill began to add up and the grocer refused to sell them any more groceries on credit, Walt pawned his prized gold cufflinks, which had been given to him by the Red Rock baseball team he'd played on and coached. That covered the six weeks' worth of groceries he owed, but Walt had nothing else to trade, and therefore there was no food. At one point food was so scarce that the family had to catch and eat songbirds, which broke Babb's and her sister's hearts.

Walt became stir-crazy. Finally, on one of his trips into town, he made a deal with the Hull family, who lived in a modest home farther down Horse Creek. The Hulls were elderly and wanted to move to town for a more comfortable life; however, they needed someone to take care of their crops and prove up their land while they were away. They were also in the market for a fancier wagon they would be more comfortable driving in town. So Walt reluctantly traded the surrey for a season of rent in the Hulls' house. Babb and her sister Dorothy were sad to see the carriage go, even though they'd only ever gotten to ride in it once, on Dorothy's birthday, when Walt had finally given in and driven the two of them down the dirt wagon road at night with both kerosene lamps lit like comets in the velvety dark.[3]

The Hulls' unique house sat directly on the bank of Horse Creek, sheltered by sandstone cliffs in a canyon. On their first visit, Babb remembered that "the gate to the . . . place, two upright posts with a long post on top, led simply into more of the plain without a house or any sign of habitation in sight. Papa said nothing. . . . We drove on and on until we came to the very edge of a precipice. Below we saw cottonwood and willow trees along one side of a shallow creek with a wide sandy shore, a beautiful scene. Tears came to Mama's eyes."[4] As they pulled closer, the house came into view: "It was simple, two rooms, a flat roof, but it was perched on a tiny rock mesa with steep shale sides and a narrow collar of the same rocky earth around it."[5] Surrounding the house were outbuildings, including an old dugout now occupied by a flock of chickens. The house itself was simple, yet it contained treasures: "In the rented farmhouse we found a book, a big, thick anthology of popular ballads and poems. The book was read ragged by all of us and added to our 'schooling.' Papa memorized and recited many of the verses, and all his long life would suddenly 'break out' with a verse (or many) appropriate to the occasion."[6]

As they unpacked on that first day, they found a tarantula scurrying across the floor of their new home. It must have been nestled in the cool dark of the vacant room, unaware that humans would soon invade. Huge spiders were just one of the many animals Babb and her family would encounter on the plains. In the dugout, they'd shared their space with sand rats. One enormous and aggressive rat had attacked Babb while she slept. When she screamed, her father got up and opened the hatch, thinking the rat would try and escape. But the rat refused to exit. Instead, it stubbornly stood its ground. Even when her father went after it with a piece of stove wood, the sand rat "turned back . . . bared his teeth, and stiffened for fight. It was as if he wished to fight rather than escape."[7] Finally, after a night-long standoff, Walt had caught the rat and killed it.

After they'd settled into their new home on the creek, Konkie, who'd stayed at his dugout, came to visit them. He arrived at dinnertime and later that evening as dusk fell and a golden color glowed on the horizon, he took Babb with him on one of his "walkabouts." After they had been wandering though the dark fields, a horse suddenly came into view.

"There's a horse!" Babb exclaimed when she saw a bay horse trotting towards her and her grandfather.[8]

To her surprise, her grandfather wasn't shocked to see the horse. Instead, he just looked at her. What he seemed shocked about was that Babb had seen the horse, but he regained his composure and nodded thoughtfully at her.

"Let him be," Konkie whispered in her ear. "That's Daft."

Babb was confused. How did her grandfather know the name of this horse that now pranced around them? The horse had the small head of a mustang and his coat "gleamed in the moonlight." Babb watched her grandfather's face, which had softened when the horse approached them.

Then, just as suddenly as he had appeared, Daft lifted his head from where he was nuzzling the buffalo grass and took off galloping towards the canyon's edge. He "streaked past" Babb and her grandfather "like a frigid wind, ears back, nostrils wide open, and his eyes wild." Babb was paralyzed and her heart dropped as she realized the horse was galloping straight towards the edge of a cliff. Then she watched him gallop right over the edge. She saw him "suspended for an instant in the empty air" before he fell, "screaming all the way down."

Silence enveloped them. Then Babb, shocked, began to cry for what she believed to be the horse's demise. Her grandfather, seeing her reaction, put his arm around her to comfort her. "Don't cry anymore, don't grieve," he told her, "and I'll try and tell you why. Daft is alright. We'll come back again, and you'll see."

Konkie started walking away from the cliff. Babb followed as he began to explain that Daft wasn't actually a *real* horse anymore, and he had brought her there to see if she, too, could see his ghost. Daft had been her grandfather's horse and he had gone mad eating loco-weed, a plant that grows wild on the plains and contains the alkaloid swainsonine. Horses and other livestock that graze on the flowering weeds for an extended time become deathly poisoned. The plant causes neurological damage, and it was this damage that triggered

Daft to run madly towards the edge of the cliff and jump to his death. Babb's grandfather explained that he had first seen Daft's ghost one night a few weeks after the horse had died. After that, Daft came to visit him often: "I've seen that horse many times. I'd walk over there on fair nights just to watch him play. He hardly ever jumps off the cliff. He just plays. I thought he had quit doing that or I wouldn't have taken you here."

As the two walked, Daft suddenly reappeared before them. To Babb, he was "so real I ran to touch him, to show him my joy and relief, but as I reached out my hand, he disappeared. He did not run away; he simply was not there." Babb's grandfather comforted her: "Don't be afraid. I am not afraid. Daft is not afraid. So, you need not be afraid. Is that clear?" When Babb nodded her head in agreement, Konkie continued, "We are privileged to see him." Konkie revealed to her that he'd never told anyone else about Daft's ghost, and he begged her not to tell anyone about what they'd witnessed that night. Babb agreed and kept her grandfather's secret until she used it in her writing decades later.

The next morning, when her grandfather left to return to his dugout, he looked back at Babb and gave a tip of his hat. She could see his eyes twinkling beneath the brim.[9]

The Babbs would continue to live on their little rented farm for another two years, until their poverty became so severe that for one week, the whole family survived on red pepper tea—hot water flavored with red pepper—which they drank to trick their stomachs into believing there was something in them. Babb remembered the dizziness she felt, the way the room swam. Jennie begged her husband to let them leave, and for once he listened.

In the fall of 1917, the Babbs decided to move to Elkhart, Kansas, where there was the promise of work and where a school had opened. Walt went ahead of Jennie and the girls to try to find a job and a place for them to live. He left extensive directions on how to pack up their belongings—what to sell, what to keep—as if Jennie were a child. Both Sanora and Dorothy didn't understand why their father always treated their mother as if she couldn't make decisions for herself. Within a week, Walt sent word for Jennie and the girls to come to Elkhart. He'd gotten a job driving a dray wagon for a coal company, most likely the Amsden Lumber Company.

During their last weeks in the rented house, before Walt had left for Elkhart, Konkie had come to say goodbye. After dinner Walt got into an intense argument with his father. "Papa made one of his one-sided quarrels with Konkie, and Konkie left. It was night and he went out for one of his customary walks on the plains to get himself together and I went along. We walked for an exceptionally long time in the dark, came back, and in the morning, he was gone. We did not see him again for years."[10] Babb, who had grown close to her grandfather, would miss his quiet presence the most. Now, as they moved to a new town, there was no buffer between her and the molten and irrational temper of her father.

The next day as she, her mother, her sister, and her mother's best friend, Bettie Gatlin, and her husband started off on the three-day wagon ride to Elkhart, Babb was both excited and terrified of what was to come. The Gatlins seemed rich compared to the Babbs, and one of the strongest memories of this journey revolves around the "grub box," essentially a cooler made for wagons in which all of the food was kept. When Babb peeked in it was brimming with food: "fried chicken, potato salad, boiled eggs, bread and butter and jam and cake and coffee."[11] It had been weeks since Babb and her sister had eaten anything more than a meager meal, and the idea that these three days would be filled with plentiful food made the journey more rewarding.

During the ride to Elkhart, Jennie sat in the front of the wagon with the adults, while Babb and her sister sat in the back, on top of a cage that contained a restless pig the Gatlins were taking to Elkhart to sell. During the trip, meals were cooked on an open fire. At night they'd camp under the stars and Babb would feel the vastness of the universe above her. Perhaps it was in moments like these that she began to dare to imagine herself somewhere else, somewhere far away from all of the hardships she had endured so far. Babb was only ten and a half years old. Indeed, when she arrived in Elkhart, her life drastically changed in two ways. First, she would be able to attend school on a regular basis. Second, she would not only begin to write, but she would also get her first job working for a newspaper.

4   *"Study Like a House Afire"*

After three long days of traveling, the town of Elkhart slowly came into view. First a few claims popped up on the flat prairies, each identified by a pole rammed into the ground and topped with strips of cloth. Next to each plot were piles of precious lumber. Then the lots began to increase in number until structures began to rise, and the town came into view. Contrary to Frederick Jackson Turner's assessment in 1893 that "the frontier has gone, and with its going has closed the first period of American history," the Oklahoma Panhandle and surrounding areas, including Elkhart, Kansas, also known as No Man's Land, was still growing, and railroads were laying down new routes as the second decade of the century neared an end.[1]

When their wagon entered the town of nearly two thousand inhabitants, all Babb could hear was the sound of construction: hammers hitting nails, the toothy rub of saws cutting wood.[2] Elkhart was founded on May 3, 1913, when one of the largest railroads in the U.S., the Atchison, Topeka and Santa Fe, extended a branch from Dodge City, Kansas, down to the far western corner of Kansas, establishing Elkhart as "the cornerstone of Kansas."[3] During the early 1900s, when a railroad line created a stop in a town, the town grew exponentially overnight, and Elkhart was no exception. As they slowly drove down the main street toward their new home, Babb watched the plentiful businesses pass by: "a bakery, drugstore, bank, stationer, dry goods, real estate, feed, and grain and two cafes, a few other shops that catered to basic needs and a large general store . . . a newspaper office, a one-story hotel, and a railroad station."⁴

When their wagon pulled up to their newly rented home near the train station, it was late afternoon. Their traveling companions, the Gatlins, dropped them off and went on to deliver their pig to the stockyard for sale. Jennie must have been sad to see her dear friend Bettie go, but looking at the size of the town around her, she likely had hopes that she'd soon meet more people. Bettie and her husband would be starting their return to Baca County that night.

When Babb's father emerged from the front door he was "tight lipped and sulky." Just weeks into his new job, Walt already felt caged in by having to work for someone else. He claimed that if it weren't for his daughters and wife, he would have already quit his job and told his boss to go to hell.⁵

The Babbs' first house in Elkhart was dramatically different from either of their residences in Eastern Colorado. The sheer amount of space they had felt luxurious. The house was shaped like a T, with a long room that they set up as their living room. This room met the straight line of a bedroom, a kitchen, and an all-purpose room. Because the house was located just across the street from the roundhouse, where incoming trains would switch their engines, all day and night they could hear the lonely call of the train whistles and the loud metallic clanking of the locomotives being turned around and detached or reattached to head in the opposite direction. The trains stirred in Babb a longing to see more, to go beyond the boundaries of the town, just as they had previously in her father. Like the trains, in Elkhart her life was being rerouted toward another destination that lingered beyond the horizon.

The family unpacked their meager belongings, setting up their beds and the small monkey stove, which they had brought with them.

Their rental was owned by the Smith family, proprietors of a local newspaper called the *Elkhart Tri-State News*. The Smiths had been drawn to Elkhart's quick growth in the fall of 1915, when they took over the newspaper and transformed it into an eight-page weekly.[6] Now, two years later, they had become well-respected members of the community. The head of the Smith family was the rotund Eugene L. Smith, whose name was emblazoned on the masthead of the *Elkhart Tri-State News* but who spent most of his time glad-handing with fellow citizens at the local café and saloon and did little of the day-to-day work of running a newspaper. His powerhouse of a wife, Corabel, who went by Cora, was the one who actually ran the paper. Cora had come to Kansas with her parents in a covered wagon and learned the printing trade in Emporia. She'd met Eugene while she was working at a paper in Topeka as the society editor. They'd married in 1892 and had four sons, Theodore (Ted), Cecil, Harold, and Donald, while running newspapers in Fairview, Strong City, Spearville, Ellinwood, and Sublette before moving to Elkhart.[7]

Women had been granted the right to vote in Kansas in 1912, eight years before the Nineteenth Amendment was ratified, so it's not surprising that Kansas was a place where independent women like Cora were not only accepted but encouraged. When Babb met Cora, she immediately connected with her strong personality, a sense of congeniality that was equally shared. A few weeks after meeting Babb, Cora told Walt and Jennie that if anything ever happened to them, she would gladly adopt their daughter.[8] Walt quickly took to the Smith boys and immediately began teaching them baseball. As Harold Smith wrote to Babb many years later, Walt "wanted to make me a professional baseball player."[9] The Smith family members spent most of their time at the *Elkhart Tri-State News* office, which was located just down the street from the Babbs' house on the main road, right next to the hardware store and the general store. It didn't take long for Babb to start visiting Cora at work, and through these visits she slowly got her first glimpse into the newspaper business, a place that would soon become important to her growth as a writer.

The morning after they arrived in Elkhart, Jennie helped her daughters dress and escorted them to the school, a two-story brick building located on Wildcat Avenue.[10] The grade school was located on the bottom floor, the high school upstairs. Poverty had taken a toll on both of the Babb children. Babb recalled, "If I had been pretty once and would be again, there was nothing attractive now about my extreme thinness, sunburned skin, and the half-starved look of my big-eyed face and dried hair."[11] The girls had attended a little bit of school here and there between planting and harvesting broomcorn crops, but this was the first time they'd be two of forty-five students attending full-time. Inside the building, a secretary ushered them straight to the superintendent's office to wait to meet with him. After they sat down, Jennie looked at her two girls more closely and took in how terrified they both looked. "Don't be scared!" she reassured them with a gentle pat on their skinny legs. "I'm so thrilled you both will finally get a proper education!"[12] For Jennie, living in a place where the girls could receive a full-time education filled her with hope. But she worried that the poverty they'd experienced over the past three years had damaged her daughters more than she could see.[13]

The door opened and in walked the school superintendent, Professor Harry J. Davis.[14] His Nova Scotian upbringing and his stiff black suit must have made him seem severe to Babb, for he made a formidable impression that stayed with her for years. Babb recalled how he swiftly removed his derby hat and hung it on the coat-tree. She stared at his gray eyes, below the red line caused by the tightness of his bowler hat, looking for kindness.[15] When Jennie explained their situation to Davis—that both girls were extremely intelligent but hadn't been able to receive proper schooling due to where they had been living in Baca County—he nodded politely. He pointed to

Dorothy and said, "No problem about the little one." Then he turned to look at Babb and said, "But the older one will have to start in second grade and be passed to where she belongs."[16]

Davis was an observant man, and when he saw Babb's face fall at the thought of being stuck in a class with younger children, he took a breath, thought about it, and went on: "Or . . . perhaps she can be given a series of oral and written examinations instead." He excused himself and went to talk to his secretary to figure out testing. When he returned, he explained that Miss Temple would give Babb her exams beginning at nine the next morning. Babb likely left the office feeling relieved. As long as she passed, she'd be okay.

The next day Babb and her sister walked the long blocks to school alone. They marveled at the treeless school yard filled with swarms of children laughing and playing on playground equipment. Neither one of the girls had ever seen so many children together in their lives, nor had they ever seen a real playground. Teeter-totters, a metal slide, and a maypole decorated the yard, fueling the children's enjoyment. Seeing this possibility soothed the trepidation Babb and her sister felt about their new home. As Babb recalled in *An Owl on Every Post*, "Without a word to each other, we took all this friendly noise in and agreed that school and town were less fearsome than we had imagined."[17] With this understanding the two girls parted: Dorothy went to her combined first- and second-grade classroom, and Babb went to meet Miss Temple to begin the testing that would determine the fate of her schooling.[18]

In her classroom, Miss Temple asked Babb a series of questions only to be surprised by the results. When she queried Babb about which books she had read, she was astounded by her answer. She wondered how this small girl had learned so much from reading *The Adventures of Kit Carson,* a book of verse, and the pages of the *Denver Post* that had been pasted to the walls of her family's dugout. What Babb didn't tell Miss Temple was that her secret weapon had been having her grandfather to teach her with these tools. Her grandfather may not have received a formal education beyond the fourth grade but he walked through the world with great wonder, and because of that he seemed to Babb wiser than most people she encountered. In those years they had shared on the plains, he'd passed along that wonder to Babb, and it would become one of the most useful tools she'd have in her future life as a writer.

Beyond what she perceived as innate intelligence, what Miss Temple must have seen in Babb was her hunger to learn. Looking at Babb, her skinny legs and arms poking through her worn clothing, she could infer how difficult her circumstances must have been thus far. She took a chance and decided to lay Babb's fate in her own hands. After the exam was over, Miss Temple shut her book, cleared her throat, then looked up at Babb and asked, "Will you study like a house afire?"[19]

Babb, who had readied herself for the worst, immediately agreed by fiercely nodding her head.

Miss Temple left Babb with a stack of worn textbooks and told her she was going to place her, conditionally, in the seventh grade: "You're ready. It's harder than eighth, which you can doubtless skip into high school. Stay home a few days and study every minute, I don't want you to be embarrassed in class."[20]

When Babb left the school that day, she was so thrilled she was ready to pull an all-nighter, if only to please Miss Temple. When she got home, she burrowed herself in a corner of the house and started studying. She barely spoke to anyone in her family for two days.[21]

Three days later, Babb entered the combined seventh- and eighth-grade class. School started promptly at 9:00 a.m. and ended at 3:00 p.m.[22] Throughout the day the students were taught reading and arithmetic, geography, and history. Babb threw herself into learning. The apprenticeship she had begun in the one-room dugout in Colorado, reading the *Denver Post* stories that were pasted to the wall, had somehow gotten her to this place, this precipice from which she could see a new horizon. It was here that her need to record and capture what she saw around her began to germinate and grow, and where she would begin to see her future as a writer. At age eleven, she wrote her first English assignment, "How to Handle Men," an essay that she wrote for her mother, protesting the shackles of male violence she saw her living under.[23] Decades later, when he interviewed Babb, scholar Doug Wixson would propose that Babb's earliest essay was one in which "she had her father in mind." Indeed, the essay took on what would become one of Babb's main themes as a writer: family relationships and women's ability to overcome the obstacles placed in front of them. As Wixson would write in the introduction to a reprint of *The Lost Traveler,* Babb's first published novel, "She made it her purpose very early on to 'figure out what had really happened to them all' even if it took a lifetime to do it."[24]

In the classroom, Babb listened attentively, and whatever didn't make sense at first due to the huge gaps in her education, she went home and read about in the books she'd borrowed from Miss Temple; finally, she had books surrounding her. She had access to knowledge she had been craving for years, and she felt as if her tremendous thirst were finally being quenched.

In the afternoons, it was Babb's job to collect the mail, as it arrived during the hour her mother was preparing dinner. Each day after school she'd walk down to the post office in the center of town. The mail was delivered by train, and once the train arrived the mail had to be driven by wagon and sorted in the post office. Babb would go down early so she could observe the people in the crowd who were also waiting for their mail. Since they'd moved back to civilization, she'd been fascinated with watching people (in the same way she had been fascinated with watching prairie dogs back in Baca County). She remembered always seeing three elaborately dressed women in the crowd who captivated her. She thought that they were the most beautiful women she had ever seen. "They were pale and they wore their tawny hair in an extravagant style new to me. When they entered the post office, it was as if this appearance were the most important social engagement of their day and evening."[25] They stood out from everyone else in town. They wore bright silk dresses that clung to their breasts, and from their arms draped long, flowing capes as if they were heading to a ball instead of the post office. "From head to toe they were immaculate like new dolls right out of a box."[26] Babb couldn't understand why these women were dressed so differently than everyone else in town, and why they were avoided.

One day an older man wearing loose coveralls saw Babb staring at the women and he scoffed, pointing at her with his fat finger. "Don't get any ideas, sis," he said. "They're sure purty but purty is as purty does."

Babb looked at him uncomprehendingly, so he clarified, "They're whores. . . . Floozies. Ladies of the Evening. Got it?"[27]

Babb soon saw that the vehemence towards the three women was shared by much of the town. Prostitution was illegal but was still tolerated in this far corner of Kansas—tolerated when it wasn't seen walking down the street in full attire, as these women so brazenly and bravely did each afternoon.

The man's lecture was interrupted by the "small wooden clatter"[28] of the general delivery window being raised, which signalled that the mail was ready to be picked up. Everyone formed a loose line and Babb took a spot, slowly inching up to the counter. When she got to the front, the postmaster asked for her name, then turned around and grabbed a large packet of letters from the cubby into which it had been sorted. Babb started looking through the letters the minute she left the post office and as she walked the few blocks home. Most were for her mother, from all of her relatives, as Jennie loved to write and receive letters, but to Babb's delight there was also a thin letter from her grandfather back in Baca County. How she must have missed the quiet, reassuring touch of his hand on her shoulder. How she must have wished she could share with him the stories of all of the new people she'd observed in town and tell him about all of her scholastic triumphs.

Their days in Elkhart began to pass without incident. Winter melted into spring. The Babb girls were enjoying going to school. They'd made a few friends but mostly played with the Smith boys. Harold Smith would write to Babb later in life to tell her that she was "always the favorite, along with your wonderful mother, of our family, especially me."[29] With Cora's help, Jennie had found a number of women friends. Only Walt remained unhappy, frustrated with driving the dray wagon.

One day when Walt came home, he slammed the door behind him. He was covered from head to toe in coal dust. "That's it," he screamed. "I'm not working for that man another day in my life."[30] At Walt's words, Jennie tensed. Her life was a kite tethered to the electricity of Walt's mercurial moods, and she never knew when lightning would strike.

As luck would have it, Walt's rash decision to quit his job didn't have much of an impact this time. The next week he found out that one of the two local bakeries was looking for a baker, and he was able to secure a new job.[31]

After that, when Walt came home, he once again smelled like baked bread, and his arms were filled with extra loaves. He was a complicated man, but for brief periods during Babb's childhood, during his tenures as a baker, he would become his best self. As Babb explained,

My father was not a lazy man, not altogether irresponsible, though I suppose the whole picture of him as a husband and a father was one of irresponsibility. . . . While the middle-class mood was upon him, he became the best baker for miles around. He had a talent for it; he used the finest ingredients; he was snowy-clean, and the bakery was scrubbed and sweet smelling. The demanding work with the great trough of dough suited his healthy strength. At that time all the work was done by hand. He loved to punch down the rising dough with his fists; the sheer pleasure of using his strength made him delight in this task. The delicate work he did with delicacy. His high spirits were always exploding in laughter or small, non-sensical often Rabelaisian comics. His temper, violent and sometimes brutal, flared as easily as his gaiety.[32]

Walt was glad to be back at his preferred trade, even though it wasn't *his* bakery and he had a boss to report to. As he liked to say, "I won't put my life in another man's pocket."[33]

In this case, however, he wasn't working for a man; he was working for, as he phrased it, a "bossy woman" named Mrs. Aiken, a fact that must have been very difficult for Walt, who tended to try to dominate the women around him.[34]

Later that year, thanks to Walt's new job, the Babbs moved into their second home in Elkhart, a duplex two blocks up the street from their first house. The house was an upgrade. As Babb recalled, "There were two large rooms and a kitchenette . . . hardwood floors . . . a new outside toilet painted white to match the house. The front door had a frosted pane with an elaborate peacock design."[35]

Despite Walt's newfound job satisfaction, in the evenings, he was soon lured back to his favorite profession: gambling. By 1910, virtually all gambling had been outlawed in the United States, but it had always been a part of the culture of the panhandle. This prohibition resulted in an underground world of back-room poker games all over the West. In Red Rock and Waynoka, Walt had profited from these back-room games. In Elkhart, they were hosted in the back of the drugstore, where Walt thrived by marking cards and making money off of the "suckers" who came through town.[36] Every once in a while, a "sucker" would catch on to Walt's system of marked cards and go to the law and try to have him arrested. When that happened, Walt would flee to a sod house located just over the state line in Oklahoma until the situation cooled off and the police stopped looking for him.[37] When Walt was gone, the bakery duties fell to Jennie. Cora helped with the girls, and she sent one of her boys out to the sod cabin with supplies for Walt.

Soon, though, Walt found that the newly elected sheriff was willing to make a deal with him: he would look the other way if Walt paid him cash from his gambling earnings. This was a lesson Walt would take with him when this sheriff left office and another took his place. He would learn to check out the "law" before he moved the family to a new town, to make sure they'd be open to bribes.

The Babbs had moved back to civilization at an momentous time, a time when the world would be rocked by two events: World War I and the Spanish flu epidemic. On April 6, 1917, the *Tri-State News* reported that the United States had officially entered World War I. Over the next year and a half, millions of Americans would serve overseas. This meant that even Elkhart would lose many boys and men overseas, and even more would be injured. To strengthen the United States military force, the Selective Service Act of 1917 was enacted on May 18, 1917, requiring all males ages twenty-one to thirty to register for potential military service. Then, in August 1918, the age range was expanded to include all men eighteen to forty-five. Walt, who was thirty-eight years old, would register for the draft as required on September 12, 1918, but he would not be called to duty before Armistice Day, November 11.[38]

Before the conflict, the people of Elkhart were divided on whether or not Europe should settle her own arguments. Babb recalled seeing men fighting in the street in front of the general store over whether or not the United States should be involved in the war. Once the United States entered the war, however, support quickly increased, and the focus shifted towards patriotism and supporting the troops. Babb remembered that "pictures of young boys who had been killed or crippled appeared in the *Tri-State News*. I cut them all out and placed them gently in a small folder that advertised seeds." It was difficult for Babb, who once held funerals for the heads of chickens her family had to kill for food, to comprehend the idea of war and why so many adults were so easily compliant with it. "I could not kill a grasshopper. He had eyes, he looked at me, and his eyes said: 'This is my life.' I respected that. Had this no place in the grown-up world?"[39]

One night, after the war had begun, Babb's father rushed into their home. Nearly out of breath with excitement, he told their family "to be dressed and ready to go to the train at eight o'clock." The family walked down to see the "troop train," filled with "boys from here and farms and towns around," who were to be shipped out to fight the war.[40] When they got down to the train station, the place was packed. Three coaches stood on the tracks, and each was crammed with young boys dressed in their uniforms. The crowd swarmed around the coaches, but the doors to the train were blocked by guards. Cora Smith was right next to one of the coaches, talking through the open window to her two oldest sons, Cecil and Ted, who were each shipping off to separate training camps. Jennie clung to Walt as they entered the crowd. She was shaken by the news she'd just read in a letter that her youngest brother, Green Berry, who was only twenty-three years old, had recently been shipped off to the front lines. Walt hoisted Dorothy up on his shoulders so she could see above the crowd.

Babb tried to scan the faces of all of the boys in the trains. At first she noticed how much better they looked in their uniforms than they did in their usual overalls and suits. Babb thought the uniforms seemed to fill the boys with more confidence. As she recalled, "Assembled and trained to kill, they were already separate from all of us on the platform. I could not understand this, but I had heard it said. It was true. It was unbelievable. When this thought came, I looked for signs that might reveal this terrible fact. But there were only laughing faces, and here and there one taut with shyness."[41]

Right after this realization, the first train whistle blew, signifying that the boys were about to depart. A skirt of steam swept across the platform as the engine heated up. Parents tried to put up a brave front, but their faces were contorted with worry. Suddenly a swarm of young girls pushed past the officers who were guarding the train doors and boarded each of the coaches. Babb watched in awe as "the girls flung themselves toward the boys. They smiled, wept, and kissed. Some kissed only the ones they loved; others kissed one soldier, then another." The girls in their bright dresses could be seen through the train windows, their warm bodies pressed against the bodies of the boys, or whispering in their ears as if to remind them there was something to come back home to. It was the first time Babb had ever witnessed such an unabashed public display of passion, especially without reprimand from the adults standing by. The experience opened up something in Babb about passion, about the sensuality and tenderness that was inside of her. As she recalled, "I watched all the kissing, the eyes shining with love and stunned with grief, and I imagined myself a part of the night's drama. I had not thought much of being a girl in relation to boys, but the daring kisses woke a nebulous longing in my body and mind."[42]

When the train whistle blew a second time and the conductor yelled "All aboard!" the girls jumped from the train. From the platform they reached up their hands to lace fingers with the boys who hung out from the windows, holding on as long as they could until the train started to move slowly away, breaking their grasp. "The people stayed on the platform. The train gathered speed and sent a long, sorrowful whistle back over the plains."[43] When the train was out of sight, a great emptiness settled onto the town.

It would only be a few months later that the second historic event happened. In the fall and winter of 1918, the Spanish influenza epidemic came to Elkhart. Many researchers are of the opinion that the Spanish flu actually originated near Elkhart, in Fort Riley, Kansas, in March 1918, when over five hundred soldiers became suddenly ill.[44] The victims of the first wave of the flu, however, only experienced mild symptoms. But by the time the flu returned from Europe in the fall, the disease had mutated and turned deadly.

Victims of this highly contagious flu experienced a sudden high fever, a dry cough, headaches, body aches, and extreme fatigue. Many who were infected with the new strain died within hours of developing symptoms, "their skin turning blue and their lungs filling with fluid that caused them to suffocate."[45] As Babb recalled, the epidemic killed "so many people . . . too many to bury separately. I remember dray wagons full of wrapped bodies."[46] Jennie was one of the first citizens of Elkhart to fall ill. Walt refused to "waste money" on a doctor, so Jennie suffered alone in the house without medical care. With her mother ill, Babb was put in charge of cooking, cleaning, and caring for her sick mother, leaving it no surprise that soon, Babb and her sister also fell ill. Even with his children deathly ill, Walt stubbornly refused to spend money on a doctor. For two weeks, Jennie and both girls were bedridden. Finally, just as Jennie was getting better, Walt's luck ran out and he caught the flu. When he did, he groaned and complained, "God, I'm sick. I'm going to die!" and demanded that Jennie get the doctor.[47] By that time, the outbreak had risen to epidemic proportions and there were no doctors available. When Babb reflected on this time period, later in life, she thought that her family had survived because they had been "toughened by the hunger" they'd suffered in Colorado.[48] For all of November the Spanish flu ravaged their community, infecting over three hundred residents.

One afternoon while Walt and the girls were still recovering, a woman came to the peacock-crowned door and knocked. When

Jennie opened the door, the woman asked her if she could read Jennie's fortune in return for fifty cents. Jennie, who believed in fortune telling, was thrilled, and given all that was going on in the world, she was equally eager for some good news. She let the woman in, made her a cup of coffee, and sat down with her at their kitchen table to have her palm read. The woman spent an hour talking about the "promising future" she saw for Jennie. Jennie was so pleased by what she heard that she sent the woman away with a fresh loaf of bread from the bakery and basked in her fortune for hours afterward, drinking coffee alone at the kitchen table.

The next day, when she went into the cupboard to pull out the coffee can where they kept their stash of money (Walt didn't believe in banks), she discovered that the money wasn't there. They'd been robbed. Jennie was more terrified about telling Walt than she was about not having any money. She went into the darkened bedroom where he lay in bed recovering from the flu and told him, weakly, "The money can's gone." Walt was so furious that he jumped out of bed "as if he had received an electric shock."[49]

"Gone!" he bellowed. "That damn gypsy took it and it's all your fault!" An intense argument followed between Walt and Jennie, with the girls cowering in their sick beds. But before it could go too far, there was another knock on the door. When Jennie answered it this time, a man handed her a telegram. As Dorothy recalled, "In our family a telegram always meant sad news. And it usually was."[50] This time was no different. The telegram was addressed to Walt. He knew what it said before he read it. The night before, he'd dreamed about his dear friend Asa, the man who'd worked with him at his Red Rock bakery and who had helped his family once he'd left for Baca County, and who had remained a close friend despite the distance that had grown between them. Since he'd awoken that morning, Walt had been worried that something bad had happened to Asa.[51] When he read the telegram, "his face contorted with grief" and he wiped the tears that streamed down from his face with the back of his hand. The telegram was from Asa's relative. Asa had volunteered and shipped off to war just a few months previously, but it wasn't combat that killed him. Sadly, he died of influenza just days before the armistice. Walt "thought his heart would break and die." The letter invited Walt to the funeral in Oklahoma. Babb remembered her father's devastation in an early draft of what would become her first published novel, *The Lost Traveler*: "Asa was good, he was the best man he ever knew, and he was wasted by a useless death for no cause at all. There was something pure and unprofaned about Asa."[52] Asa had been like a second father to the girls (and an added support to Jennie) in Red Rock, especially when Walt was off gambling. But how would Walt afford the train fare when all of their money had been stolen? Normally he would ask to borrow money from the Smith family, but both Cora and Eugene had also become ill. Cora would survive, but Eugene, who had underlying health issues, died on November 24, 1918, leaving his wife to run the news operation completely on her own.[53]

Instead, Walt swallowed his pride and asked his boss, Mrs. Aiken, for an advance. She agreed and Walt boarded the next train to Oklahoma to attend Asa's funeral. When he returned, Walt began to gamble with abandon. Losing Asa had left him ungrounded. He was home less and less, leaving Jennie to take over his shifts at the bakery for entire weeks. She began to hate the smell of baking bread.

With her mother busy at the bakery, Babb began to spend her extra time at the newspaper office helping Cora and the printer, twenty-four-year-old Blair Von Gunday, return the type to its proper cubbyholes after printing.

But the solace she found in the *Elkhart Tri-State News* office was soon ripped away by her father's insatiable appetite for gambling. In the fall of 1919, the Babbs were forced to leave the life they'd carved out in Elkhart and move to Forgan, Oklahoma, another panhandle town eighty-five miles away. Like Elkhart, the community began as a railroad town when the Wichita Falls and Northwestern Railway expanded west from Woodward, Oklahoma, to meet the needs of farmers and ranchers in the newly settled area. Walt had moved them to Forgan to start anew: to leave the life of gambling that had begun once again to consume him. Walt wasn't making a moral choice; the move was probably a necessity, as it is likely the new sheriff was no longer accepting his bribes.

Forgan was quite different from the bustling city of Elkhart. Babb's family moved suddenly, without having secured a place to live, so they spent their first few nights at the town's only hotel. As Babb and her family stood in the "dreary" lobby of the Commercial Hotel, she remembered "looking out into the unpaved dusty street, absorbing, and hurting with the utter desolate loneliness of this ugly, ugly town. A whirling dervish of sand danced through the main street and there was not a soul in sight to see it. We looked at one another in the irony of that moment, and it kept us all from bursting into tears."[54] Babb once again had been uprooted; however, with each move she grew increasingly into the writer she would become.

5   Finding Venus

In the fall of 1919, twelve-year-old Babb enrolled as a first-year student at the two-story brick Forgan High School, in a transition that was anything but easy. The high school was small; there were only twelve students in Babb's class. The school had only been in operation for six years when Babb and her family moved to Forgan.[1] Most of the students lived in town or on the farms surrounding the town. Forgan was set on the upslope of a hill. Nearby, bordering Beaver Creek, there were fifty miles of sand dunes left over from an ancient sea, some bare, most covered in tall grasses, yucca, and sage.[2] For the next four years, the Babbs would experience how the wind carried that sand into town, leaving the streets, the windows, everything covered in its fine grains.

Within a few weeks of their arrival, Walt was able to rent a storefront in order to start the town's first bakery, in a white two-story building located on the main street. The building also contained an apartment where the family could live.[3] Despite the challenging times Babb would face in the years ahead, her life at home was again filled with "the good smell of hot bread, buns, cinnamon rolls and jelly rolls, the vanilla of cakes and the fruits and crusts of pies."[4] These were smells she associated with her father's new attempt at "respectability," a brief period in which he would give up gambling and instead work hard at the trade Konkie had taught him. As usual, Walt's renunciation of gambling—if it really even happened—would not last long. He'd soon seek again the freedom that his true profession provided him, and this time his choices would have a direct impact on the trajectory of his daughter's life.

In Elkhart, school had been Babb's sanctuary, a place where she could forget her tumultuous home life and lose herself in learning. But in Forgan, her new high school was anything but a safe haven. Word about her father's past spread fast, and most of the students ignored her. In addition, Babb was two years younger than most of the first-year students in her small class. Soon, violence began to follow her home in the form of a pack of older girls. Without warning they'd run at her and push her down in the dusty street. The pack moved with the muscle of an animal, striking her repeatedly as she lay prone on the ground. But Babb, still terribly skinny from her family's lean years, refused to give up without a fight. She rose from the ground, bloody faced, wobbling on spindly legs, and faced her attackers, who were twice her size. The wall of girls who towered over her erupted into laughter. She posed no threat, and they knew it. They ran away still laughing at her.

After her beating, Babb walked the last few blocks to the bakery, trying to shake off what had happened. She was only twelve years old, but the violent attacks she experienced awoke in her a realization. She remembered the three prostitutes she'd seen every day at the post office in Elkhart, how they dressed, "immaculate like new dolls right out of a box," and how they walked with their chins raised despite the way the crowd would inch away from them.[5] She remembered the look of disgust on the face of the man in the coveralls when he warned her not to talk to the women. What came into focus was how the women had carried on despite the way the town had labeled them, and despite the fact that many of the men who turned away from them had once lain in their beds. How they leaned into their difference, proudly wearing their exquisite dresses and hairstyles, and held their heads high. The experience of moving to Forgan and being immediately ostracized by the older girls made Babb realize she had a choice. She could become defeated; she could become the gambler's daughter that she was perceived to be. Or she could ignore the hate and become who she wanted to be: a writer.

When she walked into the bakery, her father was whistling. The air was ripe with yeast and warm from a long day of baking. Walt was in the back, decorating a cake with flourish. Like his father, Walt's favorite part of being a baker was decorating cakes. He never let anyone else do it and spent so much time on it that her mother got stuck doing all of the less creative tasks: wrapping the breads and cookies in wax paper, replenishing the glass display counter, and taking customers' orders. Babb could smell the sweet scent of frosting as she walked in and saw her mother at the counter. She walked straight back to where her father was frosting the cake. When he looked up, he saw her scrapes and bruises and her bloody lip and asked her what on earth had happened to her. After he heard what had transpired, Walt told his daughter to start using what she knew to defend herself. During their long winters on the plains, he'd taught her a few boxing moves. Jennie was horrified, but as usual she did not stand up to her husband. His cruelty had worn her down, and it was just easier to follow along with what Walt decided was "right" for their family. Over the next week, the older girls continued to stalk Babb, but "in subsequent attacks, I furiously delivered a few knowing blows and was soon left alone."[6]

The days wore on in Forgan. Babb poured her attention into her studies. But as she remembered, "School was too easy, and I began to feel wild and restless." The initial challenge she'd felt attending school for the first time in Elkhart had worn off. Now, she really wanted to learn and knew that to do so, she needed books. As she recalled, "I wanted to read books and neither the school nor the town had a library."[7] When her father gambled at the Warren Hotel in nearby Liberal, Kansas, he sometimes brought home books that had been left there. But for Babb, there was never enough to read.

Like her father and grandfather, Babb also had a tough time with authority, especially her father's. As she recalled, "I had been in full tilt rebellion against his authority since I could remember, and suddenly that year I began to rebel against all authority."[8] One afternoon, Gilbert Piper, the school superintendent, called her into his office to reprimand her for speaking out against teachers and challenging their authority. But he, too, was an authority figure, and she paid little attention to his warnings. It was her English teacher, Edith Sloan, who was finally able to get through to her.[9] As luck would have it, Miss Sloan was also a newspaperwoman. She was the editor of the town's weekly, *The Forgan Eagle*.[10] She too found Babb incorrigible, but like many she was able to look past her behavior and see through to Babb's intellect and intensity. Within a few weeks, Babb asked Sloan if she could get a job as her "printer's she-devil"[11] and she agreed, offering Babb $5 a week.[12] Sloan was a young single woman living in a small panhandle town. She wasn't afraid to take risks, and perhaps she saw in Babb someone like herself. After school, she taught Babb how to set type at the newspaper office. Soon Babb was sent to collect ads and taught how to use the handpress to print auction notices. Being in the newspaper office on Main Street brought her back to the *Tri-State News* office in Elkhart, and Babb immediately felt a little bit more at home. She remembered, "I felt so happy and importantly busy in the small office with the sound of the press surrounding me with a specific kind of rhythmic solitude that I began to behave much better."[13] It was through her time in journalism, a career she would build on beginning with this position, that Doug Wixson believes Babb "trained her power of observation," which would later serve her in her writing.[14] Babb remembered how much she "loved the sound of the presses" on busy nights when an edition was being completed and she and Miss Sloan "put the paper to bed."[15] Babb documented this love in *The Lost Traveler*: "The rhythmic click and roar of the press filled all the space with its living sound and left beneath it a field of solitude."[16]

Babb had never been to a theater, but she'd read plays and seen a few "traveling stock companies" perform them.[17] What she knew about plays was that they brought people together, and Babb was desperate to find a way to connect with those around her. She also wanted to see what it would be like to write a play herself, so after school she'd sit "on a low shelf behind a cake case in the front of the bakery" and write. As she remembered, "I [wrote] several plays, all first drafts, dashed off in a matter of hours." The themes of her plays were simple. As she recalled, "They were about good and evil: war, and New York and Chicago gangsters we read about. What to do with them."[18] Once she'd written several, she wanted to see what it would be like to perform them. To do so, she realized she needed two things: a cast and a place to practice and perform. When she looked across the bakery, she saw her sister Dorothy and her new friend quietly playing in the corner. She walked over and told them they were now part of her theater group. Dorothy, who was only ten, idolized her sister and would have done whatever she asked; she didn't know what a theater group was, but she was glad to be included in her older sister's plans. Babb saw her mother sipping coffee behind the counter and asked her if she had an idea where they might perform the play she had just written. Jennie, who chatted with all of the customers as they came in, told her daughter that a customer had mentioned that she had an empty storefront on Main Street. Jennie encouraged her daughter to call on the woman to see if she'd be willing to loan them the space for their performances.

Babb grabbed the small hand of her sister, who laced her fingers with her new friend's, and the three of them walked through the bakery door out onto Main Street. They walked across the street to the empty building next to Davis Drug and the theater and knocked on the door of the apartment behind it, where the owner lived.[19] A woman answered and smiled when she saw the girls. Babb explained her plan: she'd written a few plays and wanted to perform them. Would the woman be open to letting her and a few friends perform in her empty storefront? The woman was lonely and the idea of having a group of children warm the empty store with their laughter immediately made her smile. She agreed.[20]

The next day at school, Babb was on a mission. She'd overcome the fear and inferiority she'd felt when the older girls had made her first weeks in Forgan a living hell. Now, she walked into the high school with her head held high. She asked a few girls if they'd like to be a part of her production, and surprisingly, they agreed. Knowing that her crime-themed plays would need a male lead who could pull off the look of a criminal, she walked up to "real good-looking boy of thirteen" who she already knew to be "the town's toughest boy, a real delinquent," and asked him to be the lead. He looked at her as if she were crazy. As she remembered, he "snorted his scorn of both 'sissy acting' and me." But the next day, he quietly walked up to her and asked to be included.[21]

The widow had a piano she no longer used, and she offered to have it moved into the old storefront so Babb and her troupe could use it for their productions.[22] One of the girls whom Babb had asked to be a part of their troupe could play piano well, and she agreed to be in charge of music. Now banded together, the group practiced every day after school. Whenever Babb wasn't working at the newspaper, she was writing, directing, or even starring in plays. The troupe members set off in search of old sheets to use as curtains, the widow donated "her young finery for [their] costumes,"[23] and they even gathered enough money to buy makeup. As Babb remembered, "We were all dead serious and devoted to the company."[24] They had a play, they had an orchestra, they even had costumes and makeup. They spent hours copying Babb's script for each of the actors.[25] Now all they needed was an audience. At the newly renamed *Forgan Enterprise* office after school, Babb asked Miss Sloan if she could use the small idle handpress to print handbills advertising their first performance. She agreed. That afternoon, Babb, her sister, and other members of the group took to the streets of Forgan to pass out handbills publicizing their upcoming Saturday performance.

The handbills worked. That Saturday the once abandoned storefront was packed with adults and children all there to see the free play. The audience was made up of "farmers' and ranchers' families [who] came to town on Saturdays and their children and town children."[26] All sat on the floor or stood around the edges of the room. The girl who played the piano walked out from backstage and sat down at the piano with relish. As she played, she grinned out at the audience. The first actors took the stage. What followed was a success. In between acts, the girl played the piano and Babb danced in ballet shoes she had sent away for from a magazine.[27] When the play ended, the room filled with applause. For the next few months, every Saturday Babb and her troupe performed to a packed house. As she remembered, "They loved us, whether they enjoyed our unconsciously funny dramatics or took us seriously never came into question. They came and came again."[28] Babb was thrilled at her theatrical success. Their makeshift theater would flourish for two seasons "until the building was rented for a hardware store."[29] She stopped hating the small town. In it she had found a way to creatively express herself. Babb would not become a playwright, but she would spend future years "directing" writers in the many literary magazines she would edit. That makeshift theater in Forgan had awakened in her another avenue of creativity.

From plays, Babb moved on to writing short stories, "war stories about country boys home from France trying to adjust to their old lives," a topic she later admitted she knew nothing about.[30] But she had found what would become her preferred form—the short story—and the topic that would interest her throughout her extensive career as a writer, the complicated lives of those around her.

A few years later, what also awoke in Babb in Forgan was her sexuality. While girls of Babb's age were typically not allowed to date, they did, and they had no access to birth control. Babb notes that a girl in her first-year class was visibly pregnant.[31] What had lingered in Babb at the train station as she watched the girls run onto the train to say goodbye to the boys being shipped out to war had begun to blossom into what would become her "ethic of sexual freedom in keeping with the physical and spiritual freedom she felt as part of the natural world."[32]

By sixteen, she had grown out of her spindly legs and become striking, a girl people noticed when she walked into a room. Photos from her scrapbooks from this time show her with her wavy hair cut to her shoulders, looking sultrily at the camera. She was still thin, weighing in at ninety-eight pounds, but in her scrapbook photos she carries herself like a model. Her sexuality and the freedom she felt it gave her became her escape from the intensity of her home life and the pressure of the way the town had labeled her. The fights between her mother and father were escalating. Jennie had become passive due to Walt's abuse, but some days she would break through her fear and fight back. On those days the bakery, their home, or both erupted in violence. Walt also continued to try to control his daughter, condemning her for taking a job because he thought it made him look as if he couldn't support his family, and forbidding her to date boys. He called her a whore; he told her she was worthless. But Babb was done listening to Walt. She loved her job at the paper and wouldn't give it up for anyone. She also wasn't about to listen to her father about relationships. The terrible relationship she saw portrayed between her father and mother instilled in her a wish to never marry.

Babb began to date boys at school. Her most serious boyfriend was the handsome farmer's son Este Buffalow, who was two years older than her. Este had a twin brother named Roy, and both he and his brother played basketball and football at the high school. In a letter written fifty years later, Babb recalled the lunch breaks they'd spend together and how they'd walk back hand in hand to the school after lunch.[33] Pictures from her scrapbooks show her and Este picnicking at the nearby dunes, rolling down the hills of sand, laughing.

On some Saturday nights, Babb would sneak out to go down to the big dance hall on Main Street to listen to music, dance, and be noticed by the strangers who were passing through town. As she remembered, "In those years, some of the big bands played 'out in the sticks' before they went on the road to big cities. At one of those dances, Russ [Russell Manuel] kept looking at me dancing." He walked over to her on the dance floor and "introduced himself."[34] In the dark dance hall, with the music playing, her body swaying, Babb no longer felt the burden of her family. She felt free in her body. When Manuel walked up to her and asked her to dance with him, she happily said yes. He was five years older than Babb, but she didn't care, and he immediately became enamored with her. He would visit her whenever he was in town, and they sent each other letters while he was on the road either playing the banjo in major bands or performing as part of the cowboy circuit. Her scrapbooks from this era are filled with photos of him in his full cowboy regalia, twirling a rope high above his head.

Babb's best friend, Moita Davis, lived just down the block in an apartment above her family's drugstore. She'd moved to town in 1922, when her family lost their farm near Beaver, Oklahoma, to foreclosure. She and Babb shared a ferocious love of reading and a newfound love of boys, as Moita was in love with Este's twin brother, Roy. Babb would go to the drugstore after finishing her work at the newspaper to fetch her friend, always trying to avoid Moita's mother, Luna, who loomed over the lives of her children. Mrs. Davis would stand on the balcony above the drugstore at the entrance to their apartment and shout spitefully at her son, "Doyle! Doyle?!" berating him from above in front of customers. Her husband, Noah B. Davis, was rarely seen. When she wasn't allowed to hang out with her friend, Moita would send Babb secret messages through the music she played in the store. On weekends the girls took photographs and Babb would paste them in her leather-bound scrapbook. Mrs. Davis, who considered herself a devout Christian, didn't approve of Moita's friendship with a gambler's daughter and forbade her daughter from being friends with Babb. One day, she was so frustrated by the girls' friendship that she walked across the street to the bakery and shouted at Jennie that her daughter was a bad influence on Moita. Babb, who had been in the back of the bakery, was mortified, as was Jennie. Despite her mother's wishes, however, Moita remained friends with Babb until their graduation, after which they lost touch.[35]

Even though Walt had found a bakery to run in Forgan, gambling was still what he considered to be his profession. In Forgan, Walt mastered the art of marking cards as a way to rig his game, and he set up shop. As he described to Babb in a letter in 1948, to set up shop, "you rent a room for the purpose to gamble in. Porter gets you a table and chairs. You tip the porter and give the clerk half of what you make." He claimed he ran a "square game" but also that none of the players knew he was a professional gambler. He ran games that lasted as long as three days and three nights, all the time buying drinks for his players and feeding them lunch and dinner.[36] Though set in Garden City, Kansas, Babb's first published novel, *The Lost Traveler*, draws directly from her experiences in Forgan during her high school years. Based on her writing about this time, it's likely that Walt enlisted Babb to help him set up the altered decks for his gambling use. She marked the cards with small pen marks or cut outs so her dad, whose own eyesight was beginning to fade, could read them during the game. Then he'd reseal the cards in plastic so they could be sold as new by the clerk at the hotel, who was also in on the scam. Walt frequented the Warren Hotel in Liberal, Kansas, where games were hosted on a regular basis, and he'd rent a room. It was easier to cheat "suckers," as he called them, in Warren than in Forgan (not a lot of out-of-town guests visited Forgan). Gambling, like drinking, was illegal; however, the passage of prohibition laws in 1910 and 1920, respectively, didn't mean people weren't still gambling and drinking on a regular basis. Walt felt when he was gambling that "he was living the free life he always wanted," a life that was seeping deeper and deeper into his own.[37] Walt frequently gambled with many of the businessmen of town, sometimes even the preacher, but just as those same men had condemned the prostitutes they regularly slept with, they turned on Walt and thereby turned on Babb in the end, in order to maintain an air of decency in their small town. Babb had learned not to care. She held her head high but that didn't mean there wouldn't be consequences.

As her high school graduation approached, Babb's teachers nominated her to become valedictorian.[38] She was thrilled to be asked to write a poem and a short speech to read at graduation, and she spent hours working on the pieces. Graduation ceremonies were to be held at the Methodist Church. Babb was proud to finally be receiving recognition for her hard work. Even Walt, who hated the idea of stepping into a church, would be in attendance. As she sat at the front of the church, Babb was nervous with anticipation. Her hands shook and she felt sick to her stomach. A guest speaker spoke to the graduates about the opportunities that awaited them in the world, a premise that few students growing up in a small town like Forgan would have believed, as few would ever leave the town where they grew up. Finally, superintendent Floyd B. Hayes rose and stepped to the podium; Babb noticed how his neck blushed. She anticipated her name being called, as she was supposed to be the next speaker. But instead of inviting her up to the podium to give the speech she'd worked so hard on, Hayes started announcing the names of the graduates. Babb was shocked. When her name was called, she rose and faced him, but he wouldn't even look her in the eyes. When the ceremony ended, she rushed past her celebratory classmates and the mass of families coming to congratulate them and out the back door of the church before anyone could see the tears that streamed down her face. When her family found her in their apartment, her graduation gown was crumpled on the floor and she lay in her bed weeping. She expected her father to go into a tirade, but all he said was "Those sonabitches," and the rest of the night the family sat in stunned silence.[39]

The next day Babb received an explanation of sorts when she was "told the superintendent and various church ministers felt it would be a disgrace to the town to have a gambler's daughter so honored," especially in a church.[40] Her best friend's mother, Luna Davis, and a group of other women Davis had worked into a frenzy about the way it would look if they let a gambler's daughter be valedictorian, had been instrumental in getting their pastors and then the school superintendent to revoke Babb's valedictorian title.[41] After graduation, Babb was humiliated and furious. She'd worked hard. She wanted desperately to go to college. Her newspaper editor, Edith Sloan, "wrote a praising piece in the next weekly issue, announcing that I was [valedictorian]. This took the edge off my bitterness (at the time) somewhat."[42]

One of her teachers who knew that Babb needed to get out of Forgan and into college had applied for a scholarship for her at "a fine eastern college," but as Babb recalled, "Without money for clothes and train fare I was unable to accept."[43] In the end it was Babb's mother, Jennie, who came to her rescue. Jennie had always valued education over everything and did all she could to make sure her girls received the schooling they needed to do something with their lives. She arranged for Babb to live with her youngest brother, Green Berry, who had returned from the war relatively unharmed and begun a career working for the railroad, so Babb could attend the University of Kansas. But the steep tuition still stood in her way. After her high school graduation, Babb also took her fate into her own hands. She went to speak with Hayes, the very person who had blocked her from being honored, to ask him a favor to make up for what he had done. Her meeting worked, and several months later, on September 7, 1924, she received a glowing letter of recommendation from him. Babb wrote to the president of the University of Kansas and included the glowing letter from Hayes, and the university gave her a one-year scholarship. At the time it was very unusual for a woman to be offered a scholarship to college.[44] Through the help of her mother and her own will, Babb had found her ticket out. She would attend college. She would be surrounded by books, and she would finally have everything in place so that she could move further towards her ambition of becoming a writer.

6   *The Poet of Kansas*

On September 12, 1924, Babb attended the 59th Annual Opening Exercises of the University of Kansas in Robinson Gymnasium at 10:00 a.m. As her mother had set up, she lived with her uncle Green Berry Parks, his wife Nannie, and her grandmother Parks in Lakeview, near Lawrence, where the university was located. Her uncle was a Santa Fe Railroad agent and was able to arrange a train pass for Babb so she could take the train to school in Lawrence for free.[1] At college, she loved learning about ancient history and dreamed of traveling to Greece some day. In the fall, she took classes in rhetoric, English literature, elementary Spanish, living plants, exercise, and hygiene. Courses were much more challenging then they had been at her small high school in Forgan, and Babb's grades dropped from straight As to a C average. She was discouraged, but her English professor, Charlotte Aiken, lifted her spirits by praising her papers and encouraging Babb to pursue her dream of becoming a writer. As she remembered, "This was my first big encouragement, and I am forever grateful to her."[2] Professor Aiken would invite Babb over for tea and words of support. Babb wanted desperately to stay enrolled at the University of Kansas, but due to her poor grade point average, she was not offered a scholarship for her second year. Without funding, she could not afford the tuition. So at the end of the school year she returned to live with her family, who had moved from Forgan to Garden City, Kansas.[3]

Their new home, located at 518 North 9th Street, in a working-class neighborhood just a few blocks from downtown, was simple and rundown. Garden City itself, however, offered an upgrade to the sand-filled streets of Forgan. In Garden City, the streets were lined with trees (a rarity on the prairie).

In this new city, Walt rented a room on the third floor of the Windsor Hotel, also dubbed "The Waldorf of the Prairies." This elegant structure was built in 1887. It was the setting for some of the largest business deals made in Garden City, and it was also the place where gambling and prostitution took place. As Walt would later describe in a letter to his daughter, gambling was still technically illegal, but the setup at the Windsor Hotel was standard. Traveling salespeople coming through Garden City via train would pay the clerk a dollar for entry "to see a girl" on the fourth floor or, if they wanted to gamble, they'd pay to be escorted to the third floor.[4] As Babb captured in the first draft of her novel *The Lost Traveler,* in the evenings Walt[5] would sit around the wide, open hotel lobby reading the newspaper, "trying to spot a restless fellow who with a little urging would welcome a game."[6] Walt did not get a secondary job at a bakery in Garden City; instead, he chose to gamble full-time. Even with the special arrangements Walt made at the hotel, however, the onset, during Prohibition, of organized gambling controlled by the mob made it increasingly difficult for a lone hustler like Walt to make a living gambling. Likewise, Walt's purpose for gambling had shifted. His addiction, his need to continue gambling at all costs, changed the way he gambled, causing him to lose more of the family's much-needed money.[7] Walt's luck waxed and waned, going from huge winnings, when he'd "clean out" a "sucker," to total desolation, when he'd lose everything. As his bankroll declined, Walt's moods swung sharply, and he became "increasingly frustrated and domineering."[8] As Babb remembered, she dreaded being at home: "Life at home was always like walking on the sharp edge of a neutral emotion which at any moment without warning would flash into an extreme of pleasure or pain. There was no ease, no peace . . . and this apprehension of coming misfortune."[9] In desperation, Jennie took a job at a grocery store to ensure they would at least have enough to eat regardless of how Walt's games went. Walt hated that Jennie wanted to work and he berated her daily. She rarely went against her husband's wishes, but now that they lived in a town and she no longer had to run the bakery while her husband gambled, she decided to take their finances into her own hands. It was the first step she would take toward walking away from their rocky, unhealthy marriage.

Babb, too, had tasted the freedom of being away from her father's tumultuous moods, and this taste made her thirsty for independence. She wanted to continue the college education she had begun at the University of Kansas. She began taking classes at Garden City Community College. She enrolled in classes in general psychology, public speaking, English history, sociology, journalism, ethics, and school management. She did much better in her classes than she had at the University of Kansas, excelling in Spanish literature, Spanish composition, and Spanish prose and poetry. Despite her access to education, she struggled with living once again in her father's orbit. He berated her with insults. He teased her about her drive to excel. In short, he tried to cut her down to what he had become: someone stuck in the cycle of his own addiction. Babb missed her life in Lawrence: her friends, the dances. She missed the freedom she had to leave her uncle's house without being subjected to the third degree. The junior college wasn't as exciting as the University of Kansas. There were many reasons Babb wasn't enthralled with having left her life in Lawrence, including a history professor named Dan who routinely hit on her and wrote her love letters that he left in her textbooks. She'd gone on one date with him and then didn't want to continue seeing him, but he had a challenging time letting go. On May 26, 1927, Babb graduated from Garden City Community College with an associate degree. This would be the highest educational degree she would obtain.

What saved Babb during this era was her return to what was familiar: the newspaper office. Upon her return from her year at the University of Kansas she applied to work at one of the two local papers, the *Garden City Herald*. The newspaper was owned by the famous columnist E. E. Kelley and was staffed by multiple members of his family, including his daughter Katherine, who was the paper's editor.[10] When Babb applied, the editors thought she was too young to work as a reporter (regardless of her prior experience at the *Forgan Enterprise*). Kelley, however, took a chance on her and hired her to help with office tasks such as bill collecting. He had raised his children in a newspaper office, and he liked the idea of mentoring a cub reporter. Babb's first job at the paper was to go door to door to different businesses that had placed ads and collect what they owed. Most paid up, but some were stubborn and tried to avoid her. Through this process, however, she got to know many of the shopkeepers and business owners in Garden City. It was an experience that brought her back to her early childhood in Red Rock, when she'd wander from her parents' bakery to the other shops in town. Everyone knew her. In Garden City, if she was able to collect, she'd receive ten percent of the bill.

Eventually, after several months of collecting bills, she was finally given the opportunity to prove herself as a reporter. One afternoon, a neighbor stopped by the Babb household because Kelley had called and asked her to get Babb. The Elks building on Main Street was on fire and the *Herald* didn't have anyone to cover the story. Babb didn't even think. She grabbed her coat and ran out the door to the scene of the fire. When she arrived, the building was engulfed in flames. She could feel the fire's heat from a block away. In *Lost*

Traveler, she recounts what the loss of a community building like this meant to her town: "This was the scene of student dances, of town banquettes . . . of memories unknown to the stranger's eye straying over."[11] Dozens of people were milling about the streets in front of the burning building, including many of the businesspeople she'd gotten to know from collecting bills. Each gave her his insight about what had happened, and one of them introduced her to the reporter from the town's second newspaper, the *Garden City Telegram,* who was also covering the story, and they compared notes. After a few hours of gathering information, Babb walked to the *Herald* office, where her boss was seated at a typewriter typing away at his own story. He didn't look up or stop typing. He just nodded to her and pointed to another typewriter at a nearby desk, indicating that she should sit down and draft her story at that machine. Babb had never typed on a typewriter, as she'd never before had access to one. At her old job reporting for the paper in Forgan, she'd drafted her stories in longhand. But Babb, determined to not let anything stand in her way, sat down at the machine, pulled out her notebook and began typing her story, slowly, letter by letter. She didn't leave until she'd finished. When she placed the finished copy on Kelley's desk, he read it, then looked up from beneath his green visor to tell her she'd done an impressive job. Babb ran all the way home, filled with excitement and glee. The next day the joy continued when her story appeared on the front page of the *Herald* with just a few edits.

After she covered the fire, the editor assigned her a regular column—on cooking, a topic she knew little about—called "Household Hints and Timely Recipes." To complete her assignment, in desperation Babb "reprinted magazine recipes" she found at the local library.[12] Despite this, Kelley kept giving her assignments and she kept growing as a writer. In an author bio that Babb wrote in 1939 for *Kansas Magazine,* she mentions the influence her time at the *Herald* had on her: "She owes a debt of gratitude to E. E. Kelley who encouraged her when she was going to school and working on *The Garden City Herald.*"[13]

What also saved Babb from her own disenchantment at home and at school was her ravenous appetite for books. Once she had access to more than the pages of the *Denver Post* plastered to the dugout walls and the trite *Adventures of Kit Carson,* Babb's literacy improved greatly. By the time she was living in Garden City, she had acquired an impressive personal library: twenty-five books of poetry and thirty-three books of literature.[14] Among her poetry books were three by the New Woman poet Edna St. Vincent Millay: *Renascence* (1912), *The Buck in the Snow and Other Poems* (1928), and *Poems* (1923).[15] Another notable poetry collection in her library was *Nets to Catch in the Wind* (1921), by Edna St. Vincent Millay's friend Eleanor Wylie. It's no wonder Babb was drawn to these women, who lived unconfined, in open marriages, and who held power over their lives. Between the two world wars, women had finally been granted the right to vote and were cutting their long hair into short bobs, riding bicycles, getting jobs other than the heretofore allowed profession of schoolteacher, and becoming more in touch with their own sexuality.

At the time that Babb was reading Millay, Edna—or Vincent, as she preferred to be called—was living at her upstate New York estate, Steepletop, or traveling the world and giving readings to audiences of thousands. As Millay's biographer Nancy Milford points out, at the peak of her fame, to some, Millay was more famous than Lord Byron.[16] What Babb found in Millay was a poet who was enchanted by nature and who believed in the freedom of her own sexuality. When Babb read Millay, it was the first time she'd read poetry by a woman that expressed the way she thought about these themes. In Millay's poems, women have control over their lives. Millay gave Babb a model for how she could live her life: free of the conventions and constraints that dragged down the lives of most young women. In the small-town environment of Garden City, women had achieved the right to vote; however, the freedom and agency that many women had begun to express since World War I had ended was not as prevalent there as it was in the lives of celebrities such as Millay. As scholar Carol S. Loranger observes, the influence of Millay on Babb's poetry would extend "well into the 1930s."[17]

Many of the books Babb possessed were acquired through mail order, but she also read the pocket-sized Little Blue Book editions of literary classics published by E. Haldeman-Julius in Girard, Kansas. Thousands of titles were available at drugstores. In addition, Garden City had a good-sized library, which she frequented. It was at this library that Babb first encountered the work of Russian writers like Tolstoy, Dostoevsky, Gorky, Gogol, and Chekhov. As she'd later reflect, she saw these nineteenth-century Russian works as the "greatest of any novels in the world" due to their "richness of characters."[18] Another favorite novel that she would return to repeatedly was *Madame Bovary* by Gustave Flaubert. She claimed, "It is technically almost a perfect book"[19] and that she'd read it six or seven times.[20] And she greatly admired the work of Theodore Dreiser, a writer who in years to come she would actually get to know personally.

Babb's extensive reading encouraged her creativity. She began writing short stories on a regular basis. These works still lacked the strong female protagonists and rich imagery that would distinguish her later short stories, but one sees her talent beginning to bud even in these pieces of juvenilia. For example, in "Prairie Dwellers,"[21] an unpublished short story from this period, Babb writes about a woman, Ann, and a man name John Leigh who meet in France during World War I. On a whim, the two marry in France before John heads to the front. A few months later, without word from John, Ann returns to New York, where she finishes school and bemoans the fact that she doesn't know how to find her husband. Then one autumn John suddenly shows up at her doorstep unannounced and offers to sweep her away to live with him at his farm in the Midwest. Ann agrees but struggles with adjusting to life on the farm. The two attempt to meld their different worlds by reading aloud to each other at night, Ann reading literary passages while John reads agricultural essays. In truth, they only half listen to one another. Ann gets tired of listening to John talk about alfalfa and he feels the same about her endless passages of literature. When John is suddenly killed in an automobile accident, Ann is left devastated and utterly alone on the farm. Her mother comes out from New York to bring her back home, but Ann insists on staying, claiming that she now feels closer to John because his death made her focus her interest on agricultural matters, the same ones she had found dull while he was alive.

"Prairie Dwellers" is a trite love story that hinges on an epiphany caused by death. It's written about characters who've been to war and therefore experienced things Babb could barely imagine, and this shows in her prose. While the story is anything but biographical, it feels very much like an extension of the scene of reckless abandon Babb witnessed back in 1918 at the train station in Elkhart, when the young boys were going off to war and the young girls jumped on the trains to kiss them goodbye. In that moment, Babb had absorbed how the threat of war silenced the ordinary judgments usually made about women expressing passion. Since that day, Babb had written plays, stories, and poems about the war and its effects on young men and women. The topic became a conduit through which she worked out her ideas about how the two could interact. She rarely wrote about topics she knew intimately in her short stories, a fact that would shift dramatically as she began to hone her writing skills during the coming years.

Even with the escape provided by literature and her job as a reporter, Babb felt trapped in her life with her family. She was anxious to find a way out of the house and a job that would give her more time to write. At the time, rural schools across the United States were always eager to hire young women to teach at one-room schoolhouses, so during the summer session in 1927, Babb took the courses she needed to obtain her teaching certificate.

That same summer, protests were happening all over the world regarding the sentencing of Nicola Sacco and Bartolomeo Vanzetti, two immigrant anarchists who were controversially accused and convicted of murder. After several attempts at appeals, the two remained incarcerated and awaiting execution.

Sacco and Vanzetti were scheduled to die in April 1927, but their fate became front-page news as celebrated writers, artists, and academics pleaded for their pardon or for a new trial. Most thought their conviction was largely based on prejudice against Italian immigrants and the jury's bias against anarchists. Some of Babb's favorite writers, including Theodore Dreiser and Edna St. Vincent Millay, were part of the protests. Millay was arrested while picketing the Massachusetts State House in Boston. Appealing to the governor, she wrote, "I cry to you with a million voices: answer our doubt. . . . There is need in Massachusetts of a great man tonight. It is not yet too late for you to be that man."[22] In response, Massachusetts governor Alvan T. Fuller appointed a three-man commission to investigate the case. After weeks of secret deliberation, the commission upheld the verdict. Sacco and Vanzetti were executed in the electric chair just after midnight on August 23, 1927. After the execution, which Babb and the rest of the country were attentively aware of, she began to awaken to leftist ideas.

In the fall of 1927, Babb was given a teaching appointment and she left her family to work in a one-room school in New Hope, Kansas, thirty miles northwest of Garden City, "on the prairie where scarcely a building or a tree breaks the monotony of buffalo grass sod for miles in every direction."[23] Babb begins her short story "The Flying Bird of Dreams," which is based on her time in New Hope, with a description of the school: "[A] one-room white frame building with a small coal shed attached and two unpainted grey outbuildings were enclosed by a barbed wire fence. There was a large worn spot in the buffalo grass where the children played."[24] Babb boarded with a large family that owned a nearby sheep ranch. They had three grown sons and two school-aged daughters who attended Babb's school. She and the girls often had to walk four miles a day to and from school. Teaching in this rural setting was a harrowing experience that brought back her own childhood of poverty and isolation in Baca County. As she remembered, "I was a teacher and janitor and on coldest winter days rubbed the frost from the children's ears with snow; and once in the spring the children of one family brought head lice to school." Babb's twenty-two students ranged in age from four to sixteen. When students needed one-on-one instruction, they were called up to the recitation desk. During the winter, Babb was almost fired from her job because she had chosen to wear pants and high laced boots, which made it "easier to step in and out of deep snow." But "the pants were considered 'immoral'" and she was severely reprimanded and nearly fired.[25] Luckily, the students were quite fond of her and fought to have her remain as their teacher. After several board meetings at which the moral implications of pants-wearing were discussed, Babb was told she would be allowed to stay on as long as she never wore pants again.[26]

When there were blizzards, a friend brought a sled to help haul the children and Babb home. On her days off, he'd meet her at her home and bring her one of his horses so that they could spend the day riding on the plains. Their wandering on horseback brought back memories of wandering on foot with her grandfather so many years before. Babb would draw heavily from these experiences in her short story "The Flying Bird of Dreams," named after a phrase her friend frequently said while they were riding the plains.[27] Another story that was inspired by this time period was "William Shakespeare," which was based on one of the children who lived on the sheep farm where Babb boarded.[28] "I wrote what I think is one of my best stories about him. . . . He thot he was WS [William Shakespeare]. He worked on the ranch but wrote bales every night on paper sacks, cardboard, any paper he could find. As I graded papers at the kitchen table, he wrote his manuscripts: words, words that didn't [make] sense."[29]

After a school year had passed, Babb left her teaching job. She couldn't bear to see the poverty the children had to suffer, and she was ready to focus more intently on her own writing career. Often, she used most of her earnings to buy the children food and clothing. When she returned to Garden City, though, she was fueled by the small successes she was now experiencing with her poetry.[30]

While she was teaching at the New Hope school, she wasn't just grading papers at the kitchen table, she was also writing and sending out her poetry both locally and nationally, a practice she would jump into wholeheartedly upon her return to Garden City. Babb's 1927 poem "To L_____" was published in Ben Haglund's little magazine *Northern Light,* one of the literary journals that "helped break the isolation of a new generation of literary radicals west of the Hudson, who were widely separated geographically."[31] Haglund, who lived in Holt, Minnesota, published his literary journal on an old handpress (much like Babb once used to print handbills about her theater productions back in Forgan).[32] During this time Babb also joined numerous literary organizations, including the Kansas Authors Club (1928 and 1929), the International Writers' League (1928), and the American Writers' Society (1930–32).

Babb's poetry began to be published extensively. Over the next few years, she had work published in the small literary magazines *The Harp: A Poetry Magazine, The Prism, Jayhawk,* and *Will o' the Wisp,* as well as in publications with a more national reach, such as *Stratford Magazine, The Lantern, Poet's Scroll,* and *The Grub Street Book of Verse.* One of her poems, "I Wish I Could Remember," was originally published in *The Prism* and then reprinted in *The Grub Street Book of Verse.* Her boss, E. E. Kelley, mentioned her growing fame in his

"Grass Roots" column in the *Topeka Daily Capital,* calling Babb "a talented young woman" with "the genius of industry." The *Garden City Herald* published an article praising her poetry, as did the *Hutchinson News,* the *Elkhart Tri-State News,* the *Wichita Eagle,* and the *Dodge City Globe.* In another article from January 1928, entitled "Poet of Prairies," Babb is referred to as "one of the poetic geniuses of the country." This column would not only be published locally but would be syndicated across the country.[33] Thanks to the syndication, within a few weeks Babb's reputation as a poet had grown from local to national. The literary attention she'd begun to receive spurred her toward a decision that would change her life.

As Carol S. Loranger points out in her essay "Erratic Orbit: Sanora Babb, Poet," during this time, "Babb was producing short, personal, lyric poems . . . rhymed and metrical, with passion and lost love and love affairs as the predominant subject matter. Like Millay, Babb's tone in these is one of wry self-reflection and world wisdom."[34] Much like her fiction from this era, however, Babb's poems were still only loosely autobiographical. Her early poems are written in the first person, and while they talk about intimate matters, they do so mostly with a "bright, impersonal voice."[35] But even in these early poems, one sees Babb's unique voice begin to emerge. For example, in her ten-line poem "For Future Reference," published in the 1928 *Grub Street Book of Verse,* she exclaims her deep affinity for the land, one she wants honored even after her death:

> If I must lie within a grave
> Dug from a measured plot of ground:
> The customary six by three,
> With tombstones grinning all around—
> Let there be nothing else to crowd
> My body tense for final rest,
> For I have loved above all things

The tang of mellow, dark earth best.
My dust will take too long to settle
If I must lie in silk and metal.[36]

The poem is written in stilted iambic pentameter and ends formally with a rhyming couplet. The first four lines aren't extraordinary; they offer a rote description of a grave and its dimensions, ending with the surprising image of "grinning" tombstones. But the overall motif of the poem, how the speaker does not want to be imprisoned in a coffin upon death and instead wants her body to immediately be in contact with the loam so that it may return to the "mellow, dark earth" of the prairie, offers insight into the mature voice Babb will soon inhabit in her poetry. Eventually her work will have what Wallace Stevens called "the intelligence of the soil"; she will become a writer fully immersed in the terroir of the land on which she grew up.[37] It is as if, as least metaphorically, part of her never wanted to leave the grave-like dugout she'd once lived in in Baca County. In that dark room, she communed with the land; she communed with nature in a way that she would never be able to shake. Finally, that the poem's premise is that she wants agency to make decisions about how her body will be handled after her death is also an indication of who Babb is becoming as a poet.

In other poems of this era, Babb writes simple verses about her dog Toby, who has died ("To Toby," *The Prism*, 1928), and about wishing to forget (and then forgetting) her lost love ("I Wish I Could Remember," *The Prism*, 1928, reprinted in *Grub Street Book of Verse*, 1928). These poems offer little insight into the trajectory her poetics will take in the future. They are small, controlled verses that take few risks. However, in her later poem "Coute Que Coute" (published in *The Harp* in 1929, on the brink of the next big transition in Babb's life), one finds a continuation of the agency found in her 1928 poem "For Future Reference" and insight into why Babb has begun to receive growing acclaim as a poet. Titled after the French phrase meaning "by any means possible," in this poem Babb takes on the cliché "of wanting cake and eating it" (line 3). One feels, in the opening lines, the cautious warning felt in a small Kansas town on the brink of a depression: Be careful. Plan for your future. Don't waste the riches you might find today, as you may never have the fortune of finding them again. But Babb had been raised in a family whose fortunes waxed and waned, whose circumstances fell into and rose out of starvation and destitution. A family where sometimes Walt would return to their cold home (when they had no money to buy coal or stock the pantry) in the early morning and wake Jennie and the girls and shower them with pockets full of coins and handfuls of bills that he'd won off unsuspecting suckers at the Windsor Hotel.[38] Babb had been trained by her impulsive father to spend whatever wealth she received on fine clothes while she still had the money in her pocket, and this inherited philosophy informs the poem's assertion:

> If I keep it in the cupboard
> it will grow stale untouched.
> I'll be too old to care for sweets
> My hands have never clutched. (lines 5–8)

One can infer, too, that it wasn't just material wealth about which Babb felt this reckless abandon. During those years, Babb was young and filled with passion. She spent time alone with boys. She kissed boys whom she had no intent to marry. She dated freely. And when she was questioned about her openness toward her own sexuality, she didn't back down. As her character Jennie states in the first draft of *The Lost Traveler* (written about this time in her life), when teased by Drake, a boy she's kissed and who works with her on the newspaper, that she is a "suffragette" (a derogatory term at the time), she responds:

"I want to be a free woman, but not against men, if that's what you mean. With them. That division is everything, I hate it."

"You're a suffragette, alright," he said again, teasing her, "but you don't look it."

"That's because you think they should look ugly or ridiculous. Most women are freer since the wars; do you think they look funny?"[39]

That Drake teases Jennie for her independent assertions is not surprising. And that women who stepped away from the norm, who acted out in a way that empowered their own lives, were ridiculed is also not surprising. But to see this insult so clearly tied to the idea of a suffragette is enlightening, especially the assumption that suffragettes were ugly and hated men. Instead of being insulted, Jennie tries to enlighten Drake about how "most women are freer since the wars" and they don't "look funny" now that they have this freedom. That this motif is also so clearly defined in an early poem tells us a great deal about who Babb was from a noticeably young age. This passage offers us insight into choices Babb would make throughout her life that were unconventional and out of step with the gender norms of her time.

In the end of her poem "Coute Que Coute," Babb asserts she'll "eat my cake and care not / About the hungry days . . . I shall / Walk wisely down lean ways" (lines 9–10, 11–12). Soon, Babb will use this same philosophy and the momentum that's continued to build about her poetry to find the courage to leave her family for good.

The encouragement Babb received from Kelley at the *Garden City Herald* helped her expand the reach of her journalistic efforts. In 1927 she took an associate editor position at *Opportunity,* a monthly magazine also published in Garden City and owned by Kelley, where she earned $15 a week.[40] But as the Depression pushed on, Kelley was no longer able to make a profit on the newspaper or the magazine. There was another, more successful newspaper in town, the *Garden*

City Telegram. When Kelley's finances were depleted in 1929, he lost his family's paper. One day, unexpectedly, Kelley walked into the newsroom with his rival, the owner of the *Telegram,* and introduced him to his employees as their new boss. The owner of the *Telegram* had purchased the *Herald* for a fraction of what it was worth in order to consolidate it with his own paper.[41] Babb must have been devastated to see her mentor go. Almost immediately, her new boss took away Babb's editorial duties, claiming that she'd be better suited writing a column on domestic affairs. She began writing a column called "Women's Realm," about topics like fashion. Babb agreed because she needed the work, but she also secretly decided to start looking for another position: one where she'd have the freedom to cover more important and relevant stories, as she had under Kelley's tenure. A few months later she interviewed at a paper in Amarillo, Texas, in hopes of finding a better situation, but she didn't get the job. However, when her new boss heard that she had applied for a job elsewhere, he fired her on the spot. Babb was shocked, but she used the event as a catalyst to move towards what she had been dreaming about for years.

Babb made up her mind that it was time to move away from her family. She would move to either New York City or Los Angeles to become a writer. As was typical in her household, when she told her father about her plan, he scoffed at her naïveté, telling her she'd never make it and shouting at her, "If you get hungry, don't expect me to send you any money."[42] She and her father had one of most violent fights of her life. She does not record what occurred, but in *Lost Traveler* she writes about a terrible fight between daughter and father that ends with the daughter shooting her father.[43] Whatever happened between Babb and her father was enough to make Babb finally listen to the lonely train whistle she'd grown up hearing. This time she would be the one sitting in one of the seats looking out the window as the landscape paraded by. She asked her father to roll his dice to decide where she would move. He rolled and it was decided: she'd purchase a ticket to Los Angeles.

Determined to continue being a journalist, Babb applied for her Associated Press credentials and before she left Garden City, on June 21, 1929, she received a letter from Fred Vanderschmidt, a correspondent with the AP, who said they'd be "very glad indeed to accept [her] correspondence." Babb also reached out to Frank L. Stowell, the editor at *Opportunity* with whom she'd worked, asking for a letter of recommendation. He wrote, "To whom it may concern: Miss Sanora Babb has been in my employ nearly two years and I take pleasure in recommending her to anyone desiring her services. She has been a conscientious and faithful worker, efficient and has always had the best interests of our business at heart."[44] With her credentials and letter of recommendation in hand, her books packed, and the few clothes she owned stuffed in a suitcase, Babb boarded a train heading west to Los Angeles.

7 *"Fling This Wild Song"*

When Sanora Babb crossed the red brick platform in Garden City on August 1, 1929, to board the Santa Fe line train going west, she heard the conductor's "long drawn All A-b-o-a-r-d-d-d sound along the platform." She listened to the bells quickening, signaling to the passengers that their journey was about to begin and they needed to board before the train "hitched forward once or twice and waited for running passengers." She heard the "signals and the great rhythmic slow ruuush-ruuush of the train" gathering speed until it was "lost in the fin[e], steady sound of the wheels clicking along the rails. Back from the engine came the outside whistle of the train . . . alone and lonely onto the dark plains."[1]

Outside the train window the sharp knuckles of mountains rose from the flatland in the north. Babb had never seen mountains, let alone mountains of this size; up to then, the largest peaks she'd seen were the far-off domes of Two Buttes that rose a mere three hundred feet near her family's home in Eastern Colorado. The train veered south, traveling through the desert landscapes of New Mexico and Arizona before entering California and stopping in Los Angeles.

Babb left Garden City with her AP press credentials in hand, but she didn't have a solid prospect of a job, nor had she scoped out a place to live in advance. The day she'd boarded the train, the stock market was already unsettled; it had been experiencing extreme fluctuations since March 1929. Little did she know that in just a few weeks, this volatility would plummet the United States economy into the worst depression of its history.

When Babb arrived in Los Angeles, she found a cheap room to rent and then set out to find a job.[2] The first few days she "went to employment agencies and was told [she] was not equipped for office jobs or anything they had" because she didn't know shorthand and could not touch-type. After barely learning to type on the typewriter at the *Garden City Herald,* Babb had bought an old Underwood and practiced at home, but her self-taught methods didn't impress the offices where she was applying. However, armed with her AP credentials and her experience on newspapers in Forgan and Garden City, she "went to the newspapers and [obtained] a few feature writing jobs" at the *Los Angeles Herald.*[3]

On September 1, 1929, pleased with her mild success, Babb took a day trip to Mount Lowe, a 5,000-foot mountain near Los Angeles, and wrote a poem called "Conquest" about her experience. The poem documents the incredible shift in her point of view since coming to the West Coast as embodied in her mountain climb. In the first four lines, Babb encapsulates the stasis she felt when she was trapped in her old life under the thumb of her father:

> I, of the prairies, have conquered a mountain,
> I, who have shunned the deep echo of hills,
> Fearing my song flung out always, carelessly,
> would return swiftly with vengeance that kills.[4]

However, in the four lines that follow, Babb reveals that atop Mount Lowe, "the stolid breast of a sage mountain," looking at the city of Los Angeles spread out beneath her, she is transformed. The fear she'd felt dissipates and she suddenly feels the courage to "fling this wild song" out into the world.[5] Atop the largest mountain she had ever climbed, Babb must have felt that all of her risks had paid off. She was ready to release the wild song that had been gathering in her throat for years. She'd left the grip of her father's addiction and landed her dream job: writing feature stories for Los Angeles newspapers.

The elation she felt on that mountaintop, however, didn't last long. Just a few weeks later, the unthinkable happened: over a series of terrible days, the stock market crashed. Los Angeles flew almost immediately into a panic. Babb remembered "many people crying in front of closed banks and beating on the locked doors" during the initial crash.[6] At the *Los Angeles Herald,* where she had been picking up intermittent work, she recalled that "all the women were fired first, then the men. A terrible, terrible time." For weeks, the city plummeted into chaos: "Soup lines lined the street—no work, no food, no shelter."[7] The faces on the people in those soup lines, sunken and without hope, haunted Babb. She knew what desperation looked like; she'd seen that same look written across her mother's and father's faces.

With more time on her hands, Babb started haunting local bookshops and spending time at the Los Angeles Public Library, where she began to meet other young writers who had moved to Lost Angeles to begin their careers. Babb was just one of "[m]any young writers, especially the Depression generation . . . [who] had our education interrupted or stopped; . . . became self-educated from love of books; we were wandering all over . . . looking for any little job for survival."[8] These writers included the novelist John Fante, who grew up in Denver and who'd also escaped a family that had been dominated by a father's gambling addiction. Fante would become well known for his autobiographical novel *Ask the Dust* (1939). Decades later, this novel would become Charles Bukowski's favorite; ironically, he discovered it at the library where Fante had struggled decades earlier. At the same time, Babb was beginning to write short stories again, but instead of writing about characters whose life experiences she didn't know much about, she'd started drawing from her own experiences. It is interesting that this shift happened at the same time that a similar shift occurred in Fante's writing, and it's likely that the two influenced each other during this time.

Babb also met Harold Salemson, a writer who'd just returned from Paris.[9] Salemson was the former editor of the expatriate literary magazine *Tambour*. When Babb told him she was looking to meet more writers, he invited her to join the John Reed Club. Named after the American activist and journalist John Reed and started in 1929, this nationwide organization was meant to bring together Marxist writers, artists, and intellectuals.[10] Babb later told scholar Doug Wixson that what she heard at the meeting sounded good: "All the politics involved was rather new to me, but being born a rebel, I was attracted to the left and the idealism of saving the world."[11] Ever since she'd followed the Sacco and Vanzetti case, Babb's interest in the issues of the left had begun to grow.

During the spring of 1930, Babb landed a full-time job as a secretary in the Warner Brothers Theatre building at KFWB, the radio station established by Warner Brothers cofounder Sam Warner, one of the most popular radio stations in the country. Her salary was $22.50 a week.[12] With money now coming in, she was able to rent a room from a woman and her daughter at 1731 Wilcox Avenue. The previous secretary, Kay Van Riper, had risen to the role of lead writer and was now writing, producing, and starring in the immensely popular historical drama *English Coronets*. After she would leave KFWB, Van Riper would go on to work on Andy Hardy films, beginning with *A Family Affair* (1937).

At KFWB, Van Riper became Babb's mentor, and the two quickly became friends. Babb was quickly promoted to junior writer.[13] In this new role, one of Babb's jobs was to collaborate with Van Riper on the lyrics to songs for her show, including a song they wrote together called "How Deep Is the Ocean." After they finished writing it, the lyrics were set to music and recorded by the KFWB orchestra. Like everything else Babb wrote for the radio station, the song aired without naming her or Van Riper as lyricist. At the time, Babb didn't think twice about it. But, because she and her colleague had not been documented as the authors of the lyrics, they had no rights to the song, and soon after it aired, "somebody swiped it" and claimed they'd written the song themselves. Later Babb remembered hearing the song on the radio and being completely surprised to hear her own words sung. Babb and Van Riper never received any royalties for their work on the song, which would become a standard.[14] Such acts were common during this era in Hollywood, and it wouldn't be the last time that Babb would have her intellectual property used by another author.

Regardless, the women continued to work together and for years to come. Babb would share her own creative work with Van Riper until Van Riper's untimely death in 1948. In one of their last exchanges, in 1947, Van Riper wrote to Babb, "My Lord, girl, how you can write! With what delicacy, light and shade, small and great touches of the brush! As always, after reading something of yours, I could come and smack you over the ear for not getting down to business about it."[15]

Working in the Warner Brothers building brought Babb in close contact with Hollywood professionals on a regular basis, including professionals who could get her journalism gigs. As she recalled, KFWB shared a building with "motion picture agents, magazines"; Babb sold "a few stories to a magazine called . . . *Talk of the Town.*" In addition, the "woman editor" at *Film Daily* sent Babb to review several films. This exposure to a vibrant community was everything she had moved to Los Angeles for, as she would explain to her cousin Lillie in a letter: "You asked me if I am happier here than back home?

Home was usually a series of places one after another and now that I look back, I believe it was interesting, if hard. However, I am happier here, because I could not progress there any further than I had gone . . . and I needed the contacts of other writers, editors, and the world, which I hope more than most anything else, to travel over while I live."[16]

The beauty that had begun to blossom in Babb back in Forgan and Garden City had now fully bloomed. Babb was a young attractive woman living in Hollywood, and her beauty did not go unnoticed. One night the famous Hollywood producer Irving Thalberg was having dinner at the Ambassador Hotel with his agent when he saw twenty-three-year-old Babb out on a date. Afterward, the agent, who also worked in the Warner Brothers building, at the Lyons and Lyons Agency, began following Babb. After a few days of being followed, Babb was riding the elevator and got fed up with her stalker. She wheeled around and shouted at him, "If you don't stop following me, I'm going to report you to the police!"[17]

At her outburst, the agent just chuckled and told the elevator operator to tell her who he was. Once Babb knew he was a talent agent, her annoyance lessened, and she cautiously agreed to meet with him in his office during her lunch break. It's there that he informed her about Thalberg's interest in her. The famous producer had seen in Babb his "new star," a beautiful, intelligent woman who would be a perfect successor to the actress Norma Shearer, who was also Thalberg's wife and who wanted to retire now that she had won an Academy Award.[18] Babb told the agent flat out that she didn't want to be an actor, she wanted to be a writer. She'd enjoyed writing and starring in her own productions years ago in the empty building in Forgan. What she had loved about that experience, however, had not been performing the parts; it had been sitting in the bakery at her makeshift desk dreaming up the characters she would bring to life on the stage. The agent wouldn't take no for an answer. He insisted that she at least meet Thalberg in person to discuss the matter. Babb told him she'd think about it and left the meeting.

The next day, word of her offer had already spread, and as soon as Babb walked into the *Film Daily* office her editor, Bea, blurted out, "I heard all about [your offer] from his agent next floor. Imagine having Irving Thalberg wanting to make you a star! No strings, either. Says you have the face, his new star: beautiful and intelligent."[19]

Babb scoffed and tried to explain that she wasn't interested in being a movie star.

"Listen, idiot," Bea, insisted, "you keep that appointment." Babb's editor knew what power Thalberg wielded in Hollywood.

But Babb, standing across from Bea in the small office, asked, "Why? I just want to be a writer."

Bea answered, "Nonsense. He said you suggest a secret magic he can't quite figure out. He's got you all planned out. Go for it."

Babb, having escaped the rule of her father, had no intention of being controlled in any way. She asserted, "I'll plan myself out."

But Bea insisted. "The appointment is made. At least be courteous."

Babb thought about it and finally relented: "Well, I do appreciate it. All right, I'll be courteous."

Satisfied, Bea let the thread go and got back to business, sharing Babb's next assignment with her: "While you're still among us, how about doing an interview? I'll give you some pointers. Find your way around MGM. I'll set up a lunch date with that Chinese cameraman. He's hot copy. You on?" Bea was referring to James Wong Howe (Wong Tong Jim), a Chinese-born American who was fast becoming the most sought-after cinematographer in Hollywood due to his innovative filming techniques.

Babb, happy to turn the conversation back to writing, answered, "I'd like that!" and walked away with her new assignment.

That afternoon, guided by her editor's pressure, Babb returned to Thalberg's agent's office and agreed to go with him to the MGM lot. With dozens of films being produced at once, the lot was bustling with activity. Before their meeting, Thalberg had Babb undergo a screen test, and she posed for dozens of headshots.[20] When she walked into his office later that afternoon, Babb was surprised at how young Thalberg looked.[21] From across his big desk, he promised to make her a rich movie star. For most young women working in Hollywood at the time, this would have been an offer they couldn't refuse. But to Babb, taking the offer meant selling out. And no matter what Thalberg promised her, Babb told him money didn't matter, she wanted to be a writer. One wonders what in Babb wouldn't relent in that moment. Here she was at the precipice of possibility, yet something in her didn't trust what she hadn't earned. Now that she was away from her controlling father, she didn't want to be lured into something she didn't want to do. Hollywood in the early 1930s was a toxic place to be a young woman, but Babb held her ground. If there were physical advances, she either ignored them or didn't bother recalling them in her later accounts. She rose from the couch where Thalberg promised her riches and walked out the door. It was a decision none of her Hollywood friends at the Warner Brothers building could understand.

Walking off the MGM lot that day, Babb passed a handsome Chinese man. As they went by each other, each looked at the other discreetly. Realizing he might be James Wong Howe, the cinematographer she was supposed to interview, Babb risked asking him, "Are you . . . ?"[22]

In preparation for her article on him for *Film Daily*, Babb had been reading about Howe. She wasn't surprised when he finished her sentence: "James Howe."

Babb's expression softened in a smile. "I'm supposed to interview you next week if you're available. *Film Daily.*"

Howe was surprised. "You're not an actress?"

Babb was quick to reply: "No. I've just had a narrow escape."

Curious, Howe asked what she meant. Babb explained what had just happened with Thalberg. Shock washed over Howe's face. "Mr. Thalberg! You said no?"

Babb was annoyed by yet another person who didn't understand her position and explained, "I just want to be a writer."

Howe, who'd struggled for years against the racism inherent in the film industry to get his footing in Hollywood as a cinematographer, didn't understand Babb's motives. "You should listen to Mr. Thalberg!" he said.

Babb was eager to change the subject and asked, "What is your *real* name?"

Howe, startled by her audacity, answered, "James Wong Howe. Wong is my family name."

Babb told him, "You should use it instead of that stuffy Anglo James Howe."

Howe explained, "You don't understand."

Always the reporter, Babb pressed him for more information. "Is it your idea or theirs?"

Howe explained that the decision had been up to MGM. Babb didn't yet understand the racism that stood in Howe's way. He was a handsome, successful cinematographer. She had no idea he had had to sneak into the studios to get his first job because the guards wouldn't let an Asian man onto the lots. She had no idea that Howe had had to fight an uphill battle since that first day.

Babb knew nothing of this, yet, so she answered him from her position of privilege: "Odd. Anyway, I'd insist on my own name. But that's your business."

Howe, who was eager to change the subject, asked her, "What is your name?"

"Oh, I'm sorry. I'm Sanora Babb," she answered, extending her hand to shake his, "but I've got to run and catch the Red Car back to the office."

Howe was intrigued and wanted to keep their conversation going, so he offered, "My car's here. Would you like me to drive you back?"

Babb hesitated. She didn't often accept rides from men she didn't know, but she thought he seemed nice. "Only if you are going to Hollywood."

They walked off the lot and up the street to where Howe had parked. He opened the door of his slick convertible Duesenberg to let Babb in on the passenger side. The sun was shining on Los Angeles that day, and Howe had the top down. One wonders what Babb was thinking, the wind blowing her untamed hair even wilder, the palm trees strobing by as they drove through the streets toward Hollywood. By the time Howe dropped Babb off at the Warner Brothers building, they'd set up a date for their interview in just a few weeks.

Before the interview could take place, the unthinkable happened. Seemingly without cause, KFWB let Babb go. Van Riper was moving to New York, and without her influence, Babb was just another young female writer who could easily be replaced by a man. While Babb had been picking up articles here and there, the small stipends she earned weren't enough to make rent. She stopped paying it, hoping her landlord would be lenient until she found a steadier income. One day while she was out conducting an interview in her stylish white suit, her landlord changed the locks. When she returned to Wilcox Avenue, she found her belongings had been tossed on the street. Babb was furious. She had nowhere to go.

She wasn't alone. It was the beginning of the Great Depression, after all. Hordes of people were sleeping on the streets, and Babb soon became one of them, sleeping on a bench in Lafayette Park with five other unemployed strangers for four months.[23] As she remembered, "The police were kind to us, told us to get newspapers from the trash can to sleep on for warmth." The strangers she found herself with formed a small community. A twelve-year-old boy in their motley crew was charged with gathering newspapers every evening. Luckily, during her months on the street the weather remained mild. "Whenever one or two of us managed to get a few hours of work, we shared food."[24] Babb finally found a job posing nude for students at the Otis Art Institute for forty cents an hour, but she fainted during a session because she was so weak from hunger and was immediately fired. "We were so busy trying to survive we had no idea we were storing up experience. What I remember most is the grim humor, even laughter and sometimes we sang together, very low, at night."[25]

Homeless, Babb did not give up her love of reading. While unemployed, she continued to loiter at the temple-like building of the new Los Angeles Public Library to check out books and sit on the long steps near the fountain, reading in the afternoon sun.[26] Or she'd frequent Stanley Rose's Bookshop on Hollywood Boulevard. Rose was "a swaggering, foul mouthed, large-hearted, hard-drinking Texan"[27] who would greet Babb and the other down-and-out writers who frequented his shop with his thick Southern drawl, inviting them to spend as much time as they liked reading the books on the shelves.[28] His bookshop became a gathering place for writers. Rose was a kind man who fostered community and he never kicked them out, even though none of them could afford to buy books.[29]

In desperation, Babb found work through a friend at the Warner Brothers building with whom she'd kept in touch, and she and four other young writers began ghostwriting screenplays from books in the public domain for "a rich, illiterate man who sold the screenplays under his own name." He had a whole bank of writers working for him in his massive two-floor suite at the Knickerbocker Hotel on Ivar Avenue near Hollywood Boulevard. He required his writers to read screenplay after screenplay in order to learn the form. Babb remembered sitting in the suite, the air thick with cigarette smoke, the room noisy with visitors, trying to write. But Babb was used to chaos; it's the environment in which she'd grown up. So she wrote through it and within a few weeks her screen adaptation of *Raffles, the Amateur Cracksman* was sold to MGM, it would eventually be made into a film, *Raffles*, starring Ronald Colman.[30] When the screenplay was sold, her boss threw a huge party at the suite, where, much to Babb's surprise, Louis B. Mayer himself, the cofounder of MGM, delivered a check for $13,550 to her boss. From this enormous payout, Babb received only $500 (which must have felt like a fortune given her circumstances). *Raffles* was the only screenplay Babb would write that would be made into a movie, but it bought her a ticket out of poverty, and she was once again able to secure a more permanent place to live: a top-floor apartment in a building on Hollywood Boulevard, near Rose's bookshop. The payout also gave her enough to cover her living expenses so that she could focus her time and attention on doing what she wanted to do: write.

Babb still spent time browsing the shelves at Rose's, except now when she saw a book she wanted, she could afford to buy it. Over the four months she was homeless, Rose had become a close friend, someone Babb could talk to. Because her apartment was located so close to the shop, Rose would often come by with a group of Hollywood celebrities or visiting writers he'd been dining with at Musso's, the restaurant next door to his bookshop. On one of these visits, Rose brought his new friend James Wong Howe. Babb hadn't seen Howe since their first encounter (she'd had to cancel their interview because she had lost her apartment soon after their meeting), but she saw Howe's face light up when he saw her. He clearly remembered her. But when the group came back to her apartment, Howe just sat quietly in the background with what looked like a scowl on his face, so Babb assumed he wasn't that interested in her.

With the encouragement of her literary friends, Babb began to send her work to the "little magazines" that had become popular in the early 1930s. Babb learned about all the small, national magazines at the bookshop, where Rose kept an ample supply on hand. As scholar Doug Wixson points out, "Despite their short run, little magazines of the 1930s . . . served an important role in introducing little-known writers to mainstream publishers."[31] The young Filipino writer José García Villa, who ran the literary magazine *Clay,* accepted Babb's short story "Little Pariah" for the spring 1932 issue. It was her first published short story. In it, a young, sick boy strips off his clothes and basks naked in the rain. While the story is written from the point of view of a boy, it is in this work that one begins to see Babb's shift toward writing about her own sensual experiences. As she later explained to her cousin, "I love to lie naked in the rain above all other pleasures, and I am drawn irresistibly out into it—gentle or downpours." Perhaps it was the freedom she felt in Los Angeles that caused this shift in her writing: "There is something I like of the difference here (in L.A.) . . . the bohemian freedom . . . the many types of people . . . from many lands . . . the gathering of artistic people . . . the international flavor."[32] The sexual awakening that had begun in her high school years continued and evolved during Babb's first decade in Los Angeles, where she would continue to explore her sexuality.

Another young writer, William Saroyan, read "Little Pariah" in *Clay,* and sensing he'd found a like-minded peer, wrote to Babb on April 18, 1932. In his letter, he praised her work, but he also warned her that "having stories and work in *Clay* is alright for a time, but the practice ought ultimately to be avoided. The company is generally bad or negligible."[33] Saroyan was living in San Francisco and hadn't yet published his breakthrough story, "The Daring Young Man on the Flying Trapeze," which would appear in *Story* magazine in 1934. But he had studied the literary market and was savvy about how to promote one's literary career by carefully choosing where one's work was published. Saroyan was on a mission to become a famous writer, and he was eager to share his strategies with Babb. This letter was the first in an onslaught of letters in which the two discussed literature and their lives as up-and-coming writers. Their close friendship and

Saroyan's encouragement would push Babb to write her first novel. Their friendship was equally important to Saroyan's development as a writer; however, despite the fact that their correspondence spans a decade and that the two wrote a screenplay together called *Women without Men*,[34] only one of Saroyan's biographers included his relationship with Babb in the accounts of this era of his life. For many of these biographers (such as Jack Leggett, Lee Lawrence, Aram Saroyan, Leo Hamalian, and Edward Halsey Foster), Saroyan's career didn't begin until he published his first successful short story.

One does find a different account in the Saroyan biography *The World of William Saroyan* (1998), in which Nona Balakian, who interviewed Babb toward the end of her life and who read many of Saroyan's letters to Babb, includes a brief mention of their relationship: "Saroyan fell deeply in love with [Babb] in 1932 or 1933 . . . and asked to marry her." Balakian goes on to question why no previous Saroyan biography mentions Babb and why "to this day no one who claims to have been close to the writer appears to know of Ms. Babb." Balakian boils the answer down to Saroyan's own myth-making about his pre-fame origin story: "For a long time, it was assumed that Saroyan's love life had but one object: his typewriter. The initial image that he created was of a struggling young man, locked in a cold San Francisco flat, furiously and obsessively turning out stories that he couldn't sell."[35]

Meanwhile, during the early years of her correspondence with Saroyan, Babb started making a small amount of money publishing poems and writing articles for the magazine *Town and Country*. When she interviewed an Italian antiques dealer for an article she was writing, he invited her to lunch with his friend G. Henry Stetson, one of two brothers who were heirs to the Stetson hat fortune. Babb was impressed by the striking man across the table from her. And it seemed Stetson was equally impressed with Babb, as he asked her out on the spot. Later that same day, they met at a lavish restaurant.

Babb couldn't believe that just a few months ago she'd been sleeping on a bench and now here she was, dining in one of Hollywood's finest restaurants. Stetson, who'd grown up near Philadelphia in a family that had great wealth, soon took on the role of Babb's benefactor. Within months he had proposed to Babb, but she was hesitant to agree. Stetson was used to getting what he wanted when he wanted it, so he continued to pressure her until she hesitantly agreed, and they became engaged. Babb, still recovering from the stress of being homeless and in awe of Stetson's wealth, was thrilled to no longer have to worry about money; however, she knew she wasn't ready to settle down, especially if it meant not being able to write. She knew what usually happened to a woman's career when she married: it disappeared, and she was determined not to let that be her fate. Babb remained wary. In addition to the possible erasure of her budding career as a writer that a marriage to Stetson might cause, she was also leery because the couple had a tumultuous relationship; Babb complained in letters to friends that Stetson was violent with her. Babb, who was still only twenty-five years old, had grown up in a house where abuse was the norm. She'd lived under the pressure of her father's rage. Perhaps that's why she stayed in her abusive relationship with Stetson for over a year.

For her birthday, Stetson gave Babb the ultimate gift: an adventure of travel. He bought her passage to Central America on the steamer *Antigua* of the United Fruit Company line. The steamer left from San Francisco, a city she'd never visited but had heard much about from Saroyan's letters. She tried to meet him while she was briefly in town, but their letters crossed paths and they never determined a time to get together. In San Francisco, as Babb waited for the boat to Panama, she "walked around, feeling restless and lonely, but glad to be going someplace new and strange."[36] Up to this point, Babb had never left the United States, and she was eager to discover the world beyond her country's borders.

When Babb arrived in Panama City, she immediately loved the freedom of exploring the city alone. During one of her wanderings, she befriended an old West Indian man who rode a horse and "was something of a history book" as he recounted the city's past and the names of all of the flora and fauna they encountered. The old man took Babb on several outings into the jungle to identify "the strange birds and snakes, the dense plant life that is rather frightening the way it grows before one's eyes."[37]

After a few weeks in Panama City, Babb continued to Colón and Cristóbal and then took a little boat to her first stop in Costa Rica, Puerto Limón. From there she boarded a train to the capital, San José. On the train, Babb looked out the window at the luscious jungle that lurched past. Just as the passengers were served lunch, the train slowed to a standstill and a group of starving children walked out from the jungle, their bellies swollen, their desperate hands reaching through the open train windows. Babb and most of the other passengers immediately gave their lunches to the children, along with the change in their pockets. Once the train reached San José, Babb stepped back into a life of luxury. Thanks to Stetson's funding, she stayed in an elegant hotel where cocktails were served at 4:00 p.m. and one had to dress formally for dinner. Babb was surprised by how many Americans she encountered, most of whom she found unbearable. As she recalled in a letter to Saroyan, at the hotel "I suffered the presence of the Americans in the dining room that night: they grew drunk and noisy and vulgar."[38] Babb, who wanted to distance herself from the rude Americans at the hotel, devised a plan to spend most of her time alone. Most of the residents of the hotel slept in, so she reversed her regular habit of staying up late and instead woke at five in the morning to walk by herself around the city: "At that time I could see the volcanoes smoking in a semi-circle. . . . The mountains rose magnificent and beautifully green."[39] Once she left the hotel and immersed herself in the flow of life in Costa Rica, she began to feel much as she had growing up on the prairie: as if everything around her were at the mercy of nature.

After a few more weeks exploring Costa Rica, Babb reluctantly returned home via Panama. On the way, her ship stopped in Puerto Armuelles to load a cargo of bananas. On the dock, she saw a little boy selling miniature monkeys, and Babb, who always had a soft spot for animals, immediately fell in love with one and bought it to bring home with her. Later, the monkey, who she called Patsy, slept curled at Babb's throat at night.

The next day, in the pouring rain, the ship finally set sail into "the heavy grey mist of sea and sky together." Babb felt lonely "not to be coming away, but to be coming back here."[40] The trip had altered Babb and awakened in her a need to travel and see the world. Babb's return was announced in the *San Francisco Call:* "Miss Sanora Babb, Hollywood scenario writer, arrived here today on the steamer *Antigua* with a three-month-old monkey, a souvenir of her trip through Central America."[41]

The day before Babb left for Panama, James Wong Howe had finally called Babb and asked her out on a date. Babb, who was still skeptical about this man who said little at parties, declined, partly because she wasn't sure about him and partly because she was going to be away for months. However, Howe wasn't deterred by Babb's initial refusal. He'd asked what date she returned, and he'd remembered it. Babb walked into her apartment holding Patsy's tiny body against her chest; Howe called within hours to ask her out again.

Babb's travels had given her plenty of time to think about her tumultuous relationship with Stetson. She'd tasted the freedom of being alone, and by the time she returned she was ready to try something new, so she decided to go on the date with Howe. In the early 1930s the general public did not accept mixed-race couples. Howe was well aware of how they'd be treated if he took Babb to a restaurant in Hollywood, so he took her to a restaurant in Chinatown.[42]

Babb, who was used to the extravagant restaurants that she and Stetson frequented, was surprised to be taken to Chinatown on a first date, but she soon found the small noisy restaurants there much more to her liking.

For the next several months, Babb dated both Howe and Stetson. Babb wasn't someone who believed in monogamy. The poetry she grew up on by Edna St. Vincent Millay had opened up the idea of sexual freedom to her. The horrific spectacle of her parents' marriage had further solidified in her a will to prioritize her own sensual needs above society's gender standards.

Soon Babb and Howe were going out a few nights a week and Babb began to see for herself the racism Howe constantly experienced. One night, when she insisted they go to a restaurant in Hollywood, the host couldn't find a table for them despite the fact that they had a reservation. Another time, when the two of them were driving in Howe's convertible, a finely dressed woman saw them and was so outraged that she began driving alongside them, yelling and swerving her car as if to run them off the road. When they parked in front of their favorite restaurant in Chinatown, the woman pulled up right behind them. Howe leaned over to Babb and urged her to just let the whole thing go; it didn't matter. But Babb couldn't do it. Instead, she sprang out of the car and began screaming at the woman, who in turn yelled furiously back. In a moment of rage, Babb grabbed the woman's expensive hat off of her head and threw it into the gutter. The woman fell to her knees screaming "My hat! My $100 hat!" as it floated away in the dirty water. Babb left the woman on her knees and walked back to Howe. He slipped his arm around her waist as they entered the restaurant, and though he told her she shouldn't have engaged in the conflict, she felt that quietly he liked that she'd fought back.[43]

That winter, Howe was sent by MGM on a trip via Panama to Europe to shoot background shots. By this time, Howe had made his name well known as a cinematographer and his talent far exceeded the assignment; however, as he saw it, he was being punished for having depicted the actress Myrna Loy too realistically in the film he had just shot for MGM, *The Thin Man*. The director, W. S. Van Dyke, didn't like the way that Howe had interpreted the scene in which Loy looks in the mirror and says, "I look awful." While they were shooting the scene, Howe asked Loy to "muss up her hair a bit and rub some of her makeup off." As he remembered, "She was pleased and did so." But after Van Dyke reviewed the scene, he was furious. He called Howe into his office to ask him why he'd taken the liberty of changing the shot. When Howe answered that he'd done it to make the scene more realistic, to make Loy look like she "felt awful," as the script stated, Van Dyke was livid and told him, "We're paying you to make the stars look beautiful, not realistic." As punishment for his initiative, Howe was taken off of his film projects and sent away for four months with an assistant to shoot background shots for inclusion in MGM films.[44]

Before he left, Babb saw Howe off at the dock. Over the past few months, they'd become close, and she burst into tears at that thought of his leaving. To her surprise, Howe remained dry-eyed and stoic. Later, in a letter, he admitted that as soon as he boarded the train, he hid in the men's restroom and cried as he hadn't since he'd had to leave his mother in China when he was five years old. Back in his birth city of Taishan, Howe's mother had fallen into a coma-like state after his birth, a state "in which her bodily functions nearly ceased." Not wanting to raise a child on his own, his father hastily arranged another marriage. When Howe's mother awoke, she found her husband had married someone else. In 1899, when Howe was five, his father decided to emigrate to America on his own, with the intent to return for his family as soon as he had settled. In 1904, when Howe's father returned from Pasco, Washington, where he'd been working as a laborer on the Northern Pacific Railroad and now wanted to open a general store, he insisted on not only bringing his new wife and family but also Howe, his first son. However, he did not intend to bring his first wife, and so Howe had to say goodbye to his mother.[45] Losing his mother at such a young age deeply affected Howe, and the effects would surface in his relationship with Babb as it progressed.

While Howe was away, Babb and Howe wrote frequent letters to each other processing their growing love. In January 1933, Babb wrote about how glad she was that she was able to feel the love that was growing between them: "I might have lived my whole life without it—but now you love me, and I love you—It is of beauty + the poetry of living—and it belongs to us—to you and me together."[46] By the time Howe returned, Babb had broken off her relationship with Stetson.

Without the distraction of Howe's presence, and with her relationship with Stetson cooling, Babb focused her energy almost entirely on her writing. She began sending out her work extensively, work that was becoming more and more based on what she had experienced or witnessed during her childhood. In "Poppies in the Wind," which was published in *The Windsor Quarterly* in the summer of 1933, she writes from the point of view of a young girl who despises her mother's rules and who identifies with her father's lawlessness. Babb insinuates that the father in the story is a gambler like her own, describing his nighttime movements and ample cash: "Her father would go out then, and down into the lights of the town. Hours and hours later, while it was still dark, the child would hear him return. . . . Next she would hear the hard sounds of money being taken from his pocket and placed gently on the table."[47]

The young girl in the story refuses to wear clothing, which causes her mother so much frustration that at one point she screams at the young child, "Someday you'll get raped, you little fool. Now put some clothes on before you go out."[48] The girl keeps a small "garden" of flowers she's made from salvaged paper labels of food cans she finds in the trash heap in the backyard. The garden is the place she goes to escape the chaos of her life. The story's climax occurs on the family's wash day, when her mother and father go outside to pour out the scalding wash water. Unbeknownst to her parents, the young girl follows them outside, and when she sees that the trajectory of the water will destroy her "garden" she jumps in front of it, only to be burned so severely that she dies at the end of the story. The dramatic ending is reminiscent of the one in another early story, "Lost Cry," which was published in *The Outlander: A Quarterly Literary Review* in the spring of 1933. In it, the protagonist is a married women who, dissatisfied with her life, goes out walking at night only to be hit by a car.

During this time, Babb also continued to have success publishing her poems. She published "Essence" and "Spring Wooing" in *Prairie Schooner*. In "Essence" one sees the distinct shift in Babb's poetic style. Gone are the exact and imprisoning end rhymes found in her early work. Instead, this twenty-four-line free verse poem is ruled by extended metaphor and sensory details. In it the wind is "fragrant with swollen seeds the breath / Of things unborn" (lines 9–10).

In 1933, Babb received a letter from Jack Conroy, editor of the new leftist literary magazine *The Anvil,* accepting her short story "Dry Summer." In the acceptance letter, Conroy praises "Poppies in the Wind" and compares her work to that of Grace Stone Coates, whose linked story collection *Black Cherries,* about farm life in the Midwest, was also written from a child's point of view. He suggested that Babb send her work to Gavin Arthur at *Dune Forum* and Dr. Goldberg at *Panorama.*[49] It's in "Dry Summer" that Babb first introduces the characters Ronny and Myra, who reappear in her first novel, *Whose Names Are Unknown.* It's likely the story was part of an early draft of the manuscript of the novel. "Dry Summer" is set in the Babbs' stone house on the bank of Horse Creek in Baca County. The father in the story is as troubled as Babb's own, and a sense of violence pulses throughout. It is a mature story that gives us a glimpse into the writer she grew into. This shift to writing about autobiographical material helps her find a voice that publishers were seeking. "The Old One," another short story from this era that was published in *The Midland* in the spring of 1933, is also set on a western prairie, and it tells the story of a young girl hired for domestic farm work. The story revolves around a funeral: the old man she works for has died. There are references to broomcorn farming and the way a small community comes together to mourn the dead. The story also includes sensual descriptions of the landscape that show the extent to which Babb's craft had improved: "It was a bitter day for a funeral. As if no softness could be spared for grief, the skies hung gray and sullen near the earth, closed over a day which farmers would waste for death. Though it was the high time of summer, a wind came out of the north as cold as November, and men awoke and smelled the crystal air, saying among themselves or in their minds that such a wind was blowing hail."[50] With several stories now published in well-acclaimed magazines and a novel on its way, Babb must have felt that her decision to move to Los Angeles had been a good one.

Since his first letter to her about her work in *Clay*, William Saroyan had continued corresponding with Babb. In 1933, Babb revealed to Saroyan that she had begun working on a novel that Simon & Schuster had shown interest in (based on the success of her short stories), but that she did not yet have the courage to send it.[51] It's hard to tell which novel Babb is referring to in her letter, as she started several novels during this era, including one called *Konkie,* based on her grandfather's life, and another one about an abusive alcoholic boyfriend.[52] But Babb's short story material written during this era points to the fact that she was already beginning to write what would become her novel *Whose Names Are Unknown.* In January 1935, Babb confessed to Saroyan that she had "only 50 pages of my book done—I hadn't thot of pages until a few minutes ago I started counting them expecting several hundred! I haven't any courage about the book: I have to push this feeling aside forcibly in between the times of wanting to write or I couldn't do it at all. I forget it of course when I want to write, but it would be better if I didn't feel that way at all."[53]

As time passed, Babb's letters to and from Saroyan became more and more intimate. In him she had found a writer of equal caliber who had a great ambition to be more. But this intimacy scared her. As she wrote to Saroyan on March 27, 1934, after he'd hitchhiked down from San Francisco to visit her and her sister Dorothy for several weeks, "I'm sure that everyone contains in himself some point of being that is never touched nor given out: I do not mean this when I say I cannot give myself closely. Sometimes it is almost a tangible thing: almost as if I can hold it in my hand and will not give it out of myself. As if the loss would relinquish me finally to others (another), and I would be unwhole and lost, and bound over to that other part, rather than the person who received it."[54] Saroyan slept on the couch during his visit. He and Babb went for long walks around her neighborhood near Hollywood Boulevard. She "liked him very much," but at least for Babb, the passion they exchanged on the page never flourished in real life.[55]

8 The Writers' Congress

As Babb continued to work through memories in her fiction, she kept in touch with her family back home in Kansas through frequent letters. Through their correspondence, she learned that after she left, her shy, dependent sister, Dorothy, had also left the family, following in her big sister's footsteps by taking a teaching position at a rural one-room school, and that her mother, who was still working at the grocery store, had finally gotten the courage to ask her father for a divorce. As Jennie told her daughter years later, "It took me twenty-seven years to get mad."[1] Despite what she'd seen growing up, Babb was still surprised by the news of her parents' divorce. Perhaps she never guessed that after all those years of living under Walt's control, her mother could finally see her way to freedom. To process their break, Babb wrote a poem that was not published until after her death. In it she spoke in the voice of her mother who, freed from the abusive grip of her father, was "free to grow whole again."[2] Walt was shocked and devastated when Jennie asked him for a divorce. For the first time since he had begun to court her when she was fourteen years old, nothing Walt said could change Jennie's mind.[3] Without his family to tether him down, Walt hit the road and spent the rest of his life gambling from town to town, finally settling in San Diego. He'd send Babb postcards from wherever he was, writing about his lady friends and big winnings. Whenever he was near Los Angeles, he would come by to visit. But it wasn't just Jennie who had found a way to distance herself from her abuser; Babb's relationship with her father was also changing. As she wrote in a letter to her cousin Lillie Pollard, while she feared her father as child, then loathed and hated him as a young adult, now, freed from his controlling grip, she just pitied him.[4]

When Dorothy returned from teaching in rural Kansas, Babb invited her sister to live with her in Los Angeles. In early 1933, she sent Dorothy a train ticket enclosed in a letter. Dorothy was thrilled to come to live with her older sister. The two were bound by the shared experiences of their traumatic childhood. It had been odd for them to live separately for the last three and a half years, but for Babb their separation had also been a relief. In Los Angeles, the only person Babb had to worry about was herself. But now that their parents were divorcing, Dorothy had become distraught, and Babb slipped back into the role of caretaker that she'd held since her sister was born. Throughout their tumultuous childhood, Babb had been a shield for her sister. She had tried to protect her from the force of the trauma they both experienced day in and day out, because she knew her sister wasn't as resilient as she was. Dorothy wasn't independent and she had always relied on Babb's protection. For the rest of her life, Babb would support her sister both financially and emotionally. Dorothy struggled with insecurities, ill health, and depression. But being her sister's keeper weighed on Babb's independent spirit, as she tried to explain in a letter to Saroyan:

> I have one sister, a shy, delicate poet of a girl. . . . I sent for her to join me here. . . . She is so dependent on me for all communication, activity, and even the most commonplace things necessary to existence, that I would be less busy, less tethered, if I had a dozen children on my skirts. I don't resent her because I love her very much. . . . It isn't that I plot her life, but that I am forced into being a medium for her.

I'm trying desperately to escape crippling her with having me always on hand, but I don't know how to handle the situation.[5]

On March 7, 1933, Dorothy boarded the same Santa Fe rail line her sister had taken across the plains to the Rocky Mountains and down through the deserts of Arizona to California. When she stepped off the train two days later, Dorothy saw her sister frantically waving to her from the platform. The two embraced, and Babb took her sister back to what would now be *their* apartment at 1156 North Curson Avenue in Hollywood. The apartment was one of many in what looked like a Tudor house set back from the street. After her long journey on the train, Dorothy probably fell into the comfortable bed her sister had made for her and slept soundly. But the next morning, she woke to a violent jolt. The world around her shook with such fervor that she thought it was coming to an end. Babb awoke to the same violent shock, the walls of the room rippling.[6] What Babb and her sister had experienced that morning was what would later be called the 1933 Long Beach Earthquake, a 6.4-magnitude earthquake that killed 120 people and caused millions of dollars of damage. Luckily, Babb and her sister were not harmed in the earthquake, and their apartment only sustained minor damage.

After her violent entry into the new landscape of California, Dorothy began to settle in. Babb used her savings to help pay Dorothy's tuition at the University of California at Los Angeles. But within months, Dorothy found her studies overwhelming, even though Babb supported her and even helped with her homework.[7] Dorothy left UCLA before officially graduating. Desperate, Babb encouraged her sister to enroll in Woodbury College's ten-month course in private secretarial and journalism training. However, this, too, Dorothy was unable to finish.

Still, to have her sister with her was a comfort to Babb. Her sister immediately liked Howe, who, upon his return from Europe, had continued a close relationship with Babb. The two would likely have moved in together; however, due to Hollywood's "moral code" and California's strict miscegenation laws, Howe couldn't move in, let alone marry Babb. Howe was often with Babb and her sister at their apartment. Babb and Howe purchased a matching pair of Sealyham terriers they named Cissy and Annie that Babb kept at her apartment.

In the little apartment on Curson Avenue, Babb and her sister read books together, as they had when they were young, and discussed them late into the night. Despite the burden of caregiving, having her sister there meant that Babb had someone with her who had lived through all she had lived through. One day when Babb retrieved the mail, she found a small letter addressed to her in her Aunt Stella's tight, looping script. It was odd to receive a letter from her father's sister, so she called Dorothy into the living room and they sat on the couch and opened it together. The letter explained that their grandfather Konkie had had a stroke and died while he was staying on Stella's farm near Liberal, Kansas. He was eighty-one years old.

Since they'd last lived with him in Eastern Colorado, Konkie had never slowed down. The day he died, he'd been out herding cattle. Walt would always hold a grudge against his sister for making their elderly father work on her farm; he thought she was responsible for their father's death. With her parents divorced and her beloved grandfather dead, Babb's childhood had now been completely uprooted and exposed to the air. Where would she be if she hadn't had her grandfather to help teach her how to read in their grave-like home in the dugout? Would she have had the confidence to venture out into the unknown if she hadn't had her grandfather lead her out into the wilderness of the prairie on their long walkabouts?

Dorothy, too, was deeply affected by the blow of losing her grandfather. She was so troubled by the thought of him dying in her Aunt Stella's stuffy religious household that she rewrote his death in a short story, "Konkie." In the story, she placed her grandfather in a dark movie theater, nodding off in the flickering blue light of the film: "As he watched the film, for what seemed a long time, he grew drowsy and tired. Rest and peace, they were fine things. He knew that he was falling asleep, but he didn't mind. That is the way Konkie quietly died."[8]

The next spring, Babb decided to visit her mother and for the first time since she'd moved to Los Angeles, she took the train back to Kansas. It was strange following the same route that had brought her to Los Angeles in reverse; she was returning, but she was returning changed. Her mother had also transformed. For the first time in her life, Jennie was living on her own and she was thriving. She worked in the grocery store and was as social as ever.

When Babb stepped off the train, she noticed that Garden City had also changed, but not for the better. The Depression had hit the town hard, and a drought had afflicted the High Plains all year: "For fifty-eight days that summer the temperature exceeded 100 degrees; rainfall was less than half of normal."[9] During Babb's visit a dust storm so dark it turned the noon sky as black as night struck the town. Traffic stopped dead in the street. All the businesses on Main Street closed. Residents tried to stuff rags into all the cracks in their homes to keep the dust out, but the wind blew hard for days, carrying dust everywhere. People wrapped wet towels over their heads so they could breathe. Many became sick with "dust pneumonia."

It wasn't Babb's first dust storm; she'd experienced them growing up. But it was by far the worst one she'd ever seen. It was storms like these that had begun to drive a quarter of a million refugees west, looking for work. During her trip home, Babb also visited Forgan, where she'd graduated from high school. What she found was a town devastated by drought and dust, a town where all economic prosperity had disappeared. The class differences she had suffered under when she was labeled as an outcast, as a gambler's daughter, had been "temporarily effaced by a failing economy."[10] Babb immediately wrote the scene into her notes for a novel she'd begun thinking about writing: "I saw them standing in line for the meat and potatoes of relief. I saw the people I used to know who had lived smugly in their imaginary stratas—the *best* people who had bathtubs and cars . . . the unacceptable ones who had no bathtubs . . . standing in line together. The essential differences in these people in the first place had been very slight, and now with the superficial gloss gone, and hunger a near and known thing to all of them, their stricken faces, one after another in line, looked very much alike."[11]

When Babb returned to her mother's house, she wondered what other towns throughout the Oklahoma Panhandle and beyond had become like this one. No one could predict what would happen over the next few years: the drought would continue, bringing ever more dust storms, and a plague of grasshoppers would descend on the Midwest. Soon, hundreds of thousands would have nothing left: their fields, their homes would be ruined by the dust. They would be lured away from their failing farms, from their dying towns, and would head west in hopes of finding work. Babb took the train back to Los Angeles determined to continue to write about what she had seen growing up in the Oklahoma Panhandle and what she was seeing now.

Living in Los Angeles, Babb had become deeply enmeshed in the John Reed Club and later, the newly forming League of American Writers. The league was an association of American writers and critics launched by the Communist Party USA (CPUSA) in 1935. In February 1935, the writer Meridel Le Sueur sent Babb an impassioned letter to urge her to become more involved with the party.[12] Le Sueur, who was seven years older than Babb, had been raised by a feminist-socialist mother (Marian Wharton) who lectured on the Chautauqua circuit about controversial topics such as birth control. Like Babb, Le Sueur grew up in the Midwest (Texas, Oklahoma, and Kansas) before her family settled in Minnesota and she became active in the Farmer-Labor Party. As an adult, Le Sueur switched parties, joining the Communist Party in the 1920s. When she wrote to Babb, Le Sueur had divorced her first husband and was living in Minneapolis as a single mother raising her two daughters. Le Sueur had received substantial recognition during the 1930s from such writers as Sinclair Lewis, Nelson Algren, and Carl Sandburg and was best known for her reportage, especially her piece "I Was Marching!" (1934), which had been inspired by the 1934 Teamsters trucker strike in Minneapolis, a bitter labor dispute that caused the deaths of two strikers but ended in victory for the union.

Babb had written to Le Sueur about a trip she'd taken to Boulder Dam (renamed Hoover Dam in 1947), and Le Sueur, in response, encouraged her to write it up as a story: "Do write something about it. I think reportage is very very good for a writer." The term *reportage* was widely used during this era to denote a reporting style that intended to make the reader "experience" the event recorded. As a "participant observer," the writer or reporter could "use vicarious persuasion," baring her feelings and attitudes and the sensory-rich details she witnessed to influence the reader's own. This "three-dimensional" reporting was used by the Communist Party as a way to fight back against presumed objectivity in journalism and was an example of the "proletarian art" encouraged by the party.[13] But most of Le Sueur's letter was dedicated to encouraging Babb to attend the upcoming League of American Writers' Congress in New York City: "Listen you must come to the Congress in May you simply must. Everyone is talking about you as in the clipping and we all want to see you and you must come. It is going to be amazing and thrilling. You never never felt anything like you feel when individual artists get together and talk and have a communal feeling not based on rejection and revulsion." Le Sueur had attended an earlier national convention of thirty John Reed Clubs in September 1934, when representatives "met in Chicago to assess their considerable progress and chart their future,"[14] and she had been "amazed and surprised" by the experience, claiming that she "grew about three years in that time."

Babb was deeply encouraged by Le Sueur's letter and when, in early 1935, delegates from the Los Angeles chapter of the league needed to be chosen as representatives for the First Writers' Congress, to be held in New York City, Babb eagerly volunteered. She was chosen to attend, along with the novelist Harry Carlisle, whom she knew from their local chapter. Carlisle was a "quiet, low-key"[15] English writer who'd published the 1931 novel *Darkness at Noon,* about his experiences as a miner in western England.

A third delegate, Tillie Lerner Olsen, whom Babb wasn't as acquainted with, was also chosen. Olsen had just moved from San Francisco to Venice Beach, where she was working on her first novel (which Babb had read chapters of and thought was "very good").[16]

The three delegates had a few meetings before their departure, first at Olsen's apartment in Venice Beach[17] and then at Babb's apartment in Hollywood, where Olsen discovered Babb's father's old "raggedy" coat that he'd left after a recent visit. Babb remembered that "Tillie wanted that coat to wear in New York to look like a proletariat."[18] It was the first sign that alerted Babb to what she would later judge to be performative behavior on Olsen's part, but at the time she thought little of it. To her, the coat, and how "authentic" it appeared, was almost comical. The poverty caused by her father's gambling addiction was deeply knitted to her own poverty and to the trauma she had experienced as a child. In her mind, it was clear wearing her father's coat could not transform someone into being a witness to the poverty she'd endured.

Babb said her goodbyes to Howe, her sister, and their two dogs. She was relieved to be freed from the vise of her sister's need but sad to leave Howe and the dogs. Still, aside from her trip home to visit her mother, she hadn't traveled significantly since she'd gone to Panama and Costa Rica, so she was thrilled to be off on another adventure.

The trio of writers left Los Angeles on April 9, 1935, squeezed into "a little one-seat Ford with a cloth top" that "an empathetic MGM producer" had lent them.[19] They drove through the vast desert of Death Valley and then past the "grand forests near Flagstaff." As the temperatures dropped, they all froze in the tiny, flimsy convertible. Olsen soon regretted wearing Babb's father's cheap coat, as it was thin and left her freezing.[20] As Babb recalled in a letter to Doug Wixson, they "were all poor, broke, though I had $70, and paid the bills."[21] When they arrived at their first destination, Gallup, New Mexico, they found "a virtual war zone, where [International] Labor Defense investigators had been kidnapped, beaten, and left to die." Olsen wrote about what she saw in a letter to her estranged husband, Abe Goldfarb; they had witnessed "brutalities toward women and children, Slavs and Mexicans—all at the hands of police and 'gun thugs' hired by mine owners."[22]

Babb would write one of her earliest nonfiction pieces about what she witnessed during their stop in Gallup. "The Terror" (which would be published in *International Literature* later in 1935) is one of her first attempts at writing reportage, the type of writing Le Sueur had encouraged her to try.[23] In the article, Babb investigates the police suppression of a coal miners' union using all the tools she'd learned to use in her fiction during the years she'd been writing in Los Angeles. The piece, in which the drama of what transpired is palpable, begins with a vivid descriptive scene before recounting the horrible events that led to the mass arrests. "We drove across the railroad tracks, leaving the better streets and the cleaner houses behind and came up the slope into the rough dark roads of the miners' town. Back at the station, the Indians were setting out their little pots and beaded bands and silver charms. The Seven-Fifty-Eight was roaring over the desert, whistling a signal, entering the block. For meals and a few dollars a month, the Navajos were creating atmosphere for the travelers."[24]

After setting the scene (the train tracks that divide the town into the haves and have-nots, the Native Americans who are there to provide "atmosphere" for the tourists), she details the event that has transpired: a stray bullet from a deputy's gun had killed a sheriff, and hundreds of miners and their wives had been arrested and charged with "mass murder." The shooting occurred at a small shack where a miner had been evicted for being a month late on rent. He'd paid his delinquent rent and his neighbors were helping him move his furniture back into his shack when the police came and the dispute began. The article goes on to follow Babb's visit with women whose husbands had been arrested and jailed in Sante Fe. One woman was arrested along with her three children, ages one and a half, five, and eight, all of them confined to a cell for four days. Babb describes that everywhere they went, there "was [the] confusion and disorder of a recent police search, and things not yet put back together."[25] Babb depicts the scenery and the people so vividly that one feels as if one is there, sitting in the stuffy small shacks while she speaks intimately with the victims. The reader is a witness, just as she is, and it's this sort of detail that makes her reportage pieces so incredibly powerful. What's fascinating about this account, and about her other examples of reportage in the years to come, is her focus and point of view: Babb always included the women and children who were affected by the crisis she was writing about. Her reportage often gives agency and voice to women who otherwise would have been erased from a historical moment (a trait she shares with the reportage written by her peers Le Sueur and Olsen).

After the trio of writers left Gallup, they continued north through the Rocky Mountains and Denver and on to Omaha, Nebraska, where they stayed the night at the home of Olsen's in-laws, the Goldfarbs. Olsen's daughter had been staying with them while Olsen was in Los Angeles writing her novel. Olsen was trying to balance being a mother, a wife, and a writer, which often left her feeling conflicted and which meant that any decision she made was open to judgment by society. This was one of the reasons Babb was wary of getting married, and even warier of having children. After Olsen's short visit with her daughter, the three writers got back into the convertible and continued their journey.

When they arrived in Chicago, they "stayed in fifty cent hotels, visited factories to talk to workers and looked up author Nelson Algren." Algren, a Chicago-based writer whose first novel, *Somebody in Boots*, had just been published, was deeply involved with the Communist Party. Babb remembered touring the factories in order "to see for ourselves automobiles being manufactured, steel plants in operation, and all sorts of factories." While in Chicago, tensions began to rise between Olsen and Babb. Olsen "chided Babb for being too liberal, too individualistic, and too ignorant of Marx," and Babb didn't like the way Olsen treated her.[26]

On April 26, 1935, they arrived in New York, well before the opening ceremonies of the Writers' Congress and just a little over two weeks after they'd begun their cross-country drive. The event was scheduled to last two days. Prior to leaving for the congress, Babb had arranged to stay with her old friend from KFWB radio, Kay Van Riper, who had explained to her in advance that she "didn't like the left." The two shared "a small hotel room" and Carlisle and Olsen got upset with Babb because she hadn't arranged a place for them to stay as well, a reaction that Babb still found ridiculous decades later when she recounted the trip to Doug Wixson, calling them both "impossible."[27]

Because of the tension caused by Babb's housing arrangement, she was on her own when she first arrived, an hour early, for the opening ceremonies. When she walked up to the Mecca Temple, a domed Shriners convention hall located at 130 West 55th Street, near Carnegie Hall, she saw a young Black man sitting on the curb, also waiting for the ceremonies to begin. As she remembered, when he saw her he stood up and shook her hand and "we introduced ourselves. He was Richard Wright."[28] Wright had not yet published *Native Son,* the book that would skyrocket him to fame in March 1940, but he was already an up-and-coming writer in the party, and Babb was delighted to meet him. His was the first of many significant and important introductions she would experience over the next two days.

Earl Browder, general secretary of the CPUSA, delivered the keynote address to all four hundred delegates. Other speakers included Clarence Hathaway, who conveyed greetings to congress attendees from "the entire staff of the *Daily Worker,*" the official newspaper of the Communist Party, and Joseph Freeman of *New Masses,* the party's literary magazine. In the opening ceremony, the League of American Writers declared itself to be "a voluntary association of writers dedicated to the preservation and extension of a truly democratic culture."[29] Le Sueur was there, too, the lone woman among the twenty scheduled speakers.[30] During the panels, readings, and events that took place over the next two days, delegates debated "whether they wrote for workers or for everyone, whether unschooled writers were more authentic than sophisticated ones, whether proletarian writers could borrow techniques from bourgeois writers, and whether message was more important than art."[31] Babb joined the May Day parade, finding the mass of writers marching down Broadway chanting "We write for the working class" in metered unison to be "a big thrill."[32]

Yet, while Babb was excited to be at the congress, she didn't always agree with the sentiments that the panels were exulting. She didn't know if she completely agreed with the call to create "proletarian art." Like Le Sueur and Olsen, Babb was experiencing what Elaine Showalter has called an "object/field problem."[33] She wanted to write about the poor—in fact, she embodied a deep commitment to writing about them—but she didn't want to do so with a prescribed agenda. As she recalled, "My poems and stories had been appearing in literary magazines since the late 20s and since I grew up poor, I wrote about such people, but I was opposed then and still am to slant my writing. This was a real bone of contention when I was in the left movement."[34]

On one of the nights of the congress, Random House editor Bennett Cerf, who had, like Babb, grown up in Garden City,[35] took a group of writers (which, in his private journal, he called a "mob of communists") to the Black Pit nightclub and then on to dinner at an expensive restaurant.[36] The group included Jack Conroy, Tillie Olsen, who had a book under contract with Random House called *Yonnondio* that she was struggling to finish writing,[37] and Babb, who desperately sought a contract for her own novel. At dinner, they could see a group of homeless people outside the restaurant's plate-glass windows, begging for food, the sight of which sent Olsen into a tirade about how much the restaurant charged for food and cocktails. Babb didn't agree with the scene that Olsen was making, and she praised Cerf for his charm and generosity, hoping to garner his favor (and perhaps a future contract for her book). Olsen, in response, attacked Cerf's culture and wealth. These tit for tats led Babb to denounce Olsen as "a communist patsy" and Olsen to denounce Babb as a "capitalist tool," words that wedged additional distance between the two writers.[38]

At other events during the Writers' Congress, Babb would also meet Kyle Crichton, the editor at *Scribner's Magazine* who'd reached out to her about her work in 1932. He'd read her story "Dry Summer" and though he'd rejected it, he'd wondered if she was working on a novel.[39] She was excited to meet him (and to find out that he wrote under the pseudonym Robert Forsythe in *New Masses*), and the two would enjoy a decades-long friendship.

When Babb left New York on April 29, 1935, she left fortified by the community that she'd found at the congress. Olsen and Carlisle drove back to California in the convertible without her.[40] At the talks, panels, bars, and restaurants she'd gone to, Babb had met writers from all over the country who were passionate about the topics she was also passionate about. She'd met publishers like Cerf who would soon play a significant role in her future as a writer. But she also left with the fire of her independence ignited inside her. She had no desire to shape herself into a person whom Olsen would be more likely to respect. When she'd seen Olsen marching in the May Day parade, a red scarf tied around her neck "'in the Soviet Youth manner' that rippled as she marched along Broadway,"[41] Babb realized that Olsen wanted her communism to be performed and admired, a feeling Babb did not share.[42] While she supported the cause, Babb wanted her writing to be about what she wanted her writing to be about.

Babb left New York in a car filled with "some of the Chicago writers," including Nelson Algren.[43] And by the time she arrived in Chicago, she knew what she needed to do. She needed to return to Los Angeles slowly, through the stretch of the Great Plains where she'd once spent her life. The next morning, she persuaded Algren to drop her off at the side of a highway going west, so she could hitchhike and walk home.[44] As she would later remember, when she stepped out of Algren's car, she was looking upon the journey home "as an adventure."[45]

Walking in between rides meant that time slowed. She could see the great fields of grasses swaying in the wind like a vast inland sea. She could awaken to a dawn chorus of birdsong after sleeping behind a nest of cottonwood trees on the side of the road. At night, when she looked up at the sky, it was like it had been when she was a child: stars milky thick, and she a small part of the universe as a whole beneath them.[46]

When there were large swaths of miles between towns, she'd hitchhike. As she remembered, "I was cautious, never got in a car that wasn't a family and now and then these farmers or ranchers took me home for dinner (supper) and the night and put me on the highway again next morning." When she reached the Rockies, she walked "miles and miles in those grand and beautiful spaces under the big sky." She conserved the little cash she had left to buy food, but by the time she arrived in Salt Lake City, she'd run out of both. Most twenty-seven-year-olds would be terrified in that situation, but Babb had spent her childhood surviving hunger and therefore wasn't afraid of it. She knew she had to solve the problem herself; no one else was going to save her. So she did what she always did when she needed work: she found a newspaper office. As she recalled, "I went to the newspaper looking pretty disrespectable by now, and behold I was given a few hours of reading proof because the proofreader was home sick."[47] Just as it had in Elkhart, Forgan, and Garden City, the newspaper office had welcomed her in when she most needed it. Her pockets filled with enough money to fund the rest of her journey back to Los Angeles, Babb hitchhiked and walked across the wide salt flats and the seemingly endless desert of Nevada. She crossed the snow-covered peaks of the Sierra Nevada, where the roadside was punctuated with forget-me-nots and slick orange poppies. Then she walked and hitchhiked down through the San Joaquin Valley, the place where her first novel would finally be completed in the years to come. When she returned to Los Angeles, she returned newly inspired and ready to continue on her path towards becoming a writer as she'd always dreamed about.

9 "I Demand You Write More Shamelessly and Nakedly"

Babb's travels to the Writers' Congress in New York not only solidified her commitment to writing in her own way, but also substantially
widened the reach of her literary universe. A few months after the
conference, another letter arrived from Meridel Le Sueur. Babb had
attended Le Sueur's keynote address at the Writers' Congress and
had thanked her for encouraging her to come to the event. Le Sueur
wrote to further encourage Babb to hone her craft, this time by reading more women writers who wrote about women's experiences. Le
Sueur put forward her own short story "Corn Village" and the femi-
nist-themed modernist novels and short stories of Margery Latimer
as examples.[1] Latimer wrote about growing up in a small town in her
autofiction novel *We Are Incredible*. Le Sueur praised Babb's writing,
especially the way Babb not only centered her stories on the lives of
women but put them in control of their lives regardless of the circumstances surrounding them. Le Sueur ended her letter with a direct
call to action: "There are plenty of men writing about men. I think it
is time for women to speak. . . . You must write now like a woman,
give yourself all your experiences as a woman and make a path. . . . I
demand you write more shamelessly and nakedly."[2]

As Le Sueur observed, Babb was already writing stories that from
a modern perspective are feminist themed; however, when asked in

later interviews about this, she was adamant that she had not written with this intention. As scholar Alan Wald pointed out, "Babb's stories are replete with . . . incipient feminism (although she herself might not use the term)."[3] While Babb didn't bother to adhere to the gender norms of the era when writing about women, she wrote the way she did not as a political statement but simply because that's how she saw the world. Even though Babb didn't think she was writing feminist literature, we are able to see a fuller and more representative West because of her writing, one in which women have control over their lives, a West that challenges the cliches put forward by Hollywood and most male writers. Babb would follow Le Sueur's demand to write "more shamelessly and nakedly" about the world she had grown up in and the world around her. Her need to write a novel about the people she had known growing up continued to grow in her consciousness.

After returning from the Writers' Congress, Babb was also approached by Howard Rushmore of the Communist Party publication *New Masses,* who asked her to send him more "little stories" like "The Terror: New Mexico," the piece she'd written about Gallup and published in *Reportage, International Literature.*[4] Babb would comply, and she began sending Rushmore her reportage pieces.[5] She would also publish several creative works in another Communist party publication, *The Young Worker.* These essays show her grasp of reportage and her growing focus on farmworkers and their rights. Babb's interest in writing about farmworkers had begun with her reporting days in Garden City, when she'd written news stories about local wheat farmers.[6] Through writing an essay for *New Theater Magazine* called "The Los Angeles WPA Theater Project," Babb forged a connection to *New Theater* editor and future filmmaker Herb Kline. They struck up a friendship and a few months later, Kline invited Babb to join a tour of the Soviet Union with a group of artists. Like her previous travels to Panama and Costa Rica, Babb's travels to France,

Germany, Poland, and the Soviet Union would shift her perspective of the world.

While Babb's world had grown from her trip to New York, her small one-bedroom apartment in Hollywood had begun to feel claustrophobic because of her sister's "devouring dependence" on her.[7] The previous thoughts that Babb had expressed in her letters to Saroyan about the burden she felt when her sister was around strengthened and grew during the years Dorothy was living with her in Los Angeles. Dorothy had left a trail of abandoned commitments behind her: she'd dropped out of UCLA and secretarial school, and she'd left a job working as a librarian. Babb soon realized that the mental health issues she'd observed in her sister as a child had become more debilitating as Dorothy grew up, and she felt both obligated and trapped in the role of caregiver. It wasn't only Babb who was hindered by her sister's dependence: James Wong Howe, whose life by now had become deeply intertwined with Babb's, was beginning to be troubled by Dorothy's constant presence in their lives. He wanted Babb to himself and if she was to be a caretaker, he would have preferred that she take care of him.

Howe continued to spend a great deal of time at Babb's apartment on North Curson Avenue, and they spent nearly all of their nights together. (One of them would have to sneak out of the other's apartment via the back stairs in order not to be caught by the landlord, as it was still illegal for them to live together.) Howe's career was taking off. He'd come a long way from working as a camera assistant on silent films in 1917 and was now a much sought-after director of photography. However, as Todd Rainsberger points out in his biography of Howe, despite his success, he was still considered a novelty to the American press: "Most of the American articles about Howe dealt with his race and personality" rather than focusing on his craft.[8] Because of this fact, and because Howe had learned on his last European trip that he was taken seriously by the press there, he decided to accept an offer from director Alexander Korda to film *Fire over England* at Denham Studios in London. The film would star both a young Vivian Leigh and Laurence Olivier.[9] After much thought, Howe left for England in February 1936 with the hope of convincing Babb to follow him there.

During his journey east, Howe's train passed through Babb's old hometown, Garden City, and while the train lingered at the station waiting for passengers to exit and board, Howe wrote to Babb that he imagined he saw her mother at the station, waving from the platform under a sunny sky, where he reported there were "no dust storms." Their letters were filled with passion and longing, especially as the distance between them widened. The more miles that lay between them, the more urgently Howe asked Babb to join him. Just two days out, nearing New York by train, Howe sent her a heartfelt wire: "I am very lonesome for you more than ever before never thought it would be like this to leave you."[10] One sees in their correspondence how in Howe's absence Babb took on a role like that of wife or secretary. She paid his rent and other bills and took on any other task he wrote to her about. At the same time, Babb was also being almost entirely financially supported by Howe.

The thought of leaving her sister behind and following Howe to England once he was settled was tempting to Babb, as was the idea of living abroad for an extended period, but for many months she didn't act on that impulse. She still had reservations about exclusive monogamous relationships like the one that was developing between her and Howe, and having time and distance away from him helped her better reflect on how she was feeling about their relationship. He was talented and handsome, and they adored each other, but he also had faults that worried her. Her letters reveal that Howe possessed a temper, especially when he drank, and that he was so devoted to his work that when he was deep in a movie project, the rest of the world, including her, disappeared into the background. These issues had caused some severe arguments between the two of them. In some ways the legal barriers that kept them from being able to marry were somewhat of a relief to Babb, as they imposed a space between them, a space that from this distance, she could explore and understand. Babb had witnessed what happened to people in a bad marriage. She'd seen her mother reduced to a pulp under her father's fist, and she had no wish to follow in her footsteps.

By April 30, 1936, Howe had arrived in London, and with each letter his pleas for her to join him and his declarations of love escalated: "This trip has done me some good, to get away from Hollywood and its machine. Best of all, is I suddenly realize how much I am really in love with you. What a fool I have been to [illegible] with you, and our silly arguments that never meant anything but unhappiness to us both. You are so right in all you say and have said. I realize it more and more each day."[11] After spending several weeks in a hotel, Howe rented a furnished two-story apartment near Hyde Park and tried to tempt Babb with descriptions of the home he'd set up, one they would finally be able to share as a couple, as his contract in England did not include the Hollywood "moral codes" that didn't allow him to live with her.

During his stopover in New York, upon Babb's insistence Howe had met with *New Theater* editor Herb Kline, who had invited Babb to join the group tour of the Soviet Union that summer. The trip was organized through the Soviet company Intourist, and the plan was to visit a theater festival in Moscow and Leningrad.[12] But when Babb asked Howe about the trip, his letters begged her to visit him instead, pleading that he'd arrange a better trip for the two of them in the Soviet Union later in the year, when he was finished filming. But Babb didn't relent. While she missed Howe and wanted to see him, and while she wanted to escape from caring for her sister, she wasn't willing to let go of her independence to do so. However, she would ultimately need Howe's money to pay for the trip.

In late June, Babb's mother Jennie took the train from Garden City to Los Angeles to visit her girls. Sitting on the couch in the front room of Babb's apartment, the three reminisced about their lives in Oklahoma, Colorado, and Kansas. But the stories Babb's mother told weren't the same as the ones Babb remembered living through. Her mother had bleached the worst parts out, thinking she was saving her daughters from reliving the trauma they had experienced at such young ages. But Babb's instinct as a writer was to press into those wounds. She wanted to better understand the places in which she had grown up and the people who had surrounded her, no matter how dark and painful the story might be. Once her mother returned to Kansas, Babb decided it was time for her to go to England. She left the dogs in the care of Dorothy and made sure her friends were looking out for her sister. She also encouraged Dorothy to visit her friend the writer Carlos Bulosan, who had recently been hospitalized for tuberculosis. She knew these activities would keep her sister busy.

Babb had met Bulosan through her submissions to the radical literary journal he edited, *The New Tide*.[13] Bulosan had left the Philippines for America on July 22, 1930, at age seventeen. He struggled for several years as a laborer before pursuing a career as a writer. Bulosan and Babb began to correspond, and a deep epistolary friendship soon bloomed. In February 1936, Bulosan wrote to Babb, "You have given me a key to a door I have always wanted to enter." He told her he wanted to meet in person and informed her, "I always go to the LA Central Library (5th and Hope), Literature Department. I always sit there several hours a day."[14] Babb wrote back that she'd look for him at the library.

When Babb met Bulosan at the Los Angeles Public Library, he was shy and worried that she wouldn't understand his accent, so he would only pass notes to her to communicate. The two sat on a stone bench outside the library, watching "little dark birds amongst the trees"[15] until Bulosan got up the courage to speak. Babb knew he needed that space in order to trust her enough to talk. Once he felt brave enough, the two shared their troubled childhoods. As Bulosan would later recount in his memoir, "[Sanora] was understanding. She was sensitive and lonely. She started talking of herself, revealing the background of an American life. . . . She described the terror that haunted her childhood. Then it came to me that her life and mine were the same forces; they had only happened in two different countries and to two different people."[16] On March 5, Bulosan revealed to Babb, "I am, I think, madly in love with you." He thanked her for the encouragement she was giving him about his writing career, "as you have encouraged William Saroyan."[17] In return, Bulosan encouraged Babb to finish her novel.

Later that month, Bulosan came by Babb's apartment. As he remembered in a letter to her, "The last time I saw you, the thing we can both remember, is so lovely and it keeps flowering in me, in my being. I remember the room, the little dog, the excitement, oh I remember all with a haunting memory, and I feel a certain kind of beauty growing in me."[18] However, shortly after he wrote this letter, Bulosan's health began to rapidly deteriorate, and he was hospitalized at Los Angeles County General Hospital for tuberculosis. He would stay in the hospital for the next two years, undergoing three operations. Babb visited him weekly until she left for England, and Dorothy visited him while Babb was away.

In August, Babb took her time traveling across the country by train. During a long layover in Chicago, she met with Nelson Algren and Jack Conroy, with whom she'd shared the drive back from the Writers' Congress the year before. In New York, she reunited with Kay Van Riper, her friend from the radio station, before boarding the *Queen Mary* and sailing across the Atlantic toward the adventure that awaited her: reuniting with Howe, and then visiting the Soviet Union.

When Babb arrived in England, she and Howe shared a passionate reunion. She loved the cozy apartment he'd rented. There were two fireplaces, built-in cupboards, and a Navajo rug in the living area.[19] However, when production for *Fire over England* began, Howe was swept back into long hours at work and had little time to spend with her. Babb complained in letters to friends that she rarely saw him, and though she enjoyed having most of the day to herself to write (she began a new short story based on her childhood experiences traveling to Elkhart for school, "Winter in Town"), she missed Howe's companionship. When she told him this, Howe was able to take time off from work for a weekend, and the couple traveled to Paris.

Back when their relationship had begun, Howe had liked the fact that Babb was a writer, which he'd perceived as a nonintrusive hobby. But as their relationship became increasingly serious, his expectation changed.[20] As Babb later recalled, Howe "never gave me the support of his belief [in my writing]. . . . This has hurt me for years."[21] Howe had also become increasingly jealous of Babb's close friendships with writers, especially male writers.[22] In a recent letter, Howe had written to Babb that he was jealous of her relationship with Bulosan, and Babb had responded by asserting her independence: "Let me have my friends in the movement. . . . I have to have some friends who are interested in literature."[23]

One night in Paris, after a long dinner and far too many drinks, Babb willfully flexed her independence, and in response Howe lashed out, resurrecting all their past disagreements. Howe's temper exploded, and they got into such a loud verbal fight in public that Babb, furious, left Paris immediately and returned to England. When she walked into their London flat, she found the phone in its little nook was already ringing out into the empty apartment. It was Howe, begging her to come back to Paris. He was sorry. He hadn't meant it. He wanted her to give him another chance. After thinking it over, Babb did go back. But their relationship continued to traverse rocky uprisings in the years to come. Howe was obsessed with his work, he was jealous, and he didn't understand Babb's need for independence because he, like most of the men who fell in love with her, had never met a woman quite like her before.

On August 10, 1936, Babb took a train from London to Paris to meet up with Kline's theater tour of Eastern Europe and the Soviet Union.[24] Howe had reluctantly financed the trip. When Babb arrived, she walked the petrichor-scented streets of Paris after a late summer rain. The women who passed her on the streets were dressed in fashionable dresses and shoes. Babb donned a form-fitting, fur-collared coat that made her look like a movie star. That afternoon she met Kline and the others in the group in front of the Soviet consulate. There were five people in the group in addition to Kline and Babb. Upon meeting, the seven began to talk as they walked along the Seine, browsing the booksellers' stalls. Babb took an immediate liking to the young writer Helen Riesenfeld; the two would quickly become friends. That evening they went to the Gare du Nord and boarded a train to their first stop, Berlin, where they would spend the initial week of their tour.[25]

When they arrived in Berlin they found it to be in the vise of Nazi rule (Hitler had come to power in January 1933). American newspapers had done little to capture the rise of fascism in Germany, and the members of the group had no idea just how tense Berlin had become, especially towards Jewish people. Many of them were Jewish and were not prepared for the overt anti-Semitism they would encounter. As Babb observed in her letters home, Germany was "swastika covered," with "armored cars and soldiers in the streets." At once, Babb saw that the German people were "frightened into a horrible subservience." Over the week they would spend in Berlin, group members "were shoved and laughed at and called vile names in the streets, refused a decent hotel. . . . [The group] could not go [out] alone . . . for fear of being beaten, possibly killed."[26] Still, Babb photographed what she saw. In the box of photographs she saved from the journey is a haunting picture of lanky teenage soldiers in full uniform, joking with each other and smiling for her camera like the kids they were.[27] One night, while staying at a cheap hotel on Friedenstrasse, they went out to dinner and when they returned, all of their beds had been removed and replaced with cribs.[28]

After a week, the travelers were relieved to leave the tense streets of Berlin and travel by train to Warsaw, where they visited the Jewish ghetto. Two of the people in the group had brought money to give to relatives. It would be another three years before the city would be invaded by the Nazis, but already the Jewish population had been segregated into ghettos. Babb immediately felt that Warsaw was a city with fear pulsing under its surface. In the ghetto, a woman who recognized them as outsiders became worried and called the police. Officers arrived and found the group walking down the street. The police "were very rough" and in response, Babb wheeled around and swung her camera at one of them, hitting him smack on the head.[29] The group was arrested, placed in a holding cell, and only released on the condition that they leave the country that night. So the weary group boarded another train, this time headed to Kiev, which was now a part of the Soviet Union.

Sitting on the train, getting ready to depart the Warsaw station, the group members settled silently in their seats. None had expected the atrocities they'd seen thus far. Suddenly they saw a group of people they'd met earlier in the day in the Jewish ghetto approaching on the platform. They boarded the train as it waited for passengers. The visitors had brought a big box of food. Babb recalled, "They'd made us lunches."[30] The act immediately lifted the group's spirits; it was also extremely brave, as at the time, any group of Jewish people sighted on the street by police could be arrested for conspiracy. In return for the food, Babb and her group "gathered up all of the books we had brot from the US . . . and handed them . . . to them, all on impulse and in gratitude and admiration for their coming."[31]

As the train pulled away from the station, Babb and her colleagues were pleased to finally be on their way to the Soviet Union. For Babb, the idea of communism had long been abstract, an ideal that floated in the clouds. She wasn't a registered communist, but she'd long believed in the ideals of communism and had associated with writers who were communists. Now, she was going to visit a place where communism was actually in practice, and she was excited. As Babb would later recall, in many ways she had been "brainwashed" to believe "that socialism was the best way to live."[32] This brainwashing, paired with the Intourist staff's curation of what they were allowed to see, would blind Babb and the rest of the group to the many atrocities that were already occurring in the Soviet Union.

In Kiev, the group immediately felt welcomed by the Intourist representatives who greeted them. There were no soldiers in the streets, and no one shouted slurs at them as they walked through the city. Herb Kline, who'd already traveled to the Soviet Union on several occasions, was treated like a celebrity by the Intourist staff. They attended nightly performances at venues like the neo-Renaissance opera house, its dome topped with a pair of griffins. Inside stood one of Europe's largest stages, surrounded by aisles of golden seats. The hall was always full. As Babb would report in a letter, "Theater going is a part of [Russian] lives. . . . I never saw an empty seat." She visited the Ukrainian State Theater and interviewed the director after the production.[33] What she began to notice—or what the Intourist representatives would allow her and her group to see—was how the arts were not only valued, but fully integrated into society.

Outside the city, the group was escorted to model farms, where the workers looked "happy—they have eased faces beside the others we have seen in Germany and Poland."[34] From Babb's perspective, in the Soviet Union, farmers did not suffer bad years and poverty like they did in the U.S. Little did she know that in just a few years, all that she saw would be decimated by war. Because her trip was being curated by Intourist, Babb also didn't know what violence Stalin was already enacting outside of her view. In Moscow, the first of Stalin's show trials—the Case of the Trotskyite-Zinovievite Terrorist Center—had just begun that month.

Instead, thanks to Intourist, Babb saw her ideals played out in front of her. Everything she'd heard discussed at the John Reed Club and later at the League of American Writers and the Writers' Congress, everything she'd read about in the Communist Party's literature was being enacted, and she vowed that when she returned to the U.S., she would finally become an official member of the party. What she didn't know was that she was seeing a kind of theater, a view of the Soviet Union that was a façade covering what lay rotting underneath. Her visit was a commercial steered by the Stalin-controlled Intourist agency.

In addition to the model farms, the group was taken to visit hospitals in order to understand how the medical system worked. Babb observed that in the Soviet Union, women were able to work in all professions and trades and seemed to be treated equally, an idea that delighted her. At the hospital Babb saw birth control being openly distributed to women, something she'd never seen in the U.S. When she asked someone if single women could also have access to birth control, the woman answered, "What do you mean? There's no such thing as married women and unmarried women in that sense. Every woman should know and have the same privileges; a woman is never asked if she is single or married."[35]

Babb continued to write Howe regularly on her trip; however, one sees how complicated her relationship had become unfold in these letters. As scholar Erin Boyston Battat pointed out in her introduction to Babb's collection *The Dark Earth and Selected Prose from the Great Depression,* "While Babb was emotionally committed to Howe, she espoused an ethic of sexual freedom in keeping with the physical and spiritual freedom she felt as part of the natural world." In a letter Babb wrote to Howe in 1936, she affirmed her love for him but also asserted her belief in "complete freedom of women." She even wondered why there was a double standard in regard to sexual freedom: "Why is freedom in men called promiscuity in women?"[36] These statements suggest that Howe didn't understand Babb's need for close and intimate friendships with her peers, especially those with whom she shared her writing. To add to this, because Babb had not yet published a book, Howe didn't take her seriously as an artist, an omission that would drive a wedge between them in the decades to come. While their relationship remained intimate, it also remained complicated.

After a few days of touring Kiev, Babb suddenly began to feel a sharp pain in her abdomen. She became so ill she couldn't get out of bed. Riesenfeld, the group member she'd become closest to, stayed at their suite in the hotel with her until a doctor could arrive. At first, as Babb revealed in a letter to Howe, she was afraid she was pregnant.[37] In one of the few times in her life she discussed wanting a child, she told him she would want to have a boy.[38]

When the doctor arrived at their hotel, Babb was surprised to find she was a woman. Dr. Fera assessed Babb's symptoms and told her she was suffering from appendicitis and would need an operation. Despite her positive views about the Soviet medical system, Babb didn't want to have an operation in Russia, so she waited out the pain, hoping the appendicitis would calm down. Riesenfeld had left and reunited with the tour group. Babb lay in bed in the three-room suite for five days, alone, looking out the hotel window at the Soviet people passing by. She read *Moscow Rehearsals: An Account of Production in the Soviet Theatre* and dreamed about what the group would see during the upcoming theater festival in Leningrad. She was well cared for. The doctor and other guests visited her daily, and her room was filled with flowers.

During these visits, Babb got to know Dr. Fera and soon learned her life story. Fera had been a peasant farmer stuck under the thumb of a violent husband. When she'd escaped to Moscow, she couldn't find work and soon found herself trapped in a life of prostitution. After the Russian Revolution, she was taken to a prophylactoria,[39] where she was "treated" (likely for venereal diseases) and "given the opportunity to discover a talent." When asked what career she wanted to pursue, Fera boldly chose to become a doctor, and because school was free, she was able to become one. As she recalled to Babb, "Often at night, I would weep with gratitude, but soon, I understood it was my right—to be happy and to serve my people."[40] Babb was so enthralled by her doctor's story that she wrote a reportage essay about it that would later appear in *New Masses*.

Babb was also treated by nurses who kept her abdomen wrapped in warm compresses throughout the day until the pain began to subside.[41] On August 27, Babb received the good news from Dr. Fera that she was finally well enough to travel. That evening, a lavish Lincoln car picked her up from her hotel and drove her to the train station, where she said goodbye to the doctor and boarded the first-class night train to Moscow.

In Moscow, Babb was reunited with the group, and they traveled on to attend the theater festival in Leningrad. For several days the group attended multiple plays daily and met with actors and directors. They then returned to Moscow and toured the city: its theaters and parks and newly built housing complexes, in which thousands were being relocated. Moscow presented itself as a modern city, and the soundtrack of American jazz rang out from the dance halls at night. Babb fell in love with the city and did not want to leave, but her appendicitis and Howe's insistence that she return drove her to cut her tour short and return to England instead of staying in Moscow longer and continuing with many in the group to visit the Scandinavian countries.

On her last night, Babb and Herb Kline had dinner at a restaurant near the center of the city, then walked across the Moscow River.

With the sun setting behind them, they walked the city streets, sharing their experiences with one another. Babb was trying to memorize everything she saw. They stopped to watch the red sky blanket the Kremlin, its windows golden and glowing. They continued walking until it was dark, ending up beneath the lit onion domes of St. Basil's Cathedral at Red Square. Babb had a few days left on her visa, but Howe kept writing about how miserable he was without her so, against her better judgment, she agreed to return to London. Riesenfeld agreed to leave with her.

The next morning, Babb and Riesenfeld boarded their train back to Paris via Warsaw and Berlin. The first night they slept peacefully in a sleeper car on the Russian-owned train, but once the train crossed the border into Poland, their experience shifted dramatically. The German police boarded and began to patrol the train. Passengers were awakened throughout the night for passport checks. The events they'd experienced in Berlin came rushing back and Riesenfeld, who was Jewish, was terrified that the German soldiers were eyeing her and that they would not let her over the border. Luckily her fears did not come to fruition. The pair continued to Berlin without incident and caught the midnight express train to Paris.

When they arrived at dawn in Paris, the two were tired and in desperate need of baths. They decided to stay on in Paris for a few days to recover and spend a little more time together. Riesenfeld took Babb to visit her friend the poet and critic Hans Sahl, who had fled Germany and was now living in exile in Paris. At his apartment, Babb and Riesenfeld spoke excitedly about all they had seen in the Soviet Union.

Over the next few days, they went shopping, and got appointments at an exclusive salon, Emile's. Babb was told she was given the "best man" in the place. When she sat down in the chair, her hairdresser immediately began asking Babb questions. Was she living in Paris? When she explained no, she was just returning from a trip to the Soviet Union, his eyes lit up. He admitted openly that he was a comrade, which shocked Babb. She wondered how he knew that she was a communist.

While he cut her hair, he explained that he'd narrowly escaped the rise of fascism in Italy. He'd been a controller in a railroad company and was luckily warned the day before the fascists were to come for him. He escaped to Paris, took up his new profession, and never looked back. As he cut and styled her hair with exquisite detail, he confided in Babb that although it was not widely acknowledged, the Italian people did not support fascism and had been fighting for their rights for years.

When he finished her haircut, Babb didn't recognize herself in the mirror. Her usually unruly curly hair had been not only tamed but expertly styled. She looked like an advertisement for Emile's. Her Italian hairdresser only charged her 40 francs for a haircut that should have cost 85 francs, and when she tried to slip him a tip as they embraced to say goodbye, he refused. "Not from you, Madame, not from you! We are comrades!"[42]

That night Riesenfeld and Babb finally parted ways. Hans Sahl, who escorted the pair to the train station, took a photograph of the two before they boarded their separate trains. Riesenfeld took the boat train to the SS *Berengaria,* on which she'd set sail for the United States, while Babb took the train and then the ferry across the channel to London.

On the ferry, as the waves lapped at the boat's hull, the transformation she'd experienced must have crossed Babb's mind. Her travel to the Soviet Union had begun to connect her powerful sense of community, born from her roots living with the Otoe community, to communist ideals. She wondered why women in the United States hadn't yet been granted the rights they had in the USSR. And she believed that the poverty that farmers in America now faced could be solved through the government's intervention and by farmers working together to secure their rights. But although she hadn't seen the puppeteer strings controlled by Stalin's hand in the Soviet Union, she had seen the deep wound fascism had already caused in Poland and Germany. She was troubled by how its dark roots were growing through the cities of Europe. As she'd later recall in a letter, "Fascism seems so near. . . . I've seen it now—it is worse than I ever thought, and I thought it was bad enough."[43]

Babb finally arrived back in London at 11:30 p.m. and Howe, still at work, was not there to meet her. Instead, she made her way back to their empty apartment, at 8 Caroline Place, alone. The next morning, Howe explained that *Fire over England* was nearing the end of production and he was now working nights, beginning at 5:00 p.m. Even when he was home, Babb saw little of him because he slept during the day.[44] Some nights Howe didn't even return to their apartment, instead staying at the home of director William K. Howard because it was closer to Denham Studios in Buckinghamshire. Sitting alone in their empty apartment, Babb wrote furiously to her sister that she couldn't understand why Howe insisted that she return when he wasn't going to be around anyway: "I could have been in Moscow these days!"[45]

In fact, work was just about all that Howe did for the next few months. When *Fire over England* finished production, he immediately began working on another film at Denham Studios, *Under the Red Robe*. While they were in England, he would also work on another Denham film called *Troopship*. Babb used the extended time she had to herself to focus on her writing. She revised "The Terror," the article about what she'd seen in Gallup, New Mexico, and she published the short story she'd begun when she'd first arrived in England, "Winter in Town." She also began to look for some form of employment. She took a job coediting *The Week*, a radical newspaper founded and run by the journalist Claud Cockburn. *The Week* published articles that challenged main-street press ideas about Hitler and the

Spanish Civil War. Clockburn had fought in Spain and written a book about his experience, *Reporter in Spain*. What Babb had seen in Berlin had made her realize how dire the situation in Germany had become, and she was eager to write for a journal that would not be afraid to tell the truth.

In November, Howe was finally able to leave his work at Denham Studios for a brief holiday, and the two of them set off on the trip they'd planned through Europe, visiting Paris, Prague, Budapest, Vienna, and Rome.[46] Babb wrote to her father from Paris, where she and Howe had flown on an airplane, "I love Paris. I wish I lived here instead of London."[47] The next day they traveled to Vienna, where Babb caught a cold.[48] Photographs taken on this trip show the couple laughing and enjoying each other's company. In later years, they would call this trip their "honeymoon" and claim that they had been married in Paris; however, this was a story they made up to cover up the fact that they'd been living together before they were legally able to be married. Babb was still grappling with parts of their relationship and her own feelings about marriage.

When they returned to England, Howe, who was finally in between films, had more free time, and he and Babb were able to attend more social events together. In England Howe was a celebrity, "receiving as much attention from the press as the stars did."[49] At a production party for the film adaptation of *Pygmalion* thrown in honor of George Bernard Shaw by the other major London studio, the newly opened Pinewood Studios, Howe and Babb were introduced to the striking Chinese actress Rebecca Ho Hing Du, who went by the stage name Lotus Fragrance. Lotus had been discovered by British talent scouts and had recently shot her first movie, *Incident in Shanghai*.[50] Howe and Lotus were of course introduced by their white hosts because they were both Chinese. While Lotus liked Howe, she connected more with Babb. While Howe talked show business across the room with other luminaries, the two women sat on an elegant couch in the corner of the grand ballroom, swept into the tide of an engaging conversation. Lotus told Babb about her two children, three-and-a-half-year-old Francis and Roxana, who wasn't yet a year old. After the party, Lotus invited Babb to visit her home in the Golders Green suburb of London to meet her children. At their home, Babb held baby Roxana in her arms, not knowing that in less than a decade, she'd play a much more significant role in Roxana's life. In addition to being an up-and-coming movie star, Lotus ran a beauty salon in London. Some days Babb would meet her there and the two would go shopping together, wearing low-back dresses to show off their beautiful figures.

By early 1937, the clock was ticking on Howe's visa and he needed to renew it. He wasn't yet legally able to become an American citizen, so in order to renew his visa he needed to return to the United States. He originally planned on flying to the United States and quickly returning to England. However, while he was in the U.S., Howe received a compelling offer from his old friend David Selznick to stay in Hollywood and begin working on *The Adventures of Tom Sawyer*, directed by Norman Tauroq. By the time they met to finalize the project, Selznick had also pulled him into another one, *The Prisoner of Zelda*. Howe decided not to return to London, and it was a decision he would not regret. Within a year, Howe would receive his first of ten nominations for an Academy Award for his work on the film *Algiers*.

The only problem was that Babb hadn't planned to travel back to the United States right away. Howe pleaded with her to return to Los Angeles as soon as possible to rejoin him. His telegrams and letters tell her how much he missed her, how much her sister Dorothy missed her, how much her dogs missed her. Babb, however, didn't want to leave the life she'd built in London. As she'd later write, "I had grown fond of London and friends and enjoyed those . . . good years."[51] The time she'd spent in the Soviet Union and her work writing news for *The Week* had changed her. When Howe left, she moved out of their apartment and into a small hotel on Baker Street. She continued working at *The Week* and soon began a romance with a young Irish cardiologist named Desmond MacCarthy. Babb destroyed many of their early love letters,[52] but the few that remain include memories of picnics in the countryside and other romantic outings. Each of MacCarthy's letters to Babb begins and ends by addressing her as "darling." It was a short fling, for Babb would return to the United States in April, but she would continue to correspond with MacCarthy until the late 1950s.

When Babb finally decided to leave Europe, she knew one thing: she adamantly did not want to return on a German ship. Her time in Berlin had horrified her. Instead, she returned on the *Queen Mary*, the same ship she had taken to Europe the year before. The elegant ocean liner was still in its infancy; however, the luxuries offered to her and the other 1,600 passengers were state of the art. There were two indoor swimming pools, a beauty salon, and a library, and one could make a phone call to nearly anywhere in the world from the ship. Even with these amenities, Babb's passage across the Atlantic was anything but easy. The waves churned the boat nearly all the way, sending even a ship of the *Queen Mary*'s breadth and weight veering from side to side. Great salty waves washed up on the deck, so most days were spent indoors. One wonders what Babb thought about during those weeks as she returned to her life in Los Angeles after being away for so long.

She'd seen enough in the Soviet Union to believe in communism as a solution for the poor in the United States. But it wasn't only the programs that Babb saw in the Soviet Union that impressed her, it was the Russians' cultural approach. As Babb experienced it (albeit as curated by the government officials who ran Intourist), artists and the arts were not only supported but adored by the entire community. And the belief that Babb had long held that women were equal she saw enacted in Russia, where women were given the same opportunities as men.

Crossing the stormy Atlantic, the next phase of Babb's life began to come into view. Babb began to see how she could finish the novel that had remained lingering on the horizon since 1934, when she'd first written to William Saroyan about her progress. But though she'd been collecting research about the dust storms from her mother, and memories about farming broomcorn from her father, she had not yet solidified the scope of what she wanted to write. After seeing how struggling farmers were championed in the Soviet Union through socialized farming, Babb felt a new commitment to telling the story of the people she'd grown up with on the plains. She also realized that in order to tell their story well, she needed to see who they were now. She needed to immerse herself in their lives. And though she was tied to the cause of communism, she was not going to write about the victims of the Dust Bowl through this lens. She was still determined to write, as Meridel Le Sueur had urged her, "shamelessly and nakedly" toward the truth: her truth. As always, the story Babb wanted to tell, the truth of the matter she wanted to find in her research, lay at the core of her work.

10 *"You Can't Eat the Scenery"*

In April 1937, Babb returned to Los Angeles, where Howe was engrossed in cinematography work on three films: *The Adventures of Tom Sawyer, Algiers,* and *The Prisoner of Zenda.* Once again, Howe's longing for Babb had been satisfied by her return, and now that she was home, he was too absorbed in his work to have much time to spend with her. Babb also returned to her sister Dorothy, who in Babb's absence had pivoted her obsessive attention to Babb's dear writer friend Carlos Bulosan, whom Babb had urged her to visit in the hospital. After two years of weekly visits, Dorothy had fallen in love with Bulosan and he with her. Their love bloomed from their shared loneliness. Dorothy no longer had her sister living with her, helping her with daily life, while Bulosan was trapped in the tuberculosis ward at Los Angeles County General Hospital. In addition to being lonely, Bulosan carried the deep wounds of the childhood trauma and the effects of the overt racism he'd experienced since arriving in America. Bulosan later revealed how much Dorothy's visits meant to him: "I shall treasure your loving thoughts and unforgettable actions of tenderness as the most important and significant events of my life. I know you are one of the wonderful women who make men strive all their lives for decency of the world. . . . I owe everything to you for making me what I am intellectually."[1] Just before this touching passage, however, Bulosan admitted to Dorothy that he had "thought of suicide" three times that month. Dorothy too suffered suicidal ideation, although her trauma had been caused by poverty and abuse rather than racism. At the end of his letter, Bulosan commands Dorothy to "go on living" and "be brave."[2]

In 1936–1938, while Bulosan was in the hospital, he underwent three operations for a lesion in his right lung and had nearly all of his ribs removed on one side. By the time Babb returned home from England, Bulosan was finally allowed to leave the ward for the first time, and he visited their apartment for a day. Under a technicolor-blue sky, the three had a picnic on the front lawn. Even before his sickness, Bulosan was described by author and friend John Fante as "a tiny person" who had "an exquisite face" and "lovely brown eyes."[3]

Babb made roasted chicken for the picnic and sent Bulosan back to the hospital with leftovers and a bag full of fruit. Dorothy gave him fresh notebooks to write in and a new selection of library books that she had checked out of the Los Angeles Public Library for him. Back at the hospital, Bulosan would write to tell Dorothy that it was her sister's "friendship and generosity of spirit" that had made him "unafraid to meet other Americans." He wrote, "From where did you two unusual girls materialize? . . . Neither of you has had to learn to be without prejudice: you simply have none."[4]

On June 7, 1938, Bulosan was released from the hospital to slowly recover his life. His literary career would gradually begin to rise, and he'd write extensively about both Sanora and Dorothy in his 1946 memoir *America Is in the Heart*; however, although he mentions all of his male writing friends (like Fante) by name, he does not name Babb or her sister. Instead, he calls Sanora Alice Odell and Dorothy Eileen Odell. Why he made this switch isn't revealed in the correspondence between Babb, her sister, and Bulosan that continues until just before his death in 1956. Perhaps, in the post–World War II climate, he was trying to protect the sisters from being associated with his leftist ideas, or from being associated with a Filipino writer. But it is because of this omission that later scholars did not include Babb among Bulosan's closest literary friends, even though she and her sister had been such an important part of Bulosan's life while he was in Los Angeles. Like Saroyan, Bulosan doesn't name Babb as one of the people who encouraged him during the early part of his career. Babb is a ghost who is never acknowledged, her name nearly erased from the mostly male authors who are remembered from the 1930s in Los Angeles.

Once back in Los Angeles, Babb kept the promise she had made to herself after her experiences in the Soviet Union, and she joined the Hollywood branch of the Communist Party USA (CPUSA). Although she had been deeply impressed with how Russia supported its citizens while she traveled there, Babb didn't join just for ideological reasons. She joined because she saw the party as representing the rights of the dispossessed workers who'd been left by the United States government to fend for themselves, and she believed communist principles could be used to provide assistance.[5] But just as when she'd left the Writers' Congress in 1935 fueled by the ideas of the party, she kept her writing relationship with the party on her own terms. She had no intention of using her art as a weapon, of writing with a political aim that was guided by the party's leadership. She intended to use her writing to speak for the marginalized on her own terms.

Babb was eager to do more research for the novel that she had begun writing in 1934 and that she'd shared with her friend William Saroyan.[6] Her novel had already received interest from several publishers, and she was determined to finish it.[7] From the start, the novel had been titled *Whose Names Are Unknown*, after "a legal eviction notice which begins, To John and Mary Doe whose true names are unknown."[8] On early drafts, Babb also states that the title was inspired by the Bible verse Leviticus 25:35: "Thy brother . . . tho' he be a stranger."[9]

On her journey back from England, Babb took the train from New York to Los Angeles, stopping to visit her mother on the way. However, what she saw when she stepped down from the train at the station in Garden City, Kansas, and when she visited her high school town of Forgan, Oklahoma, was shocking. The towns and their citizens had become nearly unrecognizable due to the continued drastic effect of dust storms.[10]

Between 1935 and 1940, over 600,000 impoverished people fled their homes on the "drought-stricken Great Plains" to try to find work in the West: "in New Mexico mines, Arizona cotton fields, California's harvests." These were people like Babb's father's family, who had survived for generations on the plains, often through tenuous circumstances, "in pursuit of rural independence and autonomy." But the combination of low crop prices and years of drought had left these independent farmers, and all of those within their communities, destitute. And since there were no "social programs, no farm subsidies, no price controls and no alternate sources of water," the citizens who lived in the affected area had few choices but to stay and starve or flee to Arizona and California, where they might find work.[11] However, the horror was that the plentiful jobs these desperate people were told were available to them if they traveled west were not available. Instead, what they found when they left everything they'd ever known and arrived in Arizona to pick cotton, or in California to pick peas, were hate, resentment, and prejudice.

When Babb shared her manuscript with a screenwriter friend in Los Angeles, the writer offered to connect Babb to her friend Tom Collins, who worked for the Farm Security Administration (FSA) setting up camps for Dust Bowl refugees. The FSA was founded in 1935 as the Resettlement Administration, and its sole purpose was to help displaced farmers. Collins set up his first camp in Marysville in 1935 and had been opening camps up and down the state of California ever since. Babb was pleased to make the connection and immediately began corresponding with Collins, hoping to secure a future opportunity to meet him.

For the next few months, as she waited for an appointment from Collins, Babb set off on her own on short trips to the San Joaquin Valley to do research for articles and for her novel. She went with a purpose down flat highways cradled by orchards, and she carried with her a small reporter's notebook and the Leica and Rolleicord cameras that Howe had given her so she could record what she saw.[12] Like the photographer Dorothea Lange, Babb was determined to record snapshots of what she saw, only hers would not be photographs, they would be images constructed of words.

On one of these trips, Babb recorded small, postcard-like images in her notebook that documented what she saw: "the small houses sit in the midst of a field—the small fields clinging to the hard feet of the Sierra Madre Mountains" and "the gray-green of the olive groves." She also documented the people she saw: "a girl leading (pulling, tugging) three goats along a road on the edge of town," a "man sitting along stream with only trousers on, and on all the bushes around him he had spread his washed clothes. He was sitting on a rock bare-waist and barefooted, reading a magazine."[13] To Babb, who was a poet as much as she was a writer, the image was what spoke the unspeakable. It was what stayed with her long after she left wherever or whatever she was writing about. She had come to the fields to find the language to speak about an unspeakable atrocity, and the only way she knew how to do so was to look deeply and become a mirror that reflected back the reality that she saw to her reader.

When Babb had toured the model farms in the Soviet Union, she had found a possible system where farmers could be respected. This experience had made her realize a truth about her own book: that unless her audience knew who the farmers she depicted were *before* disaster struck them, they would not see their humanity after disaster had stripped everything from them. They would not know who the farmers truly were. It was at this point that Babb's novel split in two. In one half, the reader would get to know the victims in Oklahoma, before the worst thing that had ever happened in their lives—the disaster of the Dust Bowl—struck, and in the second, the reader would then understand the depth of the atrocities they faced when they fled their homes out of desperation.

Babb knew that to do this, she'd need to really get to know the people about whom she'd be writing, so she began work on a series of reportage-style articles about the plight of the migratory workers she met. Her articles included "Farmers without Farms," which was published in *New Masses* on June 21, 1938. *New Masses* remained a prominent intellectual journal of the left that was viewed by CPUSA "as the leading vehicle of social change."[14] In "Farmers without Farms," Babb opens with a breathtaking description of the fruitful valley. Then she contrasts this beauty against what she learns in an interview with a farmworker's wife: "You can't eat the scenery . . . and you can't hardly enjoy the spring when you're hungry." The article documents the long walks during which Babb observed the most extreme poverty she'd ever witnessed: "When I walk along the roads, see families in their tents, see them at their monotonous meals of flour-and-water pancakes and potatoes or beans, see them standing in line, hungry and humiliated, waiting to ask a little help, I think that surely no one can even *know* the presence of these conditions and not wonder at and question the appalling poverty and suffering of these people who produce the agricultural wealth which surrounds them but does not even sustain them."[15]

Babb didn't just observe the plight of the migratory workers, she also acted. When Babb learned that children were harvesting walnuts at a farm near Modesto without pay, she traveled there to investigate. Then she reached out to the United Cannery, Agricultural, Packinghouse and Allied Workers of America in San Francisco to see if they could help her find support for these children, but the agency turned down her request. Undeterred, Babb organized a strike on her own, and ultimately the children were paid for their work.[16] On another occasion, Babb was arrested during a strike and spent a night in jail with Communist Party organizer Dorothy Ray Healey.[17] But while her research and activism were fulfilling, Babb was eager to get closer to her subjects so that she could adequately portray them.

When Tom Collins finally got back to her and invited her to help him interview refugees near Brawley and El Centro in the Imperial Valley, Babb jumped at the chance. The day in 1938 when Babb arrived at the Gridley Camp, the winter rain beat down on the muddy road as she stepped out of her car and walked briskly up to the lone administration "building." Rows of tents stretched out behind the building. She knocked confidently on its thin screen door. She was about to begin an eight-month stint working as a volunteer for the FSA in the San Joaquin and Imperial Valleys. The administration building, like all the other *permanent* buildings of the camp, was half tent, half solid shelter. Gridley was one of the original FSA camps that provided housing, washrooms, toilets and showers, and a community room for the ever-growing wave of migrants descending on California from the Dust Bowl.

Collins likely answered the door with his signature half-smile, the one he wears in many of the photographs taken while Babb was volunteering. Collins was a lanky man with a square jaw and thin mustache who had been raised in an orphanage, trained for the priesthood, and managed a school system in Guam before taking on the massive task of opening FSA camps up and down California. Rain drummed on the thin tin roof as Babb smiled back and stepped inside.

For the next eight months, Babb would work closely with Collins providing supplies for the Dust Bowl refugees whose overflowing "flivvers," or Model Ts, crowded the roads. Collins and Babb walked the dirt roads of the Imperial Valley, those of the Central Valley all the way up to the Feather River in Sacramento, and even those of the apple farms in Oregon, interviewing newly arrived refugees in order to find out who they were and what they needed and to spread word about the camps.

Collins, a tireless, resolute administrator, oversaw the entire camp program. His vision was to create a place that would foster self-governance among the refugees and thereby boost morale. He instituted a system he called "democracy functioning" (D.F.), in which committees of refugees made democratic decisions about the place they lived. When they returned from recruiting refugees, Babb helped Collins implement the D.F. system at many of the camps.

There were four committees that ran the camps: the central governing committee, the entertainment committee, the maintenance committee, and the Good Neighbors committee. In addition, there was an array of subcommittees offering social events, athletic contests, childcare, clubs, and a camp newsletter. Collins saw the D.F. groups as a training ground for creating a union for farmworkers. Babb immediately felt at ease in the camps. She saw who the refugees were: people who wished only to reestablish themselves.

For a few months, Babb lived among the refugees and devoted herself to the camp's operation and documentation. During her time working for the FSA, Collins estimated that Babb visited 472 families, or 2,175 men, women, and children, and that she had met with approximately 781 families (about 3,640 individuals).[18] As he calculated in a glowing letter he sent to her at the end of her service:

1. You visited tents, shacks, cabins and hovels. 472 families or 2175 men, women, and children.
2. You interviewed and signed up 309 families or 1465 men, women and children.
3. Total families you met and know 781.
4. Total individuals you met and know 3640.
5. You, therefore, spread happiness and hope to all these—and we thank you with all of our hearts.[19]

Babb spent her days helping refugees do the important menial tasks they needed to survive, like setting up tents or taking their children to the clinic. But she was also there to help them do more, like establish a newsletter and plan dances. Collins was impressed by Babb's ease with the camp's residents and with the refugees she interviewed and signed up for spots at the camps on the road. As he wrote about Babb's work, "It was she who bridged the chasm between the D.F. and the next move, the C.I.O. (Congress of Industrial Organizations). It was she who raised aloft the bigger banner for the united front. Of such stuff are the real leaders of men made."[20]

Although Collins praised the direct work Babb did organizing residents at the camp, he knew she was a gifted writer, and he felt she could make an even bigger impact using her craft to spread the word about the plight of the migrants: "I feel you can do your best work for the agricultural and industrial workers by and through the power of the written word. You have the unusual ability possessed by so few writers to do a POWERFUL bit of work. The field is rapidly being filled with organizers. Whatever you write will be of great assistance to the workers and organizers. I would like to see you WRITE and WRITE. It is your profession. You are nobly fitted for it. May you DO IT. We all HOPE YOU WILL. WE WANT YOU TO DO SO."[21]

And write she did. Babb kept detailed notes about her interactions with the refugees (she counted in her journal "493 home visits, 2512 people seen in homes").[22] In late February, when she arrived in Tulare County, she documented how desperate the situation had become regarding the cotton crops that migrants had come to pick: "Visalia 2/24/38—This year 250,000 acres less of cotton to be planted here, and that means about 60,000 people wandering around starving. (Act just passed by Congress for crop control.)" The act in question was the Agricultural Adjustment Act, passed as part of the New Deal, which created programs to reduce surplus and raise crop prices. It encouraged farmers to reduce their production of certain crops

(like cotton) in return for subsidy payments. This act, which was originally created to assist farmers in the Dust Bowl area, was now working against them in California. In another journal entry, Babb observed how "Oklahomans, referred to as 'Okies,' are held in derision."
And she noted how state officials spoke openly of eradicating the migrants: "remark made by a State official [for The California State
Emergency Relief Administration, or SERA], also local c of c [cham-
ber of commerce] man: 'You know what ought to be done with these
people? We ought to damn [sic] all the rivers in the state and drive
them into them." Or how she overheard a justice of the peace say, after having a talk with migrants, "I never realized these people are humans." Babb noticed how different the makeup of farms were in California compared to the Midwest: "The small farmer is almost extinct
in the great farm valleys of California, which are controlled by high
finance—big growers, absentee owners."

Babb observed that in the winter months of "January-February-
March the migratory workers are at their lowest ebb. There is no work
during these months." And it's during these tough times that she
records the intimate scenes she sees in the camps, such as this view
into a migrant tent: "woman in bed, too hungry and weak to get up.
Children sitting around hungry and weak. The man walking down
the road to find something to do, or something to eat, fainted from
hunger, and can't go on." The winter of 1938 was a wet one, and heavy
rains flooded camps throughout the spring. As Babb recorded, "It's
rainy and suddenly very cold. The tent floors are all wet, and most of
the bed covers damp. With nothing to do, and a need to forget hunger, they go to bed very early. . . . The rains cut out whole season of
work, adding two more months to unemployment of farm workers.
Annual incomes will be even further below decent subsistence and
have to be supplemented by some form of state or federal relief."[23]

Babb visited and spoke with residents at all three types of migrant
camps in California. These included the "U.S. Govt. camp—or

'demonstrational' camps" like the ones that Collins had opened. "Grower camps" were those set up near crops where "grower either gives free tent space or charges rent. Furnishes water and the poorest type of toilet." Finally there were "squatter camps," where large groups of migrants set up camp illegally on private land. At one point Babb estimated that there were two thousand of these "squatter camps" in the state, where people had no toilets or running water and were starving to death.[24]

Fueled by Collins's encouragement and inspired by what she saw and the stories the refugees told her, at night Babb continued to write her first novel: a book about two families who suffered through the environmental disaster of the Dust Bowl and, having lost everything, had to migrate to California. Now that she was living among the very people who had been directly affected by the Dust Bowl, she was filled with inspiration and details. As she later reflected, "These were the people I knew all of my life. . . . I knew them and lived with them through the hard pioneering days of breaking new land, of more prosperous days, of the early depression years."[25]

One sees the events that led to scenes in her novel recorded directly in her journal. To Babb, the tension in the valley between growers and farm laborers was taut. As she wrote, "I am afraid some blood will spill out on the green grass floor of the valleys this summer and next fall." Babb observes the effects of the cotton pickers' strike, where she sees a "family in cabin, company owned. Know they will be put out if strike. Sympathetic with strike, as all are save the stools [informers], but decide to and are told to get out at once. Refuse [to leave until they receive] three days' notice. . . . Finally law sets all things in road and drives car out. Put sick man out on road too."[26] This scene will later be woven in toward the end of *Whose Names Are Unknown* when the protagonist, Milt, and his family are forced out of the shack they have been renting from the cotton growers because they have decided to join the strike. The novel also includes details about how much each family must pick (nine hundred pounds a day) to retain the privilege of a cabin and the use of the three showers that served the two hundred people who lived in the camp.[27] As Wixson has observed, "Babb's field notes reveal the working methods of a writer not content to remain a detached observer or journalist. Like female regionalist writers such as Sarah Orne Jewett and Dorothy Canfield Fisher, Babb infused the particularities of time and place with an empathetic sensibility."[28]

Pleased with her storytelling and fueled by her passion to reach the widest audience possible, Babb took a risk and sent the first four chapters of her work in progress to Bennett Cerf, the esteemed editor and cofounder of Random House, whom she'd met during the 1935 Writers' Congress. Many of her peers (including William Saroyan) had experienced recent success with the press and had encouraged her to submit her work there. Over a period of five years, several presses had shown interest in her novel, but a contract had eluded Babb because she had not been able to finish the book. But now, living among the subjects she was writing about, she'd gained a confidence in what she was writing that she hadn't before possessed. She knew she could find the heart of her novel on the ground, interviewing the refugees.

The four chapters Babb sent Cerf were loosely based on childhood experiences in Red Rock, Oklahoma, the years during which, due to debt caused by her father's gambling habit, her family was forced to sell their bakery and move to Eastern Colorado.[29] The story follows Julia (the character based on Babb's mother) and her daughters (based on Babb and her sister) as they take the train to Lamar in Eastern Colorado to join Milt (based loosely on Babb's father) and move into a dugout owned by Milt's father, Konkie (based on Babb's grandfather) to begin farming broomcorn and winter wheat. Babb shifts the time period from 1912–1914 to the Depression era but relies heavily on her own firsthand experiences of life in that area of the country. Because Babb and her family had starved and suffered, she understood the hardships of those around her in the migrant camps, and she was able to translate that understanding into her depiction of them.

Contrary to the way they were typically represented, the families who sought refuge in the camps were from a variety of backgrounds. They were settlers of the plains who'd gained land in land runs and homesteading (like Babb's own family). They were sharecroppers from southeastern Oklahoma. They were Arkansas homesteaders, or tenant farmers, or they were dryland famers. Many who arrived from Oklahoma, Texas, Arkansas, Kansas, and other Great Plains states weren't farmers at all. They were tradesmen, teachers, lawyers, and small business owners who had lost everything to one of the greatest natural disasters that had ever hit North America.[30] Yet in the public's eye, all of the refugees were grouped together as "Okies," a derogatory term used to dehumanize a suffering people.

Babb wrote about the organized government camps in her journals, letters, and articles—how the camps provided shelter: tents with the possibility of a wooden floor (for $10 more); medicine and medical care from a staff nurse; baths; and much needed community. When most refugees first arrived, they refused help even though they were often desperate for it. All they wanted was what they couldn't find: work, and the ability to once again be self-sufficient. They had been lured to the Imperial Valley by the promise of work picking peas and lettuce in the winter, or they had been lured to the San Joaquin Valley by the promise of work during the long cotton season, or they had been lured to the Sacramento Valley to work picking peaches and prunes in the spring. But somehow, no matter how fast they traveled from crop harvest to crop harvest, there were never enough jobs for all who needed them. Once they settled into a camp, however, with the help of the camp's Good Neighbors Committee, even the proudest new residents eased into getting the things they needed: blankets,

a place to sleep, a meal. Babb noted in her writing that "Tom Collins
. . . is a sincere, self-sacrificing hard-working friend of these people,
and many of them, never having found anyone else willing to help
them since they came to California, believe him to be their only
friend. They are suspicious of others, but they trust him to the ut-
most."[31] Soon, Babb was equally trusted. As Wixson points out, her
natural warmth and sincerity put people at ease. As she described in
a letter to her sister Dorothy about a visit she and Collins had with a
family from Oklahoma on a rainy day when no one could work,
"When we left they said they wished we didn't have to go because it
was like visiting with old friends. That made me feel happy. These
people don't say things they don't mean, in fact, they won't say much
of anything unless they think they can trust you."[32] When Babb first
started working with Collins, she was often overcome by all she saw.
As she revealed to her sister in a May 1938 letter, "At the end of the
first day, after seeing the people living worse than I had even imagined, I suddenly started to cry while I was eating and had to come
back to my room. Once during the day, I almost broke, but I had to
hold myself tight against it, because they have enough troubles without that, and if we felt bad, they'd feel worse. They know we like
them and want to help them without seeing our tears."[33]

The camp residents had good reason to be "suspicious" of people
besides Collins and Babb, as outside the camp, prejudice against
"Okies" intensified. Local Californians saw refugees as debased,
barely human, and ignorant. Local papers played up these ideas with
caricatures that fueled the anger of taxpayers, who felt they were being forced to pay for other people's troubles. Schools refused to allow
refugee children to attend. Hospitals wouldn't admit refugees regardless of their willingness to pay in advance for services.

In her journal, Babb recorded the heartbreaking story of a couple
who "came to California in [a] Ford to find work." They had no
money and were waiting for government assistance. But when their

assistance check finally arrived in the mail, it was intercepted by their landlady, who kept it to pay their back rent, even though the family was starving. The woman was pregnant and had already lost a newborn child during the grasshopper invasion that had plagued Colorado in the spring of 1937. She was terrified that due to her malnutrition, the same would happen to this child, so she sought help. She visited the local hospital hoping to get medical care but was turned away and sent instead to the Red Cross. Babb was shocked to learn that even the Red Cross refused to treat "these people." In her notes, Babb recorded that the woman's fears had come to fruition. Due to malnutrition and lack of medical care, she miscarried and lost "the girl, so lovely."[34] It was encounters like these that she experienced while volunteering for the FSA that drew Babb back to her typewriter each night, recording the real stories that she witnessed for the camp records and trying to incorporate those stories into her own novel.

Babb accompanied the birth control activist Margaret Sanger when she visited the camps to "to talk to the farm women about birth control." Babb and Collins had witnessed and assisted "some terrible births with half-staved women and starved or dead babies; the women lying on newspapers in tents, not having been allowed to enter local hospitals."[35]

Whenever Babb left the camps, she'd be harassed in town due to her association with Collins and the FSA. One morning, when she was sitting at a "tacky little lunch counter" waiting for her breakfast, "two strongarm men knocked me hard to the floor. They helped me up and told me 'get out of town. The last organizer who came through here—they found his body floating in a canal.'" Later that day, when she returned to the camp and told Collins about the incident, he advised her to be cautious and leave; however, Babb was undeterred.[36]

11   Whose Names Are Unknown

A few months into her job volunteering for the FSA, Tom Collins invited Babb to a nearby café to have lunch with a writer he was collaborating with named John Steinbeck. Steinbeck, who had just published a best-selling novel, *Of Mice and Men,* in February 1937, had found Collins while he was writing a series of articles on the plight of the Dust Bowl refugees for *The San Francisco News* which were published from October 5 to 12, 1936. In addition to writing those seven articles for *The News,* Steinbeck had also written a short summary about the migrant situation that appeared in *The Nation* in mid-September 1936, and a pamphlet entitled "Their Blood Is Strong," published by the Simon J. Lubin Society.[1] Thinking that having a best-selling writer bring attention to the struggling camps would be beneficial, Collins agreed to accompany Steinbeck as he visited the camps. Steinbeck had been so overwhelmed the first time he accompanied Collins and saw the absolute poverty that the migrants had to suffer he told Collins, "By god! I can't stand anymore! I'm going away and blow the lid off this place."[2]

Steinbeck had again visited Collins for a few days in mid-October 1937. When the writer returned home, he began working on his first attempt at writing his Dust Bowl novel, a manuscript he called "The Oklahomans," but by January 1938 he'd abandoned this manuscript altogether and started his second attempt, "L'Affaire Lettuceberg."[3] In this second version (begun in February and finished in May 1938),[4] Steinbeck's focus shifted from writing about the refugees to mocking the growers but by the time he finished it he was so disheartened by it that he destroyed the manuscript before his agent (who was already marketing the book) had seen it.

Collins was thrilled that Steinbeck was writing a novel and hoped he might bring attention to the desperate issues faced by the refugees. As Collins wrote in his own unpublished memoir, "Bringing in the Sheaves," he pleaded with Steinbeck to write about what he had witnessed: "What you want to do, John, is to keep your impressions in your mind and when the time is ripe DO something about those conditions. If you fail to do that then you are letting those thousands of people down."[5] During Steinbeck's visits, none of the migrants knew they were being observed by a famous writer who intended to document their experiences, as Steinbeck used a fictitious name while he was in the camps.[6] According to Jackson Benson's biography of Steinbeck, the writer hid his identity while he was with Collins because he was afraid of retaliation by the Associated Farmers and other growers' organizations. As Steinbeck wrote in his 1938 diary,

> I've written an article about starvation in the valleys . . . must be careful. Must not get angry. I know perfectly well the danger I am running in exploring the Associated Farmers. They are quite capable of murder or faking a criminal charge. . . . I know they can hurt me personally but they may not be able to beat the thing I can start.[7]

However, Steinbeck did not hide his identity from Babb.[8] It was during Steinbeck's May 1938 visit with Collins, after he'd abandoned two versions of the book he wanted to write, that he met Babb. That sunny day, as Babb walked into the café, the rainy season had subsided and the earth was throbbing with the possibility of new crops and jobs for the workers. Over cups of coffee, they talked about the camps, the refugees' plight, the terrible control the Associated Farmers held over the communities where they lived, and the powerful political lobby of farm owners.[9] Little did Babb know that the copy of her field notes she would willingly give Steinbeck would not only inspire him as he began his third and final attempt at writing his Dust Bowl novel, but would also make the publishing of her own novel impossible. As she later reflected, "Tom Collins . . . had asked me to keep detailed notes of our work every day, of the people, things they said, did, suffered, worked. I thought it was for our work, or for him, but it was for Steinbeck"; and "Tom asked me to give him my notes. I did. Naïve me."[10]

Meanwhile, Bennett Cerf at Random House was impressed with the four chapters that Babb had sent him, so much so that he invited her to New York to finish writing her novel and offered her a book contract to go with it.

The refugees Babb met at the camps were not all poor, uneducated "Okies," and the people she introduces us to in her novel are varied and real. She kept the title she had originally chosen—*Whose Names Are Unknown*—which was based on an eviction notice she had seen on a decrepit worker's shack on a corporate farm, a notice that read "To John Doe and Mary Doe whose true names are unknown." Babb thought this title embodied the fact that to the big-business corporate farmers in California, the migrant workers who toiled for pennies a day were nameless. And to the local citizens who blocked the migrant workers' children from going to school, the children were nameless. And to the hospitals that would not admit migrant women who were suffering difficult births and instead sent these women back to the dirt floors of their tents to deliver their babies on newspapers, these mothers and infants were nameless. In her monumental novel, Babb endeavored to give these people back their names. More importantly, she recorded a version of Dust Bowl history that gives agency to its victims and highlights the diversity found in California in the 1930s.

In *Whose Names Are Unknown,* when we meet Babb's protagonist, Milt Dunne, on the Oklahoma Panhandle,[11] he is living with his father, Konkie, who has decided to switch from growing broomcorn to the potentially more lucrative winter wheat, a crop that needs more water than the dry-farmed broomcorn. Babb obtained background information on farming winter wheat from her father, Walt: "Winter wheat in general started sowing it about Sept. 15 . . . grows under snow . . . harvest starts 1st of July."[12] The switch would prove to be futile as dust storms began to plague the land where the family was living.

In her novel, Babb initiates us into the routine of her characters' daily lives and shows us how intimate they are with the land on which they live:

> Milt and the old man rose every morning at daybreak. . . . When they came up into the yard, the sharp high air of western autumn came into their noses, penetrated their clothes, made them go about their chores briskly. Each morning they felt renewed in themselves, and a clear unknown excitement sprang up in them with the sense of the new season. They looked at the land they had planted the day before, and the land they would plant this day, and they felt a sense of possession growing in them for the piece of earth that was theirs.[13]

As readers, we watch the catastrophe of the Dust Bowl unfold slowly, Babb's characters helpless against what has struck them. She describes what the same land looks like after a horrific night of dust storms: "All night the dust blew and by morning the yard wore that melancholy look of a place revisited after years of desertion and ruin." The deeply personal effect of the storms on the Dunne family is depicted towards the end of the first half of the novel, through a series of heart-wrenching diary entries from the month of April: "Noon.

Ate on a dirty dusty table. Took up 15 or 20 pounds of dust to make room for more. The dirt is in waves. Think someone's farm is in our house, maybe our own."[14] Babb based these intimate descriptions on ones written to her by her mother in a letter she had sent about the "Black Blizzard" dust storm that hit Garden City, Kansas, in 1935.[15]

As the dust storms increase, the reader witnesses the devastation that slowly creeps over the town and its surrounding farms like a deadly tide. Farms are lost to the banks, doctors watch helplessly as patients waste away from starvation, the owner of the general store commits suicide because he's extended too much credit to patrons who cannot pay.

Because we have witnessed "the human dimension of this ecological disaster"[16] in the daily struggles of the people in this small community, by the time Milt and Julia Dunne leave for California with their children, we know they have no other choice, and it is this tragedy that fuels our compassion for them as they are treated as outcasts by both the corporate growers and regular citizens in California. By emphasizing her characters' lives before they were forced to migrate, Babb humanizes them.

As Lawrence R. Rodgers writes in his foreword to the University of Oklahoma Press edition, "What elevates *Whose Names Are Unknown* above the level of a well-crafted story it its willingness to cast a reflective eye on so many conventional (if problematic) pieties of American identity: the near-sacred status of yeoman farmer, the benevolent bond between nature and her human benefactors, the lure of the West as a wellspring of opportunity, the inexorableness of upward mobility. . . . Babb upends the kinds of myths about poverty that allow the more well-to-do the illusion of their own essential superiority."[17]

In California, the Dunnes and their neighbors, the Starwoods, who traveled with them, soon find a fictionalized version of an FSA camp run by Woody, a character based on Tom Collins. Babb's narrative depiction of life in the camp is both personal and inclusive. She uses a lyric, free associative voice to accurately depict the dislocation caused by hunger: "*Lonnie sleeping Friday weeds carrots three feet wide a woman screaming quarter of a mile tomorrow surplus commodities walking music water running forgetting forty cents a day sleeping forgetting forty cents floating like air clear water running sparkling through the brain surplus brain commodities sleeping a feather of music tickling this is my tent sitting down like a cloud floating music faces fluffy sound in my ears flying away*" (italics in the original).[18] Babb also uses her experiences working at the camps to accurately depict what it was like to have to give birth to an already starving child in a dirt-floored tent. When the mother is unable to produce milk, she depicts how fellow campers rally to gather enough money to pay for milk, but not in time to save the child: "'That baby don't need no milk. He's dead.' One of the women sighed. 'He's better off,' she said. 'It starved to death before it ever saw the light of day.'"[19] But her depiction of women is not just as passive victims. In Babb's novel, women stand up against the atrocities they are faced with, and they make it known that they work as hard as men.

As the chapters set in California continue, we witness how the Dunnes and Starwoods are constantly moving to find work, and the lean months in between. The reader sees the Dunne children come to terms with being ostracized and called "Okies" at school, and what the term means to them and to the community around them that uses it as a slur. Babb saw her white characters as "part of a larger, interracial class struggle,"[20] and because of this her work displays the multicultural and multiethnic environment of California during this era. The workers are representative of the people who were working in the fields at the time. They are not only white, but also Mexican, Filipino, Japanese, and African American. When the farmworkers strike against low wages in *Whose Names Are Unknown,* the strike is led by Phoebe, an African American woman.

When Babb set out to write this novel, she did so with the intent to not only depict the truth of what she saw, but also to offer an idea towards a solution. In Babb's mind, this solution had everything to do with the community she'd witnessed. She believed that the only way for her characters to overcome the horrible circumstances that had befallen them was to band together and fight the giant corporate farms that were overtaking the agricultural industry. Babb's novel ends with the hopeful idea of transformation: "An old belief fell away like a withered leaf. Their dreams thudded down, like the overripe pears they had walked on, too long waiting on the stem. One thing was left, as clear and perfect as a drop of rain—the desperate need to stand together as one man. They would rise and fall, and in their falling, rise again."[21]

As scholar Christopher Bowman has pointed out, "While both Babb's and Steinbeck's books were "motivated by a genuine concern for the Dust Bowl migrants, and both approached their novels as projects with which they could cultivate public support" for the migrants in California, the story of Steinbeck's book is quite different.[22] After his two previous starts to the novel in late May 1938, Steinbeck began rapidly writing what would become the iconic book about the Dust Bowl: *The Grapes of Wrath*. He wrote it fast, completing his first draft by mid-October.[23] As biographer Jackson Benson observed, "When at last he did get into the writing of the final draft of the *Grapes of Wrath*, he made it a long sprint, rather than a marathon run, and the strain nearly destroyed him."[24] Indeed, Steinbeck would be hospitalized for exhaustion after finishing the first draft of the book.

On September 3, Steinbeck's wife Carol came up with the title "The Grapes of Wrath," an allusion to Revelations 14:19–20 and a verse from "Battle Hymn of the Republic" by Julia Ward Howe.[25] Carol Steinbeck would also help her husband by not only typing the drafts as he wrote them but with "writing the revision, that is, correcting errors and editing for contradictions and awkwardness."[26] It's because of her deep involvement in the creation of the book that Steinbeck thought of the book as his wife's novel and why he also dedicated the book "To Carol, who willed this book."[27]

Perhaps due to this breakneck speed and his lack of knowledge about the affected area, Steinbeck made serious mistakes and omissions that numerous scholars have thoroughly documented. For example, Steinbeck placed his main characters, the Joads, who'd been "tractored out" by their corporate landlords, first in Shawnee County and then in Sallisaw County,[28] Oklahoma, both of which are far from the panhandle and outside of the areas deeply affected by the Dust Bowl.[29] According to Benson, Steinbeck did travel to Oklahoma briefly in 1937, making a car trip from Chicago on Route 66 with his wife, but with little intent to do research. "The Steinbecks purchased a red Chevrolet in New York . . . and started home, stopping by Chicago. . . . They continued their trip, following Route 66 through Oklahoma, but according to Carol, John made no conscious effort to do any research for his book along the way."[30] Not only would he not do research on this trip, he would also lie about a second trip. According to Benson, Steinbeck would later encourage a false claim that in February 1938, he "followed a trail of migrants from Oklahoma to California and lived with them in roadside camps" when he was researching the book with Tom Collins. That trip never took place.[31]

In addition to the error in setting, Steinbeck's book made it seem as if the only people who were affected by the Dust Bowl were poor white farmers. As Benson points out, "The family Steinbeck was writing about was actually a composite of several families he had encountered in visiting one squatters' camp after another."[32] Steinbeck had only met the people he based his characters on briefly, and this distance shows in his characterization of them. We see little of their interior dialogue and most of them remain stereotypes. Steinbeck's novel doesn't linger for very long in Oklahoma. When the story begins, the disaster has already occurred; the Joads have lost their land. Therefore, his characters' relationship to the land is never established. Nor does his novel elaborate on the horrific effect the greatest natural disaster in the United States had on the people who were living in "No

Man's Land." Instead, his story focuses on what happened after a handful of the 650,000 Dust Bowl refugees left their homes and everything they knew and arrived in California. Because of this, *Grapes of Wrath* readers don't witness the slow terror of the natural disaster as it affected people in their homes in Oklahoma and Colorado and surrounding states, and how it left them little choice but to flee or starve.

For the source material of *Grapes of Wrath,* Steinbeck would heavily rely on the FSA field notes written by Collins and Babb.[33] Steinbeck noted using "great gobs of information" from Babb's and Collins's reports and notes, and from Collins's subsequent letters. As he recorded in the journal he kept while writing the book, "Letter from Tom with vital information to be used later. He is good. I need this stuff. It is exact and just the thing that will be used against me if I am wrong."[34] Steinbeck was "particularly worried about a conspiracy designed to discredit him" by the Associated Farmers or other growers' organizations.[35]

Babb continued to work at the camps until late October or November, when she returned home to work on her book and reunite with her sister and Howe. But she soon realized that to finish her book, she needed the time and space to write. So the following spring, she took the train to New York City to finish her manuscript while living on the Upper West Side with her friend the dancer Lotte Goslaar.[36] She loved living in New York City and knowing her first book was nearing completion. The early summer was boiling hot, but she sat at her desk and diligently completed editing her book and turned it in to Bennett Cerf, her editor at Random House.

Cerf wrote to Babb on July 27, 1939, to say the first reader's report on *Whose Names Are Unknown* had come back "exceptionally fine" and told her that he wanted to "read it myself." He promised to get back to Babb within a week.[37]

However, a week later, when Cerf invited her to the Random House offices to meet with him, she faced a situation she could never have expected. When she entered his office, he was seated formally at his desk, which was cleared of everything except "a check under his hands."[38] She knew right away that something had gone wrong. Though the reading reports about her book had been extremely positive, Cerf explained to Babb that her publishing contract for *Whose Names Are Unknown* had been canceled—due to the wide success of Steinbeck's new book, *The Grapes of Wrath.* By June 1939, *The Grapes of Wrath* had sold over 200,000 copies, and film rights to the book had been sold for $75,000. Steinbeck's fame, which had already been solidified by his best-selling 1937 novel *Of Mice and Men,* was skyrocketing.[39] Babb was speechless and left Cerf's office in utter and complete shock.

The two reader's reports about Babb's book had the same complaints that "it would almost seem as if Sanora Babb and John Steinbeck had thoroughly discussed an identical theme and set out to write their separate books—so similar are GOW [*The Grapes of Wrath*] and WNAU [*Whose Names Are Unknown*]." They go on to explain Babb's approach: "The plight of these people is described with great understanding that indicates personal experience. Whereas Grapes had color, excitement and humor, Babb's book is more uniformly intense, more a piece of the drabness of her people." What's heartbreaking is how this reviewer closes the report: "If there hadn't been a Grapes, I would say unreservedly, here is something new, something fine, we *must* publish. Moreover, an unusual talent is displayed in this first novel."[40]

In subsequent letters, Cerf, who acknowledged the craft of Babb's novel but couldn't see his way to publishing two books about the same event, advised Babb to put her manuscript away for a few years until the market might be more receptive to another novel about the Dust Bowl. As he wrote to her in a letter on August 16, 1939:

After viewing the matter from every angle and discussing it in a full editorial conference for an hour, I don't see how in God's green earth we can publish "Whose Names Are Unknown." What rotten luck for you that "The Grapes of Wrath" should not only have come out before your book was submitted but should have so swept the country! Obviously, another book at this time about exactly the same subject would be a sad anticlimax! And I think that you must face the fact just as we did here. The last third of your book is so completely like "The Grapes of Wrath" that the families and characters might basically be interchanged in the two.[41]

Before she left New York to return to Los Angeles, Babb pleaded with Cerf, but nothing she said changed his mind. When she said she'd have her agent shop her manuscript around to other publishers, he explained that she was welcome to do so, but he knew their answer would be the same as his. Sadly, Cerf was right. Babb sent her manuscript to all the main publishing houses that fall and winter, and each rejection letter echoed sentiments similar to Cerf's: her writing was good, but because of the success of *The Grapes of Wrath* and the uncertain times of a possible world war, the publishers couldn't take a risk on Babb's first novel. Charles A. Pearce at Duel Sloan & Pearce wrote,

Sanora Babb's novel is in many ways a most impressive piece of work. Much that I hate to say it, however, I think that the Random House scheme is a sound one. WNAU is bound to be compared to GOW, and when all things are taken into account, the results are not going to help Miss Babb now or in the future. She really should prove herself with some other novel first. It's particularly sad when one realizes that she went ahead and did her job completely without knowledge of Steinbeck's plan. In many respects I think that she is a more capable and exciting writer than Steinbeck. The stuff in this book is, to me, more honest, moving, and human than much of the stuff in GOW.[42]

Babb was devastated. As she recalled, "I thought after that blow, I couldn't ever write again, and I didn't for a year."[43] As Babb would later recall, "I worked in the fields for months with Tom Collins (to whom *The Grapes of Wrath* is dedicated), who asked me to make detailed nightly notes, and we passed on this great bundle to John Steinbeck who came down to the fields two weekends; and then wrote that fine book. He had sense enough to stay home and write. He was already a professional and I was young, vulnerable, sympathetic with those courageous families and innocent of publishing ways."[44]

Cerf did not let Babb leave New York empty-handed, however; instead, he sent her home with a $250 dollar advance and a contract for a new novel. Babb, still in shock about what had happened, left without signing the contract. She couldn't fathom the idea of walking away from a book she had spent years writing and starting over on a brand-new novel.

What one sees when one compares the two books is that even though Steinbeck relied heavily on source material provided by Collins and Babb, Babb's book is strikingly different from Steinbeck's due to its approach to the subject. While Steinbeck created a fable-like story whose characters are meant to be "the over-essence of the people," as he outlined in his notes for the book, Babb's novel reveals the catastrophic natural disaster as it unfolds in real human details: the daily toil of poverty met with dignity in everything from childbirth to suicides.

Though Steinbeck met Babb on at least one occasion when he was traveling with his friend Collins doing research for his book, he never acknowledged her input into his work. His second dedication in *Grapes of Wrath* (after "to Carol who willed it")—"To TOM who lived it"—only acknowledges the influence of Collins as a "chief source, guide, discussant, and chronicler of accurate migrant information."[45] He even gave Collins a real-life prototype in the character of Jim Rawley, the manager of the "Weedpatch" government camp (which is based on the Arvin camp). Although she had contributed some of the material Steinbeck used, he never acknowledged Babb's assistance. Given Steinbeck's use of his wife's labor on *The Grapes of Wrath* without acknowledgment beyond a dedication, it's likely that Steinbeck didn't think it necessary to give Babb credit for the work she was doing (in his mind, her labor—female labor—was being done for Collins, and therefore her work belonged to Collins). It's also likely that Steinbeck didn't know about Babb's novel. *Whose Names Are Unknown* was not published in any form, except short excerpts in small magazines, before Steinbeck's death on December 20, 1968, and there are no references to it or to Babb in Steinbeck's archives. Given his fame, it is also likely that when Babb met him at the camps, she didn't tell him about her own novel-in-progress, or that if she did, he didn't pay her or her work much notice.

However, Babb does acknowledge Steinbeck in her work. In *Whose Names Are Unknown,* Steinbeck even makes a cameo as "the famous writer" who pleads with a judge to release a young boy who has stolen "four scrapped radiators from a junkyard" to buy groceries for his starving mother.[46] This scene is drawn from a real-life incident that Babb witnessed and recorded in her journals.[47] In her novel, the judge thanks the famous writer, telling him this was the "first time he had thought of these okies as human beings."[48] Everyone in the community celebrates, thinking the writer has saved the day. However, when the boy comes up for trial, he receives no mercy and is sentenced to the maximum eleven years in San Quentin for his crime. After his sentencing, the judge visits the boy's mother at her tent with a basket of food, remembering what the famous writer had told him about treating "okies" like human beings, but the woman he finds is mad with grief over her imprisoned son, and she will not accept the food. Babb's tongue-in-cheek nod to Steinbeck in her book communicates how ineffective she believed his activism to be. Sure, he was able to reach a wide audience, but could he get that audience to see who these suffering people truly were, and could he motivate the general public to do something about the issue that would be effective, that would help the impoverished people she worked with every day?

The impact of Steinbeck's undercover visits to the camps is documented in Collins's memoir "Bringing in the Sheaves" (written under the pseudonym Windsor Drake), in which he records how the camp residents are furious after they find out that the man who visited them was the author of *The Grapes of Wrath:*

> The woman screamed in my direction, "Ain't it so, Mr. Drake, that you done had a guy here with you fur nigh two full weeks? And ain't it so you done let him know all 'bout us people? And ain't it so you done give him all that rotten stuff he done writes about us?"
>
> There was no sleep for me that night, so I passed the long hours by finishing the reading of John's book—my death sentence—the termination of my work and effort with the rural poor—for their confidence in me had been LOST.

And Babb didn't give up on her novel without a fight. Even after Bennett Cerf and so many other New York publishers had rejected her work, Babb continued to seek support for her work. When Babb wrote her Guggenheim application in late 1939, she asserted the difference between her book and Steinbeck's, "In *Whose Names Are Unknown* I have presented the people in a somewhat different light than in the [*Grapes of Wrath*], and I feel I know these people thoroughly and want readers to know about them in this way."[49]

At a time when so much of the American West is plagued with natural disasters and climate migrants are a growing worldwide concern, Babb's novel and her extraordinary life offer us a lesson in humility. Had Babb left the FSA camps and finished her novel just a few months earlier, perhaps it would be her Dust Bowl novel, in addition to *The Grapes of Wrath,* that would be taught in high schools across the country, and perhaps our understanding of that period in history would have been widened to include more than a single story.

12 *The Changed World*

When Babb returned to Los Angeles from New York, she was restless. Indeed, the world had become restless, as it was now hovering on the edge of a second world war. Newspapers shouted bold headlines each morning about Hitler's rise in Europe. The Soviet Union Babb had visited just a few years before was changing as the war progressed. In November 1939, the USSR signed a non-aggression pact with Germany. Then Paris fell to Nazi Germany on June 14, 1940. For the first time, the energy of the possibility of war was starting to seep into the lives of everyone in the United States, a tension that would only increase in the coming months.

Meanwhile, Howe's cinematography career continued to soar. In 1940 he was named on *The Story of Dr. Ehrlich's Magic Bullet, Saturday's Children, Torrid Zone, City for Conquest, A Dispatch from Reuters,* and *The Strawberry Blonde.* Babb supported Howe's career in many ways, including by writing articles about it under a pseudonym. In October 1939, Babb published an article titled "The Photography of James Wong Howe" in *Direction* under the pseudonym Sylvester Davis. Howe's success, paired with his inability to see Babb as a real writer because she hadn't published a book, created distance between them, especially during the time when Babb was devasted by the loss of her contract with Random House.

Babb's sister Dorothy was still in a serious relationship with Carlos Bulosan and therefore had become less dependent on her, so her two closest confidants, Howe and Dorothy, were swept up in their own lives. Babb felt alone, a state that usually felt freeing because it gave her the time and mental space to write. However, for the first time in her adult life, Babb wasn't able to write.

It was in this purgatorial state that Babb took the train across the country to attend the fourth Writers' Congress from June 6 to 8, 1941, in New York City. Since she'd joined in the 1930s, Babb remained deeply involved in the League of American Writers. She served as the secretary-treasurer of the Hollywood chapter from 1939 to 1942. As an officer, she was required to attend events in New York, where the league was housed, including the annual congress. Just as they had in 1935, leftist writers from all over the country gathered at the fourth congress to discuss how to promote the cause of communism with activism and writing, only this time the focus was fogged by the oncoming war.

At the conference, Babb met an up-and-coming Black American writer whose work she'd read in *New Masses* and *Direction* (a pro-Communist publication associated with the League of American Writers), Ralph Ellison. He, too, was the secretary-treasurer of his chapter (in New York City), and the two sat in on many of the same meetings, including a meeting about the league's new literary publication, *The Clipper*. *The Clipper* (formerly called *Black & White*) was published monthly by the Black and White Press in Los Angeles, and it was managed by a board that included Babb and writers and activists Cedric Belfrage, Wolfe Kaufman, Lester Koenig, Meyer Levin, and John Stanford. Babb had previously published her short story "Young Boy, the World," based on a young boy she'd met who lived in a storm pipe while they were both homeless in Lafayette Park, in *Black & White* in September 1939.[1] Now, in September 1940, Babb's short story "Polly" would appear in the inaugural issue of *The Clipper* alongside a piece by one of Babb's literary heroes, Theodore Dreiser.[2] "Polly" was based on Babb's experience meeting a Norwegian man who had snuck his pet bull, Polly, into the FSA camp. The bull was afraid of being in enclosed places because of an accident the man and the bull had survived. Whenever the bull saw its owner go into an enclosed space, like a bathroom, it would bellow loudly, to the chagrin of the rest of the camp.

Babb worked tirelessly as an editor of *The Clipper*. She was a self-proclaimed workhorse, and her work on the journal filled the gap that she'd begun to feel in her life. She now poured all of her creative energy into reading manuscripts, providing extensive feedback, and creating journal issues.

Ralph Ellison lived in Harlem with his wife Rose, and their marriage had been under stress for months due to financial issues and his fear of being drafted.[3] Ellison was new to the League of American Writers and had turned to the organization in hopes that it would facilitate a breakthrough in his writing career. He worked as part of the "Living Lore" unit of the Writers' Project headed by Nicholas Wirth, which emphasized New York life through the spoken word. Ellison would visit "staked out" areas in Harlem and record "the ditties, songs and improvised street games of children." This work would encourage Ellison's growing interest in "the links between folklore, myth, ritual, drama and history" that would heavily influence his future masterpiece, *The Invisible Man*.[4]

In October 1941, Babb returned to New York to attend a league meeting about *The Clipper*. It was there in the crowded, smoke-filled room that she again saw Ellison, and this time he was looking at her across the roomful of faces. Ellison had joined the Communist Party because it was the only major institution in American life that "officially defined blacks as socially and intellectually equal to whites."[5] As Ellison stated, "I was a Communist because I was a Negro."[6] But like Babb, he refused to write "proletarian art" or "the official type of fiction" endorsed by the party. He never accepted "the ideology which the *New Masses* attempted to impose on its writers."[7] This explains why he, like Babb, was so invested in *The Clipper:* a publication that valued literary merit over communist propaganda. However, Ellison was shy in groups and spoke little in the meeting. As his biographer Arnold Rampersad states, "On virtually all questions Ralph had opinions—but he did not often share them. His shyness, his discomfort with white people, intervened. When he spoke, he often stammered a little."[8] Just as she had when she first met Carlos Bulosan, who was uncomfortable about speaking because of his Filipino accent, Babb could sense Ellison's discomfort in a room filled with white people. Her life with Howe has also made her acutely aware of the racism that was ever present. She had read Ellison's essays and stories in *New Masses* and admired him as a writer. She also found him incredibly attractive. Ellison's good friend (and the first person Babb had met at the first Writers' Congress in 1935), Richard Wright, had just seen his career take off. *Native Son* sold 215,000 copies in the first three weeks after its publication in March 1940. Ellison was hungry for the same level of success but had not yet found a way to get there (it would be over a decade before *Invisible Man* would be published in 1952).

In that crowded room, something electric passed between Ellison and Babb. Ellison caught her eye and Babb looked unblinkingly back.[9] They left the meeting together, walking up Park Avenue in the dark, deep in conversation.[10] That night they connected. She brought him to her hotel, and they had sex but afterward he became withdrawn. Their union was complicated by the fact that they both had partners, as well as by their race. In 1941, Babb and Ellison couldn't simply walk through the front door of the hotel. Instead, when they tried to enter the building that first night, Ellison was ordered to use the back entrance. Even in New York City in 1941, it was dangerous for Ellison to be seen escorting a white woman. One never knew what bystanders might do.

But the two connected nonetheless, and what began that first intimate night was a passionate relationship of not just the body but the mind. Babb found in Ellison a mirror, a man who reflected the same ravenous hunger she had to uncover and tell the stories of those whom society had discarded. Unlike Howe, Ellison saw Babb as a writer first, and this fact fueled her passion for him. Later, in a note scribbled on St. Moritz Hotel stationery, Babb wrote, "My desire (and desire, I think is an unashamed and beautiful urge, and nothing to do with appetite, with which I wouldn't insult you or myself) toward you has overcome the cool caution of my mind."[11] The two spent a few weeks in New York together, walking "under autumn skies in Central Park, or strolling through the crowded streets of Manhattan, or sitting in little cafes" where over "foolish, sentimental songs" they debated and discussed their ideas about what literature could do. Both writers felt a deep connection. As Ellison would later reflect in a letter to Babb, "Someday I'll get around to telling you just what has been happening to me since I've known you. All that I can say now with certainty is that it was no surface thing. It was no 'rare holiday' but the start of a new phase in my life."[12]

In early December, the night before Babb was to take the train back to Los Angeles, the lovers' emotions became charged by their fear of leaving one another. Ellison lashed out, becoming moody and leaving Babb alone at her hotel. The next day, when he hurried back to say goodbye, he arrived too late. Babb had already checked out of her hotel and taken a cab to Grand Central Station. Ellison rushed there and found her already sitting in her compartment on the Super Chief, looking out of the window at the bustling platform. Seeing Babb about to depart from his life, Ellison's feelings overwhelmed him and he rushed onto the train. For Babb, this moment was as if that scene she'd witnessed in Elkhart years ago, when the town's young soldiers were being shipped off to World War I and the girls boarded the train, descending on the soldiers with passion, was being reversed. As she recalled in a letter she wrote to Ellison later, "When you came in [to the compartment] I kissed you so many times to brush away the fears I had in that hour."[13] When Ellison disembarked and waved goodbye from the platform as the train slowly pulled away, Babb felt certain this was only a short goodbye, that their futures would be intertwined. For the next few hours, as the train traveled farther and farther away from her love, Babb "looked out the window at the war-busy factories" in a daze. As she later recalled in a letter, "I kept remembering all the things you said, and the ways you looked, and the crazy half hour before the train left. . . . Oh, my darling . . . Ralph, Ralph, Ralph, how will it be not to see you?"[14]

Ellison called Babb on the telephone at the station in Chicago; her train would have a four- or five-hour stop there and they had arranged the call.[15] He was filled with promises. He told her he would leave his wife to be with her. Babb had never been so overwhelmed with love. She walked back to the train "in an ecstatic dream, feeling like a living poem."[16] But she only had a few hours to feel joy before the entire world shifted.

The next night, as Babb slept in her berth on the train, Japan bombed Pearl Harbor, and by the following afternoon, it was announced on the train that the U.S. had officially declared war against Japan. Years later, Babb remembered the moment vividly. When the news was announced, Babb "was so surprised. I was in a lounge car and people sat there utterly shocked. . . . All of a sudden, everybody stood up and started singing *The Star-Spangled Banner*."[17] Babb, who'd seen the rise of fascism in Europe firsthand, knew the significance of what was about to happen, but she could never have predicted the Los Angeles she'd be returning to.

By the time she disembarked the train the next day, on December 9, the West Coast had been completely transformed by the threat of war. Cities were blacked out at night and the radio was entirely dead "except for five minutes every hour and half hour." As Babb explained in a letter to Ellison that she wrote immediately upon arriving, "All social telephoning [was] banned; everyone [was] asked not to go out anymore." Days after the Pearl Harbor attack, the threat of war was very real to the people of Los Angeles. Babb continued, "Last night Japanese bombers off an airplane carrier got within 21 miles of the coast here." She reported that Eleanor Roosevelt had come to visit Los Angeles and that night and day, "Patrol planes [roar] overhead."[18]

In this tense environment, Babb was devastated to come home to an empty mailbox. None of Ellison's letters had arrived. She became frantic, writing in the same letter, "Darling why don't you write me? There isn't anything you can't say to me, surely. Anything would be better than not hearing at all." Later that day, however, she reported that she received "a special delivery," a letter from Ellison. When it arrived, she immediately left her sister Dorothy, who was bombarding her with questions about her trip, so she could go off by herself to read it "many times."[19]

It wasn't long before Babb's partner, Howe became aware of Babb's romance with Ellison. Their relationship had become strained even before Babb's novel had been rejected by Random House. In another letter to Ellison, Babb explained that previously, Howe had begun a relationship with a young Chinese girl and nearly left Babb to marry her. Babb explained to Ellison how much Howe's act had hurt her but stated that in retrospect, she wished Howe had left her to marry the young girl.[20]

But regardless of the state of their intimate relationship, Babb and Howe's lives were deeply intertwined, as the two now ran a business together. The previous year, on February 5, 1940, they had opened a Chinese restaurant named Ching How. The restaurant was located at 11386 Ventura Boulevard in North Hollywood. Babb purchased the building due to the fact that Howe legally could not under California's laws regarding those of Chinese descent.[21] According to an article written by Hollywood reporter Julia Layne, Howe had dreamed up the idea of the restaurant "during the early days of the movie industry," when he "and his friends were in constant search of good Cantonese cuisine."[22] Someone suggested that he open a restaurant near the studios "so that it would not be necessary to travel all the way to Chinatown for a Chinese dinner."[23] The menu specified that the food served there was "Chinese food in the Chinese manner" and encouraged guests to let the chef chose a set of dishes for them so that they would "become acquainted with new dishes."[24] Opening night, the restaurant was filled with Hollywood's biggest stars, including Cary Grant and Randolph Scott. In fact, that night there were so many guests that people had to be turned away.[25] The restaurant remained a hot spot for stars and Hollywood elite as long as it was in operation. Babb not only bought the property, she was deeply invested in its operation, and the restaurant quickly became a point of stress, as Babb was constantly dealing with issues involving it. Howe had his accountant teach Dorothy how to do bookkeeping for the restaurant and "she kept the CH [Ching How] books from 1941–1951."[26]

But even with the added responsibilities of the restaurant on her shoulders, the fate of Babb's last manuscript still haunted her. In the spring of 1942, when Babb attended a novel workshop where the exiled German writer Lion Feuchtwanger was the guest lecturer, she saw even more evidence that Steinbeck's version of the Dust Bowl was there to stay. During the question-and-answer period, Feuchtwanger was asked about American novels, and Babb told Ellison that "he spoke only of Steinbeck . . . at which we argued."[27] Indeed, since its publication in 1939, Steinbeck's novel had continued to receive critical acclaim and had been turned into an Academy Award–winning 1940 film directed by John Ford. But the fact that Babb argued with Feuchtwanger about Steinbeck speaks to the authority she still felt about her work.

Babb's relationship with Ellison had unblocked the writer's block that had kept her from writing ever since *Whose Names Are Unknown* had been rejected by Bennett Cerf and other New York editors. In late December 1941, Babb wrote to Ellison that she was starting to write again, and by the end of January she reported her excitement at having written three short stories since her return from New York. An excerpt from *Whose Names Are Unknown* titled "Morning in Imperial Valley" was published in *Kansas Magazine*. Given the way Babb introduced the piece as a "short excerpt from a well-documented novel," it's clear she had not given up on her first novel.[28] She'd left her manuscript of *Whose Names Are Unknown* at the office of the League of American Writers in New York in hopes that the league would pull an excerpt from it for publication in *New Masses*.[29] She'd also arranged that when the *New Masses* editors were finished reading it, they would pass it along to Ellison so that he could also read it and send her his critique. It's clear from her letters from this period that Babb still believed that it was only a matter of time before the novel would be published.

But while Babb was able to write short stories again, she was unable to move on and focus on the new, larger project looming before her: her next novel. When she left New York, Cerf was adamant about giving her a contract and an advance for $250 to write a new novel: "You know how strongly I feel that we cannot let you get away from us, come what may. . . . I do hope that you will sign the contracts and send them back to us right soon."[30] Indeed, Babb had signed the contract Random House had given her, but she was stuck. Since the blow from Random House rejecting *Whose Names Are Unknown,* Babb had been unable to write more than sketches for her next book.

Meanwhile, the war continued, and Babb's letters offer us insight into what it was like to live in Los Angeles during this tense time. As she reports in a letter to Ellison, "There was a complete blackout . . . so above the darkness of the city it was easy to see the Japanese planes and the anti-aircraft fire. The beams caught the planes in their light, turning them silver . . . and our guns roared for a long time but hit none of them!"[31] The air raid Babb thought she'd witnessed would later be called "The Battle of Los Angeles" and deemed a false alarm by Secretary of the Navy Frank Knox. What she saw was friendly fire caused by "war nerves" when a stray weather balloon was misidentified. That night the Los Angeles area was under warning of a possible attack, so it isn't surprising that citizens (like Babb) thought they were being attacked by Japan.

These occurrences made Babb desperate to do something to fight back. The war had begun to change her political ideas. Where previously she had not been in support of war, now that attacks felt imminent, she saw the need.[32] She tried to enlist to become a cargo pilot or to join the Red Cross, but when she went to the recruitment office, she failed her physical exam due to heart issues and was refused for the premature anti-fascism of her work against Franco in the late 1930s, when she worked on *The Week* in England.[33] Years of starvation as a child had damaged her heart, and years as a communist had damaged her reputation in the government's eye.[34] Undeterred, Babb set out to find a way to support the war through volunteering. Those who lived in Los Angeles at the time were "expecting a Japanese invasion of the West Coast."[35] Organizations like the Red Cross encouraged local citizens to volunteer to prepare for an invasion. Babb enlisted a group of wealthy Hollywood women who dined regularly at Ching How, at a special table set aside for "war widows"[36] (women whose husbands were away at war), to join her in what she would christen the "mink brigade." Babb taught the women how to drive the steep, winding Hollywood Hills roads, where bunkers were built into the hillsides and troops would be located if there was an attack, so that in case of a bombing, day or night, they would be able to transport victims to safety. The work wasn't as glamorous as serving the Red Cross overseas, but at least it left her feeling like she was doing something in support of the war.

By February, Ellison's letters to Babb had changed in tone, and Babb began to conclude that he perhaps did not love her as much as she still loved him. She wrote to him, "I love you so terribly much, that in all this silence my love grows instead of lessening. It is as if you had accidentally touched something folded away in the dark of my being, and that your touch had begun an endless unfolding."[37] In his letters, Ellison had made it clear to Babb that a large part of the reason he couldn't be with her was because she was white. Babb closed her letter with this response: "I think of you in this mean white world, and I want to be with you. You will have children now. I wish they were mine. This is the first time I ever wished that, except when I said it to you. Why do you mean so many things to me?"[38]

Ellison, though his tone had changed, continued to write Babb and profess his love for her. In one letter he tells her about a new literary magazine called *The Negro Quarterly,* a wartime quarterly of African American thought and opinion that he has just launched with the well-known Black communist writer Angelo Herndon. When Ellison finally picked up Babb's manuscript for *Whose Names Are Unknown* from the League of American Writers, he wrote to Babb that he hoped she had "gotten back to the novel and that it is completed for fall publication. You *must*."[39] However, he doesn't return her manuscript to her. Despite Babb's pleas for him to return it, Ellison holds on to it until July 4, 1943, claiming that he couldn't let it go because it "symbolizes so much that was meaningful and dear for so short a while."[40] In the same letter, Ellison writes that he'd just returned from visiting their friend the poet Genevieve Taggard in Vermont, where he had begun writing again about "what I believe in and out of what my people believe in, hope for and feel."[41] And he sent his manuscript for Babb to read. He had begun writing what would be his first novel, *Invisible Man.*

When Ellison does finally send back feedback to Babb about *Whose Names Are Unknown,* his notes reveal that he sees in Babb's novel a symbolism he wants her to emphasize even more. For example, he tells Babb that the scene when Milt's wife, Julia, miscarries her child (which Babb based on her mother's own harrowing experiences in Eastern Colorado) foreshadowed "the 'stillborn strike' and the frustrations which lead up to the migration and accompany it" later in the novel.[42] He also encouraged Babb to change the point of view of the novel so that the reader experiences everything through Julia's consciousness, "since her journey from bread (bakery) to breadlessness (pepper tea) furnishes the pattern for the whole."[43] When Ellison draws a comparison between Babb's novel and Steinbeck's, he senses the unique perspective her work offers: her insight into what it was like to be a woman during the Dust Bowl. "You do a much more subtle thing because, consciously or no, your novel exploits, draws upon, the wide-spread fear of pregnancy, miscarriage, and the discovery of abortion, which weighs upon the consciousness of women during periods of drought and famine." Ellison goes on to state that "Steinbeck was never for the workers in GOW but was pleading subtly for the big shots to stop their wrong doing. You, however, have been for the worker, showing his rebirth into a new consciousness." Ellison also urges Babb to not be afraid to give her Black characters more attention: "Next time don't be afraid of the Negro, you know enough to give a deeper insight into Garrison even though he doesn't demand much attention."[44] By the time Babb received Ellison's comments in 1943, however, she had all but given up on her first novel: "I had hoped long ago to hear what you thot of it, since I value your critical opinion so much, but it is rather like talking about a dead man, now."[45]

By March 1942, Babb was finally able to devote herself to working on the new novel that she'd promised to Random House. Saxe Commins, her newly assigned editor, came to visit her at her home while he was traveling out west to attend his brother's funeral, and they went over a few of the openings she had been thinking about for the novel, which she had begun calling "The Stranger."[46]

In Babb's early sketches she sets the story in a town much like Forgan, in the Oklahoma Panhandle, where she attended high school. Stevie, the main character in this version, is loosely based on sixteen-year-old Babb, while the father figure, Des, who is tragically addicted to gambling, is based on Babb's father, Walt. The early drafts include Babb's reimagining her painful graduation from high school at which she was denied the honor of valedictorian due to the intervention of her best friend's mother, who didn't want a gambler's daughter to be honored in that way.

During his visit, Commins and Babb agree that she will send him a significant draft by May.[47] Random House is eager to publish something by Babb and has offered to publish this new novel in the fall if she can finish it fast. It's a tempting offer, but even after meeting with Commins, Babb has trouble writing about this painful time during her life. Her father's abuse and cruelty, Babb states in a letter to Ellison, was "a companion of my childhood." To cope, she explained, she'd "learned how to handle it and even forget it quickly."[48] But her writing was making her go back and relive the most painful experiences of her life, and it was this pain that kept Babb from being able to make steady progress on her novel.

Babb missed her first deadline by over six months, finally, sending an incomplete draft to Commins in November 1942. What also stymied her progress, though, was the reaction of her editor. When he received it, Commins wrote back, "I want to give you all my reaction to the first draft of your partial manuscript—good and bad—for only one purpose: so that it will help to clarify some of your problems and also urge you with all encouragement to go on until you have shaped it to your heart's desire."[49] It wasn't until July 16, 1943, that Babb was able to finish the first full draft of the novel, and it was six hundred pages long.

Babb's first approach to the story was biographically accurate, clearly displaying her father's abuse and the horrible conditions she, her mother, and her sister lived under. However, Commins found Babb's reality too cruel and advised her to move from depicting Des as an evil, self-serving man (which he saw as too extreme) to one who is "more than a representation; his reality lies in the strange, uneven mixture of charm and irresponsibility, evil and decency, consideration, and brutality. He is alive and must become the core of your novel."[50] In later years, Babb would state that "Saxe's advice helped me—he was a wonderful editor."[51] But what must it have felt like for Babb to have unearthed such a personal story about the worst days of her life, only to be met with the fact that the reality she had lived was, in her publisher's opinion, too extreme for readership to consume? Commins also seems to miss the way Babb is writing honestly about Stevie, the character she based on herself, seeing the character's overt sexuality as that of "shameful youth" and wishing instead that her character showed growth into a more proper woman through "meaningful maturity."[52]

As Babb struggled with her novel and saw Ellison drifting away from her, Howe battled to keep her as part of his life. Along with the restaurant they'd opened, the two had purchased a home, a place where they could finally live together without the prejudice of property owners enforcing miscegenation laws against them. Back in 1941, on a drive through the steep winding roads of the Hollywood Hills, Howe had found a white stucco house that was for sale. The windows of the house looked out across the valley where at twilight, Hollywood's lights would begin to turn on like a carpet of stars. Howe fell instantly in love with both the house and the view and rushed to show it to Babb. She, too, loved it. Babb made an offer using Howe's money to finance the purchase, as Howe was still not legally allowed to purchase property in California. The week they were to move in, Babb attended a homeowner meeting and remembered that some women complained that a Chinese man had recently purchased a home in the neighborhood. Babb, who by that time had become used to the constant prejudice waged against Howe, stood up at the meeting and boldly introduced herself, explaining to the gossiping homeowners that "that Chinese man" was the world-famous cinematographer James Wong Howe, that she was his wife (a lie), and that yes, they were indeed moving in. After Babb finished her speech, the crowded room went dead silent, and Babb strode out. Babb would live in this house on Queens Road until the day she died.

But in January 1943, Babb was living alone on Queens Road because she and Howe remained separated. Any try at reconciliation would lead to another argument. In a letter, Howe wrote to her, "I only wish you could know just how I feel. Now, I really know how much I love you, but I am afraid it's to[o] late. . . . You have helped and given me so much in our relationship in these nine years, and I must say it has been most wonderful. The things I said about you and the way I talked yesterday was only through shear anger and hurt. . . . I am very lonely and heartbroken, but I love you."[53]

Later that month, Babb attended the release of Howe's latest film, *Air Force,* a patriotic film about the flight crew of the *Mary Ann,* a B-17 that fights the Japanese during the Pearl Harbor attack and then is sent on to Manila to help with the defense of the Philippines.[54] Like most films of the era, *Air Force* is steeped in propaganda, beginning with an opening in which the words of Abraham Lincoln are plastered across the screen. Although both Howe and Babb attended the premiere, they did not see each other. After the screening, Howe wrote to Babb, "I was so distracted being in the same theater with you and not being able to see you. I hope we can see each other soon and have a nice talk."[55] This period of separation and reconciliation would continue off and on, and Babb would document this troubled period of their relationship in her short story "Reconciliation."[56]

Babb wrote the first draft of "Reconciliation," set in the back garden of a "Moorish house" modeled after their Queens Road home, in

April 1944. Throughout the story Babb uses nature as a way to exhibit the tension that exists between the husband and wife. The husband is uncomfortable with anything that is wild and untamed (a life, a garden), while the wife, who grew up immersed in "the wild place" of the plains of Eastern Colorado, feels most at home in it. The story recalls in great sensory detail Babb's poverty-stricken childhood in the second home the Babbs lived in on Horse Creek and the intimate relationship she had with her grandfather, a relationship that is eclipsed by the mercurial anger of her father. Towards the end of the short story, the man leaves the garden to go inside to play a record and soon the discordant sounds of Scriabin's *Poem of Ecstasy* and then *Poem of Fire* begin to echo from the house. Suddenly, listening to the music as it mixes with the natural sounds around her, the woman is able to let her loneliness go. She recognizes that "some radiant energy, long bound by the weight of confusion and opposing desires, demanded release"[57] between them as a couple, and she begins to understand that though it would not be easy, a reconciliation is still possible between them. Instead of ending the story by having her protagonist step inside the house and try to resolve the conflict, however, Babb creates what I consider one of her best endings. She closes the story by looking outward into the natural world, the same natural world that first drew the husband and wife into conversation: "Under the desperate music and the quick winter dark, she could hear the foolish frogs singing as if nothing great or small would ever be changed by the world. She hesitated a moment thinking of flight. The frogs were singing of eternals, innocently, blindly. She opened the door and went in quietly, wanting to be known, and to know him whom she had not fully known before."[58]

In a story where all signs lead to the likelihood that the woman will walk away, Babb surprises us. She uses nature as both comfort and chorus; the frogs are the final crescendo that leads her protagonist not away from the relationship, as we expect, but back into the house, toward the possibility of resolution. "Reconciliation" would not only help Babb process the troubles she and Howe were facing, but it would also, through the honors the story would receive, bring her into contact with a new, empowering group of writers with whom she would write for the next forty years.

13 *She Felt Like the Wind*

As Babb continued to work on the second draft of her new novel, she began to write sections of it as short stories, one of which is the "The Journey Begun," which would eventually be published in the anthology *Cross Section* 1948: *A Collection of New American Writing* alongside an excerpt from twenty-five-year-old Norman Mailer's debut novel *The Naked and the Dead*. In this section of Babb's novel, the young female protagonist, Damon (another masculine name, like Stevie in the early version of *The Lost Traveler*) is on watch for the sheriff, a task she's been assigned by her father, who is gambling at the back of the drugstore. We see Babb's past float through the story: the prostitutes she saw when she was a young girl living in Elkhart, Kansas, and how it felt to move from town to town based on her father's need to run from the law. In the story, Damon sees her mother destroyed by her father's gambling and drunken beatings. When she was younger, Damon hadn't been able to protect her mother from becoming the victim of her father's rage. But once she gets older, she realizes "that she was his equal. Once she had thrown a knife, not wanting to, and after that she could frighten him with her eyes and her words. . . . That part of her was in everything she was, as natural as laughter, not, as he thought, a segment he could shatter and pluck out."[1] When Damon realizes that she is not a victim like her mother—that despite her gender, she is a fighter like her father—she gains confidence. In this story, Babb uses natural imagery to convey the power her protagonist gains and her connection to her environment. Damon, like Babb when she was a young child living on the flat plains of Eastern Colorado, is connected with the wind, as when "she put her arms around the wind. It was strong enough to hold but leapt away. She felt like the wind, like this clean western wind with its strength and disturbing urgency."[2]

By the end of the story, Damon pulls herself from her father's life in the remote and conventional small town. When the police break up his gambling game, and he makes a run for it, telling her to join him in a few days, she decides this time she will not follow him. The sound of the train and the wind over the prairie awaken something in Damon that previously had been dormant. She thinks "no music, no song would ever speak for her spirit as truly as the wind and the beckoning and farewelling call of a train going through lonely places."[3] It was as if the wind had finally awakened in her the wildness and freedom that were always at her core. When she boards the train and the conductor asks her name, she immediately replies "Delores O'Shea," and with those small words she separates herself from her father.[4] Damon/Delores survives because she bends the boundaries of gender, in the way many women had to leave behind conventional gender norms to survive the demands of living in the West. Her story offers another example of how Babb's female characters found a way to control their lives, even when they felt trapped.

Babb, like Damon/Delores, was struggling between her two identities, her identity as Howe's partner in the world of Hollywood and her identity as a writer. When she had been with Ellison, she felt as if her identity as a writer was being seen. But as letters from Ellison became less frequent and then eventually stopped coming, she found herself lost between worlds. Finally, in May 1944, Babb received word via Ellison's former coeditor of the *Negro Quarterly,* the writer

Angelo Herndon, that Ellison had joined the Merchant Marines as a third cook and baker.[5] Ellison would remain in the Merchant Marines until 1945.

As Ellison drifted further into the background of her life, Babb wrote him back to life as a character in the second full draft of her novel, which she finished on May 12, 1944.[6] In this version, Stevie's name had been changed to Robin and a new love interest has been introduced: Chris, who is Black. In fact, it is his character that helps her find her way back after she's run away from her father during a violent episode in which her father has attacked her.[7]

When Babb finished the second draft of her novel and sent it to Saxe Commins at Random House, he wasn't impressed. He wrote back, "I must in fairness to you . . . tell you that there are still many things wrong with your script. . . . You realize as I do that as it now stands it is unpublishable. No amount of work by anybody else could whip it into shape, merely because there isn't an editor alive who could enter the lives of these people who belong so definitely to you and make them real. That is your stint, and you have to believe in it enough to want to do it all by yourself."[8]

His words were a hard blow to Babb's now fragile ego. As a writer, Babb began to ask herself what if the stories she wished to tell, the stories that were drawn from her real-life experiences, weren't palatable to editors like Commins? Her novel's characters do not follow expected gender norms. She depicts a female protagonist who, against all odds, tries to maintain control over her chaotic life, who is sexually active, and who is growing up in a troubled home under the rule of a gambling father. While these themes may have been tolerated during the Great Depression, now, during the war era, they were not. The truth was that even during the Great Depression, other novels written by women that featured strong female characters, were based on real-life experiences, and received contracts—such as Tillie Olsen's *Yonnondio* and Meridel Le Sueur's *The Girl*—didn't actually get published during the 1930s either. Both of these books would not be published until the 1970s.[9]

In August 1944, Babb finally heard from Ellison. He explained his silence by recounting all he had been through: how his wife Rose had left him and things had fallen apart at the *Negro Quarterly*. "In December . . . I went to sea, serving as a third cook on a Liberty Ship."[10] Finally hearing from Ellison stirred up Babb's feelings for him, but their romance would never fully rekindle.

The atmosphere had changed in Los Angeles as the United States gained leverage in the war. The air raid drills ceased, and the radio began to play music again. On May 8, 1945, when World War II ended in Europe, Los Angeles remained cautious; the threat it faced from the Pacific theater was still very real. As the *Los Angeles Times* reported on May 9,

> Los Angeles paused briefly yesterday to digest the news of the victory in Europe, then turned its eyes westward toward Japan and reclenched its fists. . . . The lack of gayety with which news of the European victory was greeted here also was evident last night. Places where crowds might have been were deserted. Only the normal throng of pedestrians were out in downtown streets. . . . Mayor Bowron declared: "This is not a holiday. Work will not be stopped. The city's business should be carried on as usual. Remember, our war is not over until Japan is defeated."[11]

In fact, Los Angeles and other West Coast cities didn't let down their guard until later that year, on September 2, when President Truman announced Japan's surrender and declared the official end of World War II.[12]

Between the European and Pacific theater victories, Babb continued to battle against her past, revising *The Lost Traveler*. She sent copies of the manuscript to many of her literary friends, asking for feedback; these included her old acquaintance Paul Jarrico, whom she knew from the early days of the League of American Writers and who was now a well-known screenwriter. In a letter, he offered to read her manuscript. He had just finished boot camp and had entered active service as a seaman second class stationed in San Diego. On the weekends he was able to return home, and on one of those trips he met with Babb. The letters that follow are filled with flirtations. Babb tells him she'd like to get to know him better, that to her he seemed "generous and warm, rather cautious and shy; that you are gentle and tender, that you have a quietness that has nothing to do with an uncertainty, that you are capable of simple gaiety, which is rare. . . . I like the way you behave with women—a kind of promiscuous and sincere attention which seems to contain no real promiscuity or emotion, but a fairly large liking for them."[13] Words that according to Larry Ceplair, Jarrico's biographer, totally won him over. In a final letter Babb explains how she has been reading novels by the Kentucky author Elizabeth Maddox Roberts, whose work takes its time to develop. This has led Babb to realize that in her own writing, she has a tendency to "leap into the middle of things too quickly," and she admits to Jarrico that she's learning that "a novel requires more leisurely development."[14] The romance (if any) that happened between Jarrico and Babb was brief, but the realization she gained about her own craft was important.

As the war ended, its themes and its outcome made their way into Babb's short stories, which she continued to write even as she struggled to make her way through another revision of *The Lost Traveler.* In her short story "The Refugee," which was included in *Cross Section 1945: A Collection of New American Writing,*[15] Babb veers from her typical topics and instead writes about a German refugee who has been liberated from a concentration camp and is now living in a small apartment in New York City. Babb based the story on the real-life experiences of her friend the actor Mikhail Rasumny.[16] The protagonist of "The Refugee" is lonely in his small basement apartment. He is trying to learn to speak English, but he has no one with whom to speak. When another refugee's son gives him a few "Mexican jumping beans," he is so starved for company that he is thrilled by their companionship. He names each bean and speaks to them in his new language. In the end the beans are lost. The man, devastated, is forced to leave his apartment and face the cruelty of the city, if only to find someone to talk to. When he reaches the river's edge, he meets a young soldier who is also lonely and who asks him out for a beer. The man doesn't have enough money to buy beer but he goes anyway, and for the first time he is able to cross the boundary between refugee and citizen and make a connection with another American. One sees the deep growth of Babb's craft in this story; she's come a long way from her early attempts, written when she was in college, when she tried on stories about a world war she knew little about. The decades she's spent honing her craft and living among Dust Bowl refugees have enabled her to write from the point of view of someone very different from herself.

Frustrated by Saxe Commins's continual rejections of her work and yet another stalemate with Random House regarding her latest draft, Babb decided to take matters back into her own hands. She decided to try to find a literary agent to help her land a publisher for her work. On November 6, 1945, on the recommendation of her friend the journalist and novelist Martha Dodd, Babb wrote to New York agent Harriet Wolf, introducing herself and explaining the tricky situation she was in with Random House. After laying out her plight—"I really didn't get the kind of criticism I expected from Saxe"—she asked Wolf to represent her.[17] Wolf agreed and was soon shopping Babb's work around to literary markets she had not yet broken into. It was during these years that Babb composed some of the strongest short stories she would ever write. Although she now had Wolf's support, the work that Babb was doing—dredging up and writing about the deepest and darkest times in her life, including the abuse she suffered under her father's rule—was taxing her mentally. On top of that, Babb had been pulled into helping Howe run the now bustling restaurant to such a degree that her work at Ching How was eating up all of her time, time she would have much rather spent writing. Babb felt pulled in all directions. Added to this was the loss she felt in regard to Ellison, especially when she discovered that after he returned from the war in 1946, he married again, this time to a woman named Fanny McConnell. All of these factors likely contributed to what happened next in Babb's life.

In early 1946, Babb experienced a nervous breakdown. She was hospitalized, and while she was in the hospital, she tried to commit suicide by climbing onto a high window ledge and threatening to jump. She was saved by strangers who talked her down. As Babb later explained in a letter to her friend Roz Sharp, "I had a terrible 'crack-up' and was given drugs." Babb blamed the drugs for making her suicidal. "When I was given so many drugs in the hospital, I tried to jump out the window! I am not the kind of person who wants to die; I love to live, so I thot this most unnatural!"[18] Letters from Babb's friends called her hospitalization a "nervous setback and illness" and revealed that Babb was "resistant to analysis" as a means of recovery.[19] Her friend the poet Genevieve Taggard wrote, "Since your letter came I have had tears in my heart . . . regret. . . . Could I have stopped this and saved you?"[20]

Given the lack of information available about this event, combined with the way mental illness was perceived at this time, it is difficult to know exactly what happened to Babb. We don't know if a particular event triggered her to have to be hospitalized. And one has to ask why she later downplayed what happened to her, claiming her "crack-up" was caused by the intervention she received ("the drugs") rather than a mental health issue. The truth is, Babb had seen mental illness; she had witnessed her sister suffer in its grip since she was a child. And she had watched her sister continue to suffer from the trauma she had lived through as a child, trauma that Babb shared. Perhaps reliving that trauma as she wrote and rewrote her novel, and feeling as if her identity as a woman and a writer was being questioned, led to the breakdown. Her whole life, Babb had identified her sister as weak and herself as strong. Perhaps admitting to herself that she had also suffered from their traumatic childhood made her feel she was weak, like Dorothy.

Regardless of the cause, the nervous breakdown set Babb back and made her more cautious. When Wolf mentioned to Babb that an editor at Simon & Schuster had read "The Refugee" and was interested in reading her novel, Babb respectfully declined. Her mental health made her cautious about leaving her book deal with Random House, even though she was frustrated with the lack of feedback she was getting from Commins. In essence, she had begun to believe his criticism was correct. She wrote to Wolf that she felt like the first two drafts of her novel (still called "The Stranger") "are not good,"[21] but that after sitting with her second draft some time she knew where she wanted to go with the character development, and she wanted to give Random House one more opportunity to read her next draft.

In 1946, while Babb was still recovering from her breakdown, the Chinese actor Lotus Ma (stage name Lotus Fragrance), whom Babb had met in England in 1936, reached out to her and Howe asking for sponsorship so she and her daughter Roxana could emigrate to the United States. In England, Babb had become quite close with Lotus and adored her two children. When Lotus informed them of the harrowing events she and her small children had endured during the war and asked for help, Babb and Howe immediately agreed. During the London Blitz of 1940–1941, "Lotus had volunteered in the war effort while her husband served in the British Army. However, the war effectively ended her budding acting career, as well as her marriage."[22] Lotus's husband enlisted to work as a translator and was sent overseas, leaving Lotus and their children to flee London on their own. On their first attempt to escape, their ship was bombed, and they had to return to London. On their second attempt, they traveled by ship via South Africa to Burma (now Myanmar), then overland to Chongqing, and eventually by air to India, where Lotus set up a fashionable beauty salon called White Rose in Bombay. Before the war, Lotus had met an Indian cosmetologist at her beauty shop in London who had given her formulas for making lipstick and powder. Lotus began manufacturing and selling these products at White Rose. In late 1946, Lotus left her son, Francis, with her estranged husband, who was then working in Calcutta, and she and Roxana traveled to her family in Shanghai. After a few months, she decided their best future would be in America, and she began to plan to emigrate to the United States with her daughter.

It was August when Lotus and now ten-year-old Roxana first arrived in the U.S. and visited Babb and Howe at their Queens Road home. Babb remembered holding then baby Roxana in her arms in London over a decade earlier, but Roxana had no memory of her. Babb was still frail from her breakdown, and when Roxana playfully hid behind a door and jumped out to say "boo," Babb was so surprised she fainted. As Roxana remembers it, Babb laughed off her collapse and seemed more concerned with making the young girl feel comfortable in her home than with her own health (years later, Babb would write to Roxana that she'd worried she'd ruined that special day for her by fainting). Lotus, who was fluent in English and Mandarin, obtained a work permit to buy electronic equipment at showrooms (a deal she had arranged in Shanghai with her uncle, Henry Ma), which meant she needed to travel a lot. She needed to place Roxana in a boarding school in Los Angeles, where Babb could help take Roxana to doctors' appointments and perform other parental tasks.

Babb and Howe found Roxana a spot at the Eunice Knight Saunders School on Havenhurst, where she enrolled in September 1947. A few weeks before Roxana was to start school, Babb and Lotus took her to meet with the school's director, Eunice Knight Saunders. Because she and her mother had had to flee London with only the clothes on their backs, Roxana had no medical or schooling records. During the interview, Roxana was petrified and didn't say a word. Thinking she could not speak English, Ms. Saunders placed Roxana in the first grade. Babb, who remembered her own experience of almost being placed below her grade level when her family moved to Elkhart, Kansas, insisted this wasn't necessary, and that at home Roxana communicated with her in English all the time. But the school had its protocol and wouldn't budge on the matter. Luckily, the situation was soon righted when Roxana began to speak at school and was quickly promoted to the appropriate grade level. Roxana spent weekends and holidays with Babb. She had her own room in the Queens Road house. The experience would be the closest Babb had to having a child. While Babb was not a natural mother, she took her new role seriously and even enrolled in a sewing class. As her first project, Babb sewed a ruffled pinafore for Roxana—sewing one of the sleeves on backwards. But though it wasn't natural, Babb grew into her surrogate role.

As Babb's health improved, she began to put more time and effort into her writing. In the summer of 1948, her short story "Reconciliation" was published in *The New Mexico Quarterly Review.* The story would also appear on the Roll of Honor in the 1948 *Best American Fiction* volume edited by Martha Foley, alongside short stories by fellow up-and-coming Los Angeles writers such as Ray Bradbury ("I See You Never") and Dolph Sharp ("The Tragedy of Janice Brierman's Life").[23]

When Bradbury and Sharp saw each other's work in the volume and discovered they both lived in Los Angeles, they contacted each other with the goal of forming a writing group. When they realized that Babb, too, lived in Los Angeles, Bradbury and Sharp invited her and several other Los Angeles–based writers to join them. With this,

Babb's writing group was formed. Sessions were scheduled twice a month on Friday evenings and were held alternately at various members' homes.[24] As Dolph's daughter, Elizabeth Eve King, remembered it, whoever hosted would provide a plate of cold cuts from Canter's Deli, and after they'd finished reading each other's work aloud and providing feedback, they'd laugh over drinks and sandwiches until late in the night.[25]

A few members would come and go, but the core of the group would write together and rely on each other's criticism for the next forty years.[26] Bradbury, who never drove a car, was a staple member, sometimes riding his bike or skateboard all the way up from Venice Beach to the Hollywood Hills to attend meetings. For Bradbury, and Babb, the group was deeply important. Bradbury wrote about the group's significance to him in his essay "I Get the Blues When It Rains."[27] The essay, about a night from the early days of the group but written in 1980, details a night when the group was derailed from its usual flow. It happened when the writer and musician Elliot Grennard walked by Sharp's piano and started tinkering, then began to play the song "I Get the Blues When It Rains." The room quieted to the familiar song. Bradbury recalled saying, "My God! I haven't heard that in years," then, slowly, everyone placed the manuscript they had been talking about aside and began to join in, singing along. One tune followed another. Wine was brought out and at some point, Babb sang "By a Waterfall" from the 1933 movie *Footlight Parade*. As Bradbury remembered it, the group kept drinking and singing very late into the night. "I don't remember who drove me home or how we got there. I only remember tears drying on my face because it had been a very special, very dear time, something that had never happened before and would never happen again in just that way."[28] The group would read nearly everything Babb wrote for the next forty years and become a pillar of protection and support as she fought to get her work published.

In 1943 the Chinese Exclusion Act of 1882 was repealed through the passage of the Magnuson Act, which allowed a limited number of Chinese citizens to become U.S. citizens. Due to this, Howe was able to become a naturalized citizen in 1947.[29] At the same time he decided to end his association with Warner Brothers, and he began freelancing.[30] Howe had always wanted to return to visit China, and now that he was a U.S. citizen with a passport and knew he would be able to re-enter the United States without a hassle, he decided to make the trip. On February 23, 1948, Howe left for China to do research for a film project about rickshaw pullers based on Lau Shaw's novel *Rickshaw Boy*.

Because she wasn't Roxana's full-time mother, Babb still had her independence. So while Howe was in China, Babb, who was finally again feeling well, traveled to New York to stay alone in an apartment at 212 East 16th Street to dedicate herself to her writing. She hoped to work on her third, and, she hoped, last revision of *The Lost Traveler*. The apartment did not have a phone, so she would not be disturbed. As she explains in a letter to Ellison, in New York she was "working nearly all of the time, seeing no one but my agent, the editor at Random House and one or two old friends." She goes on to explain that she has "been quite ill for the past two years, but in the period when I began to grow well, I had time to myself, the first time in my life. . . . It is like a wonderful new life to write for long hours every day here. . . . Writing has come to mean more to me than ever before, even though it has always meant much."[31]

In addition to spending time writing her novel, Babb had also been focused on further developing her narrative craft through short-story writing. In March, she finished writing a draft of her story "The Vine by the Root Embraced," and she sent Ellison a copy to read and comment back on.[32] She was proud of the work she was writing, as was her agent; however, as she told Ellison, whenever her agent tried to place her work in anything other than a literary publication, it would immediately be rejected on the grounds that her literary style did not "fit" the popular market, a fact that frustrated Babb immensely. But Babb wasn't one to give up. Instead, she stalwartly stuck to her ideas about fiction. As she expressed to Ellison, the editors "will not change and I will not change, in a way I see compromise toward the superficial and tawdry. . . . I would rather not be published at all than do some of the things editors suggest. Fortunately, for writers such as you and I and others, the magazines now and then publish a story outside of their pattern."[33]

While in New York, Babb also spent a great deal of time with her dancer friend Waldeen (Waldeen von Falkenstein, generally known as Waldeen), whom she admired for her deep commitment to her art. Babb had first met Waldeen at a Communist Party fundraiser in Los Angeles. Waldeen had been born and raised in Texas. At the age of twenty-six, she moved to Mexico City to create a national ballet and school of modern dance under the auspices of the Instituto Nacional de Bellas Artes (Fine Arts Department) at the request of the Mexican Ministry of Education.[34] Waldeen had been sent to New York to give a performance, but when she wasn't rehearsing or performing, she and Babb would meet to discuss art.

The other friend Babb took time out of her busy writing schedule to visit with was the important communist poet and editor Genevieve Taggard. Babb spent several weekends at Taggard's home, which she called Gilfeather, in East Jamaica, Vermont. Like Waldeen, Taggard inspired Babb. When she visited, Taggard and Babb listened to Debussy, "sung by the deep-voiced Maggie Teyte," and Taggard gave her pointed advice about her relationship with Howe: "You know, no matter how much you devote yourself, you are not an easy wife for any man."[35] Taggard herself had divorced her first husband, novelist Robert L. Wolf, in 1934, and married Kenneth Durant, a representative of the U.S. branch of Soviet news agency TASS, in 1935.

Meanwhile, Howe filled the distance between them with love letters written every few days while he was traveling. This trip was his first visit to his birth country since he had left at age five, and it was an emotional journey. In his native village of Bok Sar, he was treated as a celebrity. At the same time, the political situation in China was unstable; the Communist takeover was imminent. The meaningful experience of the visit, paired with the distance between himself and Babb, finally shifted something in Howe. On April 24, 1948, when Howe was forced to return from China early due to the approach of the Red Army, he returned to an empty house, as Babb was still living in New York. But instead of reacting as he would have in the past, by scolding Babb or begging her to come home immediately, Howe wrote Babb to tell her how much he finally understood her need to work and its importance in her life: "This separation has been good for me. Now I know what a wonderful person you are. . . . I am very sorry for the past lies and deceits I have caused you. I promise that never will happen again."[36]

Babb acknowledged in a letter to Ellison that Howe had "finally come to understand—and for that I have added love for him—that I cannot be contained within a relationship of two." Howe claimed he now understood Babb's need to be alone, why she took drives up the California coast, or why she would go to the planetarium where she "soothed [herself] by looking at other worlds."[37] Howe also told Babb that he was trying to understand her need to be with people besides himself.

Thanks to these changes in Howe's perception of Babb, when Babb returned from her four months of writing in New York, she agreed to move back in with Howe.[38] Both became more and more content with their relationship. About six months after they moved back in together, something momentous happened: the California Supreme Court ruling in *Perez v. Sharp*.

The case came about when Andrea Perez, a Mexican American woman, and Sylvester Davis, a Black man, tried to get married at the Los Angeles County Courthouse. The county clerk, W. G. Sharp, refused to issue a marriage license, a refusal based on California Civil Code, Section 60 ("All marriages of white persons with Negroes, Mongolians, members of the Malay race, or mulattoes are illegal and void") and Section 69 ("no license may be issued authorizing the marriage of a white person with a Negro, mulatto, Mongolian or member of the Malay race"). California's antimiscegenation statute had banned interracial marriage since 1850. When Perez sued the county clerk, Sharp, the court determined that marriage was a fundamental right and that laws restricting that right must not be based solely on prejudice. The groundbreaking decision made the California Supreme Court the first court of the twentieth century to rule that a state antimiscegenation law violated the U.S. Constitution.[39]

With the passage of *Perez v. Sharp,* marriage between Howe and Babb became legally possible, and this change in the law happened to come at a time when Babb and Howe had resolved many of the issues they'd faced in their relationship and were ready to make a commitment. Babb was finally ready to face her fears about marriage.

Babb and Howe planned to get married at the Los Angeles Courthouse (just as Perez and Davis had tried); however, they soon realized that although the law had changed, the racism that created it still held strong. For two days, the couple couldn't find a single judge who would agree to marry them. But as usual, Babb was determined and wouldn't take no for an answer. For two days, dressed in their wedding clothes, they drove to several courthouses in small towns in Los Angeles County and then Orange County, trying to find a willing judge. Finally, in the city of Hawthorne, when a secretary refused to issue them a marriage license, Babb lost her temper. She slammed her hands on the counter and screamed at the top of her lungs that she wasn't going to leave the courthouse until she and Howe were married.[40] The secretary was visibly shaken by Babb's outburst and went to the judge to inquire about the situation. When the Hawthorne courthouse secretary called the Los Angeles courthouse and found out that Babb and Howe could indeed be legally married, the Hawthorne city judge George W. Saunders agreed to marry them, but not without calling Howe a derogatory name and shaming Babb for wanting to marry him. Regardless, on September 16, 1949, Howe and Babb were finally officially married. Howe's assistant Bernard Skadron and his wife were the witnesses.

Babb and Howe tried to keep their marriage quiet, but due to Howe's celebrity status, by the next morning, their white stucco house up in the Hollywood Hills was swarming with reporters. Just before she opened the door to the onslaught, Babb realized how lived-in their house looked. No reporter would believe they hadn't lived there together before getting married, so she and Howe came up with the plan to lie about their marriage date. According to her interview with the director Daniel Mann years later, when Babb was asked by reporters how it felt to marry Howe, she said, "Well, this is the second time. We first got married in 1936."[41] The lie worked and most accounts still repeat the lie that the couple was originally married in Paris, instead of in California in 1949.

When Babb returned from New York, she sent the third draft of her novel, now called "The Cheater," to Saxe Commins at Random House. He had been reading this draft as she wrote it and kept saying "This is it!" but when she finally sent him the finished draft, he again rejected it. Babb was floored. When she went to her agent Harriet Wolf to ask what she should do, Wolf told her that "on the third rejection [she] could automatically be free of the contract if [she] wished," so Babb called it. She sent a letter to Commins and Donald Klopfer at Random House and told them she no longer wanted to have her book under contract with them.[42]

And so it was that at the end of the 1940s, Babb found herself in a very different place than she had thought she would be a decade previous. She was now living a much more domestic life: she was a married woman living with her husband and caring for a young girl. And even though she had written two novels, she was still unable to publish either of them.

14 *"Follow That Furrow"*

Babb and her now husband Howe were flown to Mexico City in the spring of 1950 by Columbia Pictures so Howe could photograph his next film, *The Brave Bulls*. The film uses a documentary style to depict the story of a matador who witnesses the death of a colleague in the ring, a terrible event that makes him lose his will to fight. The matador descends into a dark and meaningless life until he faces his fears and returns to the ring.

Like the bullfighter, Babb had relived the trauma of her childhood and the violence of her father through her invention of her novel *The Lost Traveler*. When she began writing the book, she entered a portal, a place she'd run from all her life, and being in this place made it difficult for her to tell her story. She had stumbled through three drafts and still could not publish the novel and ultimately did not feel satisfied with the book she had created. She knew that in order to finalize her book, she had to return to this darkness; the very essence of her self depended on it. Perhaps, by confronting the figure of her childhood father in her book, she'd find a lacuna, a way out of the darkness, and in it she'd find herself.

While they were on location, the couple stayed at Latino Americano Hotel in Mexico City, and Babb reconnected with her dear friend Waldeen von Falkenstein, who was now running Ballet Nacional, a small, dedicated cohort of dancers who traveled to remote regions of the country, dancing in rural schools, village plazas, stadiums, and fields. Waldeen had also begun translating *Canto General,* an epic poem by her friend the poet Pablo Neruda, and she had recently published some of her translations in a chapbook called *Let the Rail Splitter Awake and Other Poems.*[1] Babb would soon publish the first section of *Canto General* in the spring 1952 issue of *California Quarterly.*

Meanwhile, in the United States, Joseph R. McCarthy, a little-known junior senator from Wisconsin, had begun to garner attention when he claimed to possess a list of 205 card-carrying communists employed by the U.S. Department of State. Soon, the House Un-American Activities Committee (HUAC) investigations would arise, followed by acts of Congress like the 1950 McCarran Act, which equated anyone with a connection to communism with being a subversive. Members of communist organizations could be denied the right to apply for passports or the right to renew old ones. In 1947, HUAC began to investigate Hollywood, resulting in the conviction of the Hollywood Ten for contempt of Congress. The ten included a group of screenwriters, actors, directors, and musicians: Alvah Bessie, Herbert Biberman, Lester Cole, Edward Dmytryk, Ring Lardner Jr., John Howard Lawson, Albert Maltz, Samuel Ornitz, Adrian Scott, and Dalton Trumbo. By 1950 the Hollywood Ten had begun serving prison sentences. Because so many in the writing community had been associated with communism and the League of American Writers during the 1930s, the lives of hundreds of artists would be forever transformed by these actions, and many began to flee the United States for fear of being arrested. By 1951, HUAC had created a blacklist containing the names of hundreds of screenwriters, actors, and writers, and Communist Party members were being sentenced to prison.[2]

In the late 1940s, the legal reach of HUAC had been coming closer and closer to Howe and Babb and their circles of friends and colleagues. While they were in Mexico, the producer-director of *The*

Brave Bulls, Robert Rossen, came under investigation during filming, which would delay the production of the film into 1951.[3] Even before they had left Los Angeles for Mexico, the FBI had begun stopping by their home on Queens Road to investigate both Howe and Babb.

At these meetings, the agents would ask Howe questions about his association with "communist activities." In the first interviews they asked general questions. Then, as the interviews wore on and their intelligence increased, they began to ask questions that were more and more specific: Was Howe a sponsor of the "Free People's Dinner" for the Antifascist Refugee Committee given in Hollywood in July 1942? Was he a speaker at the 25th Anniversary of the Soviet Union at Shrine Auditorium on November 8, 1942?[4] The answers to these questions were of course yes, and Howe began to worry what consequence his loose involvement would cause.

Babb was also under surveillance and was interviewed by FBI agents that came to the house. Her file contains the facts of her involvement with the Communist Party: when she joined, which branch she was a part of, and a list of all of her publications with *New Masses* and other communist-related publications. But her file also notes her travel to Russia in 1935 and claims that others the FBI had spoken to said that during that visit, she "boast[ed] of having met Stalin," a claim that Babb laughed at when asked about it later in life. Why would Stalin have wanted to meet her?[5] While they were in Mexico, Babb began to think that given Howe's birthplace in China, her membership in the Communist Party, and her association with the League of American Writers, it might be in their best interest if she stayed in Mexico and lived apart from Howe for some time while they were under investigation. The scholar Alan Wald suspects her desire to temporarily relocate to Mexico was an "effort to evade a subpoena to testify before a congressional body."[6]

During the first few weeks of their visit to Mexico City, Babb explored while Howe worked on set. During the day, she basked in the warm winter sun as she walked the city streets, flashing in and out of the cold shade. The streets swarmed with traffic and her ears echoed with the sounds of horns honking and brakes screeching. Interspersed, she'd hear countless church bells, the gong-like clamor of a garbage truck bell, the steam whistle on a food cart, and the rhythmic clapping of palms shaping small rounds of masa into tortillas. At night she listened to the contrast between "police whistles" and the sound of "warm spring rains"[7] and recorded all that she experienced in her notebook.

Mexico City is located a mile and a half above sea level, so that even walking down the street made Babb's lungs burn with effort and her heart quicken. During the day she watched barefoot "children selling lottery tickets" to passersby on street corners. Once they'd earned enough pesos, the children would run into the nearby bakery to purchase steaming hot rolls and devour them on the spot. As she had in the FSA camps, Babb felt drawn toward documenting the people and landscapes around her, including the family in the lean-to across the street who kept a pig, then a goat. She cataloged the flowers she saw all over the city: bougainvillea, gladiolas, and "siempre viva," "a delicate tall bush with clusters of small . . . long, pink bell flowers . . . [that] children pop . . . like little bombs."[8]

One day while Howe was working on the set of *The Brave Bulls*, he was approached by a man named Hal Croves, who claimed to be the literary agent for the elusive writer B. Traven. Traven was the pen name of a novelist, presumed to be German, whose real name, nationality, date and place of birth, and details of biography were all secretive and subject to debate. Traven lived in Mexico and was best known for his novel *The Treasure of the Sierra Madre* (1927), which had been made into an Academy Award–winning film starring Humphrey Bogart in 1948. According to the agent—who Babb and Howe soon realized was Traven himself—Traven was interested in Howe's films. Traven and his translator, Esperanza Lopez Mateo, had dinner with Babb and Howe in Mexico City and "there was an instant rapport all around."[9] Babb remembered years later in an interview with Alan Wald how they'd finally confirmed that Hal Croves was actually B. Traven. One night when the two couples were out to dinner, after several glasses of wine, Esperanza had let Traven's "real name slip" and Traven immediately became furious. Seeing his anger, Esperanza decided it would be best for her to leave. Babb walked the visibly upset Esperanza to the busy street, where she helped her hail a taxi, and as Babb helped her get in, Esperanza looked up at her and blurted out, "He's Traven!"[10]

When Babb returned to Mexico City on her own and Traven was also staying there for a time, Esperanza, Traven, and Babb spent a great deal of time together and would "visit back and forth several times a week." As Babb recalled, when Esperanza was busy, Traven would come to visit her. Babb would continue to correspond with Traven in the decade that followed, helping him navigate getting one of his stories adapted as a play[11] and eventually publishing Traven's story "A Legend of Huehuetonoc" in the winter 1951 issue of *California Quarterly*.

In 1950, Mexico City was filled with expatriate artists who mingled with Mexico's artistic elite. Waldeen began introducing Babb to the group of artists she associated with, including the muralists David Alfaro Siqueiros and Diego Rivera, and the Chilean poet Pablo Neruda.[12] Not only was there Waldeen's circle to connect with, but there was also a larger "exile community" that included Communist Party leaders from the United States, members of the Hollywood Ten, and several artists and writers whose lives were connected to the communist community: Martha Dodd, Albert Maltz, Dalton Trumbo, Gordon Kahn, Hugo and Jean (Rouverol) Butler, Howard Fast, John Bright, Julian Zimet, and Elizabeth Catlett.[13] The group as a whole was called the "American Communist Group in Mexico," or ACGM, by the FBI. (Both Babb and Waldeen were considered ACGM by the FBI.)[14] Waldeen offered that if Babb wanted to stay in Mexico City to write, she could stay with her and her husband, the translator Asa Zatz,[15] with whom Babb was also friends. Babb said she would think about it.

By the time Howe finished production on *The Brave Bulls,* Babb had made her decision: she would return with him briefly to the U.S. and then leave again for Mexico City, staying until March 1951. After flying home with Howe, Babb stayed a short time to make sure Roxana, who was now attending UCLA, was taken care of, and then she returned to Mexico City. During her stay, she hoped to finally complete the fourth full draft of *The Lost Traveler.*

On February 28, 1950, she recorded in her journal, "I began writing poems as soon as I woke. I wrote all day, unfazed by marketing, gardening, and cooking. I neglected my book [*The Lost Traveler*]. I know they aren't good, but it was fun. I've just read *King Lear* and maybe its grandeur woke up my old mediocre talent to sing. There is a line in Lear about man being the one thing naked put upon the earth (in other words) and that got into my poem."[16] Indeed while she was in Mexico, the atmosphere created by the artists she was surrounded by, the different flora, the stories of the people she met, all contributed to her inspiration.

Babb also continued to publish her short stories. In 1950, she finally placed the story she was proudest of, "William Shakespeare," in the *Montevallo Review.* Her friend Genevieve Taggard, who helped her revise it and whose opinion she greatly admired, called the work "a masterpiece" and "a great American short story" that has "the taste of dust and . . . blind wild aspiration."[17] The horror story had been inspired by Babb's time as a schoolteacher in Kansas, when she met a child like the protagonist of the story, a child with little to no language or writing skills who nevertheless saw himself as a writer and insisted on being called William Shakespeare. The child would write endlessly in his own language on any scrap of paper he could find, but no one could understand a word that he wrote. Babb set the story in a later era than the one in which it actually happened (the 1930s instead of the 1920s) and used the terrifying backdrop of a dust storm to create a dark setting (both literarily and figuratively) in which the child ultimately turns against his advocate, his mother, and murders her for not calling him by his chosen name. The darkness of this story and its relationship with identity and publication add to its power. For wasn't Babb like the child, continually rewriting a story in her own language (the language of trauma) and sending it out to be read and understood by editors (mainly men, or people who could not begin to understand what it was like to grow up under the rule of a manipulative gambler like her father)?

Other stories she wrote were also receiving accolades. Her 1949 short story "The Wild Flower" was chosen for *The Best American Short Stories, 1950, and the Yearbook of the American Short Story,* edited by Martha Foley.[18] Additionally, the story was selected by the United Nations Literary Pool to be translated into twenty different languages.[19] Babb's short story "A Good Straight Game," about the gambling life, which Taggard found to be "a perfect story, flawlessly made,"[20] was published in *Kansas Magazine* in 1951.

Babb realized that if she was going to properly depict gambling in her novel, she would need more specific information, so she turned to her father. He wrote to her about the specifics of card marking, the very act he'd forced her to do when she was in her teens in Forgan and then again in Garden City. As he explained in his letter to her, "All cards are not marked. . . . Lots of gamblers mark their own cards . . . I always used a knife." He goes on to explain details such as how the cards are wrapped "in transparent paper" that one could purchase to re-wrap the cards after they had been marked so they looked new.[21] In her files, one finds catalogs for companies that sold these materials, along with the detailed notes she took of her father's explanations. When one reads the sections of *The Lost Traveler* in which Babb explains the protagonist Robin's role in helping her father mark cards (he needs help because he is losing his eyesight but is too vain to wear glasses), one sees her immaculate attention to detail. She wasn't just relying on her memory; she was carefully researching the field of gambling so she could bring it to life.

By October, Babb had begun to settle in and find her own identity in Mexico. She wrote to her friend Melissa Blake that she had found her own apartment. While she liked living with Waldeen and Asa, it was good to finally have her own space again. She missed her home in Los Angeles, especially her garden, and she missed Howe, but she enjoyed space to be herself. Back in Los Angeles, Howe was gray-listed and was being denied work because of his connections to the Communist Party, but gone were the days when he would write Babb begging her to come home. Since their reconciliation and marriage, she and Howe had come to an understanding about her need to be independent.

While in Mexico, Babb had the opportunity to return to a literary role she'd always enjoyed, being an editor. After the war broke out, the literary magazine she used to edit, *The Clipper,* was shut down since most of the male editors had been drafted. In Mexico she was asked to take on an editorial role at a new journal called *California Quarterly,* a role she'd hold from the magazine's inception among the literary exiles in Mexico City until the magazine's closure in 1956. The magazine was founded by Babb, Philip Stevenson, Thomas McGrath, Wilma Shore, Dolph Sharp, and Lawrence P. Spingarn based "on the conviction that more good writing will come out of the nineteen-fifties than is likely to achieve publication. . . . Contemporary writing is threatened equally by censorship and by obscurantism. . . . We hope to encourage writing that faces up to its time—writers who recognize their responsibility to deal with reality in communicable terms. . . . If we have a claim to newness, it is this moderate position in an immoderate time."[22] During its tenure, the magazine would publish a number of noted literary figures, including

Ray Bradbury, B. Traven, Pablo Neruda, Dalton Trumbo, and Meridel Le Sueur.

While in Mexico, Babb didn't stop relying on her Los Angeles-based writing group. In fact, the group kept in close contact with her through correspondence. Babb would send her new stories to the group members, and they would send back extensive comments. And each would send her their work, on which she would comment in return. They also kept each other abreast of what was happening in their literary careers. In a letter from Ray Bradbury, he explained the origin of his breakthrough science fiction short story "The Fog Horn" (which would later be the basis for a 1953 film, *The Beast from 20,000 Fathoms)*. He also praised the stories Babb sent him and gave her ideas on how to improve them. When she sent him her story "The Flying Bird of Dreams," about a young indigenous man she knew when she was working as a schoolteacher in rural Kansas, he suggested she begin the story on the first day of school to improve the story's opening.[23]

In January, Babb traveled a hundred kilometers outside Mexico City to the town of Cuautla (which means "where the eagles roam") with her friend Elizabeth Timmerman. When they arrived, Babb immediately noticed that the town lived up to its name, noting in her journal that there were "always hawks and vultures flying—sailing—over Cuautla—white edged wings." She recorded detailed descriptions of the San Diego Hotel, where they stayed: "thatched roofed huts. Rooms surround the patio—narrow 'porch' with red tule floor and tin roof—leather chairs—handmade—the old long narrow dining room with two rows of tables—each guest taking his regular seat at the table for each meal."[24] But her observations also extended to the people she encountered in Cuautla, such as the "nite workman who also worked at the mineral baths then nite at hotel sleeping few hours. Everywhere the necessity of two jobs—to survive."

When Babb and Timmerman ventured out into the city, she described the "many *farmacias* and hat stores—with the beautiful sombreros and charro hats. The cantinas. Pool hall in cantinas. Small hotels—the walls along the street with doors opening into rooms and inner patios. Old simple floor." At the city center, in the *zocalo,* she describes the "municipal building formerly a palace . . . the plaza with wrought iron benches." And all around the vendors selling their wares: "Shoeshine new. Candy sellers at night with box on head and paper 'lamp' a square of paper around a candle. Then on horseback. The small gentle ponies. Birds. Narrow streets."[25]

While visiting Cuautla, Babb took notes under the title "Story— Mexico" that soon became her short story "The Larger Cage."[26] Set in Mexico City, the story is about an eleven-year-old boy who, after his mother dies, is left on his own. The boy is modeled after the many children Babb had watched in the city and is steeped in the minutiae she had observed. The young boy, who is determined not to have to beg, is wandering the city looking for work when suddenly he sees something in the outdoor market, "the most beautiful and wonderful sight. Four small birds on a stick held by a man who was selling them to passersby. Birds he had seen, but these birds had black feathered bands across their eyes like the masks worn at a masquerade ball! They were tame and sat sweetly on the stick, permitting strangers to caress their sleek backs with tender fingers. Their wings were not clipped, and they were *tamed* and the wonder of this would not leave Rodolpho's mind or heart."[27]

The man who sells the birds sees the young boy staring at them and asks him if he'd like a job catching and selling the birds with him. The boy eagerly agrees and is taken home with the man to sleep in his house. The next day, the man takes the young boy and his other assistant out into the jungle to catch a new batch of birds with a net. The boy is exhilarated doing the work, but soon is devastated to learn the secret to taming the birds. The birds are fed just enough buckshot to ballast their tiny, light bodies so they can no longer fly. Weighed down, the birds can only listlessly await their fate: to be purchased and to die a few days later. The boy is conflicted. Morally, he is against destroying these beautiful creatures, but he needs the work, so he lives with the lie for as long as he can. For solace, he buys himself a bird from another vendor (who doesn't weight his birds with buckshot) and teaches himself how to tame it. He names his bird Pablo, and Pablo becomes his loyal companion. Then, one day, the police come to the stall where he works. A woman who purchased one of the weighted birds is irate. When the bird she'd purchased died, her son cut it open and found the bird's secret: the nest of tiny metal balls in its belly. Rodolpho's boss is arrested, but Rodolpho is able to run away. In the end, he can't return to selling the birds; instead, he leaves the city that night, walking into his uncertain future with his tame bird, "feeling not alone in the vast dark."[28]

Just as she had in Mexico City, in Cuautla, Babb lists all the new flora she sees: the Palma Royal, "tall with clusters of berries beneath the top / trunk smooth, beautiful, white, grey—cork sound" and the laurel tree with "bark smooth grey—fine grained but not as smooth as the white (grey) trunked palms." She admires how the laurel tree has "a shallow sharp root near the surface. Not deep into the earth." When she asked about a particular old tree, a local resident told her that in 1923 a massive cyclone had blown the tree over, completely uprooting it. But because the thing that made the tree so vulnerable, its shallow roots, also made it easy to regenerate, the local people were able to save it, so that it now stood as one of the oldest trees in the town. The resident explained to her that oxen were used to set the massive tree upright again and it grew.[29]

By the time Babb returned from Mexico on an American Airlines flight in March 1951, she, too, had regrown. She seemed nearly unfazed by the fact that her fourth full revision of the manuscript she was no longer calling "The Cheater" and was now calling "The Lost

Travelers"[30] had been rejected by most major publishers, including, G. P. Putnam and Sons and Holt. However, amid all of this rejection, one publisher seemed interested, the editor and writer Millen Brand at Crown. Babb had become acquainted with Brand through his association with the League of American Writers, where he had been actively involved since the 1930s, and she had recently reached out to him, asking him to submit work to *California Quarterly*. Brand's first novel, *The Outward Room,* was published in 1937 to great acclaim and was eventually adapted for Broadway in 1939 as *The World We Make.* In 1948 he'd received an Academy Award nomination for his screenplay adaptation of Mary Jane Ward's novel *The Snake Pit.* His story "The Fire at Cat Creek Bend" and poems "Great Age" and "Ralph Berky" would all eventually appear in issues of *California Quarterly.* When he heard that Babb was writing a novel, he asked her to send it to him for consideration at Crown. He read her manuscript with interest, but when he shared it with his fellow editors, they asked Babb to make extensive edits.

Babb was excited that a publisher was finally interested in her book; however, based on the comments she received, her gut told her that Crown didn't actually understand what she was trying to do. She'd already been through so much, trying through three drafts to write the book that Saxe Commins had wanted her to write. She did not want to have to pull apart her manuscript and revise it yet again. However, she felt trapped, worried that the offer might be the only one she'd receive.

Once she got back to Los Angeles, Babb put her head down and began frantically writing for six to eight hours a day, five to six days a week, to finish the edits Crown had suggested. Babb also returned to her writing group, which now gathered at Dolph Sharp's house on Tuesday nights.[31] It was there that she shared chapters of her revision, reading it aloud to her trusted group and getting immediate constructive feedback from writers she trusted. When she wasn't writing or workshopping with her writing group, she threw herself into her work as editor of *California Quarterly,* where again she perceived herself as "the workhorse," the editor who worked the hardest.

Babb encouraged everyone in her writing group to submit their work to her literary magazine and many did, including Bradbury, who sent her his short story "The Flying Machine." In the same letter in which he enclosed his story, he told her he'd received her short story "The Larger Cage" in the mail, telling her, "I'll read it and report on it to you when we have our meeting at Dolph's." But Bradbury couldn't wait to see her in person in order to tell her that he

> glanced at the first two pages. God, how evocative and beautiful your style is. Do you realize how wonderful you are? And that you should be writing at least 5 pages a day every day from now on and to hell with everything else? When will you buckle down and give all of us the Babb work that we all deserve to see? Hmm? Jesus, that you let a talent like yours get overwhelmed with other jobs and time-takers. I wish you would get the hell out of CQ and work for yourself. It's time you considered yourself, believe me!

With comments like these, it's no wonder Babb always left her workshops feeling lifted up. However, it wasn't just glowing praise that Bradbury offered Babb. Later in the same letter, he also offered expert criticism and edits that helped her shorten the time span of the story. "I hope you don't mind my going through and cutting the thing for you, here or there, and indicating where I think it needs dramatic sharpening. This is the sort of thing I do better sitting on a sofa next to the writer and peering over their shoulder, making editorial remarks."[32]

Then on March 27, 1952, tragedy struck Babb's life. She received a call from the manager of the hotel where her father lived that he had suffered a massive heart attack. Walt had been playing catch with some kids on the beach near his hotel in San Diego, then told the kids he had to leave because he was feeling ill. The kids saw him walk down the beach toward his hotel, where he went to lie down in his room. He never got up. Walt died alone in his room. He was seventy-two years old. The fact that he had heart disease wasn't a surprise. Walt had shown symptoms months before but had stubbornly refused to "waste" money on a doctor. At the time, he had told his daughter that he had been more concerned about Mexico opening up to gambling again so he could make a "bank roll" and go back on the gambling circuit in the U.S. Walt kept a trunk in his hotel room that was opened by the hotel staff when his body was discovered so that his belongings could be placed in it and returned to his loved ones. In it were all the clippings and photos that he had saved from his time as a baseball player in the Western Association and on the team in Red Rock.[33] When Babb went to the coroner to arrange her father's service, he said he'd recognized Walt's face: "Your dad was an old baseball player, wasn't he? I remember him."[34]

Babb, who had spent the last decade working on *The Lost Traveler* and dredging up all that her father had done to her, found herself completely overwhelmed by the news, both physically and mentally. While she was grateful that she and her father had developed "a good friendship" in his last years as he "patiently helped" her with all of the details of the gambling life she hadn't known or had forgotten, and that when she recalled his past cruelties, he was troubled by what he had done, his presence had still loomed over her life every second he had been alive. Now he had suddenly disappeared, leaving a vacuum, a nothingness she couldn't resolve. Her thick, naturally curly hair began to thin and fall out.[35] Then, after she'd gone through all of the horrible tasks of burying a loved one—identifying the body, making arrangements for the burial and services, and going through Walt's personal effects—her own body broke down. One month after her father's death from a heart attack, she, too, suffered a major heart attack. Babb was only forty-five years old. Thankfully, she survived. But as she later admitted, the attack "scared me and scared my doctor, and I still sometimes wonder how much truth he is telling me. He knows me pretty well after our sessions during the crack-up [the break down she had during the 1940s], and he knows that I'd rather die in my tracks than in bed." Even though the event didn't kill her, it could have, and so it had a cleansing effect that made her distinguish between the important and the unimportant things in her life. As she reflected in a letter to her friend Asa Zatz, "It was as if [the things in my life] had been tossed in the air and had come down in new places. I have always enjoyed just being alive, but I enjoy it even more now, and somehow in spite of so many problems which still plague me . . . I have a better view of them. . . . Work is more important. My concern for others even more important, but not to the exclusion of respecting myself and my work."[36] However, although her will was determined, her body remained weak from the heart attack. One week while Howe was still gray-listed and therefore taking every job he could get, including B-list films like *Jennifer,* and was away on location, Babb wrote to him about chest pains: "I had a great deal of pain in my chest all day—I worked too long Friday and Saturday nites writing all nite." Such episodes made Babb feel as if she didn't have much longer to live. In the same letter, she urges Howe to "remember I love you most and always and that I think you are wonderful and good and rare. Darling please don't stay alone."[37]

One place Babb was able to exercise her new perspective on creating boundaries in her life was in her approach to her relationship with her sister, who continued to struggle with mental health issues and alcoholism. For years, Dorothy's mental health had been deteriorating, and when her relationship with Carlos Bulosan fell apart and he moved to New York, she began drinking. While Babb was in Mexico, Dorothy had begun to send daily letters that were often fifty to sixty pages long. Babb called them "little books."[38] Dorothy had been so overwhelmed by the news of their father's death that she had sunk into a deep depression and threatened suicide. Ever since she was a small child, Dorothy had identified most with her father, and his death pushed her over the thin edge on which she'd been teetering. In addition to dealing with her father's death and suffering a severe heart attack, Babb was burdened with managing and paying for her sister's care. As she wrote to her cousin Lillie Pollard, "The heavy, heavy weight of her all the years of my life has torn me almost to bits." In many ways, Babb's heart attack made her realize the futility of being her sister's keeper. "She is like a lost cry forever appealing to me. I am so sorry for her and the life she has. . . . I have engaged in carrying water to pour down a bottomless well and it is time I stop, or lessen the heart-breaking, health-breaking 'trips.' Nothing has helped: love, affection, care, attention, concern, attempts to provide fulfillment . . . doctors . . . psychoanalysis, and my endless catering and emotional involvement."[39]

Although Babb exerted her freedom in this letter, she was still financially responsible for her sister's care. In a letter to her friend from her writing group, Esther McCoy (who became well known for her writing about modern architecture in Los Angeles), Babb recounted that she had already paid $1,800 for Dorothy's therapy sessions. As Babb explained to McCoy, "J loves me, not my whole family, and he has always said that tho D may be ill from various family problems in the past. . . she dominates me beyond all reason by her invalidism." In addition to this financial strain, Dorothy had been living with Babb and Howe until Babb's move to Mexico. Babb revealed that she was "finally driven to a breakdown with the tensions of their two jealousies, resentments, etc." and she helped her sister find a place to live on her own.[40]

It was in this tumultuous state that Babb agreed to join Howe on a trip to New York while he worked on the film *Main Street to*

Broadway. Despite being gray-listed, Howe was landing a film here and there, and he was eager to get back to work. While in New York for the summer, they stayed at the Shoreham, in apartment 7-E, on West 55th Street. As usual, now that Howe was working again, he was often away on set, leaving Babb to explore the city by herself and connect again with East Coast friends.

Even in the state Babb was in prior to traveling to New York, she had not given up on her first manuscript, *Whose Names Are Unknown,* and feeling that she didn't know how long she had to live, she considered telling her agent about it. She only had the one copy she'd finally gotten back from Ellison and no longer felt comfortable sending around the tattered first draft so many had commented on, so before she left for New York, she asked her friend Melissa Blake if she could pay her to type a new copy. Blake agreed and while she was typing it, she fell in love with Babb's work. As she wrote to Babb in New York, "I know that this is not a very good time for you to consider what to do with this, with the other getting itself ready for publication, but I simply must urge you strongly to do something with it, as soon as you possibly can, because the dust storms have come again, to this same place, and while that is horrible, it may mean that this wonderful novel will not remain unpublished." Blake saw the importance of Babb's unique perspective about the natural disaster of the Dust Bowl: "The publication of such a moving account of this dread scourge might move public opinion to demand some sensible form of prevention of future occurrences of this 'natural' disaster." She ended her letter with a plea: "Please don't stop trying to get it published."[41]

One day Babb and her agent Harriet Wolf took a long walk down 55th Street. As their feet fell against the hot New York City pavement, the two discussed what Babb should do with *The Lost Traveler.* Babb was at odds with Millen Brand's wish that she completely revise it yet again. She'd already been through the torturous process of revising the novel three times with her previous editor at Random House, only to have to leave and find a new publisher, and now she worried she was following the same path with Brand. She had spent six months revising the manuscript based on his suggestions and now, instead of being happy with the work she had done, he was asking her for another revision. In fact, he was asking her to do things that didn't make sense to her. In the end, Babb asked Wolf whether she thought Brand actually understood her novel. In many ways, Babb was hoping that Wolf would say no, Brand didn't understand her work and she should try to place the novel somewhere else. But instead, Wolf assured Babb that Crown was a good fit. As Wolf would emphasize in a letter, "I do not think you are making a mistake in signing on with Crown. . . . I believe you will get as fair a deal with Crown as you will get anywhere, besides which you will be assured patient and painstaking editorial consideration . . . something which is very rare I assure you."[42]

As well as meeting with her agent, Babb spent time absorbing the literary culture of New York. As luck would have it, Dylan Thomas was in town, performing a read-through of his play *Under Milkwood* to an audience of over 3,000 people at the 92nd Street Y on May 14, 1953. Babb was so moved by his work that she waited in line for hours afterward so she could speak with him. There was something about the incantation of his voice as he commanded, "Time passes. Listen. Time passes. Come closer now" that drew on darkness she'd been moored in since her father had died and her own heart had failed. In November, when Thomas died, she mourned him as if he had been a friend.

Around the time of Thomas's death, *Harper's* published excerpts from Virginia Woolf's last diaries, collected and edited by her husband, Leonard Woolf, in *A Writer's Diary,* and Babb, who had now become hyperaware of death, was struck by some Woolf's last words: "I walk over the marsh saying, I am I: and must follow that furrow, not copy another. That is the only justification for my writing, living."[43] These words, along with Thomas's haunting incantation, offered Babb another definition of how she wished to live her writer's life now that she didn't know how long she had to live. At the end of 1953, she stood on a precipice. Her father, the man who had loomed over her life since she was a child, was gone. From his death, she had almost died too. Somehow, their twin deaths, his real, hers near, had dislodged her, had made her see the furrow of life in front of her in a new way, without his shadow looming over it. The deaths had sowed in her an even greater need to finally finish and publish her book.

15 "I Do Not Wish to Be Less than I Am"

Late at night, Babb sat at her desk, surrounded by piles of books, writing a letter to Millen Brand. Outside, the moon shone down over her garden, the place she'd gone for solace after Brand's letter had arrived in the mail that afternoon. No matter the season, her garden was always full of new growth, and the bird seed she scattered there kept it equally filled with black phoebes, finches, and hummingbirds. As she and her agent had decided on their walk down Fifth Avenue, Babb had sent both her latest revision of *The Lost Traveler* and the new, clean copy of *Whose Names Are Unknown* to Brand when she returned to Los Angeles. The letter revealed that Brand saw the potential of *Whose Names Are Unknown*, especially given the dust storms that had again descended on the Midwest, but just as he had with *The Lost Traveler*, he didn't like the manuscript the way it was and asked for substantial edits. He and his colleagues had ideas about how they'd like to modernize *Whose Names Are Unknown* so that it would be more palatable to 1950s readership, by setting the novel in the present time and recrafting her original novel as a flashback. In addition to this, Brand told Babb that she would have to revise the last third of *The Lost Traveler* again for them to even consider publishing it. This time, Babb wouldn't give in to his editorial strong-arming. Standing in her garden that afternoon, netted by bird song, she'd made the decision to walk away from this publishing house. She had a truth she wanted to tell and if Brand didn't see it, she would find someone who would.

As the night progressed, Babb took out another sheet of crisp white paper and rolled it into her typewriter to begin composing a letter to her agent, Wolf. Sitting there thinking about what she would write to her, she must have wondered why her agent had advised her to continue with Crown even though it was clear they didn't understand what Babb was trying to do as a writer. In her letter, she told Wolf that Brand's letter had been "one more blow after a series of blows this month. . . . The worst is even acceptance [of *Lost Traveler*] depends on the new revision." As she further explained, "Their suggesting a happier end for Stevie [the protagonist] and what I think is an entirely superficial reason for Des' leaving seems to me to have more to do with sales than literature."[1] It was edits like these that made her realize that Crown wanted to make her book into something she didn't wish it to become. Babb went on to tell Wolf that she believed that *The Lost Traveler* was finished, and she asked Wolf to read it so she could advise her on which publishers to next send it to. Babb told her she had "no time for a rewrite and my health would not permit racing for another deadline on the mere assumption that the editors might like it. . . . I am still suffering from the effects of making the last deadline. It is a little difficult right now to face writing a long novel for the fifth time, especially when this one is such a near miss."[2] She went on to explain that she didn't think that Brand even understood the book she was trying to write.

When Wolf received this fifth version of *The Lost Traveler,* she read it as Babb asked and responded almost immediately, telling Babb her manuscript was "a delight. . . . You have done an amazing job cutting and reorganizing so that the story moves with mounting emotion to the inevitable end. I read it as if it were brand new to me and enjoyed every bit."[3] Thrilled by her agent's reaction, Babb stood her ground against the drastic restructuring the Crown editors had requested. Once again, Babb chose to follow the furrow of her own voice, writing back to Wolf, "Here are my reactions to [Crown's suggested] changes: This time I believe I am not wrong to say that I shall make *no major changes,* no complete rewrite. Minor ones, yes. I wish to improve my book all I can. . . . It is not that I am afraid of work, I think you know this; for once in my long career of torturing doubts, I feel I did what I wanted with the book, knew what I was doing, and that it is the best I can do at this stage of my life as a writer."[4] When Wolf writes back to explain that Babb can't send the book elsewhere until her contract with Crown is broken, Babb tells her, "I decided, as you see, against making any revisions and resubmitting the book to Crown. This seemed to me . . . clearly a waste of time. A cool reading of the letter shows that those editors missed my book so badly that that is not the place for me. . . . The book would end a watered-down version of whatever it is now. I do not wish to be less than I am."[5]

After much back and forth, Wolf finally relented and agreed to send Babb's work to additional publishers.[6] Over the next six months, Babb's manuscript of *The Lost Traveler* was again rejected by Harper, Houghton Mifflin, Harcourt Brace, Simon & Schuster, Knopf, and Doubleday. Babb was so confident in the book's shape that she even tried sending it to Random House again, but Saxe Commins remained uninterested in Babb's novel as she conceived it. After another steep wave of rejections, Babb's self-doubt began to seep back in, and she told Wolf she was worried she wasn't a writer at all because she hadn't yet published a book. A worry began to rise in her: what if her first book didn't come out before she turned fifty in 1957? How could she have struggled so long as a writer and have nothing to show for it? Wolf tried to reassure Babb, but after over a decade of defeat and rejection, it was difficult for Babb to keep a positive attitude.

To lift her spirits, Babb turned to her literary community for advice. When she shared her plight with her co-board member at

California Quarterly, Tom McGrath, he reminded her to stick to her own ideas about her book. "I think you should go on writing the way you want to write; it is all anyone can do. It is what I do, and the fact that I didn't do it earlier has made me a late-blooming flower, if I can manage to bloom at all."[7]

While Babb's writing career remained stymied by editors in 1954, Howe's career began to emerge from the plague of the gray list. Sun Pictures offered him a promising assignment on a new film based on a Broadway play by the Pulitzer Prize–winning writer Tennessee Williams called *The Rose Tattoo.* Soon, Howe was off on assignment filming in the Florida Keys. This assignment would not only be lucrative, but it would also be the film for which Howe would achieve his first Academy Award. But just as their financial picture began to improve, another drastic emergency hit their family.

Dorothy, who'd stopped therapy and begun to drink heavily since their father died, tried to commit suicide, and nearly succeeded, ending up barely clinging to life on a respirator at Los Angeles County General Hospital. Babb was of course terribly upset about almost losing her sister. But she was also upset that the event would force her to focus back on taking care of her sister both financially and physically. She complained to Melissa Blake that she had to sell her jewelry to pay her sister's hospital bills. In addition to this, Babb also had to resign from her role as editor at *California Quarterly* and begin looking for full-time work. Once Dorothy had recovered enough to leave the hospital, Babb found a residential recovery program for her sister in Escondido, where she would stay for seven months. At the end of those seven months, Dorothy was sober and in much better physical health. As Babb would explain in a letter to Dorothy's former boyfriend, Carlos Bulosan, "Dorothy is still in a chaotic process of change, finding the way to change slow and hard, but at last making the effort. . . . [Dorothy] looks lovely again; she does not drink, and I hope she never will again; and she is living in a way to build her health."[8]

Despite these personal struggles, and despite the negative feed-back she received, Babb did not choose to give up on her own writing. She kept imagining the future she saw for herself as a young girl in Eastern Colorado, suffering under the chaotic rule of her father. There she saw her future in the vast pull of the sky overhead, the never-ending horizon. She saw herself as a writer then and there, and somehow that vast stretch of sky taught her the endurance she needed to get through—how to stay with the pain of writing about her experiences, how to live in the danger of her childhood until she finished her book. Many might think her fortitude crazy. Most would have given up, but not Babb. She knew what she wanted her book to be, and she worked toward that goal. She revised, but this time she revised toward that truth instead of an editor's ideas as to what her book should become. She kept writing and writing through long hours, her heart still weak, for eight long months. Howe was still not supportive of her career. She wrote late into the night until the sky began to lighten and the dawn chorus began to awaken in her garden. Finally on May 12, 1954, she finished what she thought would be the last draft (the fifth full draft) of *The Lost Traveler.*

She was so sure that this was her final draft that immediately after she finished, she wrote a long, emotional letter to her mother, Jennie Kemper. She was already, at this point of completion, planning her next novel (a revision of *Whose Names Are Unknown*) and told her mother that she had "the first draft done of the Baca County Book, but the part of it that takes place in California I shall now take out and write new, staying in CO. The California section is good, but the material is dated in this time; later it might not be. Too early. It is odd that this book broke my heart not to be published because. . . *The Grapes of Wrath* came out first, but here are the terrible dust storms again."[9] Indeed, dust storms had returned to the areas around the panhandle, and many were worried that measures that had been taken to save the land after the last disastrous droughts and dust storms had not worked. As photojournalist Margaret Bourke-White wrote in her May 1954 *LIFE* article, "Two decades after the nation's worst drought year in history, 1934, the southern plains were again officially labeled by the U.S. government with two familiar words— 'Dust Bowl.'"[10]

In the same letter, Babb also took the time to explain to her mother who each character in *The Lost Traveler* was based on, and she confessed that she wished her father had lived to see the book in print. As she'd later recall, "He used to say, 'Hurry up and get that book done; I'm not going to live forever.'"[11] She admitted to her mother how much her father had helped her with the details in the book's gambling scenes. She also made a point of telling her mother that she had decided to dedicate the book to her friends instead of her family or Howe, who, she claimed, "is only recently beginning to take an interest in my writing, to appreciate the hard work it is, and the writing that emerges from the work. It is the truth that he did not believe in me until he saw my work in print, or until in NY at various times, he learned that quite a lot of people had read my stories, that I had a small distinct 'standing' as a short story writer, that he might believe in me without embarrassment." It was to her mother that she was most honest about Howe's lack of support of her writing, how his inability to see her as a writer without a book in print had deepened the insecurities she'd developed over the last two decades as she'd tried to publish her first two novels. But when she closed this important letter, Babb left her mother with her current mindset, the mindset of courage, and gladness, and an imagined future in which she wanted to live, telling her, "I am going to keep right on writing books. I regret that I didn't get an earlier start; I could have a number of books by now."[12]

When Jennie read her daughter's manuscript, she admitted, "The book was so real, and it almost put me in bed for weeks reliving the past my dear. I think how tame it was in the book to some of the things I really went through and both of you, too. . . . I think of sleeping all night with gun in my ribs shot at over my head when you were in Laurence. Footprints on my chest kicked three ribs broken in G.C. Red Rock [kicked] in the head till my ear bled. . . . I can't see how I did it."[13] Babb later recalled how her mother had said that her novel's treatment of her father's cruelty was "mild compared to our real experience . . . his colossal vulgarity and insensitivity. . . . He was violent and brutal—his answer to almost everything was physical beating and verbal, vulgar shouting the like of which you never hear." Babb's mother was beaten so badly, so many times, that she was sure the abuse had "affected her personality for life."[14]

Through all of the hard work on her novel, however, Babb had also continued to write in her preferred genre, short stories. Many of the stories were small sections of *The Lost Traveler* that she had refashioned. She also continued to bring short stories to her writing group every other Tuesday night. Her trusted group had helped her improve "The Tea Party," and in March 1956, Wolf gave Babb the incredible news that this story had somehow broken through into the commercial market: *Seventeen Magazine* had accepted it, and Babb was paid $225 for its publication.[15] Her story is about a young girl named Holly (a character based on Babb's sister Dorothy and her battles with agoraphobia), who was so devastated by having been stood up by a boy for the autumn dance that she is unable to leave her home. The other main character is an old woman named Mrs. Polk, who, like Charles Dickens's famous character Miss Havisham from *Great Expectations,* always dresses for and remains stuck in an elegant moment from her past. Mrs. Polk wears her old beaded evening dresses and Holly, seeing her in these tattered, dirty dresses, muses that her "youth must have been filled with evening dresses, but after that, who knows when or why, time, for her, had stopped."[16] One afternoon, Mrs. Polk invites Holly and her mother over for a tea party at her home. Since the outing is just next door, Holly is able to leave the house at her mother's urging. They are both intrigued because neither had ever been inside their neighbor's house. Mrs. Polk leads them to her decrepit house, where time has indeed stopped and everything is covered in dust. Babb expertly employs gothic elements that set the tone for this final scene. Seeing Mrs. Polk frozen in time awakens Holly from the stasis she's been stuck in, and she is finally able to leave the house and move on with her life. The publication of "The Tea Party" in such a commercial market lifted Babb, too, out of the stop-time she'd been stuck in. It gave her the courage to again imagine that her novel would one day find a publisher that would help her find her audience.

Babb's agent Wolf sent a carbon copy of *The Lost Traveler* to an agent in London named Patience Ross, who was interested in trying to place Babb's materials in the English market. Wolf had originally advised Babb against publishing with an English press before she placed her book with an American press; however, given the trouble she faced finding an American publisher, Wolf changed her advice. Ross immediately wrote to Babb to tell her she greatly enjoyed reading her work and thought she would have no problem placing Babb's novel in the English market.

But as Wolf continued to send out the latest draft of *The Lost Traveler* to American presses, and no offers came in, Babb began to think that she might need a new agent. When Wolf wrote to inform Babb that she was closing her business, Babb was relieved. She traveled to New York and hired a new agent, Mary Abbott. Abbott immediately encouraged Babb to send her work to a new round of publishers that she'd carefully hand-picked after reading Babb's manuscript and realizing that many of the male editors at the big houses would not relate to the strong female protagonist, the abusive father, or the explicit descriptions of a gambler's life. Abbott knew what she was doing, and when she sent *The Lost Traveler* to Eugene Reynal at Reynal & Company, to Babb's utter and complete surprise, he wrote back almost immediately to say how much he enjoyed reading *The Lost Traveler* and to ask if it was still available.

Since Abbott was a new agent to Babb, Babb had to explain to her the magnitude of what this offer meant. She had to fill Abbott in on the long and tedious journey she'd traveled since 1939: first the heartbreaking loss of the contract with Random House for *Whose Names Are Unknown,* and then the decade of revisions and editorial mishaps she'd had with *The Lost Traveler.* Babb was floored by the news that she might finally have a publisher. Reynal followed up to say he only wanted her to make some minor edits and was eager to publish the book either in the fall of 1957 or spring of 1958. It was real. So real. And Babb could not believe it.

To celebrate, Babb and Howe traveled to the desert resort of Palm Springs for a ten-day holiday during which Babb ignored mail and the pull of the new edits and just relaxed under the desert sun. While she was there, she decided to buy herself a piece of jewelry to commemorate the acceptance of her first book. In a shop in Palm Springs, she saw a Zuni squash blossom necklace in a glass case. When she placed the piece around her neck, the weight and heft of the silver and the turquoise stones felt symbolic of the traumatic journey she'd traveled to publishing her first book. Babb was fifty years old and had fought to publish a book for over twenty years. She'd unearthed stories about her past that had nearly killed her. Turquoise represents a connection between heaven and earth, and when she slipped the squash blossom necklace around her neck, Babb experienced a solid counterweight against the longing she'd felt looking up at the sky as a young child in Eastern Colorado. Howe took a photograph of Babb wearing her new necklace, her face raised in joy toward the desert sky. In this photograph, one can clearly see relief written across her face. The past that she had been carrying, that she had been wrestling with, had finally been put down on the page. She had accomplished what she'd been trying to do her entire writing life. She would finally publish her first book.

16 The Lost Traveler

Once Babb returned from the healing days in the desert, she and Reynal began to work through the small changes he'd asked for, and by fall Babb had sent him a completed draft: the sixth and final revision of *The Lost Traveler.* For the first time, she'd found an editor who liked the edits she'd made and who seemed to understand her vision of the book. Reynal loved what she had done and told her to plan for a spring 1958 publication. *The Lost Traveler* would be published in March, a month before Babb would turn fifty-one years old. As it turned out, she did not make her own deadline for publishing a book *before* she was fifty, but the emotion of the moment helped her let that imaginary deadline go.

The next few months were a whirlwind of letters back and forth between Babb and Reynal about copy edits and cover designs. Then, on March 2, Babb received copies of her book in the mail, along with posters and other marketing materials. As she wrote to Reynal in an emotional letter that he later told her moved him deeply, the act of opening the box and seeing her physical novel in print left her "overwhelmed. So many good things! I am terribly pleased. I can hardly believe any of this yet."[1]

The final version of *The Lost Traveler* was greatly changed from the earliest drafts Babb wrote in the early 1940s. Instead of being centered on Robin's character (the character based on Babb's own experiences), the book's point of view moves among the members of the Tannehill family: Robin, Des (based on Babb's father), Stevie (based on Babb's sister Dorothy), and Belle (based on Babb's mother). Babb no longer begins the book at Robin's high school graduation, where she was denied the honor of valedictorian because of her father's career as a gambler. Instead, the event is referred to in the first few pages by Robin's father and mother. In this version, we begin thick in the family drama, a drama dominated by the gambling father, Des Tannehill.

The Tannehills live in "a flat, sandy town" (much like Forgan) where "no trees shaded the unpaved streets and meandering paths, and the small houses sat on their bare yards in ugly nakedness."[2] Stevie is "curled up on the bed, surrounded by thin white catalogues ... utterly absorbed in mapping out her life." Sixteen-year-old Robin "was painting the last big numbers in the field of the canvas Do-or-Don't layout, a gambling spread" her father would use to cheat a bunch of farmhands in a dice game. Even though Robin is helping her father, Des chastises her for "going around naked as a bird's ass" and calls her "a whore." When he sees her anger rise in reaction to his words, he passes his abuse off as a joke. Des's verbal and physical abuse of his daughters and his wife is abundant in this book. In this first chapter, the two daughters are contrasted. Stevie, who adores her father, is subservient and studious, while Robin is described as someone who is "independent as a man."[3]

Robin's character is deeply at odds with contemporary portrayals of female gender norms in 1950s America. As the scholar Doug Wixson points out in his introduction to *The Lost Traveler,* in the "'Silent Decade' domestic order and happiness are managed by a self-sacrificing mother and teenage daughters who extend the mother's role, participating in household work, making the home a comfortable place for father, and preparing for marriage."[4] Robin, on the other hand, does not want to get married. Instead, she seeks freedom and equality (traits that were more acceptable for women to possess and express in prewar America). We see her express this wish in her first conversation with Blackie, Des's partner, who soon becomes Robin's lover:

> "You are all girl," he said after looking at her a long time, "but you have on boy's clothes. Do you want to be a boy?"
>
> "No. I want to be a woman. It's an old idea. A lot of wonderful women have tried it."
>
> "Are you being sarcastic?
>
> "No, I'm serious. Women don't have to imitate men. I like men, but women should be themselves, equal and different."[5]

It's no wonder that an independent character like Robin, who secures a job at the local paper as a reporter well before her eighteenth birthday, rejects the idea of gender that is presented to her: stay where you are, find a nice boy, and marry him.

In *The Lost Traveler,* Babb was also not afraid to include intimate sex scenes between seventeen-year-old Robin and Blackie. Instead of watching a girl passively lose her virginity to a much older lover, we witness the awakening of Robin's sexual hunger: her erect nipples and her feeling of being "exactly herself" when she takes off her clothes to climb into bed with her naked lover. Then, after, instead of feeling shame, Robin revels in her experience: "Oh, such a pure delight of body and spirit! Let it never end! And when it did end, she was still submerged, floating slowly up, from deep primeval waters. When she looked at him, she was shining with sensuous and reverent feelings. She could not speak but could only lie close and feel, feel her quivering flesh, her bewitched emotions, her soaring mind."[6]

One sees details of Babb's parents' marriage woven into the characters of Des and Belle. Des's cruelty toward his wife is immediately evident (at the end of the first chapter. he forces her to cut her long hair into a bob, and he continually calls her dumb). By the fifth chapter, the family has relocated to Apache, Kansas (based on a combination of Garden City, Kansas, and Forgan, Oklahoma) the setting where the rest of this *roman d'initiation* takes place. It's Babb's description of this town that immediately draws the reader in. The tree-lined town is situated between "vast flat lands whose surface undulated in spring with the green of wheat and in summer with its yellow ripeness"[7] and is divided by a line of the Santa Fe railroad. On one side of the tracks is "Dirty Spoon," where the town's Black and poor white residents live, and on the other side are Main street and the rest of the town. The Tannehills live in "Dirty Spoon" and Des is infuriated that they are living next door to Black families, a feeling Robin doesn't share. Soon, Des has set up shop in "The Royal" (based on the Windsor Hotel in Garden City) and paid off local law enforcement.

As the novel progresses, Babb not only challenges female stereotypes and gender norms, but she also challenges the reader's ideas of what a gambler is. Des is portrayed as cruel yet intelligent. At one point, he quotes Greek myths even as he sinks into a downward spiral caused by his addiction to gambling. Babb also gives an accurate view of what it was like to be Black and living in a small midwestern town in the 1920s and 1930s. When the Tannehills move into a house in "Dirty Spoon" they are neighbors to a Black family, and though Des is adamantly against it, both Robin and Stevie become close friends with Chris (the character Babb based on Ralph Ellison), the young Black man who lives next door. The intimate and nonsexual relationship between Robin and Chris begins with "a shared love of literature" and grows into one based on "intellectual parity and deep emotional connection."[8]

In the end, Robin rejects Blackie's proposals for marriage: "What do I want with a nest?" she asks. "I want some wings!"[9] As scholar Erin Royston Battat points out, Robin "rejects patriarchal social norms by asserting economic and sexual freedom despite the social costs."[10] By developing her character in this way, Babb shows Robin's wish to become economically independent. To achieve this she steers from the norm and promises not to get married "until I know how to support myself. And a long time after that."[11] When Robin flees from her father's rampage, Chris is the one who finds her hiding down by the creek and brings her home, even though he puts himself at great risk by doing so and soon loses his job for being seen with a white girl. In the end, Robin escapes her father's abusive cycles, but it's telling that when she does, she takes her sister with her.

On March 20, 1958, after twenty years of waiting, after writing two novels, and after revising one of them five times, Babb finally saw *The Lost Traveler* officially published by Eugene Reynal at Reynal & Company. That same day, Babb's novel was also reviewed in *The New York Times* by critic Charles Poore: "Miss Babb has given us a living and unflinchingly honest picture of a wandering gambler and his family. This is her first novel, and she shows herself to be a searching storyteller."[12] When her friend Ray Bradbury saw her book reviewed in the *Times,* he immediately sent her an encouraging letter: "I bought the NYTIMES to read your review! I'm so happy for you! It's so important to appear here! Also, saw your lovely picture in the window at Hunter's [Bookstore]! Beautiful! As I said, it should be on the front cover of the book! Happy sales!"[13] Thanks to the hard work of her English agent, Patience Ross, to Babb's utter joy, her novel was also released in England in 1958 by Victor Gollancz. It was a banner year for Babb, one in which she felt all her hard work and fortitude had paid off.

Directly following her book's release, Reynal arranged for Babb to go on a local publicity tour in the Los Angeles area with his colleague Errett Stuart, who lived nearby. After the thrill of her first day of autographing copies at a bookstore, Babb came home and lay in her bed pulsing with joy. As she stared up at the ceiling, she tried to ground herself. She couldn't believe her book was real and out in the world for others to read.[14] For the next few weeks, she and Stuart traveled through the Los Angeles area in the pouring rain, going from one bookstore to the next. She visited Pickwick in Hollywood and Marian Hunter's in Beverly Hills, where her book was given full display windows next to a poster-sized photograph of her. As she wrote to her New York agent Mary Abbott, "It doesn't seem real to me!"[15]

To promote *The Lost Traveler* Babb was invited to be interviewed on the TV program *A Cavalcade of Books* and claimed she was "scared half to death" because although she was married to a cinematographer, she "dislik[ed] being filmed and interviewed."[16] She said that Aldous Huxley, who was also on the program, "was as calm as if he were sitting in his living room, but . . . he later admitted . . . that he used to be paralyzed at any public utterance."[17] Would she ever get used to this type of attention? She didn't know. But she was happy to ride this emotional wave of success.

In April, Eugene Reynal traveled to the West Coast and Babb and Howe met him for lunch. The following evening, Babb threw him a small dinner party at their home. Over cocktails, Reynal praised *The Lost Traveler* and Babb sat back and smiled as she sipped her glass of wine. At his insistence, she'd given him a copy of *Whose Names Are Unknown* to read; however, he admitted during his visit that he found the work "dated." To salvage the manuscript, he suggested, as Crown had, that she convert it into a present-day "farm novel" that used scenes from the book as flashbacks. His words were disappointing, but Babb didn't let them hinder the joy she was still feeling about the publication of *The Lost Traveler.* When Reynal asked what her next novel would be about, she told him that right now she was focusing on writing short stories. He suggested she write a book from the point of view of Robin from *The Lost Traveler,* starting at age twenty-one and carrying on for another twenty years. He told her the experiences she'd lived through, her political involvement with the Communist

Party during the 1930s, and her interracial marriage with Howe were extraordinary, and he encouraged her to write a book about these topics. But as Babb later admitted to Abbott, she had no desire to return to writing about her own life: "I'm so tired of my experience."[18] Babb had grown away from the Communist Party after World War II mostly, according to Doug Wixson, because she felt it was no longer progressive.[19] Ironically, it was this personal experience that she would turn to when she wrote her next book.

Even after Babb had published her first book, Howe was unable to prioritize her role as a writer over her duties as a wife. Over the summer, Howe's relatives came to visit, and while Howe was busy working on set down at the studios, Babb took on the role of hostess and tour guide, taking them to all the tourist spots in Los Angeles, including the La Brea Tar Pits. Due to this activity, she couldn't return to her writing desk or to the important task of promoting her book until late September, when the visitors finally left.

In May, Babb's review of Ann Stanford's long dramatic poem *Magellan*, "Poem-Play Tells Saga of Explorer Magellan," was published in the *Los Angeles Times*. Afterward, Stanford reached out to her asking if she'd like to do a reading with her at a Beatnik-style espresso house on the Sunset Strip called the Unicorn.[20] That October, the two performed in Los Angeles's first coffeehouse, just a few doors down from where The Doors would take the stage a few years later, Babb reading from her new novel and Stanford reading her poems.

That fall, the University of California at Los Angeles asked Babb to teach a short-story class once a week beginning October 13 and running through January 12. Babb felt pressured to take the work because of the amount of money she was spending on her sister's care. She knew these costs were troublesome to Howe, and she wanted to pay them herself. When she explained her situation to Abbott, she said she would try "not to let [the teaching] interfere with writing except on that night. . . . This has been an extremely difficult year and I need the money."[21] She received $318 for teaching the course.[22] However, her goal of not letting the teaching take over her writing was futile. Babb, ever the workhorse, took her job teaching very seriously, typing up her lectures in advance on topics that ranged from "Story Action" to "Time Elements in the Short Story" to a final class on "Writers' Inventory, Discipline, Preparing Manuscripts, Markets and Submitting."[23]

But even as she was teaching her course on the short story, Babb returned to her writing desk, at least to write and edit her short fiction. Through working with her writing group, she was able to write and revise another story that she sold to a commercial market: "The Santa Anas" was bought by *The Saturday Evening Post* for $1,000. Babb was not only thrilled by the huge readership her work would reach, but also, on a more practical level, by the fact that the $1,000 could be used to pay for "several months of my sister's living expenses."[24] She also used $100 to pay back some of the $250 advance she had received from Crown when they gave her the initial contract for *The Lost Traveler*, and she was relieved to find out that based on this payment, on November 3, 1958, Crown canceled the remaining $150 she owed.

By late September 1958, the thrill of publishing her first novel had begun to dim. Yes, she had a book out, finally. But though she had received good reviews, and even gotten a review in the *New York Times*, her book was not selling well enough. Reynal wrote to tell her that so far only three thousand copies of *The Lost Traveler* had sold (out of an initial print run of six thousand copies in March), making, as Babb wrote to her agent, "the picture" not "awfully bright" regarding the success of her first book.[25] Babb was distraught. She began to notice that even her local bookstores were no longer carrying her novel.

Babb's relationship with Howe remained complicated. Since their marriage and her heart attack, she no longer sought sexual relationships outside of their marriage. Staring death in the face had made her realize that she did want to have a partner, and she began to place more emphasis on catering to Howe's needs. Despite their previous agreements about Babb's need for independence, Howe had a very traditional idea of marriage, and he expected Babb to take care of all the details of their life. The arrangement was at odds with Babb's writing life, but she had a deep love for Howe, and she wanted their marriage to work.

On March 26, 1956, the 28th Academy Awards were held at RKO Pantages Theatre and Howe received his first Academy Award for Best Cinematography for *The Rose Tattoo,* solidifying his reputation as one of the best cinematographers in Hollywood. Even more monumental was the fact that he was the first Asian American to win an Academy Award. Babb attended the ceremony with him, but when Howe walked up to the microphone to offer thanks for the award, he only thanked the studios. He did not thank his wife. Two years later, in the fall of 1958, after Babb had published her first book, Howe, like many of the men of his generation, still assumed her first job was to be his wife. Babb, though independent and driven, complied, but not without complaint. In a letter to her agent, Abbott, she confessed, "It seems to me being a good wife (which seems to include business manager, etc.) means being a spare-time writer."[26] Babb was conflicted. How would she balance her marriage with her writing?

What the young Babb saw in the sky as a girl growing up in extreme poverty in Eastern Colorado offered the motivation she needed to get to this point in her life, no matter the cost, no matter how difficult the road had become. And she had succeeded. But the next phase of her life would ask her to descend back into the darkness of the dugout in which she grew up and not only witness what she lived through, but also find a voice in which to tell it.

17 *"Dust on [Her] Own Hills"*

As Sanora Babb descended the small plane's staircase onto the tarmac in Vienna, Austria, on Wednesday, April 29, 1959, she was greeted by strobes of camera lights flashing. Was there a movie star on the plane behind her? she wondered as she slipped on her "Hollywood" sunglasses and smiled for the cameras.[1] At the bottom of the stairs, she saw Howe waiting for her. He'd already been in Vienna for several weeks on location for the film *Song without End: The Story of Franz Liszt* for Columbia Pictures. Two weeks before, Babb had flown from Los Angeles to New York, where she'd spent time meeting with her agent Mary Abbott before boarding her first transatlantic flight to London. At their meeting, Abbott had begun pressuring Babb to consider writing an autobiography about the extraordinary experiences she'd had in her early childhood. But Babb, still tired out by writing about her "experiences" in *The Lost Traveler*, refused.

Flying from New York to London at forty thousand feet, she looked out of the plane's small window at the moon and the stars. She had come so far from seeing the contents of the sky from the flat plains of her childhood in Eastern Colorado. Now, she finally had a book out and she was soaring in the air at eye level with the celestial objects she'd once only seen from the ground. As she would recall in a letter to her writing group, "When the stars and the moon were *out there* instead of *up there,* the sensation was one of flying in the stars."[2]

When she landed in London, Babb spent the week connecting with old friends she'd known when she lived there in the 1930s and meeting with her British agent, Patience Ross, and her British publisher, Victor Gollancz, about her next book. While in London, she was "given a week's stay at the Westbury" and she left her collection of stories with Ross in hopes that Osyth Leeston, the editor at *Cornhill Magazine,* might find a story or two she'd like to take for publication.[3] Babb had turned her thoughts towards writing her next novel, but she was still struggling to find a topic. She had several stories partially written and "what may be a short novel started."[4] But every time she began, something she got stuck. Like Abbott, Gollancz and Ross agreed that instead of writing another novel, they wanted Babb to try to write an autobiography. Autobiographies had become popular, but Babb didn't really understand what gave her authority to write one. As she told Ross in a letter, she hadn't "digested [the idea of writing an autobiography] yet. It was my idea that one had to be old and famous for that sort of book"[5]—neither of which Babb felt she was. Still, the repetition of the idea of writing a straight autobiography had made it flutter in her mind like a possibility. Now, she couldn't get it out of her mind.

When Babb reached the bottom of the airplane's stairs, she kissed Howe on the lips and the cameras exploded. Their kiss would be featured in the European papers without focus on the fact that they were an interracial couple, as the focus would have been in the United States. Howe was considered a celebrity in Europe, where he received less racist coverage in the papers. When the reporters swooped in to ask Howe questions, Babb recalled that she was grateful that instead of just introducing her as his wife, as he used to, Howe now "said [she] was a writer and mentioned [her] book."[6] Behind Babb, on the stairs, stood the English star of the film, Dirk Bogarde;

the cameras quickly redirected towards him, making it possible for Howe and Babb to quickly escape in their car and check her into the lavishly decorated Imperial Hotel.

Vienna had changed so much in the years since they'd last visited in the late 1930s. As Babb recalled to her writing group friends, "We were here in the fear days of Hitler."[7] Some of the buildings remained in rubble, while others were pristine, as if untouched by the war. At first Babb had trouble renting a typewriter, but she eventually found one with a German keyboard (whose strange characters amused her). While Howe was on set, she spent her days alone, walking around the streets of Vienna, going to the houses and rooms of Mozart, Beethoven, Haydn, and Schubert. For her, their music and lives haunted the city. On these walks Babb became especially obsessed with visiting all of the places that Mozart had lived in Vienna at the end of his life. It fascinated her that someone as brilliant and esteemed as Mozart had died a pauper and had been buried in an unmarked grave at St. Marx Cemetery Park, and she was "moved to tears in Mozart's house."[8] His sad end was in stark contrast to the fact that the image of his face was seemingly everywhere around the city: on chocolates on display in shops, on monuments. Babb even noted in a letter home that there was a popular Mozart-themed pastry that "has a complicated center."[9]

Howe only worked during the day, and therefore Babb's evenings in Vienna were spent with him, dining or meeting with friends or colleagues at the Imperial Hotel bar. This left daytime as the only time available for her to work on her writing. Babb had rarely been inspired to write during the day. Her natural writing time was late at night, so it wasn't a surprise to her that no new writing came while she was in Vienna. She was, however, able to work on some revisions, including a rewrite of her essay "Picnic Mephitis: A Common Skunk," about her pet skunk, a piece she had high hopes her agents would place.[10] Babb had pets throughout her life. They were usually dogs;

however, she did have some unusual animals, such as the pet skunk she wrote this piece about and the pet monkey she brought home from Costa Rica and Panama. In 1959, Babb and Howe had a small Chihuahua named Chico who slept on their bed and was always at Babb's side when she was at home.

Three weeks into the shooting of *Song without End* in Vienna, the director, Charles Vidor, was found dead in his hotel room. He had died of a heart attack. Howe and Babb, who had seen him just hours before he died, were shocked when they heard the news. By the time film production was moved to Munich, Germany, Vidor had been replaced by director George Cukor. After her time in Germany in 1936, Babb had no wish to return, so she left Howe to travel to Greece, where she planned to stay for two weeks with dear friends, a young writer, Gina, and her philosophy professor husband, Costas Politis. Babb and Gina had met years earlier, when Babb visited a class at Columbia University taught by the writer and editor Martha Foley, who was a friend of Babb's. Gina was a student in the class, and the two had corresponded ever since.[11]

Babb had dreamed of visiting Greece since she first studied it in her freshman year of college in Kansas. While she was in Greece, Babb spent a lot of time wandering among the ruins alone, as she remembered later in a letter to Gina: "that strange and melancholy walk . . . I heard the boys singing on the hill, that high, wild lonesome singing," a moment she'd capture in her poem "Night in a Greek Village."[12] Seeing those ancient ruins brought her to the realization that in the end of civilizations, or trauma, or violence, "man is so perishable" and "only art remains."[13] While in Greece she "had five lazy days on the island of Spetsos. I went around with a lump in my throat at the very [thought] of being in Greece."[14] Before traveling to Greece, Babb's creative focus had shifted almost entirely to fiction writing, but in Greece, surrounded by such rich and deep history, she felt compelled to express herself in poetry.

In Greece, away from the pressures of her marriage and able once again to stay up late writing, her creativity began to flow freely, and she wrote a series of poems centered around Greek themes. In her sonnet "In a Field in Peloponesia" she captures, in its turn, the way the landscape and the rich history had inspired her: "In this old land I am alien, yet / I turn to climb the stony path / to a familiar place I cannot know."[15] On Babb's last day, in the morning hours before her flight, Costas woke up early to take her for a final visit to the Acropolis. Babb's heart condition made it difficult for her to climb on her own to the top, so Costas made arrangements for her to be hoisted up the steep incline on a kitchen chair on the strong shoulders of two workmen. Aloft, rising towards the Greek sky, towards the caryatid-topped pillars of the Parthenon, a temple built for a female god, Athena, Babb felt she had come into her creative self. So much so that no matter the obstacles that lay ahead of her, she was moving towards the power that would lead her to write what would become the most successful book of her life.

When Babb returned to Los Angeles via London and then New York, both her American and British publishers and agents continued to pressure her to consider writing an autobiography. Outwardly she continued to resist, writing to her friends about the project, "I can't see it."[16] But inwardly, something was opening up to the idea. The plains where she'd spent those crucial years of her childhood were deep in her, and she began to consider what it would be like to write about that extraordinary time in her life. Perhaps now that her father was dead, revisiting those times would not seem so treacherous?

Her trip to Athens left Babb deeply inspired and when she returned, she at once began writing. As she told Gina Politis, "I am writing again. . . . Work, wonderful work, of feeling a secret delight all day that in the evening I shall go to my little room and close the door and write." Babb acknowledged what has kept her from writing: "I was prevented from writing by a number of events and duties for so long that when I was again free several evenings a week, I began to write one thing and then another, sometimes a whole first draft. . . . I am in a stream of writing and I am grateful for that."[17] In a later letter, Babb would tell Politis that she had to write: "I have no choice—I obey! Writing comes forth . . . I must write out of myself, the complex of me . . . in a way that is mine." She admitted that she felt "out of place, unrelated to my contemporaries—no place, no post to tie my horse between rides. No home base. But this is part of the pattern of my whole life, and I must accept it."[18]

Indeed, Babb's writing career up to this point had felt like this, an uphill battle. Her sensibilities, her beliefs about gender and race, her upbringing in the panhandle, where women ran newspapers and wore pants and where she'd found her writing career under the tutelage of Edna St. Vincent Millay and the attitudes of the suffragettes—all of these gave Babb a unique perspective that set her apart from her contemporaries. She didn't call herself a feminist during the second wave of feminism that began to dawn during the late 1960s because she had always been a proto-feminist, and she didn't understand why the ideas being put forward by the movement were considered new.

In the fall of 1959, Babb decided to begin gathering information for her autobiography. She had written to her mother asking her to share her memories of Red Rock from before Babb was born. Jennie responded at once with a long letter filled with details about what it was like to move away from her family at the age of fifteen, to a rugged territory town. The details she included would inspire Babb to write her short story "Run, Sheepy, Run."[19] Jennie, who was just a kid when she moved to Red Rock, mentioned that she used to play the traditional hide-and-seek-like game that the story is named after with the other kids in town. Her mother's recollections about Red Rock began to stir in Babb the type of story she'd like to tell in her autobiography. She began to consider, what if she didn't tell the story of her whole life? What if instead she wrote about Red Rock and Eastern Colorado and the early days her family lived through?

However, Babb's flow of inspiration and production was drastically interrupted by another tragic event. In April 1960, Babb's mother suffered a coronary thrombosis caused by a blood clot in an artery. Jennie was extremely ill, and her doctors advised her to stay in bed for at least two months in order to recover her strength. Her stepfather, a former grocer in Garden City named Clarence Kemper, whom Jennie had met after her divorce and married in 1949, was beside himself and constantly relied on Babb for support to help him with his sick wife. Jennie and her husband had relocated to Whittier, California, to be near Babb and Dorothy in the late 1940s. During her mother's illness, Babb routinely made the thirty-mile trip to sit with her at her bedside.

Then, in response to her mother's illness, Dorothy also collapsed. Babb's precious writing time was again swept away as she traveled back and forth to her mother's and her sister's bedsides in Whittier and then home to help Howe when he returned from work. Meanwhile, the bills for her mother's and sister's medical costs began to pile up, and Babb again felt the need to make an income to help cover them. When UCLA asked her to return to teach her course on writing the short story, called "Applied Creative Writing: Short Story 827," she agreed.

According to the course description, the class focused on "short story writing, utilizing characterization, dialogue, plot, setting, subject, summary, and scene, viewpoint" and it met on Monday and Thursday nights for six weeks beginning on June 20, 1960.[20] Babb was excited to receive the news that her story "The Santa Ana," which had been published in the *Saturday Evening Post,* had been chosen for inclusion in *The Best American Short Stories 1960 and The Yearbook of the American Short Story,* edited by Martha Foley and David Burnett. Babb's story would be included among stories by

Elizabeth Hardwick, Arthur Miller, Howard Nemerov, and Philip Roth. The editor of *The Writer* had seen Babb's work in *Best American Short Stories 1960* and contacted her to see if she had any essays about the craft of fiction she'd like to publish. Babb had developed detailed lectures for her short-story classes, and over the next decade she published versions of these as essays in *The Writer*.[21] The first of these essays, "Storyteller's Street," would appear in the October 1961 issue.

That summer, as Babb was commuting to take care of her mother and sister and preparing for and teaching her classes, the house on Queens Road once again became filled with visitors. Babb enjoyed entertaining, but in her overwhelmed state she mentioned in a letter to a friend that she was "sort of tired of them." When their guests were in town, Howe expected Babb to put everything aside to entertain them. "Work is part of my very happiness and wholeness. My work has been interrupted so much and so often. I lack the ruthless drive that would cause me to put it before human demands." Later in the same letter, Babb reveals, "I had to make a choice of which came first: my work or my marriage (there is NO equity in this) and chose marriage, not because it came first with me, but because I have a good marriage and a wonderful husband, and the difficulties caused by my attempts at having both equally were certainly not conductive to preserving my marriage."[22] In Babb's mind, if she wanted to continue to have a successful marriage, she could not let her writing get in the way. She claimed Howe needed this kind of support due to "his insecurities from early racial difficulties." But though she often conceded this, with the pull of her family also upon her, Babb mourned the long, quiet nights when she had the house to herself to write. "As a writer, I'll do the best I can with what time I have, and that's that."[23]

But even with bed rest and the support Babb was able to give her, Babb's mother's complicated heart issues did not improve. On December 21, 1960, Jennie A. Kemper died at 2:00 a.m. of "a long agonizing heart attack."[24] She was remembered at a service at Lanier's Colonial Chapel in Whittier on December 23, 1960.[25] As Babb noted at the top of the last letter she received from her mother, "She seemed to get better then worse. Clarence (stepfather) called me, and I stayed with them for two weeks. Dorothy was living nearby and had been helping her too sometimes. Mama had to return to hospital again. . . . Jimmie and I went back to Whittier that evening and I was with her until she lost consciousness."[26]

During one of Babb's last visits with her mother, two days before her death, Babb and her sister witnessed their mother's final rebellion against the men who had controlled her throughout her life. Babb watched as her mother, lying in bed, removed "her wedding ring, a moment's rebellion and courage flaring in her eyes, and threw it across the room." When Jennie's husband, Clarence, returned to the room and saw what she'd done, he explained to Babb and her sister, "That ring hurts her. . . . It's always falling off in bed and getting lost." Babb and her sister were not convinced. They had seen what had really happened. The look their mother had given them, "a private look, just a glance so quick and eloquent of release at last that we smiled, and she smiled back." Later, after Clarence had left the room, Jennie whispered to her girls her last wish: "Your dad is all around me here in the room. Wherever I'm going I don't want to see either one of [my husbands] again."[27]

Babb's stepfather fell ill almost immediately after her mother died, and he died less than a year later. Their deaths, reported Babb in a letter to her friend Melissa Blake, left her depressed and barely able to write.[28] She still went through the motions, however, and she tried to never miss attending her writing group. Her photograph was featured in an article about Bradbury, "So You Want to Be a Writer," in *Friends*, January 1961.[29] But as Babb sat at her writing desk late at night, ghosts haunted her. Not the ghosts of her dead parents, as she had always expected, but ghosts who were stirred from the land that surrounded her. Mandeville Canyon, near her house, had been the place where many Chumash and Gabrielleno-Tongva people lost their lives working as slaves for the Spanish. It was also a place ravaged by floods in 1938, when over a hundred people were killed. In the early 1960s, the neighborhood had been rebuilt upon its ruins, its past forgotten. These hauntings inspired Babb, who believed in the spirit world, to write one of her first supernatural stories, "Night of Evil," a draft of which she finished on July 21, 1961. The story is about a young newspaper reporter who rents a room in an old boarding house and encounters a violent ghost she helps release from its purgatory there.[30]

Babb also wrote to Blake about how much she enjoyed reading X. J. Kennedy's newest poetry collection, *Nude Descending a Staircase,* a collection whose title poem offered an anti-blazon, a bringing together of a disparate woman into a whole, powerful force:

> One-woman waterfall, she wears
> her slow descent like a long cape
> and pausing on the final stair,
> collects her motions into shape.[31]

Babb, in these years after losing her mother, like the woman in Kennedy's poem, was collecting "her motions into shape." How would she write about her past without her mother there to send her own memories? She couldn't rely on her sister, whose mental health issues made her an unreliable narrator who often bent the truth to make it something her mind could bear. Since their mother's death, Dorothy had again been living with Babb at her home on Queens Road, and Babb complained to Blake that Dorothy's latest issue was that she refused to leave her room due to agoraphobia.[32] Having her sister around also made it difficult to write. As she admitted in a letter to Gina Politis, "You know one cannot write in the presence of such a complicated situation."[33] It took Babb some time to sit with her ghosts before she could carry forward the joys and sorrows of her past, the past she knew without the witness of anyone else.

It was about this time that Babb wrote another short story that would eventually become a scene in her autobiography. "That Presence Out There" is about an episode from her childhood, when her family was living in her grandfather's dugout in Eastern Colorado and she and Dorothy were collecting dried cow patties to burn in their dugout's stove. As they set off across the wide flat plains, they'd dare each other to go closer and closer to the shack belonging to Old Man Hoopies, a hermit who had lived by himself on the high plains since his wife died. In the story, the man sees the girls, invites them into his meager dwelling, and shows them his treasure: the scalp with his wife's hair, which he asks the girls to put on their heads. The story captures the absolute loneliness one feels in this desolate place. One fears for the young girls, as the hermit seems on the precipice of both madness and violence, yet in Babb's exquisite re-creation, even Old Man Hoopies's humanity shines through. The story was purchased for $200 and published in *Ellery Queens Mystery Magazine* in September 1962.[34]

That same fall, thanks in part, Babb claimed, to her agent Ross's encouragement, she wrote what she thought would be the second chapter of her autobiography. As she confessed to Ross, she'd still been having trouble "settling on a design" for the book that would suit her concept of autobiography. She didn't want to be at the center of the book; instead, she wanted to focus on the whole experience of the time, the setting, and the characters (in the same way she would if she were writing fiction). In many ways, Babb's approach to writing autobiography echoes the approach she took to writing news stories, whereby the action of the retelling is enhanced by rich sensory imagery and a wide-angle view of the story.

In early 1963, Babb reported in a letter to Ross that she "finished a night's work on the book," explaining to her agent that she'd only recently come out of what she called a "discouraging period," a depression when writing was all but impossible. Now, though, she had discovered that "working is the cure, one rather forgets future results when one is writing." And although Babb still took her job as Howe's wife very seriously, she admitted her wifely duties weren't conducive to her life as a writer: "I don't seem to be one of those women who can write books on the kitchen table at the end of the day." Instead, Babb explained she had to squeeze in her writing in the quiet hours of the night once Howe has gone to bed: "Lately, I've come to my work room around 11 PM tired enough to go to bed." But since her latest revelation, despite her fatigue, every night she could Babb went to her quiet desk in her office, where books were stacked like skyscrapers from floor to ceiling, and wrote until she was greeted by the dawn chorus at first light. Instead of stopping and crawling wearily into her bed, however, she'd go downstairs and outside to her beloved garden, because she found that to "plant seeds, dig, pull weeds, watch the cat and dog playing together" made her feel more like writing the next day. In the same letter, she reported to Ross that she'd written seventy pages of her autobiography and she hoped to have one hundred pages completed by the summer.[35]

Understandably, Babb wasn't able to keep up with this grueling writing schedule of long nights and little sleep, and she missed her self-imposed deadline. In another letter, she explained to Ross that she hadn't yet written a first chapter because she wanted to begin her book by writing about her early experiences with the Otoe-Missouria tribe. She'd been trying to find two free weeks so she could travel to Oklahoma to "visit the tribe with whom I lived for a while as a child. There are very few old people left who will remember me. I postpone the first chapter for this possibility."[36] However, Babb would not make her pilgrimage to the Otoe-Missouria before she published her book, and she would have to settle on beginning the book in Red Rock, just as her family was about to leave for Eastern Colorado.

Throughout the writing of the book that would become *An Owl on Every Post,* every other Tuesday night that she was at home in Los Angeles, Babb brought drafts of her chapters to her writing group.[37] The group remained a stronghold that fortified her during the decade it took her to finish writing it. The members supported one another, and as Bradbury's fame soared during the 1960s, he too remained loyal to the group. When he was filmed for a 1963 documentary, *Ray Bradbury: The Story of a Writer,* he made sure the director included scenes of him workshopping with the group (Babb even got a close-up at minute 18:25).[38]

18   An Owl on Every Post

Finally, on August 15, 1964, Babb was able to send her agents, Ross and Abbott, the first one hundred pages "of the autobiography."[1] This sample included chapters two through nine and a later chapter (which she tells them she thinks will be chapter twelve) about Daft, the ghost of her grandfather's horse he took her to see when she was a young girl. The vision of the horse would be yet another bond she shared with her grandfather. Whereas in her experience writing *The Lost Traveler* her father (fictionalized as Des) had loomed violently over her, writing her autobiography had brought the ghost of her grandfather, one of the most influential figures in her life, back from the dead.

In the letter she included with the chapters, Babb told Ross, "When I hear from you as to your reaction to these chapters, and if your reaction is favorable or encouraging, I should like to discuss with you the present plan of the book. . . . I have a sense of where I'm going and where I'd like to stop."[2] Both Ross and Abbott were quick to respond with their praise of the pages Babb sent. Ross wrote that she "very much liked what I have seen of the autobiography, particularly the last chapter about the horse."[3] In a return letter, Babb told Ross she was "very, very happy that you like the first hundred pages" and that she planned "to work on no other writing until this is completed." She also told Ross that she was happy to have found the book's form. Her plans were "to ignore the idea of 'the story of my life' and stick to a certain time period . . . the latter-day pioneer kind of living."[4] Babb also has a similar back and forth with her New York agent, Abbott, who loved the first hundred pages and was already thinking about possible publishing opportunities. Abbott asked Babb to write a summation to share with potential publishers and Babb willingly obliged. In it, she characterized the book as "a personal narrative of a place and a time and a family."[5]

But even as the momentum of her writing kicked back up—and perhaps due to the loss of her mother—Babb had begun to pour more and more of her energy into strengthening her marriage. After a long night of writing and a bright morning in the garden, she'd write Howe small, sweet love notes and leave them where he could find them when he woke up. In return, he'd answer her with a sweet response written before he left for work, so that when she woke up, she'd be greeted by his words of love. Perhaps because of this, and the sacrifices she continually made, her marriage with Howe became as solid as it had ever been.

Howe needed her support; even after winning his first Academy Award for his cinematography on *The Rose Tattoo,* since being graylisted, he was having a challenging time finding work. Finally, in 1964, the stigma caused by the Red Scare began to lift and dissolve like a coastal fog, and Howe was again considered for big studio productions. That year he was sent to the Texas Panhandle to film the handsome young actor Paul Newman in a revisionist Western entitled *Hud*. *Hud* would prove to be another career-making film for Howe; it would be nominated for seven Academy Awards and earn three, one of which Howe received for Best Black and White Cinematography. Howe would be praised by critics for his use of "stark realism" and "extravagant surrealism." In the film, he made the western skies loom over the film's complicated characters, and he used light to convey metaphorically the complexity of the characters' emotions. For example, in a scene after Hud (played by Paul Newman) and his young nephew return home from a bar fight, they are filmed, as critic Walter Chaw has pointed out, in "a night scene illuminated only by the light bouncing off the water and the warm glow coming from a nearby enclosed porch. The light coming out of the basin feels mercurial, unpredictable, in the same way that Hud's ugly temperament and venal impulses do, underlining Hud's dangerous influence on the impressionable young man."[6]

But while Howe enjoyed Babb's support, he rarely found it necessary to publicly acknowledge it. At the 36th Academy Awards ceremony, on April 13, 1964, when Howe was presented his second Academy Award by a towering James Stewart, he merely thanked the director Martin Ritt for giving him the opportunity to work on the film, and the "wonderful crew from Paramount Studios." Like the other almost exclusively male recipients of the awards, he did not thank his wife for what she had done—and sacrificed—to help him receive the award. However, for a brief second, when Howe's name was called, the camera panned to his seat and viewers could see Babb sitting next to him, clapping wildly with joy.[7]

After winning a second Academy Award, Howe's career soared to new heights. Soon he was pummeled with offers to work on new films. Over the next few years, as Babb struggled to balance being Howe's wife with continuing to write and finish her autobiography, she followed Howe as he traveled around the country to film on location. As Babb recounted to editor Margaret Hartley at the *Southwest Review,* "We have been on the go a lot the past several years . . . and these trips while very interesting really make holes in my writing time, the preparations, settling in, coming home, resettling. . . . Wherever we go, I set up housekeeping and cook. And write."[8]

Babb traveled with Howe to the hot deserts of Arizona, near Tucson, on location for *The Outrage* (1964) and *Hombre* (1967), both of which starred Paul Newman. She would take short trips to the Desert Museum to watch a prairie dog colony, an activity that reminded her of watching prairie dogs when she was growing up. Sometimes she would work her own mini writing retreats into these trips. She spent a week in New Orleans by herself before joining Howe on location in Biloxi, Mississippi, where he was filming *This Property Is Condemned* (1966), a film based on another Tennessee Williams play, directed by Sydney Pollack and starring Natalie Wood, Robert Redford, and Charles Bronson. Babb also visited Howe on set in Selma, Alabama, where he filmed the adaptation of Carson McCullers's novel *The Heart Is a Lonely Hunter* (1967) right after "the famous march which crossed the Selma bridge." As she noted to Margaret Hartley in a letter, "Many of the marchers who worked in the textile mills there lost their jobs. A movie company in town helped that problem some."[9] The film would earn the actors Alan Arkin and Sondra Locke Academy Award nominations for their performances, and Howe would earn a Laurel Award for his cinematography. In the small coal-mining town of Hazelton, Pennsylvania, Babb joined Howe on the set of *The Mollie Maguires* (1969), starring Sean Connery. While there, Babb had to take a break from finishing her autobiography to revise a screenplay adaptation of *The Lost Traveler* because she didn't like the way another writer had treated it.[10] Babb was also consulted about the script of *The Molly Maguires* (originally written by Walter Bernstein). After reading it, she warned director Martin Ritt that "it seems to me to have a number of serious lacks that in accumulation result in a thin story of violence and not much else." She saw "the characters as the main source of the trouble" because they were "one-dimensional," making it "difficult for one to become emotionally involved in their plight." She reached to the depth of the story, seeing it not only as a vendetta, but a story that "had roots in the Irish peasants' small revenge groups against the English" and "roots in the very origin of US labor history." She thought the audience needed to understand this background in order to properly understand what was happening in the film. Babb thought the film's story could have "genuine stature as a chapter in American labor history, and at the same time be an exciting, and moving, fierce and tender, cruel and gentle, violent, and high-minded human story."[11] Ritt clearly respected Babb's suggestions, as he ended up implementing many of them into the film.

During this busy schedule of moving to and from locations over several years, setting up their homes away from home and supporting Howe as he worked (which meant taking care of literally everything except photographing the films), somehow Babb found the time to "revis[e] and polish the first pages (170 or so)" of her autobiography. These pages consisted of the first eighteen chapters minus the opening chapter she still had hopes of adding, the chapter about her early life with the Otoe people.[12]

That spring, Babb brought her polished chapters to her new agent in New York, Julie Fallowfield with McIntosh and Otis (Mary Abbott was no longer representing Babb because she had to take care of her sister, who was ill).[13] Fallowfield in turn began sending Babb's work to publishers she thought would be a good fit. Fallowfield was particularly excited about a new publishing house called McCall's as a possible home for Babb's work. McCall's was a new offshoot of the McCall Corporation (which published the magazines *McCall's, Redbook,* and the *Saturday Review*).

In the spring of 1968, Babb's lengthy short story (which she considered to be "more a novella than a short story")[14] titled "A Scandalous Humility" was published in *Northwest Review,* and it is in this story that one finds one of Babb's most interesting female protagonists. Mrs. Tsiang is a determined Chinese immigrant mother who has never accepted American customs and who has been shunned for a past that was beyond her control. Although she is othered, both in America as an immigrant and within the Chinese American community as someone who has lost face, Babb depicts her as a strong protagonist: "small, sleek as a blackbird" with "dark alert eyes" and a mind "folded tight like a green bud."[15] Mrs. Tsiang believes that in order for her soul to be at rest in her homeland, her bones must be shipped and buried in China. She's driven by a need to "become the dust on [her] own hills." Nothing can stop her. Mrs. Tsiang crosses gender lines. She eats with the men in the restaurant because they are offered a wider variety of foods, and when she prays, she leaves her fate in the hands of a goddess instead of a god. Babb takes her time to reveal the past that has left Mrs. Tsiang shunned. As a young girl, she left her village an orphan and traveled to Canton (Guangdong) to become a picture bride. But "something went wrong, and the group of young girls on the long cruel trip by sea were not delivered to husbands but to an old woman with straw hair and blue eyes, a foreign ghost, who paid for them and owned them and set them to their tasks." After years of sexual enslavement, Mrs. Tsiang finally escapes, begins a new life and marries her husband. Soon, however, her past comes back to haunt her. When the people of Chinatown find out about Mrs. Tsiang's former life as a prostitute, they spurn her, and "nothing [she] did won her face." However, by the end of the story, through sheer determination, Mrs. Tsiang overcomes these obstacles by devising a way to save face and at the same time arrange to have her bones returned to her homeland. Babb celebrates this triumph with an image of Mrs. Tsiang looking out her window and seeing moonlight on the dirty stones of the street. The moon illuminates her path forward, a new path, like the one Babb herself had seen in Greece, created by her own agency. Babb, too, was about to overcome the past traumas that had been wielded against her and finally find a path towards success.

In November 1969, Babb published one of the most important scenes in what would become her memoir, an essay called "Daft," about the ghost horse that visited her grandfather, in *Southwest*

Review.[16] The publication was more literary then commercial, and Babb didn't receive any payment. But when asked by editor Margaret Hartley where her book would be published, she told her she was embarrassed that her "new book is still not completed: I persist in my hope of finishing it before this year ends."[17] Babb was disappointed with the length of time that had passed between her two books.

Then, seemingly all of a sudden, after a decade of writing, there was a seismic shift in Babb's luck, and her path towards publication of the autobiography she was now calling *An Owl on Every Post*[18] was illuminated, spurring her to rapidly finish the final chapters of the manuscript between August 1969 and January 1970.

Babb sent a copy of "Daft" to Ross in London, who was almost immediately able to sell the story to a BBC Radio 2 program called *Morning Story* for twenty British pounds.[19] The program aired on November 19, 1969. Babb didn't get to listen to the broadcast, but the wife of her old friend, the doctor with whom she'd had a brief romance in England during the late 1930s, listened to the broadcast and "was enchanted."[20]

In May 1969, Babb got word from her agent in New York that *Redbook* was interested in publishing a condensation of her autobiography based on the incomplete draft Babb had sent her. After a great deal of back and forth, *Redbook* purchased her book for the huge sum of $8,000. Babb was stunned. Then, at nearly the same time, Hy Cohen, an editor at McCall's, wrote to Babb that he not only wanted to accept *An Owl on Every Post* for publication, but he wanted to publish it soon: he wanted *Owl* to be part of the fall list. Babb was giddy with joy. As she reported in a letter to Ross, "This must be one of my best months!" She reports to Ross that Fallowfield told her that Cohen "could not be more enthusiastic about OWL."[21] What these two acceptances meant was that Babb finally had a deadline. In fact, she had a double deadline. She needed to finish *An Owl on Every Post* for both publications by December 31, 1969. A contract also meant that

Babb, in her own eyes, could now "'legally' neglect some of my duties and continue to concentrate on the book. . . . The writing can come first, duties second."[22] The duties that Babb spoke about in her letter to Ross were her wifely duties of caring for Howe, duties that had lately begun to increase due to the fact that after the release of *The Molly McGuires,* Howe had begun to experience serious health issues.

Fueled by these deadlines, Babb wrote furiously for the next few months. She wrote the early middle chapters, 19–26, and the final chapters, 36–41, before the end of the year, and then completed the late middle chapters, 28–32, and a rewrite of the ending chapters in early 1970. She would officially finish writing and editing her first draft on February 15, 1970. In addition to finishing all of these new chapters and polishing the old ones, she would also write "several transitional chapters and bits and pieces" for *Redbook* that weren't included in the novel draft.[23] For those few weeks, Babb immersed herself completely in her work, writing through every night, giving herself full permission to let go of all of the other tasks that usually disrupted her or weighed her down: her wifely "duties," her sister's care. As the moon rose over Hollywood below her home, Babb summoned back to life the early days of her childhood that shaped her into the person she had become: the low, flat plains; the smell of sage in the crisp morning air; the wild yucca plants that punctuated the wide flat horizon; geese calling to her as they circled the fields, swooping down to eat the green stalks of wheat; the soft crunch of buffalo grass underneath her feet. And her grandfather, or at least her vivid memory of him, just up ahead on the prairie, occasionally looking back at her, leading her across that great expanse, toward the next phase of her life.

Konkie's ghost, and the ghost of her mind as a child, bloomed through her in those long productive weeks. Babb painstakingly researched every plant and animal included in the book. It was deeply important to her that she got the landscape right. Babb also felt guided and supported by her English agent, Patience Ross, whose idea it had been for her to write an autobiography in the first place. As Babb wrote to her in a letter, "If it hadn't been for your interest and urging, I should never have written this autobiography because I felt who am I to write autobiography?"[24]

As Babb recalled in a letter to a friend, "At 7 PM when I finished OWL I went in the living room to tell Jimmie with a hurray but instead started crying and couldn't stop for half an hour. Part exhaustion, part loss. I suddenly felt like I had just parted with a piece of my life."[25]

In April *Redbook* published an excerpt from *An Owl on Every Post* (pages 157–79), and soon after, on her way to meet Howe, who was on location filming *The Horsemen* in Madrid, Spain, Babb visited the McCall's office in New York. Babb would later tell Cohen that she enjoyed their "working hours" and "lovely lunch."[26] While in New York, Babb also visited the *Redbook* office, where she was given the hundreds of fan letters sent by people all over the country in response to her work. As she wrote to Ross, "I was amazed. . . . I used to wonder if anyone would read it. It seems so!"[27]

After meeting them in New York, Babb felt equally encouraged by her team at McCall's, who were urging her to finish her book and who guided her through the process of bringing it into print. Over the next six months, she and Cohen corresponded over the production of her book. Jane Pasanen, the publicity director at McCall's, also corresponded with Babb extensively. And Joanne Dearcopp, who Cohen had asked to give a second read of Babb's manuscript and who had fallen in love with *An Owl on Every Post* the first time she read it, was also in correspondence with Babb during this time. Dearcopp would later play a significant role in Babb's literary career.

One issue that arose during this correspondence was whether to call the book a novel or a memoir. Originally, Babb's agent had been concerned that someone in the book might take legal action against Babb. Fallowfield was especially worried about "the 'Krouse' family and the incident of being turned out in the approaching storm and the resulting miscarriage."[28] But she'd been reassured by the fact that Babb had changed not only the name of the family, but her description of their family farm. As Babb later explained to Ross, "Many of the characters in the book are changed in some way." For example, the cowboy Cooper Loveland was "simply a composite" of many cowboys they'd met during their time in Eastern Colorado, and Babb's mother's best friend Carrie Whitehead was actually a woman named Bettie Gatlin who now lived in Arizona with her family, and who had helped Babb remember details about the broomcorn harvest.[29]

When Babb first saw the galleys of McCall's treatment of her book, however, she was not happy. As she said in a letter to Cohen, "The book cover upsets me."[30] She thought it looked like a desert instead of a prairie. After some back and forth, she and Cohen were able to come to an agreement about the cover, finalizing a much simpler design.

For book blurbs, Babb called on the literary luminaries she'd known throughout her life. Babb's longtime writing friend Ray Bradbury wrote, "We live in the eye of the hurricane. Our time moves so swiftly we are in dire need of hearthing places where we might rest ourselves, consider our fortunes, reconsider our loves, and plan a better day. Sanora Babb, with quiet humor, and a great and all-encompassing love for a land and her people, has created a warm hearth indeed in this book. I hold my hands to it to be warmed. As extra dividend, my soul knows comfort."[31]

Both Ralph Ellison and William Saroyan also sent endorsements. Sadly, all three of these important endorsements came in late, so none was included on the book's jacket. Also not included on the book jacket was Babb's photograph (which she was late to send) and any mention of Babb's hard-won publications: *The Lost Traveler* and the numerous short stories she'd published in some of the leading literary magazines of the time. As Babb would later tell Ross, "Quotes from [Bradbury's, Saroyan's, and Ellison's] letters were to have been used on the book cover, but there was so much cover trouble toward the last that, as you know, the cover came out without picture, or quotes, and no mention of my stories or TLT. I was a bit miffed."[32]

But these shortfalls did not dampen the extraordinary moment when Babb received her first physical copy of the book, "right out of the bindery," in the mail on October 22, 1970, accompanied by a letter from Cohen, who told her he thought it was "a beautiful book, inside and out." Before its release on November 22, *An Owl on Every Post* was reviewed in *Publishers Weekly,* which called it "a charming memoir . . . a thoroughly appealing book."[33]

On November 22, 1970, the day her book was published, Cohen and Pasanen sent Babb a dozen red long-stemmed roses with a note reading, "With love and best wishes on the publication of your book."[34] Shortly after the release of *Owl,* Babb was sent by McCall's to Denver for a press tour. She took the train, enjoying the trip through the mountains to the mile-high city. Babb stayed at the Brown Palace, a downtown hotel, where she received telegrams from local television and radio shows about her appearances. Even though Babb claimed she didn't like to appear on film, she was, for this short time, treated like the celebrity she should have been. She was interviewed by the *Rocky Mountain News* and the *Denver Post,* and was also interviewed at the Colorado Women's Club. She appeared on the TV shows *High Noon* and *Contemporary Denver* and was featured in radio interviews on KDEN and KTLK radio stations.[35]

That winter, Joanne Dearcopp traveled to Los Angeles to attend a conference. She called Babb ahead of time to see if she would like to meet for lunch. Instead, Babb asked to meet her at the local farmers' market. Dearcopp arrived early, so she spent some time walking among the stalls at the market, absorbing the sensory details that abounded. When she was walking past a booth, a coral and turquoise Navajo brooch caught her eye and she purchased it, immediately pinning it to her shirt. When Dearcopp met Babb a little while later, she was struck by what the woman she had only corresponded with looked like: she was "a striking, white-haired woman who flashed a warm smile that never left her face. She was smothered in turquoise jewelry—bracelets on both wrists, multiple rings, and a Zuni squash blossom necklace."[36] It was the same necklace Babb had worn in the photograph Howe had taken of her in Palm Springs, just after she'd had her novel *The Lost Traveler* accepted.

Dearcopp couldn't believe the serendipity. Here she had just bought a turquoise pin, and Babb was wearing a wealth of her own turquoise jewelry. When Joanne shared her newly purchased pin with Babb, Babb immediately admired it, and Dearcopp knew the two of them would be good friends. As they walked around the farmers' market, Babb told Dearcopp the story of each of the pieces of jewelry she wore. Later that evening, they went to dinner with Howe at their favorite Chinese restaurant in Chinatown. The next night was a Tuesday, so Babb brought Dearcopp with her to Bradbury's home for their writers' group. As Dearcopp, who was starstruck being in the same room with Bradbury, remembered, "The group was friendly and Ray quite charming and fun. Their critiquing of each other's work was serious but with the tone of camaraderie they'd forged over decades."[37]

By February 2, 1971, however, Cohen, Dearcopp, and many of the other people who had worked on the production of Babb's book were suddenly fired from McCall's as it went through a major restructuring just after the release of *An Owl on Every Post*. Babb was given a new editor, Susan Stanwood. Due to the restructuring, the remaining staff was left completely overwhelmed. Marketing efforts were redirected toward more commercial books, such as the socialite Princess

Pignatelli's book on beauty, *The Beautiful People's Book: A Straightforward Approach to Narcissism.*

Despite this turmoil, *An Owl on Every Post* easily paid off its advance and continued to sell extremely well. In its first weeks, thousands of copies were sold, and sales continued to reach nearly a thousand copies each month for the first few months of the year. By the end of 1971, the McCall's edition of *Owl* had sold over 5,000 copies.[38] In April 1971, Babb received an offer from Peter Davies Limited in England, which hoped to publish *An Owl on Every Post* in an English edition in late October 1971. Then, in May 1972, *Owl* was chosen to be part of the County Book Club and was reprinted for the club's 5,000 members in England. Babb was thrilled that her book was chosen for the club; she had been disappointed that this had not happened in the U.S. due to Cohen losing his job at a crucial time during the promotion of her book.[39] Later, in November 1972, *An Owl on Every Post* was released in paperback by American Library Editions and went on to sell over 65,000 copies.[40] And yet, even though Babb's work was finally achieving the success it deserved, she had little time to enjoy it before tragedy struck her life again.

In the fall of 1971, the morning sun was filtering in through the large picture window of the living room when Howe suddenly collapsed "as if dead" right in front Babb. Babb fell to her knees next to her motionless husband. She shook his body, trying to wake him. Unable to get him to respond, she began crying uncontrollably. In a fortuitous coincidence, just a month prior, Babb had read an article about "mouth to mouth breathing." which gave detailed instructions on how to perform the life-saving technique. As soon as she could stop crying and had called an ambulance, she calmed herself enough to catch her breath and begin administering deep breaths into Howe's mouth, pumping her palms against his ribcage and bringing her husband back to life almost, as she remembered, "at once."[41]

Soon she heard the ambulance sirens as they wove up the steep hill to their home. When they arrived, the paramedics strapped Howe, who was still unconscious but breathing, to a gurney and rushed him to Mount Sinai Hospital. Howe remained in intensive care for eight days, with Babb by his side, comforting him as he went in and out of consciousness. When they arrived and Howe was assessed, the doctor on call had taken Babb aside and told her "to brace herself" for his death. Babb was furious. She had no intention of "bracing herself" or of giving up on Howe. As she recalled to Ross, "One simply cannot!"[42] Instead, when Howe was physically able to leave the hospital four months later, Babb brought him home and "began doing everything" possible to nurse him back to health. Howe refused to hire a nurse and insisted that only Babb care for him. This meant that any and all time Babb once had to herself was now completely gone. Every minute of her day was spent taking care of Howe until the day he died, in her arms, on the deck off of their bedroom, on July 12, 1976.

For years after Howe's death, Babb continued to be his caretaker. Even though his physical body was gone, his legacy remained, and she felt it was her duty to secure that legacy. Babb focused almost all of her energy on organizing Howe's papers for the Margaret Herrick Library at the Academy of Motion Pictures and attending all of the awards and celebrations that were organized for Howe posthumously.[43] She attended a few literary events, including the B. Traven seminar held at the University of Southern California on November 12, 1977, where she spoke on a panel about her friendship with Traven: how he'd come to her apartment in Mexico City several times a week, and how, when she brought him to a party (without revealing his identity of course), her friend Waldeen took her aside and asked her, "Who is this droll man you brought to the party?"[44]

At a star-studded party celebrating director Martin Ritt's fiftieth anniversary in Hollywood, Babb was quoted in *The Hollywood Reporter* as saying that Ritt's work "represents the truth about life, even in its rough beauty." However, as was so often the case regarding the work she did to keep Howe's memory alive, her name was misremembered and her profession wasn't mentioned at all. Her quote was attributed to "Sonora Wong," who was identified as "the wife of James Wong Howe." She began to wonder who would secure her legacy when she was gone. And what legacy did she have to leave?

1. Sanora Babb's mother, Jennie Parks, at age fourteen, roughly a year before her marriage to Walter Babb.

2. Babb as an infant, wearing a custom-made uniform of her father's Red Rock baseball team. She was considered the team mascot.

3. The Red Rock baseball team, ca. 1905. Walter Babb is standing second from right.

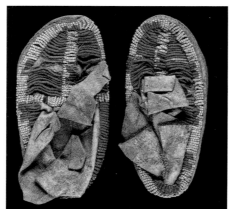

4. The beaded moccasins given to Babb by Otoe-Missoria Chief Black Hawk when she was a young girl.

5. Babb at age two, Waynoka, Oklahoma, 1909.

6. Babb's paternal grandfather Alonzo "Konkie" Babb, ca. 1930.

7. Konkie in a wagon beside his harvest of broomcorn in front of his dugout in Baca County, Colorado.

8. Babb's high school graduation photo, Forgan High School, Forgan, Oklahoma, 1924.

9. Babb with sister Dorothy in Forgan, ca. 1920s.

10. A headshot of Babb from her MGM screen test, 1930s.

11. Babb and fellow writer Tillie Lerner Olsen in Des Moines, Iowa, on their way to the First American Writers' Congress in New York in 1935.

12. Walter Babb in San Diego, California.

13. Babb in Paris, 1935.

14. Babb's photograph of two teenage Nazi soldiers in Berlin, 1935.

15. Babb with two women on a collective farm near Kiev, 1935.

16. Babb (seated in center) at an FSA migrant camp, 1938.

17. FSA administrator Tom Collins and Babb hanging laundry at a migrant camp, 1938.

18. Babb with the writers' group started by Ray Bradbury and Dolph Sharp. From left to right: Jack Gross, Ray Morrison, Dolph Sharp, unidentified man, Ray Bradbury, and Babb. The photo was taken at Jack Gross's home.

19. Cover of a menu from Ching How, the restaurant owned and run by Babb and her husband, cinematographer James Wong Howe.

20. Babb at the Acropolis in Athens, Greece, 1959.

21. Babb (wearing her trademark squash-blossom necklace) in Palm Springs after finally getting a publishing contract for *The Lost Traveler*, 1957.

22. Babb in front of a window display featuring her first published book, *The Lost Traveler,* at Pickwick Books in Los Angeles, 1958.

23. Babb and Howe at the 39th Academy Awards ceremony in 1966. Credit: Margaret Herrick Library, Academy Awards Show Photographs.

24. Babb, Howe, and their dog Chico at home on Queens Road in the Hollywood Hills.

25. Babb in the 1990s. Credit: © Joanne Dearcopp.

19 *The Recovery of* Whose Names Are Unknown

Even in the late 1930s, when she was finishing writing *Whose Names Are Unknown,* Babb knew her approach to documenting the Dust Bowl and its impacts on the people affected by it was different from the approach taken by John Steinbeck, and for the next several decades, she continued to fight to bring her version of the past into the light. But over and over again the publishing industry would remain closed to her version of the story, claiming first that her version was too much like Steinbeck's, then that a story set in the Dust Bowl era wasn't relevant to modern readers. This second and more significant erasure of Sanora Babb happened when her book wasn't published for decades and her confidence as a writer was stripped from her. This erasure of is still happening today. But it wasn't only Babb's writing that we lost; we also lost the varied perspective she added to our understanding of a catastrophic event, an omission that would leave a hole in the story of the Dust Bowl that is only beginning to be remedied.

Understandably, given the incredible success of Steinbeck's *The Grapes of Wrath,* later in her life Babb would often downplay what Steinbeck and Collins had done to her and her work. She would minimize the severity of the impact the use of her notes in Steinbeck's novel had on her ability to publish her first novel and the deep and troubling impact it had on her subsequent career as a writer. *The Grapes of Wrath* would not only become an international best seller and receive the 1940 Pulitzer Prize but would reach an even wider audience that same year, when it would be made into an Academy Award–winning film starring Henry Fonda and directed by John Ford. Eventually, *The Grapes of Wrath* would become required reading in high schools across the country (in fact, in many classrooms the book is still read today), and its narrative would solidify the single story about the Dust Bowl era that everyone—except those who lived through it—would accept as the definitive account.

It's understandable that as the years passed and *The Grapes of Wrath* became more and more famous, more and more synonymous with the Dust Bowl, Babb would try to play down what had happened to her and her book. At some point she likely assumed that there was no use in fighting back. Why would anyone listen to her version of the story when the world had chosen one story to represent the myriad experiences that made up this tragic event? However, letters and documents from this time tell a different story, one that it is important for us to remember. They remind us that truth is often not the single story that is remembered. The truth is something we have to fight to unearth.

. . .

It wasn't until the early 1980s, when Babb was nearing eighty years old, that she began to slow her work of preserving Howe's legacy and again focus on her own writing career. However, as a final gesture toward her husband's legacy, Babb sat down with Daniel Mann—the director with whom Howe had made the films *Come Back, Little Sheba, The Rose Tattoo,* and *The Last Angry Man*—for several extensive interviews that he hoped to turn into a documentary about Howe. In these interviews Babb not only talks about Howe, but she also talks about the important role she played in his life, a perspective that few who have written about Howe's career include.

Through this period, she stayed in touch with her writing group. On April 23, 1983, Babb attended the screening of her friend Ray Bradbury's film *Something Wicked This Way Comes* at the Main Theater in Walt Disney Studios, along with her friend Esther McCoy.

In April 1985, Babb was invited by her old friend Ann Stanford to attend the Associated Writing Programs Conference to present on a panel on "Celebration: Literature and the Land" with Peter Matthiessen, Patricia Clark Smith, and Barry Lopez.[1] In her speech, Babb recounted her early life living close to the land in Eastern Colorado, reflecting on how "day to day life must have intensified my awareness of nature. It gave me a mystical sense of relatedness to the natural world. No dogma, no organization, but a pure, deep perception I have never lost."[2]

In the spring of 1987, her short story collection *The Dark Earth and Other Stories from the Great Depression,* was published by Noel Young at Capra Press in one of Capra's back-to-back editions. (The second half of her edition was devoted to Lew Amster's *The Killer Instinct and Other Stories from the Great Depression.*) In the preface to the collection, Babb states, "My life began in drama and has continued so ever since. I can never live long enough to recreate the varied stories, dark and light, but I relish them all."[3] Indeed, in the last decades of her life, thanks to the help of friends and scholars, much of Babb's work that had fallen out of print would finally be resuscitated. What had once felt like a dead end now became a path out of obscurity, one where readers would become increasingly aware of her work.

Over the years after Howe's death, a few editors reached out to Babb showing interest in *Whose Names Are Unknown,* but by the time this interest arrived, Babb had lost almost all of her confidence in her first novel, and she couldn't make herself read over what she was now calling a very rough draft in order to make the changes she thought would be necessary to make it readable to a modern audience.

Then, in the midsummer of 1989, Alan Wald, who was a professor of English literature and American culture at the University of Michigan and was researching a series of books about leftist writers from the 1930s, reached out to Babb for an interview. In their correspondence leading up to Wald's visit, Babb mentioned her unpublished manuscript. She told him that "Random House had bought it" but it was never published, and that "rather recently a western publisher who had heard of it wanted to see it, but it is still in first draft and I had no time then to consider what to do."[4]

When Wald visited Babb to interview her, he asked if he could share her work with Larry Goldstein, editor of the *Michigan Quarterly Review*. As Wald explained, "I was on the editorial board of the journal and one of my tasks was to locate unpublished material by authors for the journal to bring out, with Goldstein making the final decision." Babb agreed, and later Larry Goldstein visited her to review the manuscript himself. After a few edits back and forth, an excerpt from *Whose Names Are Unknown* was published in *Michigan Quarterly Review* in the summer of 1990.[5]

A few weeks later, Joanne Dearcopp, who'd not only kept in contact with Babb since they first met while she was working with her on *An Owl on Every Post* but had become a close friend, flew back to Los Angeles to visit Babb, and while they were out to dinner at a restaurant on Sunset Boulevard, sipping glasses of wine, Babb brought up the fact that she was devastated that all of her books had gone out of print. There in the busy restaurant, she wondered aloud to herself how one could get one's books back into print. Dearcopp, who'd grown incredibly fond of Babb over the decades they'd been friends, remembers speaking before even thinking: "No problem, Sanora. We can do that."[6] Babb just looked at her across the table. "Really?" she asked. And despite having no prior experience,

Dearcopp looked back at her friend across the table and exclaimed, "I'll be your agent!"

After their dinner, Dearcopp kept her promise and took on the role of being Babb's informal agent. She began with the plan of sending Babb's work out to university presses, a plan that almost immediately worked. In 1994, *An Owl on Every Post* was republished by the University of New Mexico Press. Babb was so grateful that she inscribed the copy of her book to Dearcopp, "whose efforts and enthusiasm created this second-time around for *Owl*, this makes me a very happy writer."[7] The next year, the University of New Mexico Press republished Babb's novel The *Lost Traveler,* with an introduction by scholar Doug Wixson. Wixson had gotten to know Babb's work as he researched and wrote his dense literary work *Worker-Writer in America,* about Babb's former literary friend Jack Conroy. Conroy had been an integral player in changing the fortunes of many midwestern literary radicals. Over the next decade, Wixson interviewed Babb extensively in hopes of taking on a larger book project about her.[8]

Then, in January 1996, Babb's sister Dorothy died. Eighteen years ago, Babb had found her sister a beautiful place to live, under a doctor's care, in Hemet, California. Dorothy lived there for eighteen years. Babb was of course saddened to lose her sister, but theirs had been a complicated relationship at best. When she was finally freed from the burden of taking care of her sister, Babb revealed in a letter to Dearcopp, "Dorothy, my sister, and I were always close. We shared the same tastes or love of literature, art, music. Aside from that, she was too dependent on me, not living her own life well and was seldom happy. I hope, if there's an afterlife, she's happier. She never felt at home in this world."[9]

But Babb's freedom was short lived. A few months later, Babb's age (she was nearly ninety) and ongoing cardiac issues caught up with her, and she had to undergo extensive surgery. By July, Babb wrote to Dearcopp, she was experiencing "post surgery ups and downs, more downs."[10] She had kept writing and publishing up until this point but now did not have the stamina to stay up late into the night and write. As she told Dearcopp, "At present, no writing news from here. . . . Before I leave dear old planet Earth . . . I hope I can write a story or two and poems. Work is such a vital part of being alive, truly alive. But I love all kinds of being alive. Every minute!"[11] With the death of her sister, her last close family member, Babb had begun thinking about her own mortality. When Dearcopp asked her if she feared dying, Babb answered emphatically, "No. Who knows, it could be interesting."[12]

In 1997, when Babb turned ninety years old, Dearcopp received good news: Babb's short story collection, *The Cry of the Tinamou*, would be published by the University of Nebraska Press, accompanied by an essay by scholar Alan Wald. For Babb this was a huge accomplishment. She had always identified herself as a short story writer, and though she had received numerous honors for her work in this genre, a collection of short stories had always eluded her. Then, in September 1998, Babb was surprised to have her first poetry collection, *Told in the Seed*, published by West End Press. Though she had written and published poetry since the 1930s, Babb "never thought my poems good enough for a book."[13]

However, even in this rush of new life, one book remained out of print: Babb's first book, the one she had once thought was her masterpiece, *Whose Names Are Unknown*. As Babb's health continued to decline, both Dearcopp and Wixson began trying to convince Babb to let them help her get this important novel published. But Babb's lack of belief in the book, generated by the ordeal she'd gone through since 1938 trying to publish it, made her slow to edit her work. Finally, in 1999, Babb did some editing, and Dearcopp and Wixson sent her manuscript to one of Wixson's contacts at the University of Illinois Press. But after holding on to the manuscript for over a year, the press finally rejected it. Meanwhile, Babb's health continued to decline.

Dearcopp and Wixson realized that they needed to help Babb edit the book if she was going to have the opportunity to see it in print before she died.

The two of them rolled up their sleeves and got to work. As Dearcopp remembers, the main changes they made to the original draft were shifting the setting of the first part of the story from Baca County to the Oklahoma Panhandle. The two also "cut the first 42 pages" because they thought that they were too similar to the way Babb opened *An Owl on Every Post*. In addition, Dearcopp felt Babb's original chapter titles, which were seasonal in her earlier draft ("First Autumn," "The 4th Summer," "The 4th Winter") were difficult for the reader to follow. Instead, she helped Babb incorporate the passage of time into the text itself and changed the chapter headings to simple numbers. Dearcopp also suggested Babb change some character names: Donne was changed to Dunne, Starbuck was changed to Starwood. Finally, Dearcopp helped Babb cut back the extensive use of colloquial dialog, a style that Dearcopp attributed to Tom Collins's influence. By the time all of these edits were made and approved by Babb, she could barely get out of bed. In April 2002, Dearcopp sent this new, edited version of the manuscript to the University of Oklahoma Press, which had previously shown interest in Babb's work. As luck would have it, the press immediately accepted the book, and Dearcopp and Babb began working with editor Julie Schilling to bring Babb's lost novel into print. *Whose Names Are Unknown* was finally published on May 10, 2004. By this time, Babb was bedridden and very, very sick. But as soon as the book was printed, Dearcopp brought a copy to Babb's bedside. As she remembers it, "We expedited the process and Sanora lived to see her first-written novel, *Whose Names Are Unknown*, finally published in 2004—the one she considered her 'most important.' She was bedridden by then, sleeping most of the time and hardly speaking. When I handed her the book, her smile was nonetheless luminous. I asked her to autograph my copy and with great effort she tried. Her illegible scrawl was shocking. I had all I could do to not cry in front of her."[14]

On December 31, 2005, Babb died in her home in the Hollywood Hills. There was no formal service. Babb was not buried in a marked grave. Instead, a small group of friends gathered in her backyard, in her beloved garden, the place where she'd gone to watch the sunrise and feed the birds after a long night of writing, a place that always made her want to go back to her work the next day. Some of her ashes were scattered in her garden and others were scattered in other places that were important to her during her lifetime, including the flat land of Eastern Colorado, where the air still smelled like sage and the buffalo grass still crunched under your feet, under the sky she'd once looked to as a child, seeking a way out.

Epilogue

"She Deserved Better"

Once *Whose Names Are Unknown* was published by the University of Oklahoma Press, the fact that Steinbeck had borrowed from Babb's notes slowly began to circulate. After reading Babb's novel, some Steinbeck scholars, like Michael J. Meyer, began to substantiate the merit of the claims that Steinbeck had appropriated Babb's material. In his review of *Whose Names Are Unknown* for the *Steinbeck Review,* Meyer points out that Steinbeck called himself "a shameless magpie" and was "accused of borrowing the stories that comprise *Pastures of Heaven* from Beth Ingalls" as well as "the ideas of Edith Wagner for his short story 'How Edith McGillicuddy Met Robert Louis Stevenson.'"[1] Meyer carefully listed the similarities he discovered between the two texts, publishing a catalog of his findings in the article. He pointed out similarities between Babb's descriptions of stillborn babies as being "all dried up; even his tongue is dry" and like "a little old man," and Steinbeck's character Rosasharn's stillborn being described as a "shriveled little mummy" that "never breathed" and "never was alive." Or the overlapping scenes of the company store charging "exorbitant prices"[2] in both texts; how both books create a contrast of the fertile fields against the dying migrants;[3] or how in each novel there is an "emphasis on music as an encouragement for the human spirit."[4] He compares "the detailed description of nature that begins chapter 38 of *Whose Names Are Unknown* with that of chapter 1 of *The Grapes of Wrath*, along with the way both authors depict "the generosity and compassion of some humans, the disdain of the Okies for charity,"[5] and in addition, how both texts show the horrendous effect being called an "Okie" had on the characters.[6] He points out how both authors use a metaphor (Babb an insect, Steinbeck a land turtle) to symbolize the migrants and how they "are being toyed with by a higher, invulnerable power."[7] At the end of his article, Meyer urged his fellow Steinbeck scholars to "read Babb—if only to see for themselves the echoes of *Grapes* that abound in her prose."[8]

Then, in 2007, Babb's notes, which she had donated to the Harry Ransom Center at the University of Texas at Austin, became public through the scholarship of Doug Wixson, who published *The Dirty Plate Trail: Remembering the Dust Bowl Refugee Camps.* The book both published and contextualized the notes Babb took while she was working at the FSA camps with Tom Collins. When Meyer reviewed Wixson's book in 2010 in the *Steinbeck Review,* he noted that "chapters 2, 3 and 4 reproduce much of Sanora Babb's field notes from 193[8]. Of special interest to Steinbeck scholars is the fact that several of the reprinted entries reflect almost identical episodes in *The Grapes of Wrath.*"[9] But, though these nearly "identical episodes" were recognized and acknowledged among members of the Steinbeck scholarship community, word of them didn't permeate far into the larger world—that is, until the summer of 2009, when Ken Burns and his colleague Dayton Duncan began working on a documentary about the Dust Bowl.

Burns and his team wanted to interview survivors of the Dust Bowl, so they set out for the small towns of the affected areas to find subjects. In Guyman, Oklahoma, they met a woman named Pauline Hodges. Hodges had been a child on a farm near Forgan, Oklahoma, when the worst of the catastrophe hit. During one of her interviews, she brought up the writer Sanora Babb. The Hodges family had become destitute during the Dust Bowl, but they had stayed in Forgan, and in 1970, when Hodges was teaching at Forgan High School, she read *An Owl on Every Post* when it was published. Hodges loved Babb's work because of Babb's ability to depict the beauty and complexity found in the landscape of the panhandle and the lives of those who lived in that landscape. When Hodges found out Babb had graduated from Forgan High School, she taught the book and had her students write letters to Babb. Babb, who was thrilled to have her book taught at her alma mater, where she had once been declared valedictorian only to have the honored revoked because a small group of parents couldn't see awarding the honor to a gambler's daughter, immediately wrote back to every single student.

After that, Babb and Hodges began to correspond regularly, and it was through this correspondence that Hodges gained extensive knowledge about Babb's life and work.[10] Hodges had followed her friend's career even after Babb's death and was thrilled to learn that Babb's long-lost novel about the Dust Bowl had been published. What was most obvious to her, and what she felt she needed to say when Burns and Duncan were seeking human stories about the Dust Bowl in their interviews, was that they needed to know about Babb's novel *Whose Names Are Unknown*. Later, when Duncan followed up with Hodges about Babb, she told him all about Babb's personal connection to the place and encouraged him to also read *On the Dirty Plate Trail*. As Duncan explained in a recent interview, when he read Babb's work, he realized that she was an "important chronicler of both what occurred on the plains in the 1930s and how Dust Bowl 'refugees' were treated in California. . . . Sanora's first-person accounts added insightful and evocative texture to the on-camera interviews we filmed of the Dust Bowl survivors who were telling personal stories from their childhoods." Burns and Duncan both pride themselves on their steadfast belief that when they begin working on a documentary, they proceed with the attitude that they don't know what the story is until it reveals itself to them: "We take the time to follow different leads, to let the story tell us where it wants to go."[11] It's because of this mindset that when Duncan learned about Babb and her novel, he and his team added her story to the one they were telling about the Dust Bowl.

In November 2012, *The Dust Bowl,* a four-part documentary miniseries, aired on PBS. The film features extensive excerpts from Babb's notes and reports and showcases Babb's unique knowledge of the Dust Bowl and its victims, which greatly increased public awareness of Babb's book. In the film, the voice of Peter Coyote introduces us to Babb, who, like the refugees, grew up in the area affected by the Dust Bowl. It was her intimacy with both the place and the people who lived there that enabled her to "establish a trust and respect" with the refugees "that extended both ways."[12] Burns also notes that Babb's detailed reports, which she intended to use to write her own novel, were shared with Steinbeck. The morning after the documentary aired, *Whose Names Are Unknown* had become a best seller, and it remains one of the most purchased books in the University of Oklahoma Press catalog to this day. As Duncan said in a recent interview, "I only wish we'd done the film twenty years earlier so that Babb would have been able to experience her book sales taking off." As he put it, "She deserved better" than what happened to her and her important novel.

Joanne Dearcopp, a longtime friend who became Babb's literary executor, once promised Babb over a lovely bottle of wine that she'd get her out-of-print books back into print. Not only has she kept Babb's novel *The Lost Traveler* and memoir *An Owl on Every Post* in print, but she has also reissued Babb's short-story collection, *Cry of the Tinamou,* and published an expanded book of her poetry, *Told in the Seed and Selected Poems.* Additionally, she has published a collection of Babb's short stories and reportage from the Depression era called *The Dark Earth and Selected Prose from the Depression Era.*

While the Dust Bowl documentary gave Babb's work its first boost, interest in her work has continued to steadily grow. Babb's work has been studied in scholarly articles and book-length studies such as *Ain't Got No Home: America's Great Migrations and the Making of an Interracial Left*; *Regionalists on the Left: Radical Voices from the American West*; and *The Nature of California: Race, Citizenship and Farming since the Dust Bowl*. It has been featured in panels at the annual meetings of the American Studies Association and the Western Literature Association. In 2021, the critical collection *Unknown No More: Recovering Sanora Babb*, edited by Dearcopp and Christine Hill Smith, was published by the University of Oklahoma Press, bringing a scholarly eye to Babb's literature and life. And an extensive article about the collection, "The Vindication of Sanora Babb," by Ed Vulliamy, was featured in the *New York Review of Books* on August 19, 2021. In 2022, Babb was posthumously granted the Ralph Ellison Award from the Oklahoma Center for the Book. A documentary about Babb and her husband called *Jimmie and Sanora* is currently being developed. As Dearcopp expressed to me in a recent interview, she only wishes she could sit again with her friend, looking out the window of Babb's house on Queens Road in Los Angeles as the lights begin to come on in the city below, like a carpet of stars, and share a glass of wine to toast to her success.

One only needs to travel to the places where Babb grew up and lived to understand the power of her work and the power those places had over her. When you visit the stark landscape of Eastern Colorado, smell the scent of sage in the air, hear the sharp cry of wild geese calling out as they circle the crops of winter wheat that are still grown there, feel the crunch of buffalo grass underfoot, see the hand-carved gravestones carved by those who survived for those who did not, you can understand how the rough beauty of this place could get under your skin. Add to this the fact that this is the place where a young girl lived in a dugout, nearly starved to death, learned to read from newspapers pasted to the dirt walls, and suffered the violence of an abusive, controlling father, and you better understand why Babb felt compelled to tell her story again and again. It was a story she emerged from with fortitude, independence, and empathy for those who suffer, whether from poverty or racism or misogyny. What we lost when *Whose Names Are Unknown* went unpublished in 1939 was more than the story of our history. We lost a better way to understand the human dimension of one of the worst natural disasters of history up until that point. Now that *Whose Names Are Unknown, The Lost Traveler, An Owl on Every Post,* and so many of Babb's poems and short stories have been published or republished, we get to see the West through her eyes, and we are richer for the experience. History is like soil: you must turn it over, till it, to find the other hidden stories underneath. When we do so we find a fuller, richer story, one that is more representative of the whole of human experience. One that Sanora Babb was a master at telling.

Notes

Introduction

1. *The Dust Bowl,* directed by Ken Burns, written by Dayton Duncan, PBS Distribution, 2012.

2. HRC 52.3.

3. Douglas Wixson, "Introduction" to Sanora Babb, *The Lost Traveler* (Muse Ink, 2013), xvii.

Chapter 1. Cheyenne Riding Like the Wind

1. Babb describes this scene in her memoir *An Owl on Every Post* (Muse Ink, 2012). She also describes a fictionalized version of this scene in the 1938–39 draft of her novel *Whose Names Are Unknown.* First draft with handwritten corrections; also clippings, 1938, 1955 (original removed to box 92: restricted due to fragile condition, digital copy available for use), Sanora Babb Collection, Harry Ransom Center, University of Texas at Austin (hereafter HRC) 7.10.

2. Babb kept these moccasins her entire life, and they can be found in the Sanora Babb Collection, HRC's Personal Effects Collection.

3. Babb, *Owl,* 7.

4. The text of this letter is included in the 1938–39 draft of *Whose Names Are Unknown.* Dorothy Babb also recounts this letter in her autobiography draft "Looking Back": "Sell everything, Asa will help you. Letter soon." HRC 70.1.

5. Asa's dialogue comes from Dorothy Babb's autobiographical story "Looking Back," HRC 70.1.

6. Details are from Jennie's recollections collected in Babb's notes for her autobiography, HRC 29.3.

7. "Run, Sheepy, Run," *Cry of the Tinamou: Stories* (Muse Ink, 2021), 66–67. Babb originally wrote the story in 1959, basing it on a story her mother told her. She first published "Run, Sheepy, Run" in *Kansas Magazine* in 1969, 19–25.

8. According to Babb's biographical notes found in HRC 58.7.

9. The details from this scene are taken from Babb's early drafts of her autobiography, written as she was considering different sections of her life for inclusion in the book that would eventually become *An Owl on Every Post*. Babb's mother, Jennie Kemper, also wrote to Babb extensively about her time in Red Rock in letters she composed just prior to her death on December 23, 1960. HRC 29.3.

10. Later in her life, Jennie Kemper shared these specific details with her daughter in a letter found in Babb's autobiography files, HRC 29.3.

11. Irene Mitchell, "Early History of Red Rock," Cherokee Strip Museum, Perry, Oklahoma.

12. HRC 70.1. Babb also refers to her father's baseball career in the *The Lost Traveler*, 17–18.

13. Babb, *Lost Traveler*, 18.

14. HRC 70.1.

15. HRC 70.1.

16. Interview with Joanne Dearcopp, Sanora Babb's literary executor, 2023.

17. Alonzo's dialogue is derived from *Konkie,* the unpublished short novel Babb wrote in the 1930s. HRC 27.9.

18. HRC 29.3.

19. Kemper to Babb, October 8, 1959, HRC 29.3. On March 13, 1908, the *Red Rock Opinion* reported that Walter Babb was on the sick list with smallpox and that a yellow sign had been posted at his bakery, but it is reported that he is still playing baseball a week later.

20. *Leavenworth Weekly Times,* August 13, 1913.

21. From Babb's recollection of her early life in Red Rock, "An Indian chief first made me feel much loved and wanted. He came to my father and said with great innocence and sincerity: 'How much papoose? Me buy.' Even tho my father insisted that I was not for sale, he kept on and on, month after month, and as I kept growing, I stayed more and more with the Indians on the reservation, and in some subtle ways, Chief Black Hawk won. They dressed me in their clothes, their beads, and beaded moccasins (still have a pair of my tiny worn ones) and at pow

wow time their feathers. He gave me a spotted 'painted' pony and I learned to ride fast bare-back, holding on to the pony's long mane. The pony was always wise; when I rode him into town and went home, he took me back." HRC 28.7.

22. It was Babb's father, Walt, who originally gave her the nickname Cheyenne. Chief Black Hawk is the one who extended her name to "Little Cheyenne Riding Like the Wind." HRC 58.7.

23. HRC 58.7.

24. Kemper to Babb, HRC 29.3.

25. Babb, *Owl*, 9.

26. Babb, *Owl*, 12.

27. Babb, *Owl*, 7.

28. *Whose Names Are Unknown* was originally set in Red Rock, Oklahoma, and Eastern Colorado, drawing from many of Babb's childhood experiences. And while it was Babb's first novel, and she finished writing it in 1939, she would not publish it until 2004.

29. Babb, *Owl*, 251.

30. Babb, *Owl*, 77–78.

31. Babb to Pollard, July 17, 1935, HRC 50.1. Lillie Pollard was Babb's distant cousin; they never met but maintained a forty-year correspondence.

32. Laura Ingalls Wilder and Garth Williams, *On the Banks of Plum Creek* (rev. ed., HarperCollins, 1953), 3–4.

33. Donald W. Linebaugh, "Digging into a Dugout House (Site 21SW17): The Archaeology of Norwegian Immigrant Anna Byberg Christopherson Goulson, Swenoda Township, Swift County,Minnesota," Technical Report No. 480, Program for Archaeological Research, University of Kentucky, May 2003, https://terpconnect.umd.edu/~dwline/Goulson.pdf.

34. Babb to Wixson, 1990, HRC 58.7.

35. Babb, *Owl*, 13.

Chapter 2. A Dugout on the High Plains

1. Babb, *Owl*, 13, 14. See also the *Springfield Herald*, vol. 24, no. 4, September 9, 1910. Alonzo harvested his first broomcorn crop in the fall of 1910, which means he was likely there in the spring of 1910 to plant the crop and had been living alone in the dugout for roughly four years when Babb's family arrived.

2. Babb, *Owl*, 14.

3. Babb, *Owl*, 15.

4. Babb to Wixson, 1996, HRC 58.7.

5. Babb, *Owl,* 256.

6. HRC 29.3.

7. Babb, *Owl,* 13.

8. "The Homestead Act of 1862," Educator Resources, National Archives, https://www.archives.gov/education/lessons/homestead-act.

9. John A. Babb, "Application for Registration for Homestead Entry," 7/16/1901, Yukon, 1982.039 Wichita and Kiowa, Comanche, and Apache Ceded Lands Homestead Applications, box 1, folder 5, Oklahoma Historical Society.

10. Wallace Stegner, "Editor's Introduction," in John Wesley Powell, *The Arid Lands,* ed. Wallace Stegner (University of Nebraska Press, 2004), xvii.

11. Walter Prescott Webb, *The Great Plains* (Ginn, 1951), 8.

12. Babb, "Autobiography." These files differ greatly from later drafts of *Owl* and are found in a different part of Babb's papers at HRC. She discusses these early chapters in a letter to her agent Patience Ross on October 6, 1961, HRC 34.3.

13. Kemper to Babb, HRC 56.1.

14. Aldo Leopold first used the term "land ethic" in his *Sand County Almanac.* Jessica Hellmann, "Thinking Like the Plains: The Creation of Sanora Babb's Land Ethic," in Joanne Dearcopp and Christine Hill Smith, eds., *Unknown No More: Recovering Sanora Babb* (University of Oklahoma Press, 2021), 28.

15. Babb, *Owl,* 251.

16. Babb, "Autobiography," May 1966 (plan for *Owl* sent to Mary Abbott), HRC 28.9.

17. Babb, *Owl,* 35.

18. Babb, *Owl,* 36.

19. De Witt Clinton Peters, "Prologue," *The Life and Adventures of Kit Carson, the Nestor of the Rocky Mountains, from Facts Narrated Himself* (1858).

20. Babb, *Owl,* 78.

21. Babb, *Owl,* 79.

22. Babb to Burgess, June 3, 1963, HRC 37.9.

23. Babb, *Owl,* 83.

24. Babb, *Owl,* 141, 142.

25. This description comes from an exhibit at the Morton County Historical Society Museum in Elkhart, Kansas, as well as Babb's description in a letter to Doug Wixson, undated, HRC 58.7.

26. Babb, *Owl,* 145. Bettie Gatlin's name is changed to Carrie Mayo Whitehead in *Owl*; Babb, letter to Ross, HRC 34.3.

27. Babb, *Owl,* 147.

28. Babb, *Owl,* 147.

29. This information was found in articles in the *Springfield Herald*. These resources were provided by historian Kent Brooks.

30. Babb, *Owl*, 59.

31. Babb, "Autobiography," May 1966, HRC 28.9.

32. Babb, "Autobiography," May 1966, HRC 28.9.

33. Babb, *Owl*, 104.

34. Descriptions of the Haupmans' farm were changed by Babb in *Owl*, as she later assured her agent (who worried the family might sue her if she published her book as a memoir); Babb to Ross, March 8, 1970, HRC 34.3. She also mentions in a chronology she created for Wixson that "one daughter of the Krouses (not their name) wrote to me saying her mother was 'not like that' about the milk incident, but it did happen." HRC 58.7.

35. Babb later admitted that Maxine was a made-up character; Babb to Ross, March 8, 1970, HRC 34.3.

36. The details and dialog in the remainder of the chapter are drawn from multiple sources: the published version of *Owl*, the many versions in Babb's autobiography drafts, letters from Jennie Kemper to Babb, and Babb's letters to Doug Wixson.

Chapter 3. The House on Horse Creek

1. Kemper to Babb, 1959, HRC 56.1.

2. Babb, "Autobiography," May 1966 (plan for *Owl* sent to Mary Abbott), HRC 29.2.

3. Dorothy Babb, "The Surrey," *Direction*, July 1944 (variously titled "Happy Birthday," as published in the *Christian Herald*, July 1957); carbon typescripts, alternate version, composite version, 1944–1957, HRC 70.2.

4. Babb, *Owl*, 177.

5. Babb, *Owl*, 178.

6. Babb, "Autobiography" Notes and Materials, HRC 28.9.

7. Babb, *Owl*, 48.

8. Dialog in the following section is taken from *Owl*, 135–39; Babb's short story "Daft"; and her "Autobiography," HRC 28.9.

9. Babb believed whole-heartedly in what she saw with her grandfather. Once she published this story as part of *Owl*, she received correspondence from others who had seen the same ghost horse: "A very old woman wrote me about the ghost horse, Daft in *An Owl on Every Post* saying Daft was the wrong name, but that the horse was a familiar ghost-horse of those plains." HRC 58.7.

10. Babb, "Autobiography," May 1966 (plan for *Owl* sent to Mary Abbott), HRC 29.2.

11. Babb, "Autobiography," HRC 28.9.

Chapter 4. "Study Like a House Afire"

1. Frederick Jackson Turner, "The Significance of the Frontier in American History," paper read at the meeting of the American Historical Association in Chicago, July 12, 1893, during the World's Columbian Exposition.

2. Babb, *Owl,* 235.

3. To this day, Elkhart, and the county where it is situated, Morton County, use the "cornerstone" designation to signify the location of the town and county.

4. Babb, *Owl,* 236.

5. Dorothy Babb, unpublished autobiography drafts, HRC Container 70.

6. *Elkhart Tri-State News* was formerly known as *Richmond Republican* and *Elkhart News.*

7. Background information about Cora provided by Morton County Historical Society Museum, Elkhart, Kansas.

8. Babb, "Autobiography," HRC 28.9.

9. Harold H. Smith to Babb, HRC 16.7.

10. Details about the school's location and photographs of the school provided by Morton County Historical Society Museum, Elkhart, Kansas.

11. Babb, *Owl,* 239.

12. Babb, *Owl,* 237.

13. Babb, "Autobiography," HRC 28.9.

14. Babb would later write a short story, "Professor Coyote," about Professor Harry J. Davis and her time in Elkhart (HRC 4.4). In a letter to Patience Ross dated August 7, 1980, Babb mentions that this short story was based on the superintendent of schools in Elkhart who appears in *Owl,* where his name is Professor Waite.

15. Babb, "Autobiography," HRC 28.9. She also mentions this detail in her short story "Professor Coyote," HRC 4.4.

16. Dialog throughout this passage is from *Owl,* 238, and "Autobiography," HRC 28.9.

17. Babb, *Owl,* 239.

18. Details about what schools were like during this era were taken from an interview with Pauline Hodges, March 2022.

19. Babb, "Autobiography," HRC 28.9.

20. Babb, *Owl*, 239–40.

21. Babb, "Autobiography," HRC 28.9.

22. Interview with Pauline Hodges, March 2022.

23. Babb explained this in a letter to Joanne Dearcopp late in her life. Joanne Dearcopp private collection.

24. Douglas Wixson, "Introduction" to Babb, *Lost Traveler*, xi.

25. Babb, *Owl*, 242.

26. Babb, "Autobiography," HRC 29.2.

27. Babb, *Owl*, 241.

28. Babb, *Owl*, 241.

29. Smith to Babb, June 22, 1970, HRC 16.7.

30. D. Babb, HRC Container 70.

31. Dorothy Babb, "The Carnival," handwritten and corrected typescript, letter, 1955, 1981, HRC 70.1.

32. Babb, "Autobiography," HRC 28.9.

33. Babb, biographical notes, resumés, questionnaires, documents, HRC 58.7.

34. It is unclear, from both Babb's and Dorothy Babb's autobiographical writing, whether Mrs. Aiken was named Lucy or Nellie.

35. Babb, "Autobiography," HRC 28.9.

36. Babb, "Autobiography," HRC 28.9.

37. Babb's notes on autobiographical material for the London publisher Gollancz, Joanne Dearcopp private collection.

38. HRC Container 92.

39. Babb, *Owl*, 246.

40. Babb, *Owl*, 246.

41. Babb, *Owl*, 246.

42. Babb, *Owl*, 247.

43. Babb, *Owl*, 247.

44. Kansas Historical Society, "Flu Pandemic of 1918," *Kansapedia*, https://www.kshs.org/kansapedia/flu-pandemic-of-1918/17805.

45. History.com Editors, "The Spanish Flu," https://www.history.com/topics/world-war-i/1918-flu-pandemic.

46. Babb, biographical biographical notes, resumés, questionnaires, documents, HRC 58.7.

47. D. Babb, HRC Container 70.

48. Babb, biographical biographical notes, resumés, questionnaires, documents, HRC 58.7.

49. D. Babb, HRC Container 70.

50. D. Babb, HRC Container 70.

51. Babb to Melissa Blake, December 11, 1978; her father saw spirits before he received a telegram alerting him of Asa's death. HRC 41.5.

52. Babb, *Lost Traveler,* 75, and HRC Container 92.

53. The Smiths' oldest son, Cecil, returned from military training camp in Lawrence, Kansas, just before his father's death, and Ted returned home from Camp Zachary in Louisville, Kentucky, two days after his death, in time for his funeral. "Eugene L. Smith (Owner of Paper) Dies of Influenza 11-24-18," *Elkhart Tri-State News,* November 28, 1918.

54. Babb, "Autobiography," HRC 28.9.

Chapter 5. Finding Venus

1. "The Early History of Forgan School," HRC 58.7.

2. These dunes now make up Beaver Dunes Park in Beaver County, Oklahoma.

3. As of 2022, this building is still standing on Main Street in Forgan, Oklahoma.

4. Babb, "Autobiography," March 27, 1962, HRC 29.2.

5. Babb, "Autobiography," HRC 29.2.

6. Babb, "Autobiography," HRC 29.2.

7. Babb, "Autobiography," HRC 29.2.

8. Babb, "Autobiography," HRC 29.2.

9. Edith Sloan joined the faculty of Forgan High School when the school opened in 1913 (*Faith in Our Future: Forgan Public School Centennial Yearbook,* 2013). After leaving Forgan, Babb would lose touch with Sloan until May 20, 1958, when she'd write a letter to Mrs. Edith Sloan Williams, who was teaching at City Hospital in Baltimore at the time; HRC 43.5.

10. The paper would soon be renamed *The Forgan Enterprise.* It was owned by L. B. Tooker.

11. HRC 29.2.

12. Babb stated she made this amount at this job in her Guggenheim Application from 1939; however, the figure seems high for the work she was doing. HRC 19.5.

13. Babb, "Autobiography," HRC 29.2.

14. Wixson, "Introduction" to Babb, *Lost Traveler,* xiii.

15. Babb, *Owl,* 253.

16. Babb, *Lost Traveler,* 88.

17. According to Babb's biographical statement, "I had never been to a theater, but I had seen a few traveling stock companies. With my amateur ignorance and my mind and emotions nearly exploding I thought nothing of organizing such a project." HRC 58.7.

18. Babb, *Owl,* 253.

19. The location of this building was derived from an interview with Pauline Hodges on May 10, 2022.

20. "A generous widow let us use her storm cellar for rehearsals and making up and her empty store building on Main Street for our Saturday shows." "Autobiography," HRC 28.7. Locations for the buildings of the time were provided by Pauline Hodges on our tour of Forgan, Oklahoma, in 2022.

21. Babb, "Autobiography," HRC 29.2.

22. Babb, "Autobiography," HRC 29.2.

23. Babb, *Owl,* 253.

24. HRC 29.2.

25. Babb, *Owl,* 253.

26. Babb, *Owl,* 253.

27. Babb, *Owl,* 254.

28. Babb, "Autobiography," HRC 29.2.

29. Babb, *Owl,* 254.

30. Babb, *Owl,* 254.

31. HRC 29.2.

32. Erin Royston Battat, *Ain't Got No Home: America's Great Migrations and the Making of an Interracial Left* (University of North Carolina Press, 2014), 11.

33. Babb to Este Buffalow, June 15, 1972, HRC 43.5.

34. Russell Manuel was a cowboy and musician originally from Wichita, Kansas, who "learned all the tricks of bronco 'busting' and 'bulldogging' on a ranch in South Dakota. In addition to his abilities as an expert rope man and cowboy, he [was] also an accomplished banjo musician." Babb's recollection in the "Early Chronology" she created for Wixson, HRC 58.7.

35. Babb would learn about her friend's recent suicide in 1971, when she was corresponding with other classmates about their fiftieth high school reunion. HRC 43.5.

36. Walter Babb to Sanora Babb, December 10, 1948, HRC 13.4.

37. Babb, *Owl,* 254.

38. By her senior year, Babb and her friend Merle Landsen (who was dubbed the "Webster of FHS" in the school yearbook, and who would later become a

lawyer and a district judge) were considered the smartest people in the class of 1924. But Merle didn't enjoy their time in high school. As he would write to Sanora fifty years after their graduation, "I am sure you feel very much as I do about our school days. My high school and college experiences remain a very painful period of my life—something to be ignored or forgotten." He goes on to say that their friendship was "one of the few, very pleasant and well-remembered facets" of his high school days. Merle Landen to Babb, April 25, 1974, HRC 43.5.

39. An early draft of *Lost Traveler* contains Babb's recollection of this scene; details were taken from this account. HRC 17.10.

40. Babb, *Owl*, 254.

41. Pauline Hodges interviews, May 10, 2022, and June 7, 2022.

42. Babb to Temple Lee Reed, August 1, 1978, HRC 37.4.

43. Babb, *Owl*, 254.

44. Joanne Dearcopp's notes on her personal correspondence with Babb (from Dearcopp's private collection).

Chapter 6. The Poet of Kansas

1. Babb to Wixson, undated, HRC 58.7.

2. Babb, *Owl*, 255.

3. "When I came home from my one and only year at the university to the dusty dun-colored town in the Oklahoma Panhandle, my inner climate had changed far more than in any previous year. This I kept to myself, but not in frustration. The discoveries, expansion, assurance, no matter how small in a whole life of growing, were mine alone to savor and touch, relive and dream over. The dreams that had levitated my being since that childish revelation on the Colorado plains at the age of seven had begun to come true on my entrance to the University. With life at home deep in farm poverty in my father's romantic periods of reform, or more than less sordid and unlawful in towns, education shone with the steady brilliance of Venus, almost always visible, as a way of escape." "Autobiography," October 12, 1962, HRC 29.2.

4. W. Babb to S. Babb, December 10, 1948, HRC 13.4.

5. The character of Des is based on Babb's father, Walt. In this early draft, she unapologetically depicts her father's addiction to gambling and his physically and mentally abusive behavior. In later drafts, based on her editors' suggestions, his character would be watered down to become more palatable.

6. Early draft of *Lost Traveler,* 116, HRC Container 92.

7. Douglas Wixson, "Radical by Nature: Sanora Babb and Ecological Disaster on the High Plains, 1900–1940," in *Regionalists on the Left*, ed. Michael C. Steiner (University of Oklahoma Press, 2013), 118.

8. Wixson, "Radical by Nature," 118.

9. Early draft of *Lost Traveler*, 225, HRC Container 92.

10. Kelley was well known for his column "Grass Roots," which ran in the *Topeka Daily Capital* for nearly a decade. He bought the *Garden City Herald* in 1926.

11. Early draft of *Lost Traveler*, 140, HRC Container 92.

12. Wixson, "Introduction" to Babb, *Lost Traveler*, xiii.

13. *Kansas Magazine*, 1939, 117, HRC Container 76.

14. Phone interview conducted by Wixson with Babb, date unknown, Joanne Dearcopp private collection.

15. Later she'd add to her collection Edna St. Vincent Millay's *Fatal Interview* (1931), a book into which she pasted articles about Millay's death and an article about *The Letters of Edna St. Vincent Millay*, ed. Alan Ross Macdougall, which was published in 1952. This makes it clear that Millay remained a large influence on Babb throughout the rest of her life.

16. Nancy Milford, *Savage Beauty: The Life of Edna St. Vincent Millay* (Random House, 2001), xiv.

17. Carol S. Loranger, "Erratic Orbit: Sanora Babb, Poet," in Dearcopp and Smith, eds., *Unknown No More*, 142.

18. Babb to Carol, March 27, 1960, HRC 28.7.

19. Babb to Carol, March 27, 1960, HRC 28.7.

20. Interview with Wald, Hollywood, July 1989, HRC C3058.

21. HRC 4.2.

22. *The Letters of Edna St. Vincent Millay*, ed. Allan Ross Macdougall (Grosset & Dunlap, 1952), 222.

23. *San Bernardino Sun*, vol. 61, no. 174, February 22, 1928.

24. HRC 2.1.

25. Babb to Reed, August 1, 1978, HRC 37.4; and HRC 58.7.

26. Babb to Reed, August 1, 1978, HRC 37.4.

27. Babb to Reed, August 1, 1978, HRC 37.4.

28. Babb would also include the character of William Shakespeare in the initial draft of her first published novel, *The Lost Traveler*. "Typescript draft, 1947," 186–87, HRC Container 92.

29. Babb to Wixson, undated, HRC 58.7.

30. Babb to Reed, August 1, 1978, HRC 37.4.

31. Wixon, "Radical by Nature," 119–20.

32. Douglas Wixson, *Worker-Writer in America: Jack Conroy and the Tradition of Midwestern Literary Radicalism, 1898–1990* (University of Illinois Press, 1994), 583.

33. The article was reprinted in the *Clarion Ledger* (Jackson, Mississippi), the *York Daily Record* (York, Pennsylvania), the *Rutland Daily Herald* (Rutland, Vermont), the *Morning News* (Wilmington, Delaware), the *Stockton Daily Independent* (Stockton, California), the *Billings Gazette* (Billings, Montana), the *Idaho Daily Statesman* (Boise, Idaho), the *Fort Worth Star-Telegram* (Fort Worth, Texas), the *San Bernadino County Sun* (San Bernadino, California), the *Searchlight* (Redding, California), and the *Independent Record* (Helena, Missouri).

34. Loranger, "Erratic Orbit," 142.

35. Loranger, "Erratic Orbit," 144.

36. HRC 23.8.

37. Wallace Stevens, "The Comedian as the Letter C," The Poetry Foundation, https://www.poetryfoundation.org/poems/47428/the-comedian-as-the-letter-c, line 1.

38. Babb recounts a scene like this in the opening chapters of *Lost Traveler*.

39. HRC 7.10.

40. According to Babb's Guggenheim application, HRC 19.5.

41. Babb writes about Kelley's departure in an early draft of *Lost Traveler*, 140, HRC, Container 92.

42. Dorothy Babb to Esther McCoy, 1951 or 1954, Esther McCoy Papers, Smithsonian Institution Archives of American Art.

43. Babb, *Lost Traveler*, 232–33.

44. Both letters can be found in HRC 58.7.

Chapter 7. "Fling This Wild Song"

1. Sanora Babb, "Passenger Trains and Harvey Houses: A Writer's Tribute," Joanne Dearcopp private collection.

2. HRC 58.7.

3. HRC 58.7 and HRC 28.6.

4. HRC 24.7.

5. HRC 24.7.

6. Interview with Mann, 1982, HRC 28.6.

7. HRC 58.7.

8. Babb to Wald, 1989, HRC 54.8.

9. Interview with Wald, Hollywood, July 1989, HRC C3058.

10. The Hollywood chapter was started by Norman MacLeod in late 1931, according to Alan Wald (*Exiles from a Future Time: The Forging of the Mid-Twentieth Century Literary Left* [University of North Carolina Press, 2002], 104).

11. Babb to Wixson, February 12, 1991, Joanne Dearcopp private collection.

12. HRC 19.5.

13. HRC 58.7.

14. Interview with Mann, 1982, HRC 28.6.

15. Van Riper to Babb, 1947, HRC 4.6.

16. Babb to Pollard, July 17, 1931, HRC 49.4.

17. Interview with Mann, 1982, HRC 28.6.

18. HRC 28.6.

19. Dialog in this scene is from the Daniel Mann Papers, file 122, Margaret Herrick Library.

20. These headshots are located in HRC 66.1.

21. Thalberg was only eight years older than Babb.

22. Dialog in this scene is from the Daniel Mann Papers, file 122, Margaret Herrick Library.

23. Sanora Babb, *The Dark Earth and Selected Prose from the Great Depression* (Muse Ink, 2021), xii.

24. Babb, *Dark Earth,* xii.

25. Babb, *Dark Earth,* xii.

26. The library opened at its permanent location in 1926.

27. Hadley Meares, "Stanley Rose's Humble Bookstore Was the Center of Literary LA in the 1930s," LAist, March 19, 2019, https://laist.com/news/la-history /stanley-rose-bookstore-literary-las-hottest-spot-1930s.

28. As Babb recalled in a letter to Wixson in 1996, "Stanley Rose's Bookshop was on Hollywood Blvd. It was not a leftist bookstore, but a wonderful store that writers favored mainly because of that marvelous character (a Texan) Stanley Rose. It was truly an art hangout. An art gallery in back and good books in front. During the depression when I was flat broke, I did a lot of my good reading there, and was one of SR's longtime friends." HRC 58.7.

29. Kevin Starr, *Material Dreams: Southern California through the 1920s* (Oxford University Press, 1990), 348.

30. Babb to Saroyan, May 10, 1933: "I did an adaptation for a Ronald Colman picture about four years ago, but shortly after lost my 'wires'" (her connections to

Hollywood to sell screenplays). William Saroyan Papers, 1926-1981, Stanford University Libraries.

31. Wixson, "Radical by Nature," 120.

32. Babb to Pollard, July 17, 1931, HRC 49.4.

33. Saroyan to Babb, September 6, 1932, William Saroyan Papers, 1926-1981, Stanford University Libraries.

34. HRC 27.4.

35. Nona Balakian, *The World of William Saroyan* (Bucknell University Press, 1998), 135-37.

36. "In Progress: Costa Rica and Panama," HRC 27.11.

37. "In Progress: Costa Rica and Panama," HRC 27.11.

38. Babb to Saroyan, HRC 52.5.

39. "In Progress: Costa Rica and Panama," HRC 27.11.

40. "In Progress: Costa Rica and Panama," HRC 27.11.

41. *San Francisco Call,* Thursday, June 23, 1932, HRC 58.8.

42. Interview with Mann, 1982, HRC 28.6.

43. Daniel Mann Papers, file 122, Margaret Herrick Library.

44. Interview with Mann, 1982, HRC 28.6.

45. Todd Rainsberger, *James Wong Howe, Cinematographer* (A.S. Barnes, 1981), 11.

46. Babb to Howe, January 1933, HRC 45.2.

47. Sanora Babb, "Poppies in the Wind," *Windsor Quarterly: Modern American Literature* 1, no. 2 (Summer 1933): 175.

48. "Poppies in the Wind," 176.

49. Conroy to Babb, August 7, 1933, HRC 34.4.

50. "The Old One," *The Midland,* March/April 1933, 30.

51. Babb to Saroyan, March 27, 1933, William Saroyan Papers, 1926-1981, Stanford University Libraries. See also the letter she received from Clifton Fadiman at Simon & Schuster dated November 3, 1932, in which he asks if she has any projects afoot, "particularly if they include a project for a novel." (The letter was sent in care of *Clay* editor José García Villa, who was then living at 302 West 12th St. in New York City.) HRC 53.5.

52. HRC 70.1.

53. Babb to Saroyan, January 1935, HRC 52.5.

54. Babb to Saroyan, March 27, 1934, HRC 52.5.

55. As she recalls in a letter to her friend Nora, "He threw pebbles at my windows and shouted loud enough to be heard for blocks, 'Sanora, I love you! Let's

get married!' Jimmie was visiting me. He and Dorothy my sister were sitting talking. Then William came to the door, and I had to ask him in. He was introduced to Jimmie and then tried to pass it all off as a joke." HRC 52.5. Babb also remembers their relationship in a note written on the outside of a letter dated March 28, 1934, HRC Container 42.

Chapter 8. The Writers' Congress

1. "Early Chronology," HRC 58.7.
2. Sanora Babb, *Told in the Seed and Selected Poems* (Muse Ink, 2021), 115.
3. HRC 58.7.
4. Babb to Pollard, July 17, 1931, HRC 49.4.
5. Babb to Saroyan, April 27, 1933, William Saroyan Papers, 1926-1981, Stanford University Libraries.
6. Interview with James Wong Howe's nephew Don Lee, June 21, 2022.
7. One of these assignments was a play Babb wrote for her sister called *South Dakota Farm: A One-Act Play*. HRC 27.2.
8. Dorothy Babb, "Konkie," *Kansas Magazine*, 1949, HRC 70.1.
9. Sanora Babb, *On the Dirty Plate Trail: Remembering the Dust Bowl Refugee Camps,* ed. Douglas Wixson, photographs by Dorothy Babb (University of Texas Press, 2007), 45.
10. Babb, *Dirty Plate Trail,* 48.
11. Babb, *Dirty Plate Trail,* 49.
12. Le Sueur to Babb, February 9, 1935, HRC 47.7. All quotations from Le Sueur throughout the following paragraphs are from this letter.
13. Constance Coiner, *Better Red: The Writing and Resistance of Tillie Olsen and Meridel Le Sueur* (University of Illinois Press, 1998), 16.
14. Ann George and Jack Selzer, "What Happened at the First American Writers' Congress? Kenneth Burke's 'Revolutionary Symbolism in America,'" *Rhetoric Society Quarterly* 33, no. 2 (2003): 47–66, http://www.jstor.org/stable/3886097.
15. Interview with Wald, Hollywood, July 1989, HRC C3058.
16. Babb to Wixson, February 12, 1991, Joanne Dearcopp private collection. At the time, Olsen was under contract with Random House and writing her novel *Yonnondio.*
17. Panthea Reid, *Tillie Olsen: One Woman, Many Riddles* (Rutgers University Press, 2010), 104.
18. Babb to Wixson, February 12, 1991, Joanne Dearcopp private collection.

19. Babb to Wixson, February 12, 1991, Joanne Dearcopp private collection.

20. Reid, *Tillie Olsen*, 105.

21. Babb to Wixson, February 12, 1991, Joanne Dearcopp private collection.

22. Reid, *Tillie Olsen*, 105.

23. Le Sueur to Babb, 1935, HRC 50.1.

24. Babb, *Dark Earth*, 61.

25. Babb, *Dark Earth*, 64.

26. Babb to Wixson, February 12, 1991, Joanne Dearcopp private collection.

27. Babb to Wixson, February 12, 1991, Joanne Dearcopp private collection.

28. Wixson, *Worker-Writer in America*, 395.

29. "Guide to the League of American Writers Archives," Bancroft Library, University of California, Berkeley.

30. Coiner, *Better Red*, 81.

31. Reid, *Tillie Olsen*, 105.

32. Babb to Wixson, February 12, 1991, Joanne Dearcopp private collection.

33. Elaine Showalter, "Feminist Criticism in the Wilderness," *Critical Inquiry* 8, no. 2 (Winter 1981): 204.

34. Babb to Wixson, February 12, 1991, Joanne Dearcopp private collection.

35. Harp to Babb, January 8, 1971, HRC 16.4.

36. Reid, *Tillie Olsen*, 105.

37. Though her book was under contract, Tillie Olsen would not complete her novel during the 1930s. *Yonnondio* would not be finished and published until the 1970s.

38. Reid, *Tillie Olsen*, 106–7.

39. Crichton to Babb, July 27, 1932, HRC 42.8.

40. Babb to Wixson, February 12, 1991, Joanne Dearcopp private collection.

41. Reid, *Tillie Olsen*, 107–8.

42. This is not to say that Olsen did not also have a complicated relationship with the Communist Party. Both she and Le Sueur found themselves committed to the party while they felt "an emerging feminist critique of its androcentrism"; Coiner, *Better Red*, 16.

43. Nelsen Algren would become a lifelong friend whom Babb would often visit when she passed through Chicago on her cross-country trips, as she stated in a letter to Wixson (February 12, 1991, Joanne Dearcopp private collection).

44. Babb to Wixson, February 12, 1991, Joanne Dearcopp private collection.

45. Babb to Wixson, February 12, 1991, Joanne Dearcopp private collection.

46. Babb to Wixson, February 12, 1991, Joanne Dearcopp private collection.

47. Babb to Wixson, February 12, 1991, Joanne Dearcopp private collection.

Chapter 9. "I Demand You Write More Shamelessly and Nakedly"

1. Latimer was a writer living in New York City who published two highly acclaimed novels, *We Are Incredible* (1928) and *This Is My Body* (1930), and two collections of short stories, *Nellie Bloom and Other Stories* (1929) and *Guardian Angel and Other Stories* (1932).

2. Le Sueur to Babb, 1935, HRC 50.1.

3. Wald, "Soft Focus: The Short Fiction of Sanora Babb," *Cry of the Tinamou*, xv.

4. According to a note written by Babb found in HRC 5.2, as well as her interview with Wald, Hollywood, July 1989, HRC C3058. Rushmore would famously later become an informant for the House Un-American Activities Committee.

5. "Farmers' Holiday" (May–June 1935), "Farm in Alaska" (July 9, 1935), "Lora" (August 10, 1935).

6. Dorothy Babb, "The Years That Went Away," 18, HRC 70.3.

7. Babb to Evelyn Brewster, March 3, 1962, HRC 28.7.

8. Rainsberger, *James Wong Howe,* 20.

9. Rainsberger, *James Wong Howe,* 20.

10. Howe to Babb, April 21, 1936, HRC 45.3–4.

11. Howe to Babb, May 13, 1936, HRC 45.3–4.

12. Intourist was a Russian tour operator founded April 12, 1929, that served as the primary travel agency for foreign tourists in the USSR.

13. Bulosan to Babb, November 7, 1934, HRC 42.1.

14. Bulosan to Babb, February 14, 1936, HRC 42.2.

15. Bulosan, *America Is in the Heart* (University of Washington Press, 2014), 232.

16. Bulosan, *America Is in the Heart,* 230.

17. Bulosan to Babb, March 5, 1936, HRC 42.2.

18. Bulosan to Babb, March 31, 1936, HRC 42.2.

19. HRC 68.1.

20. Babb talks about this shift in their relationship in her interview with Daniel Mann, 1982, HRC 28.6.

21. Babb to Brewster, March 3, 1962, HRC 28.7.

22. Battat, *Ain't Got No Home,* 45.

23. Babb to Howe, August 29, 1936, HRC 46.6.

24. In 1946, John Steinbeck would also take a trip to the Soviet Union (with the photographer Robert Capa) and from this experience write *A Russian Journal.*

25. Interview with Wald, Hollywood, July 1989, HRC C3058.

26. S. Babb to D. Babb and Lillie Pollard, September 26, 1936, HRC 50.1.

27. HRC 88.5.

28. Interview with Wald, Hollywood, July 1989, HRC C3058.

29. Interview with Wald, Hollywood, July 1989, HRC C3058.

30. Interview with Wald, Hollywood, July 1989, HRC C3058.

31. Babb to Maxim Lieber, January 22, 1962, HRC 35.3.

32. Interview with Wald, Hollywood, July 1989, HRC C3058.

33. S. Babb to D. Babb and Pollard, September 26, 1936, HRC 50.1.

34. S. Babb to D. Babb and Pollard, September 26, 1936, HRC 50.1.

35. S. Babb to D. Babb and Pollard, September 26, 1936, HRC 50.1.

36. Babb to Howe, August 18, 1936, HRC 46.6.

37. Babb to Howe, August 25, 1936, HRC 46.6.

38. The only other letter in which she writes about longing to have a child is a love letter to Ralph Ellison.

39. Prophylactoria were health centers set up after the revolution for prostitutes in the USSR.

40. "Dr. Fera," HRC 26.6.

41. It's not clear what ultimately happened regarding Babb's appendicitis. There is no record of her surgery, but she did state later in a letter to Dorothy that she wanted to wait until she returned to the United States to have surgery.

42. S. Babb to D. Babb and Pollard, September 26, 1936, HRC 50.1.

43. S. Babb to D. Babb and Pollard, September 26, 1936, HRC 50.1.

44. *Fire over England* would be in production for fourteen weeks, according to Jerry Vermilye, *The Great British Films* (Citadel, 1978), 78.

45. S. Babb to D. Babb and Pollard, September 26, 1936, HRC 50.1.

46. Babb to Saroyan, October 27, 1936, William Saroyan Papers, 1926-1981, Stanford University Libraries.

47. S. Babb to W. Babb, November 8, 1936, HRC 40.4.

48. S. Babb to W. Babb, November 7, 1936, HRC 40.4.

49. Rainsberger, *James Wong Howe,* 21.

50. While in London, she would appear in three films and be part of a play at the Savoy Theatre.

51. Babb to Wixson, undated, HRC 58.7.

52. Interview with Don Lee, James Wong Howe's nephew, who lived with Sanora Babb toward the end of her life, June 21, 2022.

Chapter 10. "You Can't Eat the Scenery"

1. Carlos Bulosan, *Sound of Falling Light: Letters in Exile,* ed. Dolores S. Feria (N.p., 1960), 202.

2. Dorothy wrote a short story about her visits with Bulosan at the tuberculosis ward called "Aurelio." This was Bulosan's brother's name.

3. Fante describes his friend in the introduction to Bulosan, *America Is in the Heart*, xx.

4. Bulosan to Babb, April 7, 1938, HRC 42.2.

5. Wixson, "Radical by Nature," 123.

6. It's important to note that in John Leggett's biography of William Saroyan, *A Daring Young Man* (Knopf, 2002), there is no mention of the important relationship that Saroyan and Babb shared. However, in *The World of William Saroyan*, by Nona Balakian, she writes, "Babb (Mrs. James Wong Howe) herself attests that Saroyan fell deeply in love with her in 1932 or 1933 . . . and asked to marry her." Balakian goes on to question, as I do, why "we find no mention of either Ms. Babb or any other strong romantic attachments in the many scattered accounts of Saroyan's life in the 1930s (his own and others') and why, indeed, to this day no one who claims to have been close to the writer appears to know of Ms. Babb. Of course, there is one simple reason why this has not come up. For a long time, it was assumed that Saroyan's love life had but one object: his typewriter. The initial image that he created was of a struggling young man, locked in a cold San Francisco flat, furiously and obsessively turning out stories that he couldn't sell." Balakian, *World of William Saroyan*, 135–37.

7. Maxim Lieber to Babb, November 23, 1934, HRC 35.3. Lieber was Babb's first literary agent.

8. HRC 7.10.

9. On her 1939 Guggenheim application, Babb quotes this small part of Leviticus 25:35 as an inspiration for the title. HRC 19.5.

10. Babb, *Dirty Plate Trail*, 49–50.

11. Wixson, "Radical by Nature," 122.

12. Babb's sister Dorothy (who also was given a camera by Howe) would visit her sister and take photos. These candid and striking photos are published in *On the Dirty Plate Trail* and are housed at the HRC.

13. Babb, *Dirty Plate Trail*, 88–89.

14. "New Masses," *Encyclopedia of the Great Depression*, Encyclopedia.com, https://www.encyclopedia.com/economics/encyclopedias-almanacs-transcripts -and-maps/new-masses.

15. Babb, "Farmers without Farms," *New Masses*, June 21, 1938.

16. Babb, *Dirty Plate Trail*, 33.

17. Babb, *Dirty Plate Trail*, 33.

18. "SRA Form 101: California State Relief Administration Transmittal," HRC 18.7.

19. Collins to Babb, March 3, 1938, HRC 18.6.

20. Collins to Babb, March 18, 1938 HRC 18.7

21. Collins to Babb, March 18, 1938, HRC 18.7.

22. Quotes throughout this paragraph are from *Dirty Plate Trail,* 62–68.

23. Babb, *Dirty Plate Trail,* 63, 72.

24. Babb, *Dirty Plate Trail,* 65–66.

25. HRC 19.5.

26. Babb, *Dirty Plate Trail,* 78, 72.

27. In *Whose Names,* chapter 34, Babb writes about the immense volume workers had to pick in order to be allowed to live in a shack on the farm. Her notes about this can be found in *Dirty Plate Trail,* 83.

28. Babb, *Dirty Plate Trail,* 89.

29. HRC 7.10.

30. Babb, *Dirty Plate Trail,* 13.

31. Babb, *Dirty Plate Trail,* 102.

32. Babb, *Dirty Plate Trail,* 122.

33. Babb, *Dirty Plate Trail,* 130.

34. HRC Container 18.

35. "Babb," March 1978, HRC 58.7.

36. "Babb," March 1978, HRC 58.7.

Chapter 11. *Whose Names Are Unknown*

1. Jackson Benson, *The True Adventures of John Steinbeck* (Viking, 1984), 373.

2. Babb, *Dirty Plate Trail,* 130.

3. Robert B. Harmon, *John Steinbeck: An Annotated Guide to Biographical Sources* (Scarecrow Press, 1996), 181.

4. Harmon, *John Steinbeck,* 240.

5. Thomas A. Collins and John Steinbeck, "From *Bringing in the Sheaves,* by 'Windsor Drake,'" *Journal of Modern Literature* 5, no. 2 (1976): 225.

6. Benson, *True Adventures of John Steinbeck,* 368–69.

7. John Steinbeck, Autograph manuscript journal, February–March 1938. The Morgan Library & Museum, New York, purchased on the Drue Heinz Fund for Twentieth-Century Literature, 2023; MA 23866.

8. This is clear in the way she identifies Steinbeck in her letter to her sister. Babb, *Dirty Plate Trail,* 130.

9. Wixson, "Radical by Nature," 125.

10. Babb recounts her experiences during this time in several of her biographical statements found in HRC 58.7.

11. In early drafts, the first half of the book is set in Eastern Colorado, while in the final version, published in 2004, the setting has been changed to the Oklahoma Panhandle.

12. HRC 18.5.

13. Sanora Babb, *Whose Names Are Unknown* (University of Oklahoma Press, 2006), 6.

14. Babb, *Whose Names Are Unknown*, 86–87, 91.

15. This letter is found in HRC 18.5. The fact that Babb used her mother's letter as a source for this passage has been well documented by Erin Battat, *Ain't Got No Home*, 55, and Christopher Bowman, "'Today Is a Terror': *Whose Names Are Unknown* and the 'New' Dust Bowl Novel," in Dearcopp and Smith, eds., *Unknown No More*, 103.

16. Rogers, "Foreword" to Babb, *Whose Names*, vii.

17. Rogers, "Foreword" to Babb, *Whose Names*, viii.

18. Babb, *Whose Names*, 147.

19. Babb, *Whose Names*, 144.

20. Battat, *Ain't Got No Home*, 45.

21. Babb, *Whose Names*, 222.

22. Bowman, "The 'New' Dust Bowl Novel," 96.

23. Benson, *True Adventures of John Steinbeck*, 361.

24. Benson, *True Adventures of John Steinbeck*, 375.

25. From "Battle Hymn of the Republic," by Julia Ward Howe: "Mine eyes have seen the glory of the coming of the Lord / He is trampling out the vintage where the grapes of wrath are stored."

26. Benson, *True Adventures of John Steinbeck*, 380–81.

27. Benson, *True Adventures of John Steinbeck*, 380–81.

28. Anne Loftis, *Witnesses to the Struggle* (University of Nevada Press, 1998), 31.

29. Bowman, "The 'New' Dust Bowl Novel," 97.

30. Benson, *True Adventures of John Steinbeck*, 360.

31. Benson, *True Adventures of John Steinbeck*, 362.

32. Benson, *True Adventures of John Steinbeck*, 334.

33. Wixson, "Radical by Nature," 125.

34. John Steinbeck, *Working Days: The Journals of "The Grapes of Wrath,"* ed. Robert DeMott (Penguin, 1990), 33.

35. Benson, *True Adventures of John Steinbeck*, 369.

36. Goslaar lived at 310 West 73rd St.

37. Cerf to Babb, July 27, 1939, HRC 23.4.

38. "Babb," March 1978, HRC 58.7.

39. It's important to note that John Steinbeck and Bennett Cerf knew each other and that Cerf admired Steinbeck's work. In July 1938, when Steinbeck was looking for a new publisher, Cerf wrote to him offering to publish *The Long Valley*. Cerf wrote to Steinbeck, "I can tell you, in all honesty, that I'd rather add you to the Random House list than any other author in America today" (July 27, 1938). When Steinbeck got picked up by Viking, Cerf congratulated Steinbeck, saying, "Viking is a fine press, and I know they will do a brilliant job for you" (April 18, 1938, Random House Files, Rare Book and Manuscript Library, Columbia University).

40. Reader's report, HRC 23.4.

41. Cerf to Babb, August 16, 1939. HRC 23.4.

42. HRC 23.5.

43. "Babb," March 1978, 3, HRC 58.7.

44. Babb to Ross, June 28, 1974, HRC 34.3.

45. Steinbeck, *Working Days*, xxvii.

46. Babb, *Whose Names*, 213.

47. "Call on woman who screams out: 'You're too late! You're too late!' No food for 4 days. Mother and son in tent; daughter & husband & 2 children in trailer. Won't ask for relief but neighbors have said, Gov't man will come find them. Finally, son goes out and steals from junk shop 4 radiators ($3.00) & when he sells them is arrested and jailed. Charged with burglary for breaking in place & felony for going to another county to sell them. (11 years in San Quentin.)" Babb, *Dirty Plate Trail*, 73.

48. This statement can also be traced back to Babb's journals as reprinted in *Dirty Plate Trail*, 67.

49. HRC 19.5.

Chapter 12. The Changed World

1. Babb publishes "Young Boy, the World" in *Black & White*. This story is reprinted in Maxim Lieber, ed., *The American Century* (Seven Seas, 1960). HRC 5.3.

2. HRC Container 88.

3. Arnold Rampersad, *Ralph Ellison: A Biography* (Knopf, 2007), 146.

4. Rampersad, *Ralph Ellison*, 116.

5. Rampersad, *Ralph Ellison*, 117.

6. Rampersad, *Ralph Ellison*, 117.

7. Rampersad, *Ralph Ellison*, 122.

8. Rampersad, *Ralph Ellison*, 147.

9. Rampersad, *Ralph Ellison*, 148.

10. Ellison to Babb, November 19, 1942, HRC 43.3.

11. Babb to Ellison, November 1942, HRC 60.9.

12. Ellison to Babb, April 10, 1942, HRC 43.3.

13. Babb to Ellison, February 7, 1942, HRC 60.9.

14. Babb to Ellison, February 7, 1942, HRC 60.9.

15. Babb to Ellison, February 7, 1942, HRC 60.9.

16. Babb to Ellison, February 7, 1942, HRC 60.9.

17. Interview with Wald, Hollywood, July 1989, HRC C3058.

18. Babb to Ellison, December 9, 1941, HRC 60.9.

19. Babb to Ellison, December 9, 1941, HRC 60.9.

20. Babb to Ellison, February 7, 1942, HRC 60.9.

21. HRC 71.5 includes letters addressed to Babb as the owner of the building where the restaurant was in 1956.

22. HRC 71.5.

23. HRC 71.5.

24. HRC 71.5.

25. HRC 71.5.

26. HRC 58.7.

27. Babb to Ellison, December 9, 1941, HRC 60.9.

28. "Morning in Imperial Valley," an excerpt of *Whose Names* that was published in *Kansas Magazine*. HRC Container 8.

29. HRC 23.5.

30. Cerf to Babb, August 16, 1939, HRC 23.4.

31. Babb to Ellison, undated, HRC 60.9.

32. Babb to Brewster, March 3, 1962, HRC 28.7.

33. Babb to Ellison, July 3, 1944, HRC 60.9.

34. Babb to Ellison, July 3, 1944, Ralph Ellison Papers, Library of Congress.

35. "Babb," March 1978, HRC 58.7.

36. *Los Angeles Times,* June 21, 1942.

37. Babb to Ellison, February 7, 1942, HRC 60.9.

38. Babb to Ellison, February 7, 1942, HRC 60.9. This was the second time in her life that Babb wrote about having children. (She also wrote about the possibility in a letter to Howe when she was in the Soviet Union and thought she was pregnant.)

39. Ellison to Babb (circa late February 1942, based on Ellison's responses to lines in Babb's letter to him dated February 7, 1942), HRC 43.3.

40. Ellison to Babb, July 4, 1943, HRC 43.3.

41. Ellison to Babb, July 4, 1943, HRC 43.3.

42. Ellison to Babb, undated, HRC 43.3.

43. Ellison to Babb; this letter is undated but a note on it says "ca. 1943." HRC 43.3.

44. Ellison to Babb, "ca. 1943," HRC 43.3.

45. Babb to Ellison, July 13, 1943, Ralph Ellison Papers, Library of Congress.

46. "The Stranger" is the first title she chose for the book that would eventually be called *The Lost Traveler*.

47. Commins to Babb, April 20, 1942, HRC 23.4.

48. Babb to Ellison, February 21, 1942, HRC 60.9.

49. Commins to Babb, November 28, 1942, HRC 23.4.

50. Commins to Babb, November 28, 1942, HRC 23.4.

51. HRC 23.3.

52. Commins to Babb, November 28, 1942, HRC 23.4.

53. Howe to Babb, January 1943, HRC 45.6.

54. Other films Howe worked on during this era include *Shining Victory, Out of the Fog, King's Row, Yankee Doodle Dandy, The Hard Way, Hangmen Also Die, Armored Attack, Passage to Marseille, Objective Burma, Counterattack, Confidential Agent, Danger Signal,* and *My Reputation*. William Faulkner helped write the script for *Air Force*.

55. Howe to Babb, January 1943, HRC 45.6.

56. The story would be published in *New Mexico Quarterly* in summer 1947 and would appear on the Roll of Honor in *The Best American Short Stories 1948*, ed. Martha Foley (Houghton Mifflin, 1948).

57. Babb, *Tinamou*, 40.

58. Babb, *Tinamou*, 40.

Chapter 13. She Felt Like the Wind

1. Babb, *The Dark Earth*, 35.

2. Babb, *The Dark Earth*, 32.

3. Babb, *The Dark Earth*, 47.

4. Babb, *The Dark Earth*, 47.

5. Herndon was a well-known political prisoner who wrote the influential memoir *Let Me Live* (Random House, 1937).

6. HRC Container 92.

7. Babb to Glenn Brown, undated: "Chris was based on a Negro friend much later in my life, a Negro novelist." This version also contains a scene that includes

the sheep farmers she lived with while working as a schoolteacher in Finney County, Kansas, and their disabled son, who called himself William Shakespeare. HRC 28.7.

8. Commins to Babb, July 16, 1943, HRC 36.3.

9. Olsen's *Yonnondio* was published in 1974 and Le Sueur's *The Girl* was published in 1978.

10. Ellison to Babb, August 18, 1944, Ralph Ellison Papers, Library of Congress.

11. "Los Angeles Reacts to Victory in Europe," *Los Angeles Times,* May 9, 1945.

12. On September 2, 1945, formal surrender documents were signed aboard the USS *Missouri,* designating the day as official Victory over Japan Day (V-J Day).

13. Babb to Jarrico, August 4, 1945, "Letters" folder, box 4 of unprocessed Paul Jarrico papers, accession 2010–2011-M172, Rare Book and Manuscript Library, Columbia University.

14. Babb to Jarrico, August 27, 1945, "Letters" folder, box 4 of unprocessed Paul Jarrico papers, accession 2010–2011-M172, Rare Book and Manuscript Library, Columbia University.

15. Edwin Seaver, ed., *Cross Section 1945: A Collection of New American Writing* (L. B. Fischer, 1948), 40–52. Drafts of "The Refugee" and copies of the published story can be found in HRC 4.5, and a bibliography reference can be found in HRC 33.3.

16. *Daily News,* April 6, 1946.

17. Babb to Wolf, November 6, 1945, HRC 60.9.

18. Babb to Sharp, Wednesday, HRC 1954.

19. Waldeen to Babb, April 7, 1946, HRC 54.5.

20. Taggard to Babb, May 8, 1946, HRC 33.4.

21. Babb to Wolf, 1946, HRC 60.9.

22. See the brief biography of Lotus Fragrance by her daughter, Roxana Newman, at IMDb, https://www.imdb.com/name/nm0289612/.

23. Also in this issue are Wallace Stegner and M. F. K. Fisher.

24. Jonathan R. Eller, *Becoming Ray Bradbury* (University of Illinois Press, 2011), 187.

25. Interview with Elizabeth Eve King, September 2, 2022.

26. The group included Bradbury, Sharp, and Babb; Esther McCoy (author and architectural historian); Joseph Petracca (novelist, short story writer, screenwriter, and television writer); Wilma Shore (writer and teacher); Elliot Grennard (song writer and author); Bonnie Wolfe (author of the novel *Love in Atlantis*); Peg Nixson (author); Richard Bach (author); Ray Morrison (author); and Dan Greenburg (author).

27. Ray Bradbury, *The Cat's Pajamas* (William Morrow, 2005), 205.

28. Bradbury, *Cat's Pajamas*, 210.

29. California, U.S., Federal Naturalization Records, 1843–1999 for James Wong Howe, District Court, Los Angeles, California Petitions, 1950–1951 (Box 0436), National Archives.

30. Rainsberger, *James Wong Howe*, 22.

31. Babb to Ellison, March 19, 1948, Ralph Ellison Papers, Library of Congress.

32. This story was published in the first issue of *California Quarterly*.

33. Babb to Ellison, May 16, 1948, Ralph Ellison Papers, Library of Congress.

34. Babb to Ellison, undated, Ralph Ellison Papers, Library of Congress.

35. Babb to Ellison, undated, Ralph Ellison Papers, Library of Congress.

36. Howe to Babb, March 15, 1948, HRC 45.6.

37. Babb to Ellison, undated, Ralph Ellison Papers, Library of Congress.

38. Interview with Mann, 1982, HRC 28.6.

39. This case happened before *Loving v. Virginia* was passed in 1967.

40. Babb's anecdote about this event was related to director Daniel Mann during her interview with him in 1982. HRC 28.6.

41. Interview with Mann, 1982, HRC 28.6.

42. HRC 36.8.

Chapter 14. "Follow That Furrow"

1. Waldeen's translations of Neruda's poem were the first to be made in English. They appeared in *Let the Rail Splitter Awake and Other Poems* (Masses & Mainstream, 1950).

2. Wald, *Exiles from a Future Time*, 328.

3. *The Brave Bulls*, IMDb, https://www.imdb.com/title/tt0043359/?ref_ = fn_al_tt_1.

4. Ralph H. Van Deman Papers, Hoover Institution, Stanford University, File 7052a.

5. Ralph H. Van Deman Papers, Hoover Institution, Stanford University, File 6901.

6. Alan Wald, "Sanora Babb in Her Time and Ours," in Dearcopp and Smith, eds., *Unknown No More*, 20.

7. Impressions of what Mexico City sounded like at this time are from Diana Anhalt's description in her memoir, *A Gathering of Fugitives: American Political Expatriates in Mexico, 1948–1965* (Archer Books, 2001), 23.

8. HRC 30.4.

9. Babb to Ross, August 7, 1977, HRC 36.8.

10. Interview with Wald, Hollywood, July 1989, HRC C3058.

11. HRC Container 52.

12. Babb to Wixson, HRC 55.1.

13. Kathlene McDonald, *Feminism, the Left, and Postwar Literary Culture* (University Press of Mississippi, 2012), 98.

14. Anhalt, *A Gathering of Fugitives*, 29.

15. "She met Asa Zatz [NYC] and they were married soon, divorced some years later." Babb to Wixson, 1996, HRC 58.7.

16. "'In Work,'" HRC 23.12.

17. Taggard to Babb, May 8, 1946, HRC 33.4.

18. Martha Foley, ed., *The Best American Short Stories, 1960, and the Yearbook of the American Short Story* (Houghton Mifflin, 1961), 1–10.

19. Taggard to Babb, May 8, 1946, HRC 33.4. Babb's "The Wild Flower" was also reprinted from *Kansas Magazine* (1950) in *Senior Citizen* 7, no. 7 (July 1961): 49–55. HRC 33.3.

20. Taggard to Babb, May 8, 1946, HRC 33.4.

21. W. Babb to S. Babb, March 12, 1949, HRC 40.4.

22. *California Quarterly* 1, vol. 1 (1950). Also reprinted in Jim Burns, *Radicals, Beats and Beboppers* (Penniless Press, 2011).

23. Bradbury to Babb, November 1951, HRC 2.8.

24. HRC 30.4.

25. HRC 30.4.

26. This story would be published in the Antioch Review 13, no. 2 (Summer 1953): 168–80 and later in *Cry of the Tinamou*. Babb would also sell film options for this story for $500.

27. *Antioch Review* 13, no. 2 (Summer 1953): 170.

28. *Antioch Review* 13, no. 2 (Summer 1953): 180.

29. HRC 30.4.

30. The title is based on a line from "Epilogue" by William Blake: "The Son of Morn in weary night's decline, / The Lost Traveler's Dream under the Hill."

31. Bradbury to Babb, November 15, 1953, HRC 13.4.

32. Bradbury to Babb, April 18, 1952, HRC 13.4.

33. It's possible that he played in St. Joseph, Missouri, as part of the St. Joseph Saints, a minor league team; *Lost Traveler*, 18.

34. HRC 58.7.

35. Babb to Sharp, 1954, HRC 52.1.

36. Babb to Zatz, HRC 55.5.

37. Babb to Howe, 1952, HRC 46.7.

38. Babb to McCoy, 1951, Esther McCoy Papers, Smithsonian Institution Archives of American Art.

39. Babb to Pollard, January 1953, HRC 50.5.

40. Babb to McCoy, 1951, Esther McCoy Papers, Smithsonian Institution Archives of American Art.

41. Blake to Babb, August 31, 1953, HRC 13.4.

42. Wolf to Babb, February 16, 1953, HRC 2.1.

43. Babb to Blake, November 9, 1953, HRC 13.4.

Chapter 15. "I Do Not Wish to Be Less than I Am"

1. Babb to Wolf, July 6, 1954, HRC 36.8.

2. Babb to Wolf, July 6, 1954, HRC 36.8.

3. Wolf to Babb, October 20, 1954, HRC 36.8.

4. Babb to Wolf, July 24, 1954, HRC 36.8.

5. Babb to Wolf, August 31, 1954, HRC 36.8.

6. Babb to Wolf, September 9, 1954, HRC 36. 8.

7. McGrath to Babb, February 7, 1954, HRC 48.1.

8. Babb to Bulosan, February 24, 1956, jstor.org/stable/10.2307/community .29380751.

9. Babb to Kemper, May 12, 1954, HRC 37.

10. "Dusty Plague upon the Land," *LIFE*, May 3, 1954, 35.

11. Babb to Glenn Brown, December 21, 1959, HRC 28.7.

12. Babb to Kemper, May 12, 1954, HRC 37.

13. Kemper to Babb, May 21, 1958, in response to reading *The Lost Traveler*. Babb recounts her mother's reaction in a letter to her cousin Glenn Brown, December 21, 1959, HRC 28.7.

14. Babb to Brown, December 21, 1959, HRC 28.7.

15. This scene from "The Tea Party" would be cut from the final draft of *The Lost Traveler,* but the albums that Holly keeps in the story are still referred to in chapter 1.

16. Babb, *Tinamou,* 120.

Chapter 16. *The Lost Traveler*

1. Babb to Reynal, March 2, 1958, HRC 13.7.

2. Babb, *Lost Traveler,* 3.

3. Babb, *Lost Traveler,* 10.

4. Wixson, "Introduction" to Babb, *Lost Traveler,* xvii.

5. Babb, *Lost Traveler,* 124.

6. Babb, *Lost Traveler,* 152.

7. Babb, *Lost Traveler,* 51.

8. Battat, "Discovering Ecofeminism in Sanora Babb's Narratives," in Dearcopp and Smith, eds., *Unknown No More,* 49.

9. Babb, *Lost Traveler,* 144.

10. Battat, "Discovering Ecofeminism in Sanora Babb's Narratives," 48.

11. Babb, *Lost Traveler,* 131.

12. HRC 13.9.

13. Bradbury to Babb, October 21, 1959, HRC 13.4.

14. Babb to Abbott, March 29, 1958, HRC 35.5.

15. Babb to Abbott, March 29, 1958, HRC 35.5.

16. Babb to Ross, August 7, 1977, HRC 36.8.

17. Babb to Abbott, April 28, 1958, HRC 35.5.

18. Babb to Abbott, April 28, 1958, HRC 35.5.

19. Wald quotes Wixson in his article "Sanora Babb in Her Time and Ours," 19.

20. The Unicorn was located at 8907 Sunset Boulevard.

21. Babb to Abbott, September 26, 1958, HRC 35.5.

22. HRC 64.4.

23. HRC 64.2.

24. Babb to Abbott, October 2, 1958, HRC 35.5.

25. Babb to Abbott, August 27, 1959.

26. Babb to Abbott, March 13, 1959, HRC 35.5.

Chapter 17. "Dust on [Her] Own Hills"

1. Babb to Esther McCoy et al., June 12, 1959, HRC. 34.3. McCoy was a member of Babb's writing group. Her short story "The Cape" was featured in *The Best American Short Stories of 1950* (alongside Bradbury's, Sharp's, and Babb's). McCoy would go on to become a well-known architectural historian.

2. Babb to McCoy et al., June 12, 1959, HRC 34.3.

3. Ross to Babb, April 28, 1959, HRC 34.3.

4. Babb to Abbott, April 7, 1960, HRC 35.5.

5. Babb to Ross, May 29, 1959, HRC 34.3.

6. Babb to McCoy et al., June 12, 1959, HRC 34.3.

7. Babb to McCoy et al., June 12, 1959, HRC 34.3.

8. Babb to Ross, May 29, 1959, HRC 34.3.

9. Babb to McCoy et al., June 12, 1959, HRC 34.3.

10. "Picnic Mephitis," *Women's Journal* (September 1960): 44–45, 78, 81. The story was reprinted in *Outdoor World*, May–June 1969.

11. HRC 51.3.

12. Babb to Politis, November 11, 1959, HRC 51.4. "Night in a Greek Village" would be published in *Southern Review* 26, no. 3 (Summer 1990): 679–80.

13. Babb to Pollard, undated, HRC 50.7.

14. Babb to Ross, December 6, 1959, HRC 34.3.

15. "In a Field in Peloponesia," *Arizona Quarterly* 37, no. 2 (Summer 1981): 126.

16. Babb to McCoy et al., June 12, 1959, HRC 34.3.

17. Babb to Politis, May 29, 1960, HRC Container 63.

18. Babb to Politis, May 29, 1960, HRC Container 63.

19. This story would be published in *Kansas Magazine* in 1966. HRC 4.5. Babb complained that it was often rejected because of the taboos it contained: "This seems to be my literary history." (The story depicted an abusive relationship much like Babb's parents', and the girl in the story is only fifteen when she marries her twenty-five-year-old husband.) Babb to Politis, December 11, 1959, HRC Container 63.

20. University of California Los Angeles Extension Short Story Class teaching materials, HRC 64.6.

21. "Storyteller's Street," *The Writer* 74, no. 10 (October 1961): 5–7, 36. Another essay, "The Challenge of Words," was published in *The Writer* 81, no. 1 (January 1968): 12–13.

22. Babb to Brewster, March 3, 1962, HRC 28.7.

23. Babb to Brewster, March 3, 1962, HRC 28.7.

24. HRC 58.7.

25. HRC 58.7.

26. Kemper to Babb, December 2, 1960, HRC 40.1.

27. Babb, "Autobiography," May 25, 1962, HRC 29.2.

28. Babb to Blake, April 6, 1962, HRC 41.6.

29. Photographs of the writing group were taken for this article and can be found in HRC 62.6.

30. "Night of Evil" was also called "The Meeting." The story was revised and eventually published in *Southwest Review* in winter 1982.

31. Babb to Blake, April 6, 1962, HRC 41.6; X. J. Kennedy, *Nude Descending a Staircase* (Doubleday, 1961), 69.

32. Babb to Blake, April 6, 1962, HRC 41.6.

33. Babb to Politis, November 22, 1958, HRC Container 51.

34. HRC 5.5. Babb wrote several drafts of this story. The earliest is dated October 27, 1952. This piece had many titles, including "The Secret," "A Star and a Planet at Night," and "The Dung Hunters." She revised the story again in February 1961.

35. Babb to Ross, February 22, 1963, HRC 34.3.

36. Babb to Ross, May 12, 1964, HRC 34.3.

37. Babb to Pollard, February 2, 1963, HRC 50.7.

38. David L. Wolper, "Ray Bradbury: Story of a Writer by David L. Wolper," 1963, Internet Archive, https://archive.org/details/RayBradburyStoryOfA WriterByDavidL.Wolper.

Chapter 18. *An Owl on Every Post*

1. Babb to Ross, August 15, 1964, HRC 34.3.

2. Babb to Ross, August 15, 1964, HRC 34.3.

3. Ross to Babb, August 25, 1964, HRC 34.3.

4. Babb to Ross, September 20, 1964, HRC 34.3.

5. HRC 14.1.

6. Walter Chaw, "James Wong Howe's Way with Light," Criterion Collection, September 9, 2022, https://www.criterion.com/current/posts/7915-james-wong -howes-way-with-light.

7. "*Hud* and *Cleopatra* Win Cinematography: 1964 Oscars," YouTube, https://youtu.be/fox8vDECd1w (minute 01:14).

8. Babb to Hartley, November 22, 1968, HRC 43.10.

9. Babb to Hartley, November 22, 1968, HRC 43.10.

10. While Babb received payment for movie rights, a film has never been made.

11. Babb to Ritt, March 19, 1968, HRC 51.6.

12. Babb to Ross, October 31, 1969, HRC 34.3.

13. Abbott to Babb, July 10, 1968, HRC 35.7

14. According to a note from Babb found in HRC 4.7.

15. All quotes from "A Scandalous Humility" are from the version in *Cry of the Tinamou: Stories* (University of Nebraska Press, 1997), 13–30.

16. *Southwest Review* 54, no. 1 (Winter 1969): 72–78. (Copies of the story are in HRC 1.9.)

17. Babb to Hartley, November 22, 1968, HRC 43.10.

18. Babb settled on the title on March 23, 1969.

19. Ross to Babb, October 28, 1969, HRC 34.3.

20. Babb to Ross, November 28, 1969, HRC 34.3.

21. Babb to Ross, November 14, 1969, HRC 34.3.

22. Babb to Ross, November 14, 1969, HRC 34.3.

23. Babb to Ross, November 28, 1969, HRC 34.3.

24. Babb to Ross, March 8, 1970, HRC 34.3.

25. HRC 28.7.

26. Babb to Cohen, June 7, 1970, HRC 16.4.

27. Babb to Ross, June 1, 1970, HRC 34.3.

28. Babb to Ross, March 8, 1970, HRC 34.3.

29. Babb to Ross, March 8, 1970, HRC 34.3.

30. Babb to Cohen, June 7, 1970, HRC 16.4.

31. Bradbury to Cohen, September 20, 1970, HRC 16.4.

32. Babb to Ross, April 13, 1971, HRC 34.3.

33. Cohen to Babb, October 22, 1970, HRC 16.4. The *Publishers Weekly* review is at HRC 16.4.

34. Pasanen and Cohen, November 22, 1970, HRC. 16.4.

35. HRC 17.2.

36. Interviews with Joanne Dearcopp, 2022, 2023.

37. Interviews with Joanne Dearcopp, 2022, 2023.

38. Babb to Ross, April 2, 1971, HRC 34.3.

39. Babb to Ross, May 12, 1972, HRC 34.3.

40. Babb to Ross, July 29, 1979, HRC 34.3. This edition would go out of print in 1979.

41. Babb to Ross, November 20, 1971, HRC 34.3.

42. Babb to Ross, November 20, 1971, HRC 34.3.

43. She donated Howe's papers on April 28, 1982, to the Margaret Herrick Library at the Academy of Motion Picture Arts and Sciences.

44. "1977 November 12 B Traven Seminar" Recordings, HRC C3060.

Chapter 19. The Recovery of *Whose Names Are Unknown*

1. Babb was paid $250 plus expenses; HRC 58.5. However, after the meeting, in a letter dated May 7, 1985, Babb sent them a $100 check and offered to donate all the proceeds from her book sales (her donation went to the Endowment for American Letters fund).

2. "Babb Talk," HRC 58.5.

3. Babb, *Dark Earth*, xi.

4. HRC 54.3.

5. Interview with Wald, March 30, 2023.

6. Interviews with Dearcopp, 2022, 2023.

7. Photographs of these inscriptions were sent to me by Joanne Dearcopp.

8. While Wixson's notes survive, he never published a book-length study of Babb. He did publish articles on Babb, as well as Babb's archival documents, in *Dirty Plate Trail.*

9. Babb to Dearcopp, August 21, 1998, HRC 34.9.

10. Babb to Dearcopp, July 14, 1996, HRC 34.9.

11. Babb to Dearcopp, September 2, 1996, HRC 34.9.

12. Interviews with Dearcopp, 2022, 2023.

13. Babb to Ross, August 7, 1980, HRC 34.3.

14. Interviews with Dearcopp, 2022, 2023.

Epilogue

1. Michael J. Meyer, "Review: *Whose Names Are Unknown* by Sanora Babb," *Steinbeck Review* 4, no. 1 (Spring 2007): 135.

2. Meyer, "Review: *Whose Names,*" 135–39; Babb, *Whose Names,* 180; John Steinbeck, *The Grapes of Wrath* (Penguin, 2006), 373–76.

3. Babb, *Whose Names,* 222; Steinbeck, *Grapes of Wrath,* 56, 349; Meyer, "Review: *Whose Names.*"

4. Babb, *Whose Names,* 24; Steinbeck, *Grapes of Wrath,* 199, 328, 342–43; Meyer, "Review: *Whose Names.*"

5. Babb, *Whose Names,* 84, 115; Steinbeck, *Grapes of Wrath,* 159–60; Meyer, "Review: *Whose Names.*"

6. Babb, *Whose Names,* 164; Steinbeck, *Grapes of Wrath,* 233; Meyer, "Review: *Whose Names,*" 138.

7. Meyer, "Review: *Whose Names,*" 138.

8. Meyer, "Review: *Whose Names,*" 136–37.

9. Michael J. Meyer, "Review: *On the Dirty Plate Trail: Remembering the Dust Bowl Refugee Camps* by Douglas C. Wixson, Sanora Babb and Dorothy Babb," *Steinbeck Review* 7, no. 2 (Fall 2010): 133.

10. This correspondence can be found in HRC 16.6, 43.5, 43.10.

11. Interview with Dayton Duncan, November 29, 2023.

12. *The Dust Bowl,* directed by Ken Burns, written by Dayton Duncan, PBS Distribution, 2012.

Bibliography

Collections

Sanora Babb Collection, 1968–1973, Department of Special Collections, Boston University

Sanora Babb Papers, Harry Ransom Center, University of Texas at Austin

Carlos Bulosan Papers, University of Washington Libraries, Special Collections

Cherokee Strip Museum Collection, Noble County Genealogy Society, Perry, Oklahoma

Frederic Dannay Papers, Rare Book and Manuscript Library, Columbia University

Eastern Colorado Land Records, Bureau of Land Management, United States Department of the Interior

Ralph Ellison Papers, Library of Congress

Records of the Farmers Home Administration, 1918–1975, National Archives

James Wong Howe Collection, Margaret Herrick Library, Academy of Motion Picture Arts and Sciences

Charles Humboldt Papers, Manuscripts and Archives, Yale University Library

Paul Jarrico Papers, Columbia University Libraries

Kansas Historical Society

League of American Writers Archives, Bancroft Library, University of California, Berkeley

Daniel Mann Papers, Margaret Herrick Library, Academy of Motion Picture Arts and Sciences

Esther McCoy Papers, Smithsonian Institution Archives of American Art

National Archives, San Francisco

National Archives, Seattle

Edward Flanders Ricketts Papers, Department of Special Collections and University Archives, Stanford University

Harry Roskolenko Papers, Special Collections Research Center and University Archives, Syracuse University

William Saroyan Papers, Bancroft Library, University of California, Berkeley

William Saroyan Papers, Department of Special Collections and University Archives, Stanford University Libraries

The Sitting Room, Cotati, CA

Springfield Herald Archives, Springfield, Baca County, Colorado

Philip E. Stevenson Papers, Wisconsin Historical Society

Genevieve Taggard Papers, Dartmouth Libraries Special Collections, Dartmouth College

Genevieve Taggard Papers, New York Public Library

Ralph H. Van Deman Papers, Hoover Institution, Stanford University

Van Deman Files, 1971–1975, National Archives

Kay Van Riper Papers, Margaret Herrick Library, Academy of Motion Picture Arts and Sciences

Interviews

Kent Brooks, 2022

Larry Ceplair, June 19, 2023

Mike Conklin, 2023

Joanne Dearcopp, various dates, 2021–2023

Dayton Duncan, November 29, 2023

Kevin Hearle, February 20, 2023

Pauline Hodges, May 10, 2022; June 7, 2022; November 30, 2023

Timothy Hume, 2022

Elizabeth Eve King, September 2, 2022

Don Lee, June 21, 2022

Roxanna Newman, October 19, 2022

Books, Articles, and Films

American Stuff: An Anthology of Prose & Verse by Members of the Federal Writers' Project. Viking, 1937.

Anhalt, Diana. *A Gathering of Fugitives: American Political Expatriates in Mexico, 1948-1965*. Archer Books, 2001.

Babb, Sanora. *Cry of the Tinamou: Stories*. University of Nebraska Press, 1997.

———. *Cry of the Tinamou: Stories*. Muse Ink, 2021.

———. *The Dark Earth and Other Stories from the Great Depression*. Capra, 1987.

———. *The Dark Earth and Selected Prose from the Great Depression*. Muse Ink, 2021.

———. *The Lost Traveler*. Reynal, 1958.

———. *The Lost Traveler*. Muse Ink, 2013.

———. *On the Dirty Plate Trail: Remembering the Dust Bowl Refugee Camps*. Ed. Douglas Wixson, photographs by Dorothy Babb. University of Texas Press, 2007.

———. *An Owl on Every Post*. Muse Ink, 2012.

———. "Poppies in the Wind." *Windsor Quarterly: Modern American Literature* 1, no. 2 (Summer 1933).

———. *Told in the Seed*. West End, 1998.

———. *Told in the Seed and Selected Poems*. Muse Ink, 2021.

———. *Whose Names Are Unknown*. University of Oklahoma Press, 2006.

Baird, David W., and Danney Goble. *The Story of Oklahoma*. University of Oklahoma Press, 1994.

Balakian, Nona. *The World of William Saroyan*. Bucknell University Press, 1998.

Battat, Erin Royston. *Ain't Got No Home: America's Great Migrations and the Making of an Interracial Left*. University of North Carolina Press, 2014.

Benson, Jackson J. *Looking for Steinbeck's Ghost*. University of Nevada Press, 2002.

———. *The True Adventures of John Steinbeck*. Viking, 1984.

Benson, Jackson J., and John Steinbeck. "'To Tom, Who Lived It': John Steinbeck and the Man from Weedpatch." *Journal of Modern Literature* 5, no. 2 (1976): 151-210. www.jstor.org/stable/3830940.

Bradbury, Ray. *The Cat's Pajamas*. William Morrow, 2005.

Bulosan, Carlos. *All the Conspirators*. Anvil, 1998.

———. *America Is in the Heart*. University of Washington Press, 2014.

———. *If You Want to Know What We Are: A Carlos Bulosan Reader*. Ed. E. San Juan Jr. West End Press, 1983.

———. *The Laughter of My Father*. Bantam, 1946.

———. *Sound of Falling Light: Letters in Exile*. Edited by Dolores S. Feria. N.p., 1960.

Burke, Bob, Kenny A. Franks, and Royse Parr. *Glory Days of Summer: The History of Baseball in Oklahoma.* Oklahoma Heritage Association, 1999.

Burns, Jim. *Radicals, Beats and Beboppers.* Penniless Press, 2011.

Burns, Ken, and Dayton Duncan. *The Dust Bowl: An Illustrated History.* Chronicle Books, 2012.

Carlisle, Harry. *Darkness at Noon.* Horace Liveright, 1931.

Carpenter, Berther. "Morton County Pioneers Recall the Early History of Morton County / Tenth Anniversary Edition." *Morton County Farmer* (Rolla, Kansas), January 31, 1936. Kansas Historical Society, microfilm reel NP 3874.

Catren, Lorene L. *Before and after the Railroad Came to Elkhart and Southwest Morton County, 1885–1963.* N.p., 1963. Kansas Historical Society.

Ceplair, Larry. *The Hollywood Motion Picture Blacklist: Seventy-Five Years Later.* University Press of Kentucky, 2022.

——. *The Inquisition in Hollywood: Politics in the Film Community, 1930–1960.* Anchor/Doubleday, 1980.

——. *The Marxist and the Movies: A Biography of Paul Jarrico.* Lexington: University Press of Kentucky, 2007.

Ceplair, Larry, and Steven Englund. *Anti-Communism in Twentieth-Century America: A Critical History.* Praeger, 2011.

Chaw, Walter. "James Wong Howe's Way with Light." Criterion Collection, September 9, 2022. https://www.criterion.com/current/posts/7915-james-wong-howes-way-with-light.

Clark, Blue. *Indian Tribes of Oklahoma: A Guide.* University of Oklahoma Press, 2020.

Coates, Grace Stone. *Black Cherries.* Alfred A. Knopf, 1931.

Cohen, Jonathan. "Neruda in English: Waldeen's 'Lost' Translations from *Canto General.*" *Translation Review* 88 (2014): 56–74.

Coiner, Constance. *Better Red: The Writing and Resistance of Tillie Olsen and Meridel Le Sueur.* University of Illinois Press, 1998.

Collins, Thomas A., and John Steinbeck. "From *Bringing in the Sheaves,* by 'Windsor Drake.'" *Journal of Modern Literature* 5, no. 2 (1976): 211–32.

Comer, Krista. *Landscapes of a New West: Gender and Geography in Contemporary Women's Writing.* University of North Carolina Press, 1999.

Commins, Dorothy. *What Is an Editor? Saxe Commins at Work.* University of Chicago Press, 1978.

Cooper, Stephen. *Full of Life: A Biography of John Fante.* North Point, 2000.

Davis, Robert Murray, ed. *Steinbeck: A Collection of Critical Essays.* Prentice-Hall, 1972.

Dearcopp, Joanne, and Christine Hill Smith, eds. *Unknown No More: Recovering Sanora Babb.* University of Oklahoma Press, 2021.

Debo, Angie. *And Still the Waters Run.* Gordian Press, 1966.

———. *Prairie City: The Story of an American Community.* University of Oklahoma Press, 1998.

Dodd, Martha. *My Years in Germany.* Victor Gollancz, 1939.

———. *Through Embassy Eyes.* Harcourt and Brace, 1939.

Donohue, Agnes McNeill, ed. *A Casebook on "The Grapes of Wrath."* Thomas Y. Crowell, 1968.

Edson, A. B. "Chronology of the Farmer's Ten Years of Existence in Rolla." *Morton County Farmer* (Rolla, Kansas), January 31, 1936. Kansas Historical Society.

Egan, Timothy. *The Worst Hard Time.* Mariner Books, 2004.

Elkhart Chamber of Commerce. *Welcome to Elkhart Oil Hub of Kansas.* Elkhart Chamber of Commerce, 1973. Kansas Historical Society.

Eller, Jonathan R. *Becoming Ray Bradbury.* University of Illinois Press, 2011.

———. *Bradbury beyond Apollo.* University of Illinois Press, 2020.

———. *Ray Bradbury Unbound.* University of Illinois Press, 2014.

Ellison, Ralph. *Invisible Man.* Vintage Books, 1995.

———. *The Selected Letters of Ralph Ellison.* Ed. John F. Callahan and Marc C. Conner. Random House, 2019.

Entin, Joseph B. *Sensational Modernism: Experimental Fiction and Photography in Thirties America.* University of North Carolina Press, 2007.

Fante, John, and Stephen Cooper. *The John Fante Reader.* William Morrow, 2002.

Foley, Barbara. *Wrestling with the Left: The Making of Ralph Ellison's Invisible Man.* Duke University Press, 2010.

Foley, Martha, ed. *The Best American Short Stories, 1950, and the Yearbook of the American Short Story.* Houghton Mifflin, 1951.

———. *The Best American Short Stories, 1960, and the Yearbook of the American Short Story.* Houghton Mifflin, 1961.

Folsom, Franklin. *Days of Anger, Days of Hope: A Memoir of the League of American Writers, 1937–1942.* University Press of Colorado, 1994.

Foster, Edward Halsey. *William Saroyan.* Boise State University, 1984.

Frémont, John Charles. *Memoirs of My Life: Including in the Narrative Five Journeys of Western Explorations during the Years 1842, 1843–4, 1845–6–7, 1848–9, 1853–4.* Belford, Clarke, 1886.

French, Warren. *A Companion to "The Grapes of Wrath."* Viking, 1963.

Garrett-Davis, Josh. *What Is a Western? Region, Genre, Imagination.* University of Oklahoma Press, 2019.

George, Ann, and Jack Selzer. "What Happened at the First American Writers' Congress? Kenneth Burke's 'Revolutionary Symbolism in America.'" *Rhetoric Society Quarterly* 33, no. 2 (2003): 47–66. http://www.jstor.org /stable/3886097.

Gregory, James N. *American Exodus: The Dust Bowl Migration and Okie Culture in California.* Oxford University Press, 1989.

Griffith, Sally Foreman. *Home Town News: William Allen White and the Emporia Gazette.* Johns Hopkins University Press, 1989.

Hamalian, Leo, ed. *William Saroyan: The Man and the Writer Remembered.* Fairleigh Dickinson University Press, 1987.

Hannah, Kristin. *The Four Winds.* St. Martin's, 2021.

Harmon, Robert B. *John Steinbeck: An Annotated Guide to Biographical Sources.* Scarecrow Press, 1996.

Herring, Scott. "Regional Modernism: A Reintroduction." *Modern Fiction Studies* 55, no. 1, Regional Modernism Special Issue (Spring 2009): 1–10.

Higham, Charles. *Hollywood Cameramen: Sources of Light.* Indiana University Press, 1970.

"The History of Morton County." *Morton County Record* (Rolla, Kansas), June 3 and 10, 1949. Kansas Historical Society.

Horne, Gerald. *Class Struggle in Hollywood, 1930–1950: Moguls, Mobsters, Stars, Reds, and Trade Unionists.* University of Texas Press, 2010.

"*Hud* and *Cleopatra* Win Cinematography: 1964 Oscars." Broadcast TV clip. https://youtu.be/fox8vDECd1w.

Jensen, Joan M., and Gloria Ricci Lothrup. *California Women: A History.* Boyd and Fraser, 1987.

Kansas Historical Society. "Flu Pandemic of 1918." *Kansapedia.* https://www .kshs.org/kansapedia/flu-pandemic-of-1918/17805.

———. *Morton County Clippings, 1888–1990.* Kansas State Historical Society, n.d.

———. "Sinners and Saints." https://www.kshs.org/p/sinners-and-saints -introduction/10718.

"Kansas Pioneer Rounds Out 85 Years of Events." *Elkhart Tri-State News,* February 15, 1934. Kansas Historical Society.

Kansas State Historical Society and Department of Archives. *History of Kansas Newspapers: A History of the Newspapers and Magazines Published in Kansas from the Organization of Kansas Territory, 1854, to January 1, 1916.* Kansas State Printing House, 1916.

Kennedy, X. J. *Nude Descending a Staircase.* Doubleday, 1961.

Ketchum, Ida M. *The Morton County Pioneer.* Elkhart Lions Club, n.d. Kansas Historical Society.

Kolodny, Annette. *The Land before Her: Fantasy and Experience of the American Frontiers, 1630–1860.* University of North Carolina Press, 1984.

———. *The Lay of the Land: Metaphor as Experience and History in American Life and Letters.* University of North Carolina Press, 1975.

Lazendorfer, Joy. "The Forgotten Dust Bowl." *Smithsonian Magazine,* May 23, 2016.

Lee, Lawrence, and Barry Gifford. *Saroyan: A Biography.* University of California Press, 1998.

Leggett, John. *A Daring Young Man: A Biography of William Saroyan.* Knopf, 2002.

Le Sueur, Meridel. *Ripening: Selected Work.* Feminist Press, 1990.

Lieber, Maxim, ed. *The American Century.* Seven Seas, 1960.

Limerick, Patricia Nelson. *The Legacy of Conquest: The Unbroken Past of the American West.* W. W. Norton, 1987.

Linebaugh, Donald W. "Digging into a Dugout House (Site 21SW17): The Archaeology of Norwegian Immigrant Anna Byberg Christopherson Goulson, Swenoda Township, Swift County, Minnesota." https://terpconnect.umd.edu/~dwline/Goulson.pdf.

Loftis, Anne. *Witnesses to the Struggle.* University of Nevada Press, 1998.

Manzella, Abigail. *Migrating Fictions: Gender, Race and Citizenship in U.S. Internal Displacements.* Ohio University Press, 2018.

Marshall, Collin. "Los Angeles in Buildings: The Central Library." KCET, August 2, 2017. https://www.kcet.org/shows/lost-la/los-angeles-in-buildings-the-central-library.

Martin, John H. "Broomcorn: The Frontiersman's Cash Crop." *Economic Botany* 7, no. 2 (April–June 1953): 163–81.

McCoy, Esther. *Piecing Together Los Angeles: An Esther McCoy Reader.* Ed. Susan Morgan. East Borneo Books, 2012.

McDonald, Kathlene. *Feminism, the Left, and Postwar Literary Culture.* University Press of Mississippi, 2012.

McWilliams, Carey. *Factories in the Field.* University of California Press, 2000.

Meares, Hadley. "Stanley Rose's Humble Bookstore Was the Center of Literary LA in the 1930s." LAist, March 19, 2019. https://laist.com/news/la-history/stanley-rose-bookstore-literary-las-hottest-spot-1930s.

Meyer, Michael J. "Review: *On the Dirty Plate Trail: Remembering the Dust Bowl Refugee Camps* by Douglas C. Wixson, Sanora Babb and Dorothy Babb." *Steinbeck Review* 7, no. 2 (Fall 2010): 130–34.

———. "Review: *Whose Names Are Unknown* by Sanora Babb." *Steinbeck Review* 4, no. 1 (Spring 2007): 135–39.

Milford, Nancy. *Savage Beauty: The Life of Edna St. Vincent Millay.* Random House, 2002.

Millay, Edna St. Vincent. *The Letters of Edna St. Vincent Millay.* Ed. Allan Ross Macdougall. Grosset & Dunlap, 1952.

———. *Rapture and Melancholy: The Diaries of Edna St. Vincent Millay.* Ed. Daniel Mark Epstein. Yale University Press, 2022.

Mitchell, Irene. "Early History of Red Rock." Monograph. The Cherokee Strip Museum, Perry, Oklahoma.

Morantte, P. C. *Remembering Carlos Bulosan (His Heart Affair with America).* New Day, 1984.

Morgan, Dan. *Rising in the West: The True Story of an "Okie" Family from the Great Depression through the Reagan Years.* Knopf, 1992.

Morton County Book Committee. *Morton County, 1886–1986: Cornerstone of Kansas.* N.p., n.d.

"Morton County History . . . Homesteaders." *Morton County Record* (Rolla, Kansas), June 17 and 24, 1949. Kansas Historical Society, microfilm reel NP 3876.

Nekola, Charlotte, and Paula Rabinowitz, eds. *Writing Red: An Anthology of American Women Writers, 1930–1940.* Feminist Press, 1987.

Neruda, Pablo. *Let the Rail Splitter Awake and Other Poems.* Masses & Mainstream, 1950.

Novak, Estelle Gershgoren, ed. *Poets of the Non-Existent City: Los Angeles in the McCarthy Era.* University of New Mexico Press, 2002.

Olsen, Tillie. *Yonnondio: From the Thirties.* Delacorte/Seymour Lawrence, 1974.

Peters, De Witt Clinton. *The Life and Adventures of Kit Carson, the Nestor of the Rocky Mountains, from Facts Narrated Himself.* N.p., 1858.

"The Pioneers." *Frisco Pioneer,* April 28, 1886. Kansas Historical Society.

Powell, John Wesley. *The Arid Lands.* Ed. Wallace Stegner. University of Nebraska Press, 2004.

Pringle, Robert W. *Historical Dictionary of Russian and Soviet Intelligence.* Rowman & Littlefield, 2015.

Rainsberger, Todd. *James Wong Howe, Cinematographer.* A.S. Barnes, 1981.

Rampersad, Arnold. *Ralph Ellison: A Biography.* Knopf, 2007.

Raskin, Jonah. *My Search for B. Traven.* Methuen, 1980.

Reid, Panthea. *Tillie Olsen: One Woman, Many Riddles.* Rutgers University Press, 2010.

Rosenfelt, Deborah. "From the Thirties: Tillie Olsen and the Radical Tradition." *Feminist Studies* 7, no. 3. (Autumn 1981): 371–406.

Ryan, Frances. *History of Taloga: The Town and the School.* N.p., 1957. Kansas Historical Society.

Saroyan, Aram. *Last Rites: The Death of William Saroyan.* William Morrow, 1982.

———. *William Saroyan.* Harcourt Brace, 1983.

Seaver, Edwin, ed. *Cross Section 1945: A Collection of New American Writing.* L. B. Fischer, 1945.

———. *Cross Section 1948: A Collection of New American Writing.* Simon & Schuster, 1948.

Shockley, Martin Staples. "The Reception of *The Grapes of Wrath* in Oklahoma." *American Literature* 15, no. 4 (January 1944): 351–61.

Short Histories of Taloga, Kansas. N.p., n.d. Kansas Historical Society.

Showalter, Elaine. "Feminist Criticism in the Wilderness." *Critical Inquiry* 8, no. 2 (Winter 1981) 179–206.

Souder, William. *Mad at the World: A Life of John Steinbeck.* W. W. Norton, 2020.

Starr, Kevin. *Material Dreams: Southern California through the 1920s.* Oxford University Press, 1990.

Stein, Walter, J. *California and the Dust Bowl Migration.* Greenwood Press, 1973.

Steinbeck, John. *"America and Americans" and Selected Nonfiction.* Ed. Susan Shillinglaw and Jackson J. Benson. Viking, 2002.

———. *The Grapes of Wrath.* Penguin, 2006.

———. *The Harvest Gypsies: On the Road to "The Grapes of Wrath."* Heyday, 1936.

———. *In Dubious Battle.* Penguin, 1992.

———. *A Russian Journal.* Penguin, 1999.

———. *Steinbeck: A Life in Letters.* Ed. Elaine Steinbeck and Robert Wallsten. Penguin, 1975.

———. "Their Blood Is Strong." Simon J. Lubin Society, 1938.

———. *Working Days: The Journals of "The Grapes of Wrath."* Ed. Robert DeMott. Penguin, 1990.

Steiner, Michael C. *Regionalists on the Left: Radical Voices from the American West.* University of Oklahoma Press, 2013.

Stott, William. *Documentary Expression and Thirties America.* Oxford University Press, 1973.

Traven, B. *The Night Visitor and Other Stories.* Hill and Wang, 1966.

Vermilye, Jerry. *The Great British Films.* Citadel, 1978.

Villa, Jose Garcia. *Doveglion: Collected Poems.* Penguin, 2008.

Vulliamy, Ed. "The Vindication of Sanora Babb." *New York Review of Books,* August 19, 2021.

Wald, Alan. *Alan M. Wald's Literary Left Trilogy.* Includes *Exiles from a Future Time, Trinity of Passion,* and *American Night.* University of North Carolina Press, 2012. Kindle.

———. *American Night: The Literary Left in the Era of the Cold War.* University of North Carolina Press, 2012.

———. *Exiles from a Future Time: The Forging of the Mid-Twentieth-Century Literary Left.* University of North Carolina Press, 2002.

———. *Writing from the Left: New Essays on Radical Culture and Politics.* Verso, 1994.

Wald, Sarah D. *The Nature of California: Race, Citizenship, and Farming since the Dust Bowl.* University of Washington Press, 2016.

Wartzman, Rick. *Obscene in the Extreme: The Burning and Banning of John Steinbeck's "The Grapes of Wrath."* Public Affairs, 2008.

Webb, Walter Prescott. *The Great Plains.* Ginn, 1951.

Weller, Sam. *The Bradbury Chronicles: The Life of Ray Bradbury.* Harper, 2005.

Wilder, Laura Ingalls, and Garth Williams. *On the Banks of Plum Creek.* Rev. ed. HarperCollins, 1953.

Wixson, Douglas. "Radical by Nature: Sanora Babb and Ecological Disaster on the High Plains, 1900–1940." In *Regionalists on the Left.* Ed. Michael C. Steiner. University of Oklahoma Press, 2013.

———. "Review: *Whose Names Are Unknown* by Sanora Babb." *Western American Literature* 40, no. 2 (Summer 2005): 215–17.

———. *Worker-Writer in America: Jack Conroy and the Tradition of Midwestern Literary Radicalism, 1898–1990.* University of Illinois Press, 1994.

Wohl, Ellen. *Of Rocks and Rivers: Seeking a Sense of Place in the American West.* University of California Press, 2009.

Wolper, David L. *Ray Bradbury: Story of a Writer by David L. Wolper.* TV documentary, 1963. Internet Archive, https://archive.org/details /RayBradburyStoryOfAWriterByDavidL.Wolper.

Woolf, Virginia. *A Writer's Diary: Being Extracts from the Diary of Virginia Woolf.* Ed. Leonard Woolf. Harcourt, Brace, 1953.

Worster, Donald. *Dust Bowl: The Southern Plains in the 1930s.* Oxford University Press, 2004.

Index

NOTE: Sanora Babb is sometimes referred to as "SB" in this index. References to the photograph section (beginning after page 284) refer to figure number (e.g., Fig. 1).

Babb, Alonzo *(continued)*
young Jennie, 9; disapproval of
Walt's wandering, 15; and the
ghost-horse ("Daft") sighting, 45–47,
270, 275–76, 303n9; ghost of, writing
of *An Owl on Every Post* as bringing
back, 270; and hardtack, 37;
homeschooling SB, 33, 54–55, 123;
letters to SB, 57–58; nickname
("Konkie") given by SB, 26; reading
The Adventures of Kit Carson to SB
and Dorothy, 31–32; in Red Rock
living with the family, 12, 15; in
Waynoka, 17; and wonder, sense
of, 55
—DUGOUT HOUSE: overview, 21,
22–23, *Fig. 7*; bathing and outhouse
arrangements, 28, 36; bedbugs,
24–25, 28; claimed to be temporary,
22–23, 27; clothing, lack of replace-
ments, 44; cooking in, 27–28; and
development of SB's "land ethic,"
29; Jennie's third pregnancy and
prematurely born son (Rex), 36–42,
43, 197, 279; as like a grave, 23, 28,
92; the piano and, 20, 43; sand rats,
45; sleeping arrangements, 24;
starvation conditions, 21–22, 27, 29,
37–41, 43–44, 195; wallpapered with
pages of the *Denver Post*, as reading
material, 28, 32, 54, 55–56, 85; Walt's
cruelty and, 36; winter isolation in,
35–36
—HOMESTEAD: as arid land, 26,
29–30; arrival of Babb family, 21,
301n1; broomcorn crops, 26, 30,
33–35, 43, 301n1, *Fig. 7*; close
relationship formed by SB with the
newly sober Konkie, 31, 48, 201;
harsh conditions of, 21–23, 27;
leaving Red Rock for, 17; nearby

land purchased as gamble by son
Walt, 5–6, 26, 27, 35, 43, 44; proving
up his homestead claim, 19, 26;
rattlesnakes, 34; romanticized
letters enticing Walt, 19; water
transport, 30, 35. *See also* Baca
County, Eastern Colorado; Two
Buttes, Colorado
Babb, Dorothy Marcella (sister of SB):
abandoned commitments of, 122,
137; agoraphobia of, 245–46, 266;
alcoholism of, 234, 242; "Aurelio"
(short story), 317n2; birth of (1909),
17; as bookkeeper for Ching How
restaurant, 193; and Carlos Bulosan
relationship, 140, 141, 156–57, 187,
234, 317n2; death of (1996), 289,
290; and death of father, 235; and
death of grandfather, 123–24; and
death of mother, preceded by
serious illness, 263, 264; dependence on SB's financial and
emotional support throughout life,
121–22, 137, 139, 140, 153, 235, 242,
254–55, 263, 266–67, 277, 289; in
Forgan, *Fig. 9*; home in final years
under doctor's care, 289; Howe
and, 122–23, 137, 235, 254; and
journey to Eastern Colorado, 5, 20;
"Konkie" (short story), 123–24; in
Los Angeles living with SB, 119, 121–
23, 137, 140, 235, 266–67, 312–13n55;
massive daily letters sent to SB in
Mexico, 234–35; mental health
issues of, 157, 209–10, 234–35;
personality differences with SB, 17;
photos taken of Dust Bowl
refugees, 317n12; in residential
recovery program, 242; school in
Elkhart, 53–54, 58; suicidal ideation
and attempt, 157, 235, 242; surrey

—FAMILY. *See* Babb, Alonzo
("Konkie") (grandfather of SB);
Babb, Dorothy Marcella (sister of
SB); Babb, Jennie (née Parks)
(mother of SB); Babb, Walter
(father of SB)
—CHILDHOOD: birth (1907) and
infancy, 13–15, *Fig. 2, Fig. 5*; freedom
to roam and be social, 15, 18, 31; full
given name, 13; illnesses during, 16,
63; made mascot for father's
baseball team, 15, *Fig. 2*; named
"Cheyenne, Riding like the Wind"
by Chief Black Hawk, 19, 301n22;
nicknamed "Cheyenne," 15,
301n22; starvation conditions of, 21–
22, 27, 29, 37–41, 43–44, 47, 195;
taken in as family by the Otoe-Missouria people, 5, 18–19, 31, 150, 268,
300–301nn21–22. *See also* Baca
County, Eastern Colorado; Elkhart,
Kansas; Forgan, Oklahoma; Garden
City, Kansas; Red Rock, Oklahoma;
Waynoka, Oklahoma
—ANIMALS, LOVE OF: beloved
horse, 30; and Thornton Burgess's
animal stories, 32–33; dog co-owned
with Howe (Chihuahua, "Chico"),
260, *Fig. 24*; dogs co-owned with
Howe ("Cissy" and "Annie"), 123,
127, 140, 153; funerals for chickens,
33, 61; pet monkey ("Patsy"), 113,
260; pet skunk, 259–60; pets
throughout her life, 259–60, 268;
prairie dogs, 56, 273; starvation
conditions and eating songbirds,
44. *See also* nature as solace
—AND THE SPIRIT WORLD:
ghost-horse ("Daft") sighting with
grandfather, 45–47, 270, 275–76,
303n9; haunted by the ghosts of

those who died, 265–66, 267; her
grandfather's presence while
writing *An Owl on Every Post,* 270;
supernatural stories, 266
—EDUCATION: *The Adventures of Kit
Carson,* 31–32, 54, 85; anthology of
ballads and poems at the Horse
Creek house, 45, 54; and authority,
rebellion against, 70; college
(Garden City Community College),
associate degree, 82–83; college
(Garden City Community College),
teaching certificate, 87–88; college
(University of Kansas) and
scholarship, 78–79, 80–81, 82,
308n3; *Denver Post* pages wallpa-
pering the dugout, 28, 32, 54, 55–56,
85; as escape from her childhood
privations, 308n3; homeschooling
at the homestead, 31–33, 54–56, 123;
and libraries, personal and public,
85–86; memorizing flora and fauna,
33, 56; reading materials, early
paucity of, 32–33, 45, 54–55; school
in Elkhart (KS), 53–56, 58, 68, 212;
school in Forgan (Forgan High
School), 67, 69–70, 77–78, 198,
306n9, *Figs. 8–9*; school in Red
Rock for a few weeks after
broomcorn harvest, 35–36; Spanish
language and literature studies, 82;
theater group of SB in Forgan,
71–73, 102, 307n17; valedictorian
honor revoked due to prejudice
against SB as "gambler's daughter,"
77–78, 79, 124–25, 198, 249
—HEALTH: appendicitis, 147–48,
316n41; depression following her
mother's death, 265, 267–68;
depression following loss of
Random House contract for *Whose*

Babb, Sanora *(continued)*
feminist writer who did not see
herself that way, 135-36, 262;
husband Howe's lack of support for
her career, as hindrance, 142, 147,
186, 243, 244, 254, 256, 264, 268;
husband Howe's traditional ideas
of marriage and expectation for SB
to spend her time caretaking their
life, as hindrance, 254, 255-56, 263,
264, 268, 271, 272-73, 274, 276-77;
and language of trauma, 226; late
nights as productive writing time
of, 243, 259, 264, 268, 277, 290; and
Le Sueur's demand to write "more
shamelessly and nakedly," 135, 136,
155; literary agents of (*See* Abbot,
Mary; Fallowfield, Julie; Lieber,
Maxim; Ross, Patience; Wolf,
Harriet); literary organizations
joined by, 90, 100, 125 (*See also*
John Reed Club; League of
American Writers); Ralph Ellison
Award granted (2022), 297;
short-story classes taught by
(UCLA), 254-55, 263, 264; sister
Dorothy's dependence on SB, as
hindrance, 242, 254-55, 263, 266-67,
277; writing employment (*See.*
California Quarterly, SB as editor
of; *Clipper, The*; film and SB;
journalism and SB; KFWB radio,
employment of SB; Warner
Brothers building, employment
of SB via). *See also* Babb, Sanora—
writings; gender norms challenged
by SB; poetry; romanticization
and omissions in SB's writing;
short stories; West, the: SB as
writing against the grain of the
myths of; women's agency and
voice, SB as centering; writing
group
—WRITINGS: "The Battle of Los
Angeles," 195; "Conquest," 98-99;
"Coute Que Coute," 92-93, 94;
"Daft," 275-76; "Dry Summer,"
117-18, 132; "Essence," 117;
"Farmers without Farms," 161;
"The Flying Bird of Dreams,"
88-89, 228; "For Future Reference,"
91-92; "A Good Straight Game,"
226; "How Deep Is the Ocean"
lyrics (lack of credit or royalties for),
101; "How to Handle Men" (earliest
essay), 56; "In a Field in Pelopo-
nesia," 261; "I Wish I Could
Remember," 91, 92; "The Journey
Begun," 203-204; *Konkie* (unpub-
lished), 118, 300n17; "The Larger
Cage," 229-30, 325n26; "Little
Pariah," 109; "The Los Angeles
WPA Theater Project," 136; "Lost
Cry," 117; "Morning in Imperial
Valley," 194; "Night in a Greek
Village," 260; "Night of Evil," 266;
"The Old One," 118; "The
Photography of James Wong Howe"
(pseudonym Sylvester Davis), 186;
"Picnic Mephitis: A Common
Skunk," 259; "Polly," 187-88;
"Poppies in the Wind," 116-17;
"Prairie Dwellers" (unpublished),
86; "Professor Coyote," 304n14;
"Reconciliation," 200-202, 212,
322n56; "The Refugee," 207-8, 210;
"Run, Sheepy, Run," 6-7, 262,
300n7, 328n19; "The Santa Ana,"
255, 263-64; "A Scandalous
Humility," 274-75; "Spring
Wooing," 117; "Storyteller's Street,"
264; "The Tea Party," 245-46,

326n15; "The Terror," 128–29, 136, 151; "That Presence Out There," 267, 329n34; "To L___," 90; "To Toby," 92; "The Vine by the Root Embraced," 215; "The Wild Flower," 226; "William Shakespeare," 89–90, 225–26; "Winter in Town," 142, 151; *Women without Men* (screenplay written by SB and William Saroyan), 110; "Young Boy, the World," 187. *See also The Lost Traveler*; *An Owl on Every Post*; *Whose Names Are Unknown*

Babb, Walter (father of SB): anger at and attachment to father (Alonzo), 10, 27, 48; boxing lessons for SB, 69; and children, expressed desire not to have, 13; death of, 232–33, 235, 237–38; and death of his friend Asa, 64–65; and death of mother, 10; decision to leave Colorado for Elkhart, Kansas (1917), 47–48; decision to leave Elkhart for Forgan (1919), 65–66; decision to leave Forgan for Garden City (1924), 80–81; decision to leave Red Rock for Eastern Colorado (1914), 5–6, 19–20; decision to leave Red Rock for Waynoka (1908), 16–17; divorce from Jennie, 120–21; as dray driver in Elkhart, 48, 51, 58; extravagant clothing and expenses, 9, 93; fluency in Native American languages, 7; love letters to Jennie, 8, 14; and prematurely born son (Rex), 36–37, 40–42; reciting verses, 45; registering for the draft (1917), 60; research material given to SB, 174, 226–27, 233, 244; SB's relationship with after leaving the family, 121, 233; wedding to Jennie, 9

—ABUSIVENESS TOWARD JENNIE AND HIS DAUGHTERS: and adversarial relationship with SB, 21–22, 31, 48, 70, 82, 95, 121, 203–4; anger, 14–15, 21–22, 48; in Baca County, Eastern Colorado, 21–22, 36; biographical details considered too extreme for readership, 199, 205, 328n19; as "companion of my childhood" (SB), 198; divorce as Jennie's escape from, 120–21; Dorothy's mental health difficulties and, 157, 209–10, 234–35; dysfunction of her parents' marriage as influence on SB's relationship choices, 111, 114, 139; in Garden City, 81–82, 245; "How to Handle Men" as protest of, 56; Jennie as unable to stay in Lansing for her father's funeral, 16; Jennie's social outings as triggering, 15; mood swings, 81–82; nervous breakdown of SB and, 210; in Red Rock, 11–12, 19, 245; refusal to call a doctor, 13, 63; reliving while writing *The Lost Traveler*, as painful, 198, 208–9, 210, 220, 233, 270; and SB's language of trauma, 226; SB's move to Los Angeles as escape from, 95–96, 121; and SB staying in abusive relationship with G. Henry Stetson for a year, 111; treating Jennie as if she were a child, 47–48; violent beatings, 19, 95, 139, 244–45

—AS BAKER: Alonzo (Walt's father) working in bakeries, 12–13, 15, 69; at Doc Sweeney's café (Red Rock), 7; in Elkhart (KS), 58–59, 65; Forgan bakery owned by, 67–68, 69, 76, 306n3; as his best self, 58–59; Jennie working in bakeries, 12, 15,

Babb, Walter (*continued*)
17, 18, 60, 65, 69, 71; Otoe-Missouria tribe's appreciation for, 7, 12; Red Rock bakery owned by, 6, 12–13, 15, 17, 64–65, 167; smallpox and, 16, 300n19; in Waynoka, 16–17
—AS BASEBALL PLAYER AND TEAM MANAGER: as absent father, 13, 14–15; archive of clippings, 233, 325n33; bringing the baseball team to live with the family, 17; drafted into the Western League, 10, 233; in Elkhart (KS), 52; gold cufflinks awarded to, 44; recognized by the coroner, 233; Red Rock team, 7, 14–15, 17, *Fig.* 3; SB made mascot of team, 15, *Fig.* 2; smallpox brought home by, 16, 300n19
—AS GAMBLER: as addiction, 81–82, 127, 233, 251; Baca County land purchase as gamble, 5–6, 26, 27; background of becoming, 10; bribing the sheriff, 60; in Elkhart, Kansas, 59–60, 65, 66; fleeing for safety, 59–60, 66, 203; in Forgan, 68, 76–77, 226; in Garden City (Windsor Hotel), 81–82, 93, 226; in Liberal, Kansas (Warren Hotel), 70, 77; marked cards system of, 59–60, 76–77, 226–27; portrayed in *The Lost Traveler*, 76, 81, 204, 226–27, 249, 251, 308n5; poverty of family caused by, 127, 167, 308n3; prejudice against SB as "gambler's daughter," 77–78, 79, 124–25, 198, 249; in Red Rock, 10, 19, 59; research information provided to SB, 226–27, 233, 244; in San Diego after the divorce, 120–21, *Fig.* 6; in Waynoka, 59

—BACA COUNTY LAND: bought outright vs. proving-up claim, 5–6, 26, 27; failure of second broomcorn crop, 43; improvements after first broomcorn harvest, 35, 44; loss of land due to inability to pay taxes, 43
—FAMILY RESIDENCES. *See* Baca County, Eastern Colorado; Elkhart, Kansas; Forgan, Oklahoma; Garden City, Kansas; Red Rock, Oklahoma; Waynoka, Oklahoma
Baca County, Eastern Colorado: adversarial relationship of SB with her father, 21–22; ashes of SB scattered in, 292; boxing lessons for SB, 69; broomcorn crop, failure of second, 43; broomcorn crop, farmers pooling resources to plant and harvest, 33–35; decision of Walt to move to, and journey, 5–6, 20–21; decision to move to Elkhart (1917) from, 47–48; and desire for education, 308n3; and desire to see the world, 25–26, 49; as "empty land" and "true wilderness," 21; and the ghost-horse ("Daft") sighting, 45–47, 270, 275–76, 303n9; harsh conditions of, 21–23, 27; Horse Creek house (1914–1917), 44–47, 201; and "land ethic" of SB, 29, 287, 302n14; milk purchased from the neighbor (Mrs. Haupman), 37–40, 279, 303nn34–35; and nature as solace, 25–26, 56; Old Man Hoopies, 30, 267; romanticization and omissions in SB's writing about, 21, 29–30; starvation conditions of, 21–22, 27, 29, 37–41, 43–44, 47, 195; teaching in rural setting as harrowing reminder of, 89; voice of SB as immersed in the terroir of, 92;

Bright, John, 224
British editions: *The Lost Traveler,* 252;
An Owl on Every Post, 282
Bronson, Charles, 273
Browder, Earl, 131
Brown, Doris Stella (sister of Walt), 35,
123–24
Buffalow, Este, 75
Bukowski, Charles, 99–100
Bulosan, Carlos: *America Is in the Heart,*
157–58; and Dorothy Babb relationship, 140, 141, 156–57, 187, 234,
317n2; background, 140; friendship
with John Fante, 157, 317n3;
friendship with SB, 140–41, 142,
157–58, 189, 242; hospitalization for
tuberculosis, 140, 141, 156, 157; and
racism, 156; SB as rarely mentioned
in biographies of, 4, 157–58
Burgess, Thornton, animal stories of,
32–33
Burnett, David, *The Best American
Short Stories* 1960: *and the Yearbook
of the American Short Story* (eds.
with Martha Foley), 264–65
Burns, Ken, *The Dust Bowl* documentary featuring SB's notes and
reports, 2, 294–96

Caddo people, 7
California Quarterly, SB as editor of:
closure of (1956), 227; founding of
journal (1950), 227; resignation due
to money problems, 242; as
workhorse, 232; writers published
in, 221, 224, 227–28, 231, 232
Capra Press, *The Dark Earth and
Selected Prose from the Great
Depression,* 146, 287, 296
Carlisle, Harry, 127, 130, 132; *Darkness
at Noon,* 127

Carson, Kit, 31–32
Central America, SB's travels in,
111–13
Ceplair, Larry, 207
Cerf, Bennett: contract for a new
novel offered by, 182, 194; dinner in
New York City with, 132; as having
grown up in Garden City, 132; and
Whose Names Are Unknown
contract, 132, 167, 173, 179; and
Whose Names Are Unknown,
contract cancelation, 180–81. *See
also* Random House
*Charmian Kittredge London: Trailblazer,
Author, Adventurer* (Dunkle), 3
Chekhov, Anton, 86
Chicago: journey of SB back to Los
Angeles by hitchhiking and
walking, 133–34; phone call with
Ralph Ellison during train stop, 191;
as stop on SB's journey to and from
First Writers' Congress, 130, 133; as
stop on SB's journey to London, 141
China: Howe's loss of mother in
childhood and emigration from,
115–16; Howe's visit to (1948), 214,
216
Chinese Exclusion Act (1882), repeal
of, 214
Ching How restaurant owned by
Howe and SB, 192–93, 195, 209, *Fig.*
19
Chumash people, 266
The Clipper (literary publication of the
League of American Writers,
formerly called *Black & White*):
meeting Ralph Ellison via meetings
of, 187, 188; SB on the board and as
editor of, 187, 188; shut down
during World War II, 227; stories of
SB published in, 187–88

about the plight of, 161; SB's firsthand experiences of life in the Dust Bowl region and understanding of, 166, 167–68; schools denying refugee children to attend, 169, 173; state officials' prejudice toward, 165, 183–84; striking workers evicted from housing, 166; volume of work required to retain privilege of a family cabin, 166–67. *See also* Farm Security Administration (FSA); *Whose Names Are Unknown*

Eastern Colorado. *See* Baca County, Eastern Colorado

Elkhart, Kansas: decision to move to (1917), 47–48; founding and growth of, 50–51, 304n3; homes in, 51, 59; Jennie robbed by fortune teller, 63–64, 65; Jennie's social circle in, 58; journey to, 48–49, 50–51; letter from her grandfather, 57–58; mail collection by SB, 56–58; prostitutes, SB's encounter at the post office with, 56–57, 68–69, 203; school for SB and Dorothy, 53–56, 58, 68, 142, 212; Spanish influenza epidemic, 63–65; Walt as dray driver in, 48, 51, 58; Walt's gambling in, 59–60, 65, 66, 203; World War I, 60–62, 65, 87, 306n53. *See also* Forgan, Oklahoma

Elkhart Tri-State News (Kansas), SB's exposure to the newspaper business, 52–53, 65, 70

Ellison, Ralph: book blurb for *An Owl on Every Post,* 279, 280; correspondence with SB, 192, 193, 196, 198, 214–15, 216; critique of SB's work by, 214; critique of *Whose Names Are Unknown,* 194, 196–97, 236; divorce from first wife (Rose), 206; *The Invisible Man,* 188, 189, 196; and the League of American Writers, 187, 188–89; love affair with SB, 189–92, 196, 204–5, 206, 209; meeting SB via *The Clipper* meetings, 187, 188–89; in Merchant Marines, 204–5; *The Negro Quarterly,* 196, 204, 206; and "proletarian art" prescriptions, disagreement with, 188–89; racism experienced by, 189; Ralph Ellison Award (Oklahoma Center for the Book), 297; SB as rarely mentioned in biographies of, 4; SB discussing children with, 196, 316n38; SB's identity as writer seen by, 190, 204; second marriage (Fanny McConnell), 209; shyness of, and discomfort with white people, 189, 196

"Essence," 117

Fallowfield, Julie, as SB's literary agent: and *An Owl on Every Post,* 274, 276, 278–79; talking to McCall's as publisher, 274

Fante, John: *Ask the Dust,* 99–100; friendship and mutual influence with SB, 99–100; friendship with Carlos Bulosan, 157, 317n3; SB as rarely mentioned in biographies of, 4

"Farmers without Farms," 161

Farm Security Administration (FSA): camp services offered, 162, 168–69; Tom Collins as administrator, 159, 162–63, 169, *Fig.* 17; democracy functioning (D.F.) system of committees for self-governance of camps, 163, 168–69; emotional toll of the work on SB, 169; founding of and mission to help displaced

Farm Security Administration
(continued)
farmers, 159; Gridley Camp, 162;
harassment and violence against
SB during work for, 170; notes of SB
made during work for, 164–65,
166–67, 168–70; notes of SB
published (See *On the Dirty Plate
Trail*); SB as volunteer in the
Imperial and San Joaquin Valleys
(eight-month stint), 162–66, *Figs.*
16–17; SB working on *Whose Names
Are Unknown* during, 166, 170;
short stories based on SB's
experiences with, 188; trust of
migrants for SB, 2, 169; trust of
migrants for Tom Collins, and loss
of, 169, 184; and unionizing, 163,
164. *See also* Collins, Tom; Dust
Bowl refugees seeking work; *Grapes
of Wrath, The* (John Steinbeck)—appropriation of Babbs's material
farm workers: big agriculture as
dominating California, 165;
communism as alleviating
difficulties of, 155; SB's Soviet
Union tour of model farms, 145–46,
150–51, 155, 160, *Fig.* 15; as subject
of interest for SB, 136, 155. *See also*
Dust Bowl refugees seeking work;
Farm Security Administration
(FSA); *Grapes of Wrath, The* (John
Steinbeck)—appropriation of
Babbs's material; grower-run
camps for migrant farm workers;
growers' associations, threats and
violence against labor organizers
and observers; labor organizing;
Whose Names Are Unknown
fascism: anti-Semitism, 143–44, 149;
in Germany and Poland during SB's

Soviet Union tour, 143–44, 149, 151,
152, 154, *Fig.* 14; in Italy, 150; SB on
experience of, 151; SB refused for
WWII enlistment due to her
anti-fascist work in England, 195;
The Week as challenging, and SB as
co-editor, 151–52, 154–55, 195. *See
also* World War II
Faulkner, William, 322n56
FBI and the Red Scare: "American
Communist Group in Mexico"
(ACGM), 224–25; investigation of
Howe and SB, 222
feminism: critique of androcentrism
in the Communist Party, 314n42;
SB as feminist writer, 135–36, 262.
See also Babb, Sanora—independence, need for; birth control;
gender equality; gender norms
challenged by SB; voting rights for
women; women's agency and voice,
SB as centering; women's stories
Feuchtwanger, Lion, 193
Filipino characters, in *Whose Names
Are Unknown*, 176
film and Howe. *See* Howe, James
Wong (husband of SB)—as
cinematographer
film and SB: *Film Daily* reviews and
interviews, 101, 103, 104–6;
ghostwriting screenplays from the
public domain, 107–8, 311–12n30;
The Lost Traveler screenplay (not
filmed), 273, 329n10; *The Molly
Maguires* consultation, 273–74; Irving
Thalberg, turning down offer from,
102–3, 104–5, 311n21, *Fig.* 10; *Women
without Men* (screenplay written by
SB and William Saroyan), 110
Film Daily, SB's reviews and interviews for, 101, 103, 104–6

gender equality: and sexual freedom, 146–47; in the Soviet Union, SB's observations of, 146, 147–48, 150, 154–55

gender norms challenged by SB: in *The Lost Traveler,* 249–50; SB rejecting in her own life, 93–94, 114; in "A Scandalous Humility," 274–75; and women's agency and voice, SB's writing as centering, 136, 204, 205. *See also* Babb, Sanora—independence, need for; women's agency and voice, SB as centering

Germany, Nazi: SB's travel through (1936), 143–44, 149, 151, 152, 154, 260, *Fig. 14. See also* World War II

Germany, refusal of Babb to return postwar, 260

Gogol, Nikolai, 86

Gollancz, Victor, British publisher: *The Lost Traveler,* 252; pressure to write an autobiography, 258, 261

"A Good Straight Game," 226

Gorky, Maxim, 86

Goslaar, Lotte, 179, 319n35

Grant, Cary, 193

The Grapes of Wrath (John Steinbeck): abandoned first and second versions, 171–72, 177; as bestseller, 180, 286; Carol Steinbeck (wife) as deeply involved in creating, 177, 183; characterizations as "over-es-senced," 178–79, 182; compared to SB's *Whose Names Are Unknown,* 177, 180, 182, 197, 293–94; film version (Academy Award-win-ning), 180, 193, 286; hospitalization of Steinbeck following completion of, 177; lack of research done by Steinbeck (and false claims of),

178; previous writings about the Dust Bowl, 171; Pulitzer Prize (1940), 286; as rejected by those who lived through the Dust Bowl, 2, 184, 286; as required reading in high schools, 286; serious errors and omissions made in, 177–79; Steinbeck's fear of retaliation from the growers' associations, 1723, 179; success of, and SB as unable to publish *Whose Names Are Unknown,* 180–82, 184, 193, 285–86; third and final version, 177; title of, 177, 319n24

—APPROPRIATION OF BABBS'S MATERIAL: analysis showing, 293–94; camp visits (two), 171, 182; Tom Collins (FSA camp administrator) acknowledged in book with dedication and character based on, 182, 183; Collins's hope that a bestselling author would bring attention to the camps and plight of the refugees, 171, 172, 184–85; *The Dustbowl* documentary by Ken Burns and Dayton Duncan featuring extensive excerpts from SB's notes and reports, 2, 294–96; fictitious name used by Steinbeck and anonymity among the migrants, 171, 172, 184; SB never acknowledged by Steinbeck, 182–83; SB's meeting with Steinbeck and handing over her notes at Collins's request, 171, 172–73, 182, 183, 285–86, 296, 318n7; Steinbeck's false claim of extensive trip with Collins and lack of research, 178; Stein-beck's journal entries citing heavy reliance on field notes written by SB and Collins, and subsequent letters

Howe, James Wong *(continued)*
Stetson, 114, 116; dating SB as
mixed-race couple, 113-14, 123;
death of, 282-83; dogs co-owned
with SB, 123, 127, 140, 153, 260, *Fig.*
24; and Dorothy, sister of SB,
122-23, 137, 235, 254; *Film Daily*
assignment for SB to interview, and
meeting, 103, 104-6; as financially
supporting SB, 138, 139, 143; health
issues, and caregiving by SB, 277,
282-83; mutual commitment to the
relationship, 116; naturalized
citizenship of (1947), 214; racism
experienced by, 105, 113-14, 189,
199-200, 217-18, 258, 264;
relationship with young Chinese
girl, 192; SB's friendships, jealousy
of, 142-43, 147; SB's friendships,
understanding of need for, 216; SB's
need for independence, coming to
understanding of, 216, 227, 256; SB's
work as writer, lack of support for,
142, 147, 186, 243, 244, 254, 256,
264, 268; SB's work as writer,
understanding of importance of,
216, 258; separation from SB,
200-202; and sexual freedom of
women, SB's assertion of, 147-48;
strains in relationship with SB, 186,
192, 200; as surprised by SB's
refusal of Irving Thalberg's offer,
105; temper of, 138-39, 142-43;
traditional idea of marriage and
expectation for SB to spend her
time taking care of their life, 254,
255-56, 263, 264, 268, 271, 272-73,
274, 276-77; and B. Traven, 223-24;
visitors of, SB expected to play
hostess to, 254, 264; Wong Tong Jim
as given name of, 103. *See also*

London, SB and Howe in; Queens
Road house
—AS CINEMATOGRAPHER:
absorption in work, and exclusion
of all else, 138, 142, 151, 156, 236;
Academy Award nominations and
wins, 153, 242, 256, 271, 272, *Fig.* 23;
The Adventures of Tom Sawyer, 153,
156; *Air Force,* 200; *Algiers,* 153, 156;
The Brave Bulls, 220, 221-22, 223, 225;
celebrity status of, 152, 216, 218,
258-59; China visit and film
research (1948), 214, 216; *Fire over
England,* 137-38, 142, 151, 316n44;
freelancing career begun, 214; as
gray-listed during Red Scare, 227,
234, 235, 271; *The Heart Is a Lonely
Hunter,* 273; *Hombre,* 272-73; *The
Horsemen,* 278; *Hud,* 271-72; Laurel
Award, 273; legacy of, SB as
caregiver for, 3, 283-84, 286-87,
330n43; Myrna Loy depicted too
realistically, 115; *Main Street to
Broadway,* 234-35; *The Molly
Maguires,* 274, 277; as novelty to the
American press, 137; *The Outrage,*
272-73; *The Prisoner of Zelda,* 153,
156; pseudonymous articles written
by SB in support of, 186; relocation
for work in London, and pressuring
SB to join him, 137-39; *The Rose
Tattoo,* 242, 256, 271, 286; SB's
support not acknowledged by
Howe in Academy Award speeches,
256, 272; SB traveling on location
with Howe while writing *An Owl on
Every Post,* 272-74; sent to Europe to
shoot background shots, 114-16;
*Song without End: The Story of Franz
Liszt,* 257, 258-59, 260; as sought-after due to innovative filming

techniques, 103, 137, 186, 271–72; *The Thin Man,* 115; *This Property Is Condemned,* 273; *Troopship,* 151; *Under the Red Robe,* 151; in World War II, 200, 322n54

Howe, Julia Ward, "Battle Hymn of the Republic," 319n24

"How to Handle Men" (earliest essay), 56

HUAC (House Un-American Activities Committee) investigations, 221–22. *See also* Red Scare

Huxley, Aldous, 253

"In a Field in Peloponesia," 261

Ingalls, Beth, *Pastures of Heaven,* 293

International Writers' League, 90

"I Wish I Could Remember," 91, 92

Japan, and U.S. in World War II, 191–92, 194–95, 206, 323n12

Japanese characters, in *Whose Names Are Unknown,* 176

Jarrico, Paul, 207

Jewett, Sarah Orne, 167

Jewish people: friendship extended to SB's tour group in Warsaw, 144. *See also* anti-Semitism

John Reed Club, 100, 125, 126–27, 311n10; ideals espoused, and SB's Soviet Union tour, 146

journalism and SB: Associated Press credentials obtained, 96; the *Elkhart Tri-State News* as awakening to the business, 52–53, 65, 70; film reviews for *Film Daily,* 101, 103, 104–6; at *The Forgan Eagle* (later *The Forgan Enterprise*), 70–71, 73, 306nn10,12; letter of recommendation from editor at *Opportunity,* 96; *Los Angeles Herald,* 98, 99;

in *The Lost Traveler,* 71; *Opportunity* (magazine), 94, 96; poems and articles sold to *Town and Country,* 110; proofreading work saving her from starvation in Salt Lake City, 134; reportage, 126, 128, 136, 148, 161, 267; review of Ann Stanford's poem (*Magellan*), 254; stories sold via connections at Warner Brothers building, 101; typewriter use, 84, 98; at *The Week* (London), 151–52, 154–55, 195. *See also Garden City Herald* (Kansas), SB employed by

"The Journey Begun," 203–204

Kansas: women granted vote (1912), 52. *See also* Elkhart; Garden City; Lansing; Liberal

Kansas Authors Club, 90

Keirns, Lulu May ("Mae") (sister of Jennie): death of, 17–18; sewing clothes for her nieces, 13, 17; and wedding of Jennie and Walt, 9

Kelley, E. E.: as famous columnist, 83, 90–91, 309n10; forced to sell the paper, 94–95; *Opportunity* (magazine), 94, 96; as SB's boss at the *Garden City Herald,* 83–85, 94–95, 309n10

Kelley, Katherine, 83

Kemper, Clarence, second husband of Jennie Babb, 263, 265

Kemper, Jennie A. (formerly Jennie Babb) (mother of SB): death of, preceded by serious illness and caregiving by SB (1960), 263, 264–65, 266; letter from SB about *Whose Names Are Unknown* and *The Lost Traveler,* 243, 244; letters to SB, 174, 262–63, 300nn9–10; relocation to Whittier, California, to be near

meeting Richard Wright, 130–31;
opening ceremonies, 130–31, 135;
tensions with Tillie Lerner Olsen,
127, 130, 132, 133

Lee, Don (nephew of Howe), 316n52

leftist political ideas: awakened by
Sacco and Vanzetti execution, 88,
100; disagreement with "proletar-
ian art" agenda for writing, 131–32,
133, 155, 158, 188–89; poverty
alleviation, 155. *See also* Communist
Party USA (CPUSA); Farm Security
Administration (FSA); John Reed
Club; labor organizing; League of
American Writers; Red Scare

Leopold, Aldo, 29, 302n14

Le Sueur, Meridel: background of,
125–26; in *California Quarterly,*
227–28; and the Communist Party
(CPUSA), 126, 131, 314n42; "Corn
Village," 135; demand that SB write
"more shamelessly and nakedly,"
135, 136, 155; *The Girl,* 205–6, 323n9;
"I Was Marching!," 126; and John
Reed Club, 126–27; and "object/
field problem," 131; urging SB to
come to the First Writers' Congress, 125, 126–27, 135; urging SB to
do *reportage,* 126, 128; and women's
voices, 129

Lewis, Sinclair, 126

Liberal, Kansas: Walt's gambling
setups in the Warren Hotel, 70, 77;
Walt's sister Stella living near, 35,
123–24

Lieber, Maxim, as SB's first literary
agent, 316n31, 317n7, 320n1

little magazines, 108–9

"Little Pariah," 109

Locke, Sondra, 273

London, Charmian Kittredge, 3

London, Jack, 1, 3

London, SB and Howe in: apartment,
139, 141–42; friendship with Lotus
Fragrance (Rebecca Ho Hing Du),
152–53; "honeymoon" trip, 152;
Howe as celebrity, 152; Howe's
focus on work leaving SB alone,
142, 151; journeys of SB to and from,
141, 153, 159; living together as a
couple, 139, 152; Paris sojourns, 142,
152; relocation of Howe for film
work, and pressure on SB to join
him, 137–39; return of Howe to Los
Angeles, 153; romance of SB with
Desmond MacCarthy, 154, 276; SB
as co-editor of *The Week* (London),
151–52, 154–55; SB remaining
behind, 153–54; writing work of SB,
142, 151

London, SB in: enroute to Vienna, 258;
flying to, 257–58. *See also* Ross,
Patience

Long Beach Earthquake (1933), 122

Loranger, Carol S., "Erratic Orbit:
Sanora Babb, Poet," 86, 91

Los Angeles: cheap room on arrival,
98; decision of SB to move to
(1929), 95–96; Dorothy living with
SB in, 119, 121–23, 137, 140, 235,
266–67, 312–13n55; ghostwriting
screenplays from the public
domain, 107–8, 311–12n30;
happiness of SB in, 101–2; homeless
and living on the streets (four
months), 106–8, 111, 187; job posing
nude for art students, 107; Long
Beach Earthquake (1933), 122; and
Perez v. Sharp (end of anti-miscegenation laws in California), 216–18;
Stanley Rose's Bookshop as
gathering place for writers, 107,

Miller, Arthur, 263–64
"Morning in Imperial Valley," 194
Morrison, Ray, and the writing group, 323n26, *Fig.* 18
Mozart, Wolfgang Amadeus, 259
Mulhaul, Oklahoma Territory, 10
Musso's restaurant, 108

Native Americans: and baseball, 7, *Fig.* 3; children removed and sent to boarding schools for assimilation, 18; Dawes Act (1887), 8–9; exploitation by white "guardians" appointed for, 9; ghosts of those who lost their lives working as slaves for the Spanish, 266; hired to create atmosphere for travelers at railroad stations, 128, 129; land dispossession of, 8–9, 26, 30; Walt as learning languages of, 7. *See also* Otoe-Missouria people
nature as solace: airplane transport and, 257–58; and desire to see the world, 25–26, 49; ethic of sexual freedom, 146; flora and fauna, childhood memorization of, 33, 56; flora and fauna, extensive notes and research about, 223, 230, 277–78; the garden at Queens Road house, 227, 239, 268, 292; in "The Journey Begun," 204; land ethic, 29, 287, 302n14; mountains, 97, 98–99; mystical sense of related-ness to, 29, 287; the night sky, 25, 29, 133; in "Reconciliation," 201–2; and SB's Central American trip, 112–13; the sky, and vision of herself as a writer, 25–26, 29, 133, 243, 247, 256, 257, 292, 308n3; sunrise on the prairie, 25–26; voice of SB as immersed in the terroir of Baca

County, 92; in walking and hitchhiking from Chicago to Los Angeles, 133–34; and the wind, 204; and wonder, sense of, 21, 55. *See also* Babb, Sanora—and the spirit world; Babb, Sanora—animals, love of
Navajo people, 128, 129
Nebraska, Big Blue Reservation of the Otoe-Missouria people, 8
Nemerov, Howard, 263–64
Neruda, Pablo: in *California Quarterly,* 221, 227–28; *Canto General,* 221; in Mexico City, 224; Waldeen as translator of, 221, 324n1
New Hope, Kansas, teaching appointment of SB, 87–90, 225–26, 228
Newman, Paul, 271, 272–73
Newman, Roxana (daughter of Lotus Ma): biography of her mother, Lotus Fragrance (stage name), 323n22; SB as godmother to, 153, 211–12, 214, 225
New Orleans, Louisiana, 273
New York City: and the Fourth Writers' Congress (1941), 187; with Howe filming *Main Street to Broadway,* 235–37; meetings with agents and publishers for *An Owl on Every Post,* 278; and relationship of Ralph Ellison and SB, 189–90; sojourn for third draft of *The Lost Traveler,* 214, 215, 216, 218–19; sojourn to finish writing *Whose Names Are Unknown,* 179, 319n35. *See also* League of American Writers, First Writers' Congress (1935)
"Night in a Greek Village," 260
"Night of Evil," 266
Nixson, Peg and the writing group, 323n26

"object/field problem," 131–32

Oklahoma Center for the Book, Ralph Ellison Award granted SB (2022), 297

Oklahoma Panhandle: Dust Bowl effects on, 124–25, 159, 174; gambling, as illegal in the U.S. but part of the panhandle culture, 59; as growing frontier in early 20th century, 50; as "No Man's Land," 50; prostitution as illegal but tolerated in, 57; railroads and the growth of towns, 50, 65–66; return of dust storms to (mid-1950s), 239, 243–44. *See also* Dust Bowl; Elkhart, Kansas; Forgan, Oklahoma; Garden City, Kansas; Red Rock, Oklahoma

"The Old One," 118

Olsen, Tillie Lerner: background of, 127; and the Communist Party (CPUSA), 314n42; as delegate with SB at First Writers' Congress, 127, 130, *Fig.* 11; dinner with Bennett Cerf, 132; on the Gallup, New Mexico police suppression of miners' union, 128; and "object/field problem," 131; performative behavior of, SB's perception of, 127, 133; struggle to find balance between motherhood and being a writer, 129–30; tensions with SB, 127, 130, 132, 133; wearing Walt's raggedy coat, 127, 128; and women's voices, 129; *Yonnondio,* 132, 205–6, 314n37, 323n9

On the Dirty Plate Trail: Remembering the Dust Bowl Refugee Camps (Doug Wixson, 2007): and analysis of Steinbeck's appropriation of SB's notes, 294; and Burns and Duncan's *Dust Bowl* documentary,

296–97; publication of, 294, 331n8; sister Dorothy's photos in, 317n12

Opportunity (magazine), SB employed at, 94, 96

Osage people, 7

Otoe-Missouria people: baseball team and, 7, *Fig.* 3; children removed and sent to boarding schools for assimilation, 18; as customers of Walt's bakery, 7, 12; greeting the train, 6–7; Jennie's friendships with women of, 12; Jiwere language of, 7, 18; origins of, and history of land dispossession, 8–9; sadness of SB in leaving, 5; and smallpox, fear of, 16; taking in SB as family, 5, 18–19, 31, 150, 268, 300–301nn21–22; Walt learning the language of, 7. *See also* Black Hawk, Chief; Red Rock, Oklahoma

An Owl on Every Post: "all life is One," 29; American Library Editions (paperback edition), 282; arithmetic lessons, 33; Baca County, Eastern Colorado as source for, 21, 29; book blurbs, and author's photograph and information, coming in too late to be printed with, 279–80; claim of meeting grandfather for the first time, 31; County Book Club edition (England) published, 282; cover redesign, 279; Joanne Dearcopp as keeping in print, 289, 296; early drafts, 300n9; fan letters sent to SB, 278; the ghost-horse ("Daft") sighting, 47, 270, 275–76, 303n9; Pauline Hodges as teaching in Forgan, 295; McCall's as publisher of, 274, 276–77, 278, 279, 280, 281–82; as memoir vs. novel, issue

An Owl on Every Post (continued)
of, 278–79; Old Man Hoopies story,
267; Peter Davies Limited (British
edition) published, 282; the
prematurely born brother's story in,
42; pressure to write an autobiography, 257, 258, 261; promotion and
publicity tour, 280, 281–82; *Redbook*
publishing condensation (and
excerpt) of, 276, 277, 278; reportage-style approach to, 267; research
for, 262–63, 268, 277–78, 279;
reserving first chapter in failed
hopes of writing her experiences
being taken in as family by the
Otoe-Missouria people, 268, 274;
review in *Publishers Weekly*, 280;
romanticization and omissions in,
29–30; Ross and Abbot (literary
agents), unstinting support for,
270–71; school in Elkhart in, 54,
304n14; success of, 282; summation
written for, 271; University of New
Mexico Press, republishing (1994),
289; wifely duties to Howe, "legal"
neglect of, 276–77; wifely duties to
Howe, struggle to balance writing
life with, 268, 271, 272–73, 274; the
writing group and, 269; writing of,
as bringing back the spirit of her
grandfather, 270, 277; writing
schedule, 267–68, 270–71, 272–74,
276–78

Palm Springs holiday, 247, 281, *Fig.* 21
Panama, SB's travels in, 111–12, 113
Paris: fall to Nazi Germany (1940),
186; haircut of SB at Emile's,
149–50; lie that SB and Howe got
married in (1936), 152, 218; sojourns
with Howe, 142, 152; as starting/

ending point for Soviet Union tour
(1936), 143, 149–50, *Fig.* 13
Parks, Anna Jenny Myers (mother of
Jennie): caring for Jennie and birth
of SB, 13–14; clippings of Thornton
Burgess's animal stories sent to
Baca County, 32–33; mother's hard
attitude toward Jennie's choice to
marry Walt, and regret for, 11–12;
and SB's college year (University of
Kansas), 80; at wedding of Walt
and Jennie, 9
Parks, Green Berry (brother of
Jennie), 61, 79, 80–81
Parks, Green Berry (father of Jennie):
and birth of Sanora, 13, 14; death of,
16, 17; at wedding of Walt and
Jennie, 9
Parks, William ("Will") Henry
(brother of Jennie), 16–17
Peter Davies Limited, British
publisher of *An Owl on Every Post*,
282
Petracca, Joseph, and the writing
group, 323n26
"The Photography of James Wong
Howe" (pseudonym Sylvester
Davis), 186
"Picnic Mephitis: A Common Skunk,"
259
plays and the theater: *South Dakota
Farm: A One-Act Play* (SB's
homework assistance to Dorothy),
122, 313n7; theater group of SB in
Forgan, 71–73, 102, 307n17
poetry: emerging unique voice in,
91–92; free verse, 117; in Greece,
260–61; in Mexico City, 225;
national reputation of SB as poet,
90–91, 310n33; *Told in the Seed*
(collection published by West End

Press), 290; *Told in the Seed and Selected Poems* (collection), 296; writing and sending out during and after teaching appointment, 90. *See also specific titles*

Poland, SB's travel through (1936), 144-45, 149, 151

Politis, Gina, 260, 261-62, 266-67

Pollard, Lillie (cousin of SB, correspondence with), 21, 101-2, 109, 121, 235, 301n31

"Polly," 187-88

"Poppies in the Wind," 116-17

poverty: of migratory workers during the Dust Bowl, 161, 165, 169-70, 175-76; SB's belief in communism as solution for, 150-51, 154, 155; and starvation conditions of SB's childhood, 21-22, 27, 29, 37-41, 43-44, 47, 195; *Whose Names Are Unknown* as upending myths about, 175

Powell, John Wesley, 26

"Prairie Dwellers" (unpublished), 86

"Professor Coyote," 304n14

Prohibition, 77, 81

prostitution and prostitutes: SB's encounter in Elkhart, as teaching her to trust her inner guide, 56-57, 68-69, 203; in "A Scandalous Humility," 274-75; in the Soviet Union, 147-48, 316n39

Queens Road house, *Fig.* 24; dog Chico, 260, *Fig.* 24; FBI stopping by to investigate Howe and SB, 222; garden of, 227, 239, 268, 292; ghosts of the land surrounding, as haunting SB, 265-66; Howe's visitors, SB expected to play hostess to, 254, 264; purchase of, 199; and

racism experienced by Howe, 199-200; reconciliation and marriage, 216-18; and Roxana (daughter of Lotus Ma), SB as godmother to, 211, 212; and separation from Howe, 200

racism: anti-miscegenation laws, as complicating relationship of Ralph Ellison and SB, 189; anti-miscegenation laws, as preventing marriage of Howe and SB, 123, 137, 139, 217; anti-miscegenation law struck down in California, racism as continuing in wake of, 217-18; and claims of "black Irish" to pass as white, 31; experienced by James Wong Howe, 105, 113-14, 189, 199-200, 217-18, 258, 264; experienced by Ralph Ellison, 189; Howe as unable to own property, 192, 199; *The Lost Traveler* as portraying, 251, 252; SB and understanding of what Howe faced, 105, 114

radio: "Daft," 276; *An Owl on Every Post* publicity tour, 280. *See also* KFWB radio, employment of SB

Raffles (film made from SB's ghostwritten adaptation), 108, 311-12n30

railroads and trains: and the frontier as growing into the early 20th century, 50; and growth of towns, 50, 65-66; journey to Los Angeles, 97-98; journey to Los Angeles and saying goodbye to Ralph Ellison, 190-91; and land dispossession of Native Americans, 8-9; Native Americans hired to create atmosphere at rail stations, 128, 129; whistle of, as call to freedom, 14, 51, 95, 204

extreme for readership, 199, 205, 328n19; in *The Lost Traveler,* 199, 244-45, 308n5; in *An Owl on Every Post,* 29-30; in stories her mother told her, 140; of Walt's gambling addiction and abusiveness, 308n5

Roosevelt, Eleanor, 192

Rose, Stanley, Bookshop and friendship with SB, 107, 108, 311n28

Rossen, Robert, 221-22

Ross, Patience, as SB's literary agent in the English market: correspondence with SB, 283; "Daft" sold to BBC Radio 2, 276; English publisher found for *The Lost Traveler,* 246, 252; introduced by Harriet Wolf, 246; and *An Owl on Every Post,* 267-68, 270-71, 276, 279, 280; pressure to write an autobiography, 258, 261, 278

Roth, Philip, 263-64

"Run, Sheepy, Run," 6-7, 262, 300n7, 328n19

Rushmore, Howard, 136, 315n4

Russian novels, as influence, 86

Sacco, Nicola, and Bartolomeo Vanzetti, execution of, 88, 100

Sahl, Hans, 150

Salemson, Harold, 100

Salt Lake City, Utah, 134

Sandburg, Carl, 126

Sanger, Margaret, 170

"The Santa Ana," 255, 263-64

Saroyan, William: book blurb for *An Owl on Every Post,* 279, 280; correspondence with SB, 109-10, 112, 118-19, 311-12nn30,51; "The Daring Young Man on the Flying Trapeze," 109; mutual influence of SB and, 109-10, 141; and Random

House, 167; SB as rarely mentioned in biographies of, 4, 110, 317n6; SB attempting to visit in San Francisco, 111; self-created image of the typewriter as his one love object, 110; unrequited love for SB, 110, 119, 312-13n55, 317n6; *Women without Men* (screenplay written with SB), 110

"A Scandalous Humility," 274-75

Schilling, Julie, 291

Scott, Randolph, 193

Selective Service Act (1917), 60

Selma, Alabama, 273

Selznick, David, 153

sexism: Steinbeck's lack of acknowledgment of SB's contributions, 182-83; Steinbeck's use of his wife (Carol's) labor, 177, 183. *See also* gender norms challenged by SB; women's stories

Sharp, Dolph: and *California Quarterly,* 227; "The Tragedy of Janice Brierman's Life," 212; and the writing group, 212-13, 231-32, 323n26, *Fig.* 18

Sharp, Roz, 209

Shearer, Norma, 102

Shore, Wilma, 227; and the writing group, 323n26

short stories: autobiographical material, shift to, 117-18; commercial market and, 214-15, 245-46, 255, 267; compromise for marketability, refusal of SB to consider, 215; *The Cry of the Tinamou* (collection), 290, 296; extensive reading as encouraging, 86; first publication of ("Little Pariah"), 109; the Great Depression and beginning to turn to her own experiences as source,

Warsaw, Poland: arrest of SB's tour group, 144; fascism and anti-Semitism (1936), 144–45, 149, 151

Waynoka, Oklahoma, 16–17, 20, 31, 59, *Fig. 5. See also* Red Rock, Oklahoma

Webb, Walter Prescott, *The Great Plains,* 26

The Week (London), SB as co-editor challenging fascism, 151–52, 154–55, 195

West End Press, as publisher of *Told in the Seed* (poetry collection), 290

the West, SB as writing against the grain of the myths of: and Kit Carson stories, exposure to, 31–32; "land ethic" of SB, 29, 287, 302n14; rugged individualism, starvation as dispensing with, 29; women's agency and voice and, 32, 136. *See also* gender norms challenged by SB; women's agency and voice, SB as centering

Wharton, Marian, 125

Whose Names Are Unknown: overview, 301n28; agency of women portrayed in, 173, 176, 197; Baca County, Eastern Colorado as source for, 21; as bestseller, 296; Melissa Blake typing new copy and encouraging publication, 236; Tom Collins–based character in, 175; comparisons of *Grapes of Wrath* to, 177, 180, 182, 197, 293–94; diversity of refugees and, 174; "Dry Summer" as introducing characters Ronny and Myra, 117–18; *The Dustbowl* documentary by Ken Burns and Dayton Duncan featuring extensive excerpts from SB's notes and reports, 2, 294–96; dust storms returning to the Panhandle area and relevance of, 239, 243–44; editing final version for publication, 290–91; Ralph Ellison critique of, 194, 196–97, 236; Pauline Hodges and, 295; images constructed with words, 160; *Kansas Magazine* publishing excerpt from (1942), 194; *Michigan Quarterly Review* publishing excerpt from (1990), 288; miscarriage of pregnant refugee, 42, 176, 197; multicultural and multiethnic environment, and their interracial class struggle, 176–77; New York City sojourn to finish writing, 179, 319n35; plot based on SB's firsthand experiences, 42, 167–68, 175–76, 183–84; plot of, 167–68, 173–77; and positionality of the researcher, 2–3, 4; prejudice and hate toward refugees ("Okies"), 175, 176, 183–84, 294; realization that she must depict the farmers prior to the disaster (humanization), 160–61, 175; research for (*See* Dust Bowl refugees looking for work; Farm Security Administration); return from her Soviet Union tour and commitment to, 155; review in *Steinbeck Review,* 293–94; and solution of labor banding together, 176–77; starvation depictions, 175–76; Steinbeck-based character in, 183–84, 320n45; Steinbeck's lack of knowledge of, 183; title of, 158, 173; University of Oklahoma Press as publisher (2004), 175, 291–92, 293, 296; as upending conventional pieties of American identity, 175; writing while also volunteering with FSA, 166, 170

praise for, 135; in *The Lost Traveler*, 203–4, 205–6; in reportage, 129, 148; SB as feminist writer who did not see herself that way, 135–36, 262; in "A Scandalous Humility," 274–75; the Soviet Union and gender equality, 148; and the West, SB as writing against the grain of the myths of, 32, 136; in *Whose Names Are Unknown*, 173–74, 176. *See also* gender norms challenged by SB; prostitution and prostitutes

women's stories: from the 1930s, generally not published until decades later, 205–6, 323n9; and blacklisting during the Red Scare, 4; and the postwar "Silent Decade," 4, 249–50; previous accusations of Steinbeck as borrowing, 293

Women without Men (screenplay written by SB and William Saroyan), 110

wonder. *See* nature as solace

Wood, Natalie, 273

Woolf, Leonard, 237

Woolf, Virginia, *A Writer's Diary*, 237–38

workers' rights. *See* labor organizing

the world, SB's desire to see: the Central American trip as fully awakening, 111, 113; "honeymoon" trip in Europe (Howe and SB), 152; nature as inspiration for, 25–26, 49; train whistles as call to freedom, 51, 95, 204. *See also* Soviet Union tour group; *specific places*

World War I, 60–62, 65, 86, 87, 306n53; as subject of SB's writings, 73–74, 86–87

World War II: *The Clipper* shut down, 227; destruction in Vienna, 259; end of the war, 206, 207, 323n12; films made during, 200, 322n54; Hitler's rise in Europe, 143–44, 149, 151, 152, 154, 186; Japan, U.S. war with, 191–92, 194–95, 206, 323n12; Lotus Ma and, 210–11, 212; SB's volunteer work ("mink brigade"), 195; SB turned down for enlistment, 195. *See also* fascism; Red Scare

Wright, Richard, 130–31, 189; *Native Son*, 131, 189

Writers' Congress. *See* League of American Writers

writing group: by correspondence while traveling, 228, 257–58, 259; critiques of *The Lost Traveler*, 231–32; critiques of *An Owl on Every Post*, 269; critiques of short stories in, 228, 232, 245, 255; Joanne Dearcopp brought by SB to, 281; faithful attendance by SB, 265, 287; formation of, 212–13; members of, 323n26, *Fig.* 18; the night they sang together, 213; as pillar of protection and support for SB for forty years, 213, 269

Wylie, Eleanor, *Nets to Catch in the Wind*, 85

"Young Boy, the World," 187

Young, Noel (Capra Press), *The Dark Earth and Selected Prose from the Great Depression*, 146, 287, 296

Zatz, Asa, 225, 234, 325n15

Founded in 1893,
UNIVERSITY OF CALIFORNIA PRESS
publishes bold, progressive books and journals
on topics in the arts, humanities, social sciences,
and natural sciences—with a focus on social
justice issues—that inspire thought and action
among readers worldwide.

The UC PRESS FOUNDATION
raises funds to uphold the press's vital role
as an independent, nonprofit publisher, and
receives philanthropic support from a wide
range of individuals and institutions—and from
committed readers like you. To learn more, visit
ucpress.edu/supportus.